Joshua Rozenberg

Joshua Rozenberg studied law at Oxford and then trained as a solicitor, qualifying in 1976. He joined the BBC in 1975 and was appointed its first Legal Correspondent in 1984. He is married with two children and lives in west London. His previous books include *Your Rights and the Law* (with Nicola Watkins), Dent, 1986 and *The Case for the Crown*, Thorsons, 1987.

D1102720

SCEPTRE

TO ABIGAIL, GABRIEL AND MELANIE

The Search For Justice

An Anatomy of the Law

Joshua Rozenberg

SCEPTRE

First published in 1994 by Hodder and Stoughton
A divison of Hodder Headline PLC
First published in paperback in 1995 by Hodder and Stoughton
A Sceptre Paperback

A C.I.P. catalogue record for this title is available
from the British Library

ISBN 0 340 62859 6

Printed and bound in Great Britain by
Cox and Wyman Ltd, Reading, Berkshire

Hodder and Stoughton Ltd
A division of Hodder Headline PLC
338 Euston Road
London NW1 3BH

Contents

3 Lawyers and the Courts

4 Access to Justice

6 Planning Criminal Justice

7 When Justice Miscarries

Preface

During the summer months, law students traditionally offer up a silent prayer that parliament and the judges will not change the law until after the exams are over. Legal authors have a subtle variant: they pray that any proposals they make for reforming the law will reach the book-shops before the government puts those proposals into effect.

I have described access to justice as the key issue facing the legal system today. In the hardback edition of this book, I supported demands led by Lord Woolf for reform of the civil justice system. But in March 1994, shortly before this book was published, the Lord Chancellor took the wind out of our sails by asking Lord Woolf himself to review the rules and procedures of the civil courts in England and Wales. There was every sign that Lord Woolf's energy and determination would lead to a rather more fundamental review than Lord Mackay might have been expecting.

I wrote in the first edition that the Lord Chancellor would do well to announce that the next judge found guilty of a drink-driving offence will be expected to resign. In July 1994 Lord Mackay made it clear that Circuit judges convicted of driving while under the influence of alcohol could expect the sack: a High Court judge, the Lord Chief Justice added, might well feel he 'ought to go'. Lord Taylor announced on the same occasion that there would now be a limited system for monitoring trainee judges, again something I had called for. It may prove to be the thin end of the wedge.

As the first edition of this book was going to press, with its plea on page 82 for academic lawyers to join the judiciary, the Lord Chancellor announced that Professor Brenda Hoggett would become a High Court judge in January 1994. There was just time to squeeze in a reference to the new Mrs Justice Hale, as she became when she decided to revert to her maiden name. My demand that women members of the Court of Appeal should be called 'Lady Justice' instead of 'Lord Justice' was accepted by the Master of the Rolls a week after this book was published, but any claims I was planning to make for the power of my advocacy were dashed when it turned out that Sir Thomas Bingham had been intending to make the change anyway.

On the criminal justice side, it was gratifying to find that the government shared my suggestions on committal proceedings. I had backed the Royal Commission's view that they should be abolished, but expressed doubts abut the Commission's recommendation that stipendiary magistrates – rather than lay justices – should decide if there was no case to answer.

Not all my suggestions have been well received. The Lord Chancellor devoted his lecture at the Lord Mayor's dinner for the judges in July 1994 to a defence of his position as judge and minister (criticised on page 12). Lord Mackay said it was 'moonshine to think that difficulties over pay, budgets, and all the other grist that exists between the judicial and executive millstones in the Lord Chancellor's office would disappear if a Secretary of State was appointed.'

Most of this book was finalised in November 1993, although some passages in the first edition were updated in January and February 1994. The book first appeared in April 1994. This may seem a little slow to a broadcaster whose words are often published within a matter of minutes but is gratifyingly fast by the standards of book publishing, especially when compared with traditional academic presses.

In preparing the paperback edition I have incorporated amendments in the first seven chapters while keeping the existing page numbering. Chapter 8 has been more extensively re-written to take account of developments since the Royal Commission on Criminal Justice published its report, notably the new legislation abolishing the right to silence.

Joshua Rozenberg, September 1994

Introduction

We are all part of the search for justice. Everyone wants to see the judges acting fairly and properly, everyone wants to see the courts reaching the right results. All too often we are disappointed.

This book takes a critical look at the state of justice in England and Wales today. At its heart is an objective, factual description of our legal institutions – an anatomy of the law. It is aimed firmly at the general reader: the sort of person who knows what a judge is but is not sure why some judges are called Judge while others are called Mr Justice; the sort of person who knows there is a European Court but is not quite sure why it sometimes seems to be enforcing trade directives from Brussels and sometimes seems to be imposing human rights on a reluctant British government. (The answer, incidentally, is that there are two different European Courts, just as there are two different types of judge.)

However, the law is as much about issues as it is about institutions. *The Search for Justice* charts the key issues in the law today, the issues which dominate news coverage of our legal system. No serious survey of these issues can avoid taking sides. Sitting on the fence can be comfortable enough: it is the position which the BBC very properly expects of its reporters. It is not the position this book will take. There would have been little point in a flat description of the status quo, partly because the status quo has been changing so quickly and partly because there is now a major debate raging over what the legal system should be doing. As a result, the book has become something of a personal quest. It seeks not just to state what the law is, but to suggest what the law should be: it started as an anatomy of the law but it soon became a search for justice.

It is easier to seek justice than to find it. That is not because our judges are malign or corrupt: far from it. The senior judiciary is brighter and better than it has ever been before. However, money lies at the root of all justice, as it does with so much else in life, and money is now in short supply. So too are a sense of vision, a sense of purpose and a sense of continuity: too often we have seen short-term measures used to deal with long-term problems. Legal aid, for example, should never have been allowed to reach the crisis we saw in 1993; the judiciary should never have had to battle so long for the appointment of a few more judges. And increasingly we have seeen grand projects bogged down for years in a mass of detail: for example, Lord Hailsham's planned reforms of the civil courts and Lord Mackay's attempt to break the barristers' monopoly.

The key challenge facing our civil justice system now is access to justice. People must be able to enforce their rights against others, and those people must get the legal advice they need in order to do so. All too often this is not the case. Doing justice to all manner of men and women must be the ultimate objective of any legal system; this book finds the English legal system singularly unable to provide that elusive quality. For most people, going to court is just too expensive.

Finally, and above all, people are entitled to justice from our criminal courts. We expect the courts to convict and punish the guilty, just as we expect that innocent people will never be found guilty by mistake. It is in this last area that the picture is the most alarming.

For years we deluded ourselves into believing our courts were the best in the world. Finally the dam burst and miscarriages of justice started flooding out. For a few months it looked as if things might change. That was in 1991: looking back, it now seems like something of a golden year. The Birmingham Six were finally cleared (and Judith Ward, wrongly imprisoned for even longer, had her case referred to the Court of Appeal). The Royal Commission on Criminal Justice was appointed in order – it was assumed at the time – to prevent further miscarriages of justice. Lord Woolf published a liberal and enlightened report on prisons. Parliament passed a Criminal Justice Act which, though significantly flawed, fully accepted that prison was an expensive way of making bad people worse.

In 1993 everything started to go wrong. The Lord Chancellor cut eligibility for legal aid. In repairing flaws in the Criminal Justice Act, the government sent out an implicit message that prison was available for all offenders, not just those for whom there was no alternative. That message was made explicit by a Home Secretary who had apparently convinced himself that 'prison works'. The Royal Commission's report turned out to be something of a disappointment, but at least it attempted to strike what it saw as a reasonable balance between conflicting pressures within the criminal justice system: the government chose to push ahead with its own priorities (such as universal compulsory DNA testing, and abolishing the right to silence) regardless of the Royal Commission's recommendations. As the all-party human rights and law reform group JUSTICE put it in its Autumn 1993 *Bulletin*:

> The Royal Commission on Criminal Justice was set up in an atmosphere of deep distrust in the ability of the criminal justice system to deliver justice to those wrongly suspected of criminal offences. Its report has been released into quite a different climate: a state of near-panic at the level of criminality and the inability of the criminal justice system to stem it . . . The Royal Commission, initially under attack from reformers for being too anodyne, now faces marginalisation by decision-makers for being insufficiently tough.

When David Hare's play *Murmuring Judges* was first performed in 1991 it portrayed a reforming Home Secretary confronting a no-nonsense judge: the politician attacked the judiciary for sending too many people to prison while the judge made it clear that this was no concern of his. By the time the play was revived in 1993 this vignette, something of a caricature when it was first written, had become totally inappropriate: the real Home Secretary was extolling the virtues of imprisonment while the real judges were warning him of the dangers that lay ahead. In late October 1993 the Lord Chief Justice expressed his concern that the zeal for reform of the criminal justice system might lead the Home Office into over-hasty legislation: he reminded the Home Secretary that the government had promised to keep the judges fully informed about its proposals. But although the judges were now speaking to ministers, the gulf between the executive and the judiciary seemed as wide as it ever had been.

Our system of justice is no longer at a crossroads: it has already gone several miles down the road to ruin. The worse it gets, though, the more hope there is that people will cry 'Halt!' Like the traditional red telephone boxes which suddenly sprang up in central London during the summer of 1993, perhaps some of our finer legal traditions will eventually reappear in their former strength, as people realise that cheap modern substitutes are no substitute at all.

I must apologise to those who find my language sexist. I do not wish to win a prize for political incorrectness but I am not prepared to write 'he or she' throughout this book – or indeed 'she or he'. Nor would readers thank me for slewing my sentences round to avoid personal pronouns. As lawyers invariably say on these occasions, the masculine shall embrace the feminine.

It is a pleasure to thank my publisher, Richard Cohen, for his inspiration and encouragement. Jane Birkett was a meticulous copy editor. Lord Mackay and his staff gave generously of their time. Roger Smith was kind enough to help me through the intricacies of legal aid. Joanna Pollard supplied some of the references and saved me from many errors. Above all, David Pannick QC gave me the benefit of his wise counsel. Needless to say, none of them is responsible for the mistakes I have undoubtedly introduced since the manuscript left their hands. A book like this can never be totally accurate or up to date, even on the day it is completed, and those readers who enjoy pointing out errors to authors are encouraged to write to me at the BBC.

Authors traditionally thank their families for allowing them time to slave away over a hot word processor. Having put up with continued absences for almost a year, my own family were justifiably horrified when they discovered I had hidden the laptop in the luggage when we set off for our annual two weeks in France. This book is therefore dedicated to my wife and children for their tolerance and forbearance in the face of journalistic adversity.

Joshua Rozenberg, February 1994

1

Her Majesty's Judges

A judiciary for the nineties

In 1936 the Lord Chief Justice, Lord Hewart, said: 'His Majesty's Judges are satisfied with the almost universal admiration in which they are held.'[1] In 1992 his successor, Lord Taylor of Gosforth, acknowledged that 'no judge today would express such sentiments: if he did he would be lambasted by the press, and rightly so.'[2]

Lord Taylor was speaking at a time of crisis in the criminal justice system. Miscarriages of justice had left people shocked and bewildered. A Royal Commission was searching for ways to restore public confidence in a structure which seemed to be crumbling away. With rising despair at the inability of the system to protect them, most people believed there were times when they would be justified in taking the law into their own hands.[3]

The newly appointed Lord Chief Justice argued that the judiciary of the nineties was more deserving of public confidence than ever before. He conceded that this was not widely recognised and accepted that because of their self-imposed isolation the judges themselves had been partially responsible for people's misconceptions. Lord Taylor felt that judges could be more closely in touch without prejudicing their judicial independence but he maintained that the judges today were drawn from an increasingly broad spectrum of society: 'they are younger, better trained, more in tune with current social problems and needs than ever before.'

Is this really so? It is a question we shall examine in this opening chapter. Who are the people who sit in judgment over us? Lord Taylor realised that many people saw the judges as 'white, male, public school, Oxbridge and Establishment-minded', an image which he maintained was becoming increasingly inaccurate. White and male the judges certainly still are, in overwhelming numbers. Public school and Oxbridge perhaps less so, although the rest certainly went to good grammar schools and well-established red-brick universities.[4] But no longer Establishment-minded? There Lord Taylor may be on to something.

Of course it would be hard to find many anarchists or subversives on the bench; the judicial appointments process does tend to weed out those who wish to wreck the system or overthrow society. But, as we shall see, the modern judiciary is less likely than ever before to support the Establishment, whether it is the government of the day in civil cases or the Crown in criminal prosecutions.

Why should this be? First, there is now a new generation at the top. In 1992 the two most senior full-time judges were each replaced by men some twelve or thirteen years younger than their predecessors. In addition, many of the newly promoted judges have come from the more thoughtful end of the bench: far from inhibiting promotion, progressive views and a liberal temperament now seem to be prerequisites for advancement in the judiciary. This is just as true in the House of Lords (Lord Woolf, for example) as it is in the Court of Appeal (Lord Justice Steyn, among others) and the High Court (Mr Justice Sedley was a particularly striking appointment).

The third reason for this change of judicial attitude is perhaps the most remarkable of all. The Establishment – in the form of the Conservative government – has succeeded in alienating the judges to such an extent that it has forfeited the support it could naturally have expected from them.

There were some striking examples of this in 1993. The courts' decision that it would not be unlawful under trade union legislation for teachers to boycott the Education Secretary's tests[5] did great damage to John Patten's policies and, it seemed at the time, to his political career. The successful challenge by the miners' union to the government's pit closure plans[6] was something which would have been unlikely only a few years earlier. Finally, and potentially most embarrassing of all, the courts allowed a private citizen, with no particular standing in law, the right to challenge the government's plans to ratify the Treaty of Maastricht.[7] These were not the decisions of a cautious, Conservative judiciary. As we shall see in the initial chapters of this book, Her Majesty's judges are no longer the right-wing ideologues some people still imagine them to be.

Why, then, have the judges stopped giving unthinking support to the political party that most of them must have voted for? If there is one man above all who can be held to account for that remarkable shift in the natural order of things it is the Lord Chancellor, Lord Mackay of Clashfern.

The Lord Chancellor

The most senior legal figure in England and Wales[8] holds a unique position under our unwritten constitution. The Lord High Chancellor of Great Britain alarms those who believe in the separation of the powers by simultaneously holding all three: he presides over a department of the executive when he sits as a government minister in the cabinet; he presides over the judiciary when he sits in the highest court in the land as a law lord; and he presides over a branch of the legislature when he sits on the Woolsack[9] as Speaker of the House of Lords.

The Lord Chancellor is effectively appointed by the prime minister of the day and so can be dismissed at a moment's notice.[10] There is no job specification as such but the post usually goes either to a party politician of sufficient standing in the law or to a leading barrister (or judge) who is sympathetic to the government.[11] The Lord Chancellor receives a peerage on appointment if he (or she) docs not have one already.

A person becomes Lord Chancellor on receiving the Great Seal of England from the Sovereign. This takes the form of two heavy metal plates which form the matrix, or mould, for creating a seal measuring six inches across: for centuries, such a seal has been affixed to documents in the Sovereign's name (the only difference nowadays is that the seals are made out of plastic rather than wax).[12] The Great Seal is kept personally by the Lord Chancellor: he occasionally shows it to visitors.

People are often confused about the respective roles of the Lord Chancellor and the Attorney General. That confusion was compounded until 1992 by the expedient of having the Attorney General answer for the Lord Chancellor in the House of Commons.[13] In fact their jobs are quite different.

The Attorney General is the government's chief legal adviser: he advises ministers on the lawfulness or otherwise of their actions and answers questions in the House of Commons. He can call for cabinet papers but he does not attend cabinet meetings unless invited to. He sits on certain key cabinet committees. By statute, the Attorney General 'superintends' the work of the Crown Prosecution Service and the Serious Fraud Office. This seems to mean that the Director of Public Prosecutions – who leads the Crown Prosecution Service – should have enough independence from the government to avoid being subservient to it, and enough supervision by the government to ensure that she or he is ultimately answerable, through the Attorney General, to parliament.[14] By convention, the Attorney General is also consulted by other major prosecutors (such as HM Customs and Excise) in the most important criminal cases. The Attorney General has a tiny department but he does have the advantage of a parliamentary deputy, the Solicitor General.[15] Together they are known as the *law officers* and are usually both MPs and barristers.[16] From time to time they appear in court to argue important cases on behalf of the government, both in England and at the European courts. Both men are offered knighthoods on appointment: a woman would be made DBE.[17]

By contrast, the Lord Chancellor must not give his fellow ministers legal advice. This is because he is responsible for a legal system which may ultimately have to decide whether those ministers have broken the law. Lord Mackay has made it clear that some of his predecessors did not observe this important rule as fully as he did.[18]

There is a close working relationship between the Lord Chancellor, the Attorney General and the Home Secretary – an approach known within Whitehall as 'trilateralism'. Ministers and officials meet regularly to co-ordinate criminal justice policy.

The Lord Chancellor runs a large government department with 12,000 staff working in the 400 or more courts for which he is responsible. His annual budget – including the huge sums spent each year on legal aid – is rapidly approaching £2,500,000,000.[19] The Lord Chancellor is the minister responsible for reform of the civil law; if the government wanted, for example, to change the law on divorce, it would fall to him to steer a bill through parliament. As a minister he sits in the cabinet; by nature of his office (which is many centuries older – and better paid – than that of the prime minister) he has a leading position in the cabinet hierarchy. As one of the few cabinet ministers in the House of Lords, the Lord Chancellor may be called upon to speak in the upper chamber on any aspect of the government's policy.

8

The Lord Chancellor should be someone who can command respect both as a politician and as a judge. Such people are not easy to find. However, the Lord Chancellor has one important advantage over his cabinet colleagues: he is the only head of a substantial government department who never sits in the House of Commons. The Lords is an altogether kinder place to ministers, and the parliamentary skills needed for survival there need be less finely honed.

Perhaps the greatest responsibility of all in the hands of the Lord Chancellor is to choose the judges. He himself appoints the lower judicial officers, and most magistrates. He also advises the Queen on appointments to the High Court, which means that the Queen has to accept the names he puts forward. But appointments to the Court of Appeal and above are different. These are made by the Queen on the advice of the prime minister.

At first sight this may seem one of those meaningless formalities designed to buttress the status of senior judges. But the reality is very different. It is nothing less than naked political control over appointments to the most senior levels in the judiciary – the Lord Chief Justice, the Master of the Rolls and the appeal judges.

Potential candidates for these posts are first selected by the Lord Chancellor. That process is itself questionable (and indeed it will be questioned in chapter 2). But with the system as it is one might assume that the Lord Chancellor would simply pick a name and then send it round to 10 Downing Street so that the prime minister could redirect it to Buckingham Palace. Not so.

The former Lord Chancellor, Lord Hailsham, generally gave the prime minister a shortlist of two or three names. But he always put them in order of merit, giving reasons, and indicated why he thought any rival candidates would have been unsuitable. Even so, on one occasion the prime minister picked Lord Hailsham's second choice.[20]

It seems Lord Mackay had a similar experience. He always put more than one name on the list he submitted to Mrs Thatcher and Mr Major, indicating the strengths and weaknesses of particular candidates and making his own preference perfectly clear. Asked[21] whether the prime minister had always accepted his recommendation, Lord Mackay hesitated for an uncharacteristically long time before answering: 'My experience of both prime ministers is that they have very fully respected the advice which I have given them.'

Pressed on whether one could infer from this that the prime minister had not always accepted his first choice, Lord Mackay smiled enigmatically. He would not say whether one of the prime ministers he had served had respected his advice more fully than the other. However, it would not be surprising if the prime minister who rejected one of Lord Hailsham's choices was the one who also rejected a name put forward by Lord Mackay. That could only be Mrs Thatcher.

This approach may not have been confined to Conservative prime ministers. The Labour government of 1974–9 is widely believed to have blocked the promotion of Sir John Donaldson to the Court of Appeal.[22] However, it is not clear whether this was a decision of the prime minister or of the Lord Chancellor, Lord Elwyn-Jones.

As we shall see in the next chapter, there are those who think it bad enough that a member of the government should have sole responsibility for judicial appointments; but at least the Lord Chancellor is a judge as well as a politician. It is even more alarming to realise that the prime minister, who is never questioned in parliament about judicial appointments, exercises a veto over the selection of our most senior judges.

In 1993 Lord Mackay made or recommended nearly 1,000 professional judicial appointments. As well as appointing the judges, the Lord Chancellor has to work closely with them. He holds monthly meetings with the Lord Chief Justice, the Master of the Rolls, the President of the Family Division, the Vice-Chancellor and other senior judges. In Lord Mackay's view these arrangements do not threaten the judges' independence; quite the contrary, he has argued, they help to preserve judicial independence from the possibility of a violent collision with the executive.[23] By linking the executive and the judiciary, by explaining the problems of each to the other, the Lord Chancellor is said to make a constitutional clash less likely.

This argument is unconvincing. The 'constitutional buffer' theory, as it is called, assumes a potential clash between the judges on one side and the government on the other – with a kindly Lord Chancellor in the middle, keeping the peace. But most of the judges' recent political battles have been with the Lord Chancellor himself. As we shall see, these included the challenge to Lord Mackay's Green Papers on reform of the legal profession; the fight to get more judges appointed; disagreements over legal aid eligibility; and even Lord

Mackay's decision to replace the High Court shorthand writers. Lord Hailsham was also at odds with the judiciary towards the end of his period in office over his plans to reorganise the civil courts.

Lord Mackay has managed, in particular, to infuriate the two Lords Chief Justices who have served him – Lord Lane and Lord Taylor. Asked publicly in May 1993 about his relationship with the Lord Chancellor, Lord Taylor said he got on 'extremely well' with Lord Mackay on a personal level and that they agreed on most things – though not everything – on an operational and policy level. He then added, revealingly: 'Relations are considerably warmer since the provision of the new judges.'[24] It was clear they had been pretty frigid until then.

Lord Hailsham summed up the Lord Chancellor's role as 'constitutional buffer' in 1971.[25] 'In the absence of a paper constitution, the separation of the powers is the primary function of the Lord Chancellor, a task which he can only fulfil if he sits somewhere near the apex of the constitutional pyramid armed with a long barge pole to keep off marauding craft from any quarter.' That barge pole has now snapped. The Lord Chancellor has been no match for the marauding forces of the Treasury. They are thought to have inspired Lord Mackay's attempts to reform the legal profession; they were certainly behind his cuts in legal aid eligibility. Indeed, he could not even appoint a few more judges without asking the Treasury first.[26] The judiciary cannot defend itself against economic reality.

And neither should it. It is quite wrong that the judges should expect to have unlimited resources. It is equally wrong that the head of a major spending department *should* use a 'long barge pole' to stave off parliamentary accountability. On the contrary, the Lord Chancellor should now be directly answerable to the House of Commons – not for every decision taken by a judge but for every decision taken by a key member of the cabinet.

We may not like the Lord Chancellor's political agenda. Indeed, we may be alarmed at the effect the government's policies are having on our system of justice. We may applaud the judges for fighting their corner. But ultimately policies are for parliament to decide.

Asked about his predecessor's theories, Lord Mackay himself offered a subtly different view of judicial independence.[27] In his opinion it meant 'the duty of a judge to decide the case before him according to his oath, applying the law and free from improper pressure'. It did not mean the judges were detached from the rest of society. Lord Hailsham's 'long barge pole' was needed to prod other ministers into realising that they came under the rule of law as much as anybody else.

For years the only way MPs could question the Lord Chancellor was by letter. This constitutional lacuna was recognised – though not removed – by two recent changes. First, the Lord Chancellor agreed in 1991 that the 'policy, administration and expenditure' of his department could be monitored by the House of Commons Select Committee on Home Affairs.[28] Second, since the General Election of 1992 there has been a junior minister in the House of Commons, the Parliamentary Secretary to the Lord Chancellor's Department. He answers oral questions for fifteen minutes every six weeks about all aspects of the Lord Chancellor's work. He also answers written questions from MPs. However, it was made clear on his appointment that the junior minister would have no responsibility within the department for any of the Lord Chancellor's most important ministerial roles, such as the appointment of the judiciary.[29] His distance from the seat of power is demonstrated by the fact that his grey workmanlike office is a brisk ten minutes' walk away from the Lord Chancellor's magnificent gothic room in the House of Lords.[30]

The first holder of the Parliamentary Under-Secretary's job – John M. Taylor MP – proved no threat to Lord Mackay on matters of policy even though he was a lawyer himself (he had practised as a solicitor in Solihull). Perhaps the kindest thing that could be said about Mr Taylor was that he was a good House of Commons man, assiduously cultivating MPs in the tearoom on behalf of a department which until then had virtually ignored the elected chamber. But occasional Commons appearances at Question Time by a junior minister with limited powers should not satisfy any parliamentary opposition worth its salt. They should be calling for the organ grinder, not his monkey.

At the same time as the Lord Chancellor is running a government department and presiding over a branch of the legislature, he may also exercise important judicial responsibilities. It is quite wrong that a cabinet minister should be sitting as a judge in the House of Lords, particularly as he automatically assumes the most senior position on the panel of law lords by virtue of his office.[31] Some Lord Chancellors have rightly hesitated before setting themselves over judges with many years of judicial experience. Others, like Lord Hailsham and Lord Mackay, have not. Lord Mackay, at least, had previously been appointed a law lord on merit. Future Lord Chancellors may prove to have no judicial experience or skills whatsoever.

According to convention, the Lord Chancellor does not sit in cases where the government is directly involved. Otherwise one might find an Attorney General who went on to become Lord Chancellor arguing a case before the Court of Appeal and then, some months later, hearing the same case on appeal to the House of Lords. But it seems this convention does not exclude the Lord Chancellor from presiding over cases in which the government has a direct interest. In 1992 Lord Mackay sat in an appeal involving the Inland Revenue.[32] As it happened, the Revenue lost; if the appeal had gone the other way, there would have been a significant improvement to the government's tax receipts. Although the law lords were unanimous in allowing the taxpayer's appeal, Lord Mackay was in a minority of one on a subsidiary point with crucial implications for the resources of his own department.[33] No judge should have any interest in the outcome of his decision, even if that judge is the Lord Chancellor: justice must be seen to be done.

It is also wrong for a member of the government to be Speaker of the House of Lords. The constitutional conflict is clear to see for anyone who watches proceedings in the chamber: the Lord Chancellor has to take two steps to the left of the Woolsack when he stops speaking as the Speaker and starts speaking as a minister or as a judge.[34] There is also a practical conflict: the Lord Chancellor's parliamentary duties take up a good deal of a cabinet minister's limited time. He must seek the leave of the House if he is going to be away at the start of the day's proceedings. Every afternoon when the Lords are sitting he has to change into and then out of his court dress (black tights, buckled shoes, full-bottomed wig and silk gown);[35] important meetings in his room are sometimes interrupted when the division bell summons him to a vote.

There are increasing signs that this view is gaining ground. Sir Francis Purchas, a retired Lord Justice of Appeal, said in November 1993 that the Lord Chancellor of the day should no longer be head of the judiciary. The former judge said that the Lord Chancellor had increasingly encroached on the independence of the judiciary and Treasury constraints had outweighed concerns of justice. Sir Francis also said it was fair to ask 'whether one man, however skilled, sincere and hardworking as is the present incumbent of that high office, can expect to do two jobs which increasingly present him with mutually conflicting pressures'.[36]

Lord Mackay has consistently rejected any significant changes to the office of Lord Chancellor: in his view it provides 'a link between the judiciary, the executive and the legislature that is broken at our peril'.

> However anomalous they may seem when taken together in one job, [these three features] do represent a practical and, I would say, a sensible answer to the difficult question how best to manage the relationship between a sovereign legislature, a powerful executive government springing from it, and an independent judiciary.[37]

'There's no doubt about it,' Lord Mackay conceded, 'it's a big job which history has developed.'[38] But nobody should be expected to do the three main jobs of the Lord Chancellor; because they are in conflict, nobody can do all three of them properly. It is time for the Lord Chancellor to hang up at least one and preferably two of his three wigs.[39] We would then have an independent Speaker in the House of Lords, an independent judiciary without a government minister presiding over it, and a Minister of Justice sitting in the House of Commons.

A Minister of Justice?

It might be imagined that this is a new idea. Far from it: the solicitors' professional body first called for a Minister of Justice in 1918. In a speech to solicitors Samuel Garrett, then president of the Law Society, said there were 'many . . . functions now spread among different departments which it would be found convenient and economical to commit to the Minister of Justice. The gain to the public from having these duties concentrated in one office, in the hands of a single Minister with a seat in the House of Commons and responsible to Parliament, would be immense.'[40]

Even in 1918 the idea was not new. Mr Garrett quoted from an article in the *Law Magazine* which had said that 'the office of Minister of Justice has become an admitted want'. That assessment was published as long ago as 1856. The Law Society's views were passed to a government inquiry chaired by Lord Haldane and in 1919 the Haldane Committee concluded: 'We think that a strong case is made out for the appointment of a Minister of Justice.'[41] Under Haldane's proposals the Home Secretary would, in effect, have become the justice minister, and the Lord Chancellor would have remained in the cabinet as the government's principal legal adviser.[42]

The main advantage of creating a Minister of Justice today would be to place in the House of Commons a cabinet minister who was fully accountable for our system of justice. It would also be an opportunity to rationalise the division of responsibilities between the Home Office and the present Lord Chancellor's Department. This currently produces a number of anomalies: marriage is a matter for the Home Secretary but divorce is a matter for the Lord Chancellor; reform of the criminal law is a matter for the Home Office while reform of the civil law is a matter for the Lord Chancellor's Department. The new Minister of Justice should become responsible for all aspects of law reform. However, the Attorney General should keep his separate responsibilities, advising the government and supervising the prosecution process. The appointment of judges would ideally become the responsibility of a Judicial Appointments Commission.[43] And there would be a new Select Committee to keep the department under review.

Perhaps the most difficult question of all is what the new government department should be called. 'Ministry of Justice' sounds slightly threatening and rather foreign. The best solution (and one traditionally used in Britain) is to keep the style and change the substance: the new ministry, though very different in structure, would still be called the Lord Chancellor's Department. Other possible titles might include:

- Department of Legal Administration

- Ministry of Legal Affairs

- Courts and Legal Services Department

- Justice Department

Whatever he or she was called, the Minister of Justice would be a member of the cabinet with the status of a Secretary of State. If the new ministry was known as the Lord Chancellor's Department then its ministerial head would clearly be called the Lord Chancellor.[44] On the other hand, some reformers think that changing the title should be the outward expression of a determination to change the job: Lord Gifford QC said that 'creating a Ministry of Justice would signify that the senior law minister is not just there to oversee the courts and appoint the judges, but to ensure that people can get access to justice'.[45]

It would certainly be a shame to abolish the title of Lord Chancellor after all these centuries. But that need not happen. The title could be allocated to either of the Lord Chancellor's other current roles.

Thus the Speaker of the House of Lords might in future be called the Lord Chancellor. In that event, one might hope that the Lords would elect their own Speaker – as the Commons do – instead of accepting the person chosen by the prime minister (which is the present procedure).

Another possibility would be to give the title to a leading judge. In fact the Lord Chancellor is already President of the High Court Chancery Division although his duties are performed by the Vice-Chancellor. It would be simple enough to change the title of the presiding Chancery judge from Vice-Chancellor to Lord Chancellor. We would then have a Lord Chief Justice presiding over one division of the High Court and a Lord Chancellor presiding over another. If this idea did not appeal, a further option would be for the senior presiding law lord to be known as the Lord Chancellor. At present he does not have a title of his own.

Supporters of a Ministry of Justice have always said it would be of great value to have a government department directly responsible for reform of the law. One might argue that this is less a priority now that we have an independent Law Commission.[46] But the Law Commission has not always found it easy to get its recommendations enacted by parliament and its creation in 1965 did not sweep aside the arguments in favour of a Ministry of Justice.

As Lord Chancellor, Lord Mackay of Clashfern has been firmly against the idea of a Ministry of Justice. The present system, he believes, emphasised the independence of the judiciary. His predecessor, Lord Hailsham, took the same view. He feared that a Minister of Justice would be questioned in the House of Commons about the qualities of particular judges, about remarks they had made in court and about sentences they had passed. 'In short', said Lord Hailsham, 'judicial independence would be at an end.'[47]

It is difficult to see why this should be so. In theory, any peer can put such a question to the Lord Chancellor in the House of Lords. By convention they do not ask, and by convention he would not answer. The same convention applies in the House of Commons where there has not been a rash of improper judicial questions to the Lord Chancellor's junior minister. A Minister of Justice in the House of Commons could, would and should follow the same conventions. He or she could be accountable for our system of justice without being answerable for specific decisions.

Opponents of change might argue that we have already achieved a Ministry of Justice by stealth: the Lord Chancellor now has overall responsibility for the funding and organisation of the magistrates' courts,[48] he has a junior minister in the Commons, he is accountable to a Select Committee and so on. All this is true, and we are closer to the ideal than we were. But although the Lord Chancellor has gained some of the trappings of a modern government minister he has not lost the attributes of a benign dictator; he is still in the House of Lords, and he is still a judge as well as a politician.

The office of Lord Chancellor goes back more than nine hundred years.[49] It has shown a remarkable genius for adapting to current needs. The process of change should continue.

Lord Mackay of Clashfern

Lord Mackay of Clashfern became Lord Chancellor in October 1987. He succeeded Lord Havers who was asked by Mrs Thatcher to resign on grounds of ill-health after he had been in office for just four months. Lord Havers had the unique distinction in modern times of combining the shortest period in office as Lord Chancellor with the longest service as a law officer. He had been Attorney General for eight years.

James Mackay was born in Edinburgh in 1927, the son of a railway worker. Like Lord Denning he was a mathematics scholar; he took degrees at Edinburgh and Cambridge before starting his legal studies. He was called to the Bar of Scotland in 1955 where his practice included crime, tax, patents, and rating; he became a QC after only ten years. By the time he entered politics in 1979 James Mackay had risen through the ranks of the Scottish Bar to become Dean of the Faculty of Advocates – the leading Scottish QC.

In 1979, when Mrs Thatcher made him Lord Advocate (the Scottish counterpart of the English Attorney General), James Mackay was not even a member of the Conservative Party (although he subsequently joined). In 1984 he was appointed to the Scottish judiciary, serving for little more than a year before he was promoted to the House of Lords where he served as a Lord of Appeal – a law

17

lord – until he became Lord Chancellor.

Lord Mackay was certainly not the first Scottish lawyer appointed as Lord Chancellor although he was the first who had never been called to the English Bar. As he once pointed out, he was therefore the first Lord Chancellor to be wholly unqualified to sit as a judge in any English court, except perhaps as a lay magistrate.[50]

Lord Mackay of Clashfern will be remembered as the Lord Chancellor who tried to change the face of the English legal system. His aim was to sweep away the restrictive practices which he felt were preventing the system from working as efficiently as it could. Getting his plans through parliament was difficult enough but putting them into practice turned out to be an agonisingly slow process (as we shall see in chapter 3).

It is clear that Lord Mackay would not have done as he did if he had been brought up in the traditions of the English Bar. Lord Hailsham and Lord Havers would certainly have taken more notice of the barristers' objections than their successor did.[51] The barristers had beaten off attempts at reform in the past, notably from Lord Benson's Royal Commission on Legal Services,[52] but they completely misjudged this canny outsider from north of the border.

Lord Mackay himself believed that his background in a different legal system gave him a broader perspective. In Scotland solicitors have always had rights of audience in jury trials. It was therefore not so 'blindingly obvious' to him as it was to the judges that English solicitors could not act as advocates in the Crown Court.[53]

Lord Mackay will also be remembered as the Lord Chancellor who dedicated himself to reducing costs, notably by trying to bring some measure of control to the spiralling increase in legal aid. That alarmed many people, including his fellow judges: the Lord Chief Justice said Lord Mackay's proposals were 'deplorable'.[54] But what really lost him the confidence of the judiciary was what seemed to be his lack of support for them. The judges inferred this from his efforts to reduce their incomes by making them work longer for their pensions, while at the same time increasing their workloads by refusing for some months to increase their numbers to what they considered an adequate level.[55] Some senior judges privately despised him.

In April 1989 there was a twelve-hour debate in the House of Lords on Lord Mackay's plans to reform the legal profession,

·during which Lord Lane, Lord Donaldson and a number of the law lords made their opposition clear.[56] In May 1989, they published a 50-page response to his proposals. The Master of the Rolls even agreed to be interviewed about the controversy on the television news.

All this was clearly very painful for Lord Mackay. He is a charming man who hates unpleasantness of any kind. While maintaining his dignity, he is modest and utterly without pomposity. He has a dry sense of humour.[57] In interviews he appears calm and relaxed – even serene. Everything he says is 'on the record'. In media interviews he displays a mastery of his brief: he is never caught out by unexpected questions.[58]

Many people know about Lord Mackay's religious faith but few realise the impact it has on his working week. He was originally a member of the Free Presbyterian Church; after he parted company with it in 1989 he was not formally a member of any Church. James Mackay is not teetotal as some people supposed but, like an orthodox Jew, he would not work on the Sabbath – and the concept of work was similarly extended to watching television, travelling and using the telephone. This could cause severe problems for a government minister, particularly as Lord Mackay did not have a deputy for his first four years in office: his officials would only telephone him on Sunday in a real emergency. Lord Mackay stressed that this was not a rigid, unbreakable rule: it was simply that he tried to avoid unnecessary work on the Sabbath.

Not only would Lord Mackay not watch television or listen to the radio on Sundays; not only would he not read the Sunday newspapers; he would not even be interviewed in advance for a programme or article which was to appear on a Sunday. He said he tried to keep the Sabbath as a special day for rest and worship. Some people might think it was even more amazing that he crammed all the responsibilities of being Lord Chancellor into six days, but Lord Mackay believed it was only by resting on the seventh day that he found the energy to work on the remaining six.

It is ironic that the Lord Chancellor who did most to antagonise the judiciary should have been the Lord Chancellor who did so much to enhance it. The senior appointments Lord Mackay made in the early 1990s were generally very well received. Among them were judges who would sit with him from time to time in the House of Lords.[59]

19

The House of Lords

In theory, the House of Lords is the highest court in the land. In reality, the position is much more complicated.

The House of Lords has two roles. Above all, it is a branch of the legislature: every bill must be passed by the House of Lords before it becomes law.[60] The Lords also functions as an appeal court and it is that role which will be discussed in this book. Those judges who are appointed to the House of Lords in its judicial role are known as the *law lords*.

They really are lords: they are given life peerages on appointment.[61] In that sense they are different from members of the Court of Appeal who have the title 'Lord Justice' but are not members of the House of Lords.[62] A law lord is always a member of the Privy Council, so he would be known formally as the Rt. Hon. The Lord Smith.[63] Outside court he would be Lord Smith. Any law lord whose name really was Smith might have to take a place-name as well ('Lord Smith of Smithstown') to distinguish him from a previous Lord Smith. Or he might take a different title.

There are special rules for Scottish life peers. If a Scottish peer has the same surname as another peer, then like an English peer he or she must take a place-name as well. However, Scottish peers must also take a place-name if their surname happens to be that of a Scottish clan. This is because the unadorned clan name is always reserved in the peerage for the clan chief (whether he happens to be a peer at the moment or not).[64]

The Lords of Appeal in Ordinary, to give them their formal title, are full-time judges who have generally been promoted from the Court of Appeal.[65] There are normally around ten active law lords, with two from Scotland, perhaps one from Northern Ireland and the others reflecting a broad mix of English and now European judicial experience. To hear appeals, their lordships generally sit as a panel of five. In difficult or important cases there are seven or more, an uncommon but desirable practice which lessens the risk that the final outcome will not represent the views of the law lords as a body.

From time to time the full-time law lords are joined by other peers who have held high judicial office – a former Lord Chief Justice, for example, or a former Lord Chancellor. There can be advantages in having a former minister as one member of the panel: Lord Woolf, who was promoted to the House of Lords in 1992, believed that a retired Lord Chancellor or Attorney General could bring with him an understanding of the problems of government which other law lords might not share.[66]

Although the law lords are judges they do not sit in what would normally be thought of as a court. They can be found instead in the Palace of Westminster, in an ornate room at the Lords end of the mighty committee corridor. Their tables are arranged in a horseshoe pattern with shelves alongside for books and papers: they are not raised on any kind of dais and so, while other judges look down on counsel, the law lords look up.

When the law lords give judgment on a case, they move downstairs to the chamber of the House of Lords.[67] Counsel stand at the bar of the House: QCs wear court dress with full-bottomed wigs. The law lords make formal speeches proposing that the appeal be allowed or refused for reasons which are available in writing: there is then a formal vote. Theoretically, other peers might try to join in the 'debate' at this stage but any who did so would be frozen out.

Constitutionally the law lords are a committee of parliament, and their political role will be explored in chapter 2. Are they also a 'court'? It would appear not. In 1992 they agreed to allow the BBC to televise their proceedings – subject to a number of conditions which, as it turned out, the BBC could not accept.[68] If they had been a court they could not have granted anyone permission to bring in the cameras: it is against the law to take photographs in an English court.[69] But in practice the law lords are treated as if they are a court, and Lord Mackay maintained they were recognised as such by other provisions.[70]

It may also be misleading to think of the law lords as the highest judges in the land. There are several reasons for this.

First, the law lords are bound by decisions of the European Court of Justice at Luxembourg. When the United Kingdom joined the European Community in 1973 European law became part of the laws of the United Kingdom.[71] As a result, if the law lords consider that the outcome of a case turns on a point of European law they must refer the case to the European Court and give effect to its decision.[72]

Second, although the law lords hear appeals from Scotland and Northern Ireland as well as England and Wales, there is no right of appeal from the Scottish courts in criminal cases. The highest Scottish criminal court is therefore in Edinburgh.

Third, although the law lords can overturn the decisions of a lower appeal court, an appeal will only be heard by the House of Lords if leave has been granted first, either by the Court of Appeal or the law lords themselves.[73] In addition, there can be no appeal to the law lords in an English criminal case unless the Court of Appeal certifies that the case raises a point of law of general public importance. The effect of these rules is that the Court of Appeal is the end of the road for the vast majority of cases.

But not all. Why should there be two appeals in some cases and only one in others? Do we really need the law lords at all? It is not unknown for someone to win a case, and sometimes huge costs, by getting the support of just three law lords. The contrary decisions of the remaining two law lords, three judges in the Court of Appeal and one trial judge – six in total – would then count for nothing.

The present system means increased cost, delay and uncertainty. Set against that is the value of having important cases considered in a less pressurised environment, by judges from different legal traditions who can perhaps take a broader view of all the issues involved. It is also desirable to have one judgment which applies throughout the United Kingdom – although, as we have seen, criminal decisions are not binding in Scotland.

If the law lords were abolished there would have to be some changes in the Court of Appeal: for one thing, the Court of Appeal judges would need the power to overturn their own decisions if they had changed their minds, a power which the law lords gave themselves in 1966.[74] Also the Court of Appeal would need more judges and more back-up staff if it was to produce judgments as polished as those handed down by the law lords. But it is difficult to see what would be lost by making the Court of Appeal the highest court in England and Wales.

Change of this nature is not on the political agenda at present. In these cost-cutting times it would perhaps be dangerous for the law lords to assume that their long-term future is secure but there seems to be no immediate pressure for change.

It is worth looking in some detail at how the law lords reach a decision. Between three and four hundred claimants each year want to take their cases to the House of Lords. From these the law lords select around a hundred cases which they consider to be of general public importance.

During the weekend before the case is to be heard, members of the panel will read all the court papers including, of course, the judgments delivered by the lower courts. On the first morning, before they go to the committee room where they sit, the five law lords will meet in their library. Lord Templeman explained what happens next.

> One of the five will say: 'Looks to me as though the Court of Appeal got it quite right.' And somebody else will say: 'Oh, I'm not at all happy about the way they argued this point.' And at that we'll go up and listen to the argument. And in the course of the argument, we'll argue amongst ourselves: when a law lord makes a point to a counsel he's asking for the answer from the counsel, but he is also pointing out to his colleagues the way his mind is working. And then another law lord, who perhaps at that stage takes a slightly different view, comes in. Well then, of course, we have lunch. And at lunch, as we're going down, we'll have a sort of mild discussion about it, and at the end of the day we'll have a mild discussion, and then the first serious discussion comes when counsel have finished. We throw everybody out, the doors are shut, and the five of us sit in our horseshoe – five of us rather like the forward line of Manchester United. And the outside left who's the junior, he gives his opinion, he says he would dismiss this appeal for the following reasons, and we each do the same in turn. If we're agreed then the presiding judge asks one of us, usually an expert in the particular field, to write the first judgment. If we're not agreed, we have a further discussion and then we all write separate judgments.
>
> The next thing that happens is that whoever drafts a judgment circulates it to all the others. And even if we're all agreed on it, each goes through and criticises it, each asks for amendments. And so even if there's one judgment, it's a concerted team effort.
>
> If we're not agreed, we might have lots of discussions. Although people don't believe this, it is a fact that one changes one's mind in the course of a case, if it's one of those knife-edge cases, in deference to the views of other law lords. Sometimes I have said 'Well, I'm not convinced you're right, but I think it would make for unease and uncertainty if I dissented on this particular point, and therefore I'm not going to dissent although I have my doubts.'[75]

Other law lords have confirmed the accuracy of this account. They say they spend a great deal of time preparing their written decisions.[76]

It is therefore all the more surprising that the law lords have such meagre resources. Ten law lords share three secretaries. These redoubtable women are so busy typing letters and judgments that they have no time to perform such basic tasks as filing the law lords' correspondence. Lord Slynn, who had formerly been a judge at the

European Court, had seven people working for him in Luxembourg (including a driver); at the House of Lords he had one-third of a secretary.

It is even more remarkable that the law lords have no research support. In other countries the judge is given a 'law clerk': a first-class graduate law student, preparing to enter the legal profession, who spends a year working closely with his or her judge. A government which cavils at the extra cost of ten new lowly-paid posts might care to reflect on the increased judicial productivity that they would generate, quite apart from the invaluable training it would offer the graduates of the future.[77]

However, Lord Mackay rejected the idea of providing legally qualified assistants for the law lords.[78] Unlike the Luxembourg court (and others in continental Europe), he said, the English courts are given all the help they need with the law in the course of arguments by counsel. As a result each side can challenge the other's interpretation of the law before the judges retire to consider their decision. Some people, said Lord Mackay, would not think it right for judges to do their own legal research without giving the parties a chance to comment on it. As Lord Chancellor he received no help in preparing his judgments in the House of Lords. After all, he added, 'it's the judge's mind you're entitled to get, not some clerk's idea'.[79]

Despite their lack of support, the law lords manage to turn out remarkably polished written decisions, or *speeches* as they are called. That is largely because of the curious arrangements they have with the official law reporters, the lawyers who compile the law reports which form the foundation of the English system of binding precedents. These law reporters, who are quite separate from the legal correspondents working in newspapers and broadcasting, are shown confidential drafts of the proposed speeches *before* the law lords deliver their rulings. They check the references, pick up errors and no doubt from time to time suggest improvements. This is normal procedure before a case gets into the law reports. In the lower courts it is done after the judgment has been delivered to the parties and the public – not before.

Judges seem to get more conservative as they get older, and one effect of the Judicial Pensions Act 1993 was to prevent law lords aged 75 or over from coming out of retirement and changing the balance of the panel appointed to decide a particular case.[80] Even so, the most senior law lords are generally well into their seventies. In January

1995 the law lords, in order of appointment and therefore of precedence, were:

> Lord Keith of Kinkel, 72
> Lord Goff of Chieveley, 68
> Lord Jauncey of Tullichettle, 69
> Lord Browne-Wilkinson, 64
> Lord Mustill, 63
> Lord Slynn of Hadley, 64
> Lord Woolf, 61
> Lord Lloyd of Berwick, 65
> Lord Nolan, 66
> Lord Nicholls of Birkenhead, 61

Lord Browne-Wilkinson was promoted to the House of Lords in 1991. He and the three judges who followed him were widely acknowledged as liberal, humane, broad-minded and thoughtful – exactly the sort of people who should be sitting in the highest court of appeal. The four were not the obvious choices for a Conservative prime minister to make, although they were all appointed on the advice of Mr Major rather than Mrs Thatcher: one can only speculate on whether she would have objected to any of them had she still been in power.

Lord Lloyd and Lord Nolan were slightly older than the men appointed before them and less obviously associated with the liberal end of the bench. But they had both demonstrated their determination to root out miscarriages of justice. Lord Lloyd was the judge chosen to preside over the last, successful, appeal of the Birmingham Six, a case which he handled in exemplary fashion. Lord Nolan was a member of the court which released Judith Ward in 1992, strongly criticising those responsible for what they called 'a grave miscarriage of justice'. Lord Nolan had the distinction of proceeding from the High Court to the House of Lords in little more than two years.

The Lord Chancellor has always maintained that judicial appointments are made on merit, and many of the appointments from 1991 onwards clearly support that argument. It may be some time before the true impact of these judges is felt: panels of law lords are chaired by the most senior judge sitting, and it will be a few years before the new recruits acquire the necessary seniority to impose their views on others. However, a glance at some cases from 1992 and 1993 makes it clear that some of the younger law lords are already exerting an influence on their more experienced brethren.

Recent cases

● In *Woolwich Equitable Building Society v. Inland Revenue Commissioners*[81] the law lords had to decide whether a building society was entitled to the repayment of £76 million which had been wrongly paid in tax. As the law then stood, tax paid under protest was not recoverable even if the Inland Revenue had exceeded its powers in demanding it. The issue which divided the law lords was whether that law should be changed.

The key speech came from Lord Goff. Though quite senior in appointment he is not much older than Lord Browne-Wilkinson and Lord Slynn.[82] As it turned out, all three were with the Woolwich. The remaining two judges, in the minority on this occasion, were the oldest members of the panel, Lord Keith and Lord Jauncey. They sided with the Inland Revenue, arguing that the problem could only be tackled by parliament.

Lord Goff pointed out that to change the law would be to 'overstep the boundary which we traditionally set for ourselves, separating the legitimate development of the law by the judges from legislation'. He added: 'Although I am well aware of the existence of the boundary, I am never quite sure where to find it. Its position seems to vary from case to case.' In Lord Goff's view, other factors were more persuasive: 'The first is that this opportunity will never come again. If we do not take it now, it will be gone for ever. The second is that I fear that, however compelling the principle of justice may be, it would never be sufficient to persuade its legislative recognition by parliament; caution, otherwise known as the Treasury, would never allow this to happen.'

This seems an admirable approach. We shall be taking a more detailed look at the law lords' law-making functions in chapter 2.

1993

● In *Derbyshire County Council v. Times Newspapers Ltd*[83] the law lords had to decide whether a local authority could sue for libel. They concluded it could not: Lord Keith said it was contrary to the public interest for a government body – whether central or local – to bring an action for defamation, 'because to admit such actions would place an undesirable fetter on freedom of speech'. He added that it was 'of the highest public importance that a . . . governmental body should be open to uninhibited public criticism'.

What was remarkable about the *Derbyshire* case was that Anthony Lester QC, as counsel for Times Newspapers, had virtually persuaded the Court of Appeal, at an earlier hearing, to incorporate the European Convention on Human Rights into Britain's domestic law.[84] The lower court ruled that where English law was uncertain – as it was in this case – it should be interpreted consistently with the Human Rights Convention.[85] So the Court of Appeal applied Article 10 of the Convention, which prohibits interference with freedom of expression except where this is necessary in a democratic society (in other words, where there is a 'pressing social need').

That too was an admirable ruling but the law lords apparently had doubts over whether it was constitutionally sound. The European Convention has not – yet – been directly incorporated into the legal systems of the United Kingdom.[86] But instead of overturning the Court of Appeal's decision, the law lords discovered that the same result could be achieved by applying hitherto undiscovered principles lurking deep within the common law. Lord Keith said: 'I find it satisfactory to be able to conclude that the common law of England is consistent with the obligations assumed by the Crown under the treaty in this particular field.'

By ruling that the common law would stand up for freedom of speech in this way, the law lords had effectively incorporated a key part of Article 10 by the back door. Lord Keith was the only law lord to deliver a full opinion: the others merely nodded in agreement. That one opinion fully reflected the behind-the-scenes influence of the younger law lords, including Lord Browne-Wilkinson and Lord Woolf.

● The case of the five sado-masochists demonstrated clear differences of approach between the older law lords and their more liberal successors. In *R. v. Brown and others*[87] the more conservative-minded were in a majority of three to two over their more youthful brethren. A differently selected panel of law lords might well have tipped the balance.

The law lords were asked whether consent was a defence to charges of assault and wounding under the Offences against the Person Act 1861. The five appellants – unremarkable middle-aged men – had inflicted severe pain on other men for the purposes of sexual pleasure. Those who read the full evidence could hardly believe that what these men did to one another was physically possible, still less that it would cause no permanent damage. Yet, as one of the appellants said, they did not believe they were breaking the law: 'Everything was done with people's consent; everyone was over 21; there was no harm or injury done to anyone; nothing was done against their wishes; no one made an official complaint or any complaint at all to the police; no medical attention was needed; so where's the harm?'[88]

Three of the law lords disagreed strongly with this point of view. Lord Templeman said he was 'not prepared to invent a defence of consent for sado-masochistic encounters which breed and glorify cruelty'. Lord Jauncey said, 'It would not be in the public interest that deliberate infliction of actual bodily harm during the course of homosexual sado-masochistic activities should be held to be lawful.' Lord Lowry said there was 'no legal right to cause actual bodily harm in the course of sado-masochistic activity'.

In a powerful dissenting judgment Lord Mustill maintained that these were questions of private morality. In his view:

> the state should interfere with the rights of an individual to live his or her life as he or she may choose no more than is necessary to ensure a proper balance between the special interests of the individual and the general interests of the individuals who together comprise the populace at large. Thus, whilst acknowledging that very many people, if asked whether the appellants' conduct was wrong, would reply 'Yes, repulsively wrong,' I would at the same time assert that this does not mean that the prosecution of the appellants under sections 20 and 47 of the Offences against the Person Act 1861 is well founded.

Lord Slynn agreed with Lord Mustill that 'adults can consent to acts done in private which do not result in serious bodily harm, so that such acts do not constitute criminal assaults for the purposes of the Act of 1861'. But – by a majority – the five law lords upheld the men's convictions for assault. Some of the men immediately set in train an appeal to the European Court of Human Rights.

Running through the dissenting speeches in the House of Lords was a non-interventionist approach: a feeling that the law should not interfere unless intervention was clearly required by an act of parliament. However, such cases reach our highest court of appeal precisely because there is no clear statute law to deal with the subject.[89] This reluctance to usurp what was seen as the role of parliament was a feature of Lord Mustill's speech in a case decided a month earlier.

● Tony Bland was the young man whose dreadful injuries at the Hillsborough football disaster in 1989 had left him in what doctors called a 'persistent vegetative state': he was able to survive if fed through a tube, although he was unable to see, hear, think or feel. Asked what was to become of him, on this occasion the law lords all agreed – as did the judges in the courts below – that doctors could stop feeding him and allow him to die.[90]

Again there was a difference of approach. Lord Keith said it was up to the doctors to decide: 'a medical practitioner is under no duty to continue to treat a patient where a large body of informed and responsible medical opinion is to the effect that no benefit at all would be conferred by continuance.' Lord Goff agreed that it was not in Tony Bland's 'best interests' to continue treatment which had the effect of artificially prolonging his life. Lord Lowry went further and said that if it was 'not in the interests of an insentient patient to continue the life-supporting care and treatment, the doctor would be acting unlawfully if he continued the care and treatment and would perform no guilty act by discontinuing'.

Yet from Lord Browne-Wilkinson, one of the younger law lords, there was an altogether more thoughtful approach:

> On the moral issues raised by this case, society is not all of one mind. Although it is probably true that the majority would favour the withdrawal of life support in the present case, there is undoubtedly a substantial body of opinion that is strongly opposed . . .
> If the judges seek to develop new law to regulate the new circumstances, the law so laid down will of necessity reflect judges' views on the underlying ethical questions, questions on which there is a legitimate division of opinion . . . It is not for the judges to seek to develop new, all-embracing, principles of law in a way which reflects the individual judges' moral stance when society as a whole is substantially divided on the moral issues.

Even so, for Lord Browne-Wilkinson 'the critical decision to be made is whether it is in the best interests of Anthony Bland to continue the invasive medical care involved in artificial feeding'. In his view, the doctors could reasonably say that there was no affirmative benefit to this young man in continuing such care.

It was Lord Mustill, making the last speech of all, who grasped the nettle. 'The distressing truth which must not be shirked,' he said, 'is that the proposed conduct is not in the interests of Anthony Bland, for he has no best interests of any kind.' Lord Mustill was saying, in effect, that withdrawing feeding was in the best interests of those who were caring for Tony Bland – his parents and the nursing staff – rather than of the young man himself. However, with 'profound misgivings about almost every aspect of this case', Lord Mustill was able to find an argument which he felt was 'logically defensible and consistent with the existing law'. It was simply this: 'Although the termination of his life is not in the best interests of Anthony Bland, his best interests in being kept alive have also disappeared.' That meant the doctors were no longer under any duty to continue feeding him, and failure to do so could not be a criminal offence.

● The last judgment delivered by the law lords in the legal year 1992–3 showed how far the newer law lords were making their views felt. Lord Woolf, though the most junior member of the panel, knew more than any of the others about judicial review; he therefore delivered the main speech, leaving the others to agree with him. To preserve the anonymity of the applicant, his name was not disclosed. The case was known simply as *M. v. Home Office*.[91] This concern for *M.*'s welfare may have come too late: he had disappeared long before his case came before the House of Lords. And although he certainly had more substance than the famous snail in the ginger-beer bottle in *Donoghue v. Stevenson*[92] – which created the entire modern law of negligence although its existence was never proved – *M.* never met the lawyers who took his case to the House of Lords and may never have learned what impact he had on the British constitution.

M. was a young teacher who came to London from Zaïre and immediately claimed political asylum. He told the authorities he would be in danger if he was sent back but the Home Office decided he did not have the necessary 'well-founded fear of persecution'. The young Zaïrean sought judicial review to challenge that decision but he was not well served by the solicitors who were then representing him, and the courts rejected his application.

New solicitors were instructed only hours before *M.* was due to be put on a plane at Heathrow on 1 May 1991. There followed a series of emergency hearings, court orders, mistakes and misunderstandings which culminated in a visit by *M*'s new solicitor, David Burgess, to a judge's home after midnight. The judge, Mr Justice Garland, ordered the government to keep *M*. in its care and return him safely to England. By then *M*. was on a plane heading for Zaïre. But with exemplary devotion to his client, and no guarantee that he would ever be paid for his work, Mr Burgess made sure the British Embassy in Kinshasa knew of the judge's ruling. Embassy officials arranged for *M*. to be put on a flight back to London that evening, 2 May.

In the meantime, Home Office officials had arranged a meeting with the Home Secretary, Kenneth Baker MP. At the meeting Mr Baker was advised that Mr Justice Garland had exceeded his powers in ordering the Zaïrean to be returned because, under the law as it was then understood, no court could make a mandatory order against the Crown. If *M*. was brought back to Britain, officials told Mr Baker it would be extremely difficult to remove him – even if, as they expected, the judge's order was subsequently overturned.

Mr Baker decided that *M*. should not be returned to Britain. He gave two reasons: the assurance he had received from his junior minister, Peter Lloyd MP, that 'the underlying asylum decision . . . was the right one' and legal advice that Mr Justice Garland had no jurisdiction to make the order he did. This legal advice was subsequently confirmed by John Laws,[93] the independent barrister retained to advise the government. That evening Mr Laws advised the Home Office to challenge the judge's order at a hearing which had been arranged for the following morning. Until then, he thought the Home Office 'might reasonably hold its hand'. As a result *M*. was told there was no longer any urgent need for him to return to Britain, which presumably meant that the government had no urgent need to bring him back. He was asked to keep in touch with the British Embassy in Kinshasa but nothing was done to protect him.

The next morning, 3 May, Mr Justice Garland agreed that he had not had jurisdiction to make his original order. He pointed out that he had only granted the order in an attempt to make Home Office officials comply with their undertaking that *M*. would be kept in Britain until the case had been resolved. He believed that undertaking had been given at an earlier hearing on 1 May, and indeed he had said as much in his overnight order.

Home Office lawyers had not in fact thought they had given such an undertaking but, in the circumstances, they decided that *M*. should be returned to London. By then, however, the young Zaïrean could not be traced at the addresses he had given the British Embassy. He eventually contacted his solicitors from Nigeria but by the time arrangements were made to bring him back from Nigeria he had disappeared again. That was the last anybody heard from him.

The question for the courts was whether the Home Secretary, Kenneth Baker, was guilty of contempt of court for not complying with Mr Justice Garland's order to return *M*. to London. In the High Court Mr Justice Simon Brown decided he had no power to make a finding of contempt against either the Home Office or the Home Secretary. But by a majority the Court of Appeal overturned that decision. Lord Donaldson and Lord Justice Nolan found Mr Baker guilty of contempt, the first such finding against a minister of the Crown. Mr Baker was ordered to pay costs.

The key question for the law lords was whether the courts had the power to make coercive orders against ministers. After an extensive review of previous cases Lord Woolf concluded that they did. The courts, he decided, had power to grant interim and final injunctions against officers of the Crown.

It therefore followed that Mr Justice Garland did have the power to order the Home Secretary to bring *M*. back to Britain. However, there was no way this could have been known at the time because the existing court decisions suggested that the contrary was true. That was the advice given to Mr Baker. Was he to blame for not complying with the judge's order?

The problem for Mr Baker was that he did not challenge Mr Justice Garland's ruling at the first practicable opportunity and he did not take sufficient steps to protect *M*.'s position in the meantime. Hence the law lords upheld the finding of contempt. The Court of Appeal had believed it was not possible to make a finding against a government department or a minister of the Crown in his official capacity, although they did find Mr Baker personally liable. But Lord Woolf considered that no such restriction existed. Indeed, he thought it would be fairer to make the finding against Mr Baker in his official capacity as he was acting on advice and others were involved. In the end the finding of contempt was made against the Secretary of State for Home Affairs.[94]

It fell to Lord Templeman to produce the only quotable comment of the day. 'My Lords', he said, 'the argument that there is no power to enforce the law by injunction or contempt proceedings against a minister in his official capacity would, if upheld, establish the proposition that the executive obey the law as a matter of grace and not as a matter of necessity, a proposition which would reverse the result of the Civil War.'

If only it were that simple.

The Lord Chief Justice of England

The Lord Chief Justice is the most senior full-time professional judge in England and Wales: in the legal hierarchy he is therefore second only to the Lord Chancellor. His main role is to preside over the criminal division of the Court of Appeal. Accompanied by two other judges drawn from the Court of Appeal or the High Court, he hears the most important appeals against conviction (which these days are frequently alleged miscarriages of justice referred to the court by the Home Secretary). He also takes difficult sentencing appeals, thereby providing guideline decisions to be followed by other judges in future cases. Since 1989 those cases have included requests by the Attorney General to increase what he believes is an unduly lenient sentence.[95]

The Lord Chief Justice is also head of the High Court Queen's Bench Division, the largest of the three High Court divisions (the others are Chancery and Family). It deals mainly with debts, contract claims, actions for personal injuries and libel actions.

In addition, the Lord Chief Justice sits from time to time in what is called the Divisional Court of the Queen's Bench Division. This is the court that hears applications for judicial review of decisions taken by government departments, local authorities and public bodies. It has an important role to play in preserving citizens' rights.

The Lord Chief Justice has many other duties. For example, every time a sentence of life imprisonment is passed in a murder case the papers are sent to the Lord Chief Justice for his opinion on how long a term the prisoner should serve. As the senior judge sitting at the Royal Courts of Justice in London, he is consulted by the Courts Administrator on major decisions affecting the building and its use. He is the first point of contact between the Lord Chancellor's Department and other judges.

He also has a key role in selecting lawyers for promotion to the judiciary. The Lord Chief Justice is one of the four *Heads of Division* who gather together with the Lord Chancellor to decide who should join them on the judicial bench: the others are the Master of the Rolls, the Vice-Chancellor, and the President of the Family Division. All are known by their title followed by their name: hence 'the Lord Chief Justice, Lord Smith' or 'the Vice-Chancellor, Sir John Smith'.

One of the Lord Chief Justice's most important roles is to act as the judges' shop steward. It is to him that they take their complaints; it is his job to try to ensure that those complaints are resolved. He can do this by having a quiet word with the Lord Chancellor or by speaking more publicly in the House of Lords (of which he becomes a member on his appointment).[96] He will also find the media more than willing to publicise his views.

Perhaps his most important task is to act as the public figurehead of the judiciary. Whether he likes it or not the Lord Chief Justice will get the blame if the system appears to be working badly, if justice appears to be miscarrying. He must therefore act as a lightning-conductor, drawing in the charges and neutralising them by persuading the public that enough is being done to put the faults right, or at least by making it clear that the fault lies elsewhere. That role was taken on with enthusiasm by Lord Taylor in 1992. It had been rejected by his predecessor.

Lord Lane

Until his retirement in April 1992 the Lord Chief Justice of England was Lord Lane. Geoffrey Lane held the country's most senior judicial office for twelve years. He was humane and liberal when dealing with non-violent offenders, firm and unyielding when dealing with drink-drivers and rapists. He rescued the courts for which he was responsible from the administrative chaos sadly bequeathed to him by his prematurely senile predecessor Lord Widgery.[97] He made new law by ruling that a man could be guilty of raping his wife: until the case of *R. v. R.*[98] it had been thought that a husband was immune. And he fought long and hard – but without success – for an end to the mandatory sentence of life imprisonment for murder.

Yet to some extent Lord Lane was the architect of his own ignominy. Passionately concerned to protect an independent judiciary, he confused independence with isolation and never understood the need to communicate with the outside world. He thus allowed himself to be characterised, quite wrongly, as an arch-reactionary out of touch with ordinary life.

It was his passionate opposition to the mandatory sentence of life imprisonment for murder which persuaded Lord Lane to give his first on-the-record interview to a journalist in December 1993. The Prison Reform Trust had invited the former Lord Chief Justice to chair an inquiry which, to nobody's surprise, recommended that judges should be able to pass whatever sentence they thought appropriate in a case of murder. Lord Lane gave a news conference to publicise his report and agreed to a radio interview with the BBC.[99]

Under Lord Lane the Court of Appeal issued a series of guideline judgments which were circulated to every Crown Court in England and Wales in an attempt to encourage consistency in sentencing. Two of Lord Lane's earliest cases established his liberal credentials. In *R. v. Upton*,[100] in March 1980, he said, 'Non-violent petty offenders should not be allowed to take up what has become valuable space in prison. If there is really no alternative . . . to an immediate prison sentence, then it should be as short as possible.' He returned to his theme a few months later in *R. v. Bibi*,[101] when he said it was no secret that our prisons were 'dangerously overcrowded'.

Lord Windlesham, a former Home Office minister and chairman of the Parole Board, writes revealingly in a recent book about Lord Lane's relationship with the government.[102] He says the *Upton* and *Bibi* judgments corresponded so closely with the views of William Whitelaw, then Home Secretary, that discreet soundings were taken to see if Lord Lane would be willing to meet Mr Whitelaw:

> The answer was favourable and in the autumn of 1980, in conditions of great secrecy, a dinner party was held on neutral ground in a private room at a West End club . . . The meeting was sufficiently successful for it to be agreed that it should be followed up by a series of buffet suppers at which Leon Brittan [then Minister of State at the Home Office], accompanied by some of the Home Office officials, would meet a number of judges for an off-the-record discussion. Only one of the projected series of four had taken place when the fragile concord was shattered by a disagreement arising out of media coverage of a change in policy.

A newspaper report[103] accused the judges of thwarting Home Office plans to try to reduce the prison population. Lord Lane was furious at this inaccurate story which was directly attributed to the

Home Secretary himself. According to Lord Windlesham's account, in Lord Lane's eyes the episode bore out what he had always suspected: that no politician could be trusted, that political expediency would always come first, and that they were all the same under the skin.

When the two men next met, early in 1983, it seemed they had put the incident behind them; but formal relations between the Home Secretary and the Lord Chief Justice were not resumed until 1986. By then Douglas Hurd had taken over at the Home Office. Lord Lane and his trusty deputy, Lord Justice Watkins, had regular and less clandestine meetings with the Home Secretary, culminating in the first of a series of national conferences held at Ditchley Park, Oxfordshire, in September 1989.

In the privacy of his room at the law courts, invariably dressed in a comfortable brown cardigan and standing slightly shorter than one might have expected, Lord Lane looked like a wise old uncle who had found that the world was changing too quickly for his liking. Those changes were indeed rapid. People no longer showed as much deference and respect to those in authority as they had when Geoffrey Lane had become a judge a quarter of a century earlier. When something went wrong the public now looked for someone to blame. If there was a miscarriage of justice, they blamed the man who presided over the trial. If there was a series of miscarriages, the public blamed the man who presided over the judicial system.

Lord Lane's fellow judges maintained that this was monstrously unfair. On Lord Lane's retirement the Master of the Rolls, Lord Donaldson, said the judiciary were outraged by attempts to make the Lord Chief Justice a scapegoat for the failings of the criminal justice system.[104] Lord Justice Russell – a close colleague of Lord Lane – said the judges had no control over the evidence given in a trial: 'If juries are misled by police officers who are economic with the truth, or scientists who are less than frank, then so can judges be misled. But nowadays it seems to be the judges who are at fault. People seem to forget it's the verdict of the jury that counts.'[105]

This statement sums up the confusion of thought from which the judges were suffering. Why should the jury's verdict count if the jury itself had been misled? Why should it not be reversed on appeal? Under Lord Lane, the Court of Appeal went to great lengths to avoid overturning a jury's verdict: the appeal judges said it was not up to them to substitute their own views for those of the people who had seen and heard all the witnesses. But those witnesses may not have been telling the truth. If that was reasonably clear, it was right for the Court of Appeal to overturn the verdict. Far from diminishing respect for the jury system, as judges like Lord Lane feared, effective machinery for correcting mistakes would actually have enhanced it.

It was said[106] that judges of Lord Lane's generation refused to believe that police evidence could be institutionally corrupt. The truth is probably more subtle. They knew perfectly well that police officers told lies on oath, but they generally preferred to believe that the police had arrested the right people. If that was the case, what was said in the witness box became less important.

In some cases that approach may have led to rough justice of a sort. Even if the police witnesses had concocted all the evidence, judges of a certain disposition tended to believe that those before the court might well have committed the crime with which they were charged – or at the very least something similar on a previous occasion. On that basis, where was the harm in locking them up? It was what public opinion wanted.

Of course this was no way to run a criminal justice system. As Lord Lane was eventually to accept, turning a blind eye to police malpractice only encouraged officers to think they could get away with it, indeed to think that manufacturing evidence was what was demanded of them.

In his brief retirement speech Lord Lane referred to 'orchestrated and ill-informed attacks on the judiciary'.[107] He was right to say that the attacks were generally ill-informed but that does not mean they were wrong. Lord Lane was his own worst enemy. Because he was the leading judge in the criminal justice system it was his job to reassure an increasingly worried public that everything possible was being done to make the criminal justice system as effective as possible. He never accepted that. People were relieved to find his successor had a different approach.

Lord Taylor

On the day his appointment was announced Lord Taylor of Gosforth held a news conference at which he acknowledged public anxiety about the criminal justice system. 'Indeed', he stressed, 'the judiciary is anxious about cases that have gone wrong. We have all got a job to do to restore confidence and try to improve those aspects of the system that need it.'

He agreed to speak regularly to journalists during his period in office but appeared irritable when relations with the media did not go entirely as he had planned. At least one journalist wondered how much he really cared for the press. Hugo Young said that while Lord Taylor was 'anxious to court the media, and perhaps even redeem it, he can't escape the instinctive belief, found in the bones of every judge I know, that the media are the enemy'.[108]

Certainly Lord Taylor thought the press painted a blacker picture of the criminal justice system than was merited by the facts. He criticised the media on what seemed like countless occasions for digging up and reproducing generations of thoughtless remarks made by Circuit judges because one of their number had just said something silly in court. And he complained from time to time that the press unfairly criticised 'perfectly sensible and reasonable sentences' passed by his fellow judges, accusing reporters of slanting their accounts.

The Lord Chief Justice maintained that he fully understood that 'good news is boring, while bad news is considered better copy'. So, in Lord Taylor's view, the tendency was to interview someone who disagreed with the sentence:

> If the sentence is on the light side, there is an interview with the victim or the victim's relatives. They can usually be relied on to say that the sentence was outrageously lenient. If, on the other hand, the sentence is on the heavy side, the defendant's wife or relatives will be interviewed to say how cruel and brutal the judge was. No wonder, in these circumstances, the impression the public gain from newspapers and the television is that judges frequently impose unsatisfactory sentences.[109]

This is something of a caricature. If a sentence is thought to be broadly right then it will attract little media interest. The sort of sentences seen as too severe are life terms for domestic murders (where the judge has no choice) and imprisonment for offending young mothers (typically, where an eccentric Circuit judge has decided to make an example of somebody). The defendant's angry relatives will be interviewed only on these comparatively rare occasions. It is much more common for the victim of the crime – or even the police these days – to complain that the sentence was too lenient; and in many such cases the sentence is subsequently increased by the Court of Appeal on a reference by the Attorney General. Indeed, the judges rely on the newspapers to reflect public disquiet, a factor they ignore at their peril. If the sentence really is correct, perhaps for reasons which are not widely known, then it is the judge's business to explain these reasons and make sure that his explanation reaches the press.

Lord Taylor rejected the popular view of the judiciary as Establishment-minded. That reflected his own background: although he won an exhibition[110] to Cambridge the new Lord Chief Justice was not himself a traditional Establishment figure. Peter Taylor was born in Newcastle and educated at the famous grammar school there. While making no claims to be religiously observant, he believed his Jewish background made him more sympathetic to the needs of minorities in society.[111] Asked why he thought he had become Lord Chief Justice he replied, 'I would like to think that I am not thought to be, rightly or wrongly, wholly out of touch – that I am in the mainstream of life in the country.'

Compared with his predecessor Lord Taylor was seen as something of a liberal. The true picture is more subtle. It was Lord Lane, as we have seen, who said that prison sentences should be 'as short as possible, consistent only with the duty to protect the interests of the public and to punish and deter the criminal'.[112] It was Lord Taylor who spoke out against the 'penologists, criminologists and bureaucrats in government departments' whom he blamed for imposing a sentencing regime in the Criminal Justice Act 1991 – which prevented the judges from sending persistent offenders to prison. There were powerful arguments for custody, he said; 'it may not necessarily reform the offender, but at least it punishes him in a way society would regard as just.'[113]

Lord Lane was never comfortable when talking to the Home Office although he did respect one Home Secretary, Douglas Hurd. Lord Taylor, on the other hand, had no hesitation about speaking to the government. He had met the then Home Secretary, Kenneth Clarke QC, to discuss ways of amending the Criminal Justice Act 1991, and he was invited to meet Mr Clarke's successor, Michael Howard QC, on Mr Howard's first day in office. Lord Taylor said he hoped there would be sensible and regular contact between the Home Office and the judiciary, and that they would be able to work together 'in harness'.[114] It seemed that Michael Howard agreed.

The Master of the Rolls

The Master of the Rolls is the second most senior full-time judge in England after the Lord Chief Justice. He heads the Civil Division of the Court of Appeal. He can expect a peerage but not immediately on appointment like the Lord Chief Justice.

The title 'Master of the Rolls' dates from at least as far back as the thirteenth century but the roles he has to master have changed greatly over the years. He used to keep the rolls or records of the Chancery – and he is still responsible for supervising the enrolment of solicitors: every solicitor admitted to the roll receives a certificate signed by him. Some 4,400 admission certificates were issued during the year 1992–3: Lord Denning used to sign them while watching television.

Lord Denning

Although it is more than a decade since he laid down his battered wig Lord Denning is still linked in the minds of many people with the title Master of the Rolls. In an age when judges shunned publicity Lord Denning became the one judicial figure everyone had heard of.

He presided over the Civil Division of the Court of Appeal for twenty years, from 1962 to 1982. As such he generally had the last word: relatively few cases were appealed further to the House of Lords. But in seeking justice Lord Denning seemed to think he was entitled to get round – or even change – any rule of law that stood in his way. In his view, there was generally no need to wait for legislation. 'Parliament makes the law too late,' he once said. 'The judge should make the law correspond with the justice that the case requires.'

Lord Denning's critics maintained that his willingness to overturn decided cases made for uncertainty in the law. Although he saw himself as the champion of the underdog – the ordinary citizen, the consumer, the deserted wife – he supported employers against trade unions, education authorities against students and the Home Office against immigrants.

Towards the end of his thirty-eight years on the bench, Lord Denning formed the habit of publishing a popular book every year. One was to bring his career to an end. In *What Next in the Law* he seemed to be suggesting that some black people were unsuitable to serve on juries. His remarks followed a riot trial in Bristol, and two jurors on the case threatened to sue him. Asked to comment, Lady

Denning uttered the immortal words: 'My husband is taking legal advice.' Shortly afterwards Lord Denning apologised and announced that, at the age of 83, he would finally be retiring.[115]

His comments in retirement added nothing to his reputation: another apology followed his claim that the Guildford Four, acquitted on appeal, were probably guilty of murder all along. That allegation was clearly libellous and cannot be justified. Lord Denning's personal prejudices demonstrated the risks of letting one man dispense 'palm-tree justice'.

This should not be allowed to detract from a unique judicial career. Tom Denning was the greatest law-making judge of our century. His achievement was to shape the common law according to his own highly individual vision of society. He stood firm for freedom under the law, a phrase he himself coined more than forty years ago.

Lord Donaldson

Lord Denning was succeeded in 1982 by Sir John Donaldson. Sir John, a former local councillor,[116] had served as president of the ill-fated National Industrial Relations Court from 1971 until it was abolished in 1974 by the incoming Labour government.[117] At that point, as a highly regarded High Court judge of eight years' standing, he could reasonably have expected rapid promotion to the Court of Appeal. But, as we have seen, Sir John Donaldson had to wait until 1979 when there was a change of government. According to the Lord Chief Justice, Lord Taylor, political feelings were the sole explanation for the delay. Speaking at a ceremony to mark Lord Donaldson's retirement in 1992[118] Lord Taylor said it was the only example in recent memory of political influence playing a part in judicial appointments.

Lord Donaldson's achievement was to transform the running of the Court of Appeal Civil Division. He computerised the court lists and introduced annual progress reports on the number of cases heard during the previous year. He saved time in court by insisting that barristers should hand in written 'skeleton arguments' rather than read everything aloud; in exchange he handed down written judgments whenever possible. He also tried to discourage what he saw as 'hopeless' cases by arguing that no appeal should be heard by his court unless a judge had looked at the papers beforehand and decided there was a case to argue.

Sir Thomas Bingham

On Lord Donaldson's retirement as Master of the Rolls in 1992 he was succeeded by Sir Thomas Bingham, the ninety-third holder of the post. Nowadays most candidates for high judicial office are expected to have carried out a successful public inquiry for the government at some time; shortly before his promotion Lord Justice Bingham had investigated the collapsed Bank of Credit and Commerce International.

Sir Thomas Bingham is formidably clever. He won a scholarship to Sedbergh School in Yorkshire and was considered to have been its most brilliant pupil this century.[119] After a taking a First in Modern History at Balliol, and coming top of his year in the Bar finals, he was made a QC in 1972 at the age of 38, specialising in commercial work. His name became public currency in 1978 when he published a report which concluded that oil corporations had knowingly violated trade sanctions against Rhodesia with the complicity of British civil servants. He became a judge in 1980.

Elegant and eloquent, Sir Thomas was the first judge to support plans announced by the Lord Chancellor in 1989 for solicitors to appear in the higher courts. He sought to make the courts more efficient by continuing the shift away from oral argument towards more paperwork. He believed that the public had a false impression of the judges who, he said, were not 'senile old fuddy-duddies dribbling over their papers'. On the whole, he thought, they were rather brisk, alert, up-to-date sort of people.[120]

A few days before he took over as Master of the Rolls Sir Thomas Bingham renewed his call for a Bill of Rights: he had already declared his support for the idea in a BBC interview on the day his appointment was announced.[121] Speaking at the Bar Conference in September 1992, Sir Thomas said the need to incorporate the European Convention on Human Rights into domestic law had never been greater. 'We are signatories to the European Convention, we ratified it and in large measure we drafted it. But the British courts are unable, save in a marginal way, to pay any attention to it.'

According to the Master of the Rolls, this had three undesirable results. First, it weakened the confidence of the public in the British courts: people who lost their cases often felt they had to go to Strasbourg to get their rights protected. Second, it led to the frequent reversal of British court decisions at an international tribunal: it was better to have our dirty linen laundered at home. And third, there was the delay and cost of going to the European Court: a simple case about corporal punishment had just taken seven years to reach that court.[122] We shall be looking more closely at this issue in chapter 4.

The Vice-Chancellor

The Chancery Division of the High Court deals with topics such as companies and partnerships, patents and copyright, bankruptcies, trusts, land, mortgages and wills. As we have seen, the senior judge is theoretically the Lord Chancellor but in practice he never sits. It was decided in 1970 that the Chancery Division needed an active head and so the nineteenth-century title of Vice-Chancellor was revived and awarded to a Chancery judge nominated by the Lord Chancellor.

Sir Richard Scott

In July 1994 the Prime Minister announced that Lord Justice Scott would become Vice-Chancellor at the beginning of October. Sir Richard Scott was well known in Downing Street: Mr Major had been cross-examined by him during Sir Richard's inquiry into the sale of arms to Iraq. The Prime Minister was apparently undeterred by the prospect of criticism from Sir Richard in the report he was planning to publish early in 1995. Sir Richard Scott was educated in South Africa before being called to the English Bar. He demonstrated a fearless independence both in his inquiry and when sitting as a judge.

The President

The grandly named President is simply no more than head of the Family Division, created when the old Probate, Divorce and Admiralty Division ('wills, wives and wrecks') was abolished in 1971.[123] The Family Division deals with all aspects of family law, especially the breakdown of marriage and the resulting problems relating to children and property.

Sir Stephen Brown

Sir Stephen Brown became President in 1988 after five years in the Court of Appeal. As a High Court judge he had served in both the Family Division and the Queen's Bench Division. A charming man of the old school, in 1992 he found himself dealing with profound moral and ethical questions, sometimes at a moment's notice – for example, should a woman in labour be forced to have a caesarian section to save her life and that of her baby; should a hospital have the right to stop feeding someone in a 'persistent vegetative state'; and should a fourteen-year-old girl have the right to decide to live apart from her parents? His judgments were marked by common sense rather than profound ethical insights.

The Court of Appeal judges

There are 29 judges in the Court of Appeal, the maximum allowed by statute. All of them were promoted from the High Court.[124] They are called *Lords Justices of Appeal* and they become members of the Privy Council on appointment. In court they would be known formally as the Rt. Hon. Lord Justice Smith, which is abbreviated to 'Smith LJ' in the law reports and elsewhere. In the world outside they become the Rt. Hon. Sir John Smith or the Rt. Hon. Dame Jane Smith DBE (although the 'Rt. Hon.'[125] is often omitted). The knighthood (or DBE) arrived at an earlier stage in the judge's career, when he or she was first appointed to the High Court.

A woman appointed to the Court of Appeal has to take the same judicial title as a man. The Supreme Court Act 1981[126] says: 'The ordinary judges of the Court of Appeal . . . shall be styled "Lords Justices of Appeal".' This anomaly caused some difficulties. When sitting in the Court of Appeal Dame Elizabeth Butler-Sloss was always addressed as 'My Lady', as she had been when she was a High Court judge. But barristers who referred to her when addressing a court of which she was a member had to speak of her as 'My Lady, Lord Justice Butler-Sloss.' As Sir Thomas Bingham said in April 1994, this was an absurd usage. In a statement from the Bench, the Master of the Rolls said that while the formal statutory position could not be changed for the time being, it was desirable that she should in future be referred to in court as Lady Justice Butler-Sloss.

The Lords Justices of Appeal sit in London to hear both criminal and civil appeals. They also sit from time to time in the Divisional Court to hear important cases involving judicial review of administrative decisions. When the Court of Appeal is short of judges (and when is it not?) the Lord Chancellor may ask High Court judges and retired judges from both the Court of Appeal and the High Court to hear cases. It is wrong in principle that the latter should be called upon, except as a temporary expedient. Judges lose their judicial titles on retirement: a retired Lord Justice of Appeal would therefore sit as Sir John Smith.[127]

High Court judges

By November 1993 the number of High Court judges in post had reached the Lord Chancellor's target of 95; the maximum number now allowed is 98. The statutory qualification for appointment is to have held rights of audience in the High Court for ten years or to have been a Circuit judge for at least two years.[128]

This means it is now possible for a Circuit judge who was previously a solicitor to be appointed to the High Court without having qualified as a barrister first. In June 1993 the first such appointment was made: Mr Justice Sachs had practised as a solicitor in Manchester before becoming a Circuit judge in 1984.

It used to be quite unusual for a Circuit judge to be moved up to the High Court although such promotions are becoming more common.[129] However, most High Court judges are still appointed from among the leading Queen's Counsel – men and women in their middle to late forties or their early fifties.[130] Lord Mackay was keen to appoint judges at a younger age than before. Before appointment judges are expected to prove themselves by sitting part-time as a Recorder (or as a Deputy High Court judge).

Few things irritate lawyers more than a report of a case which gets the judge's title wrong. Journalists gain credibility if they can name a judge correctly; they tend to be disbelieved – however accurate their reports – if they confuse a High Court judge with a Circuit judge, or mix up a Lord of Appeal and a Lord Justice of Appeal. It is worth spending a moment longer on judicial titles.

A male High Court judge would be called the Hon. Mr Justice Smith. A woman would become the Hon. Mrs Justice Smith, whether she was married or not – to avoid any suggestion of a 'misjustice'.[131] Both are abbreviated to 'Smith J' in the law reports. The prefix 'Hon.' is usually omitted except on formal documents. High Court judges are sometimes called 'puisne judges'[132] or 'red judges'.[133]

It is normally a solecism to include the judge's first name in his or her judicial title. The exception to this rule arises when two judges share the same surname. If that happens, the judges would be known as Mr Justice John Smith and Mr Justice Peter Smith (and the equivalent for Lords Justices).[134] Judges in the higher courts (the High Court, the Court of Appeal, and the House of Lords) are addressed in court as 'My Lord' or 'My Lady', as appropriate.[135]

Confusingly, the judges do not keep the titles 'Mr' and 'Mrs' outside the courtroom. All High Court judges receive a knighthood or DBE on appointment. They would therefore become the Hon. Sir John Smith or the Hon. Dame Jane Smith DBE.

Letters to a High Court judge may begin 'Dear Sir John/Dame Jane', or one can simply write 'Dear Judge'. In conversation outside the courtroom a judge would nowadays be addressed as 'Judge' rather than 'My Lord'.[136]

On retirement a High Court judge gives up the title 'Mr Justice' or 'Mrs Justice'. They are also dishonoured – in the sense that they lose the right to call themselves 'the Honourable'. This seems unfair. A retired member of the Court of Appeal is still 'Rt. Hon.'. Even retired Circuit judges remain 'His Hon.' or 'Her Hon.'.

The government announced in March 1993 that High Court judges would continue to receive knighthoods on appointment even though other worthies like Permanent Secretaries would receive them only on merit. This exception to the prime minister's reform of the honours system was justified on the ground that it would preserve the independence of the judiciary: that was presumably intended to mean that the judges should not feel under any pressure to be nice to the government. While this sentiment is admirable, its logic is flawed; the same independence could be preserved by ruling that, in future, *no* judge would receive an honour. But that would make it even harder to recruit them in the first place.

Deputy High Court judges
Queen's Counsel may be appointed to sit part-time as Deputy High Court judges 'where it is expedient as a temporary measure'.[137] In addition, Circuit judges may be invited by the Lord Chancellor to sit as Deputy High Court judges.

Some of the QCs are being tried out for a full-time appointment in the High Court; others do not want to sit full-time (or would never be offered the opportunity). In the spring of 1993 more work was being done by deputies in the Queen's Bench Division in London than by High Court judges.[138] Except in emergencies it must be quite wrong to expect litigants who are bringing or defending proceedings in the High Court to appear before judges who are not suitable or not willing to sit permanently in that court, particularly as they do not have the same measure of judicial independence as those appointed full-time.

Circuit judges

In July 1994 there were 510 Circuit judges in post: the number has been increasing steadily in line with the judicial workload. The statutory qualification is to have had rights of audience in the Crown Court or the county courts for ten years; or to be a Recorder; or to have served for at least three years in one of a number of more junior judicial offices.[139] Solicitors have been eligible for appointment as Circuit judges since the species was created in 1971[140] although they needed to clock up five years' experience as Recorders first and so the first solicitor Circuit judges were not appointed until 1976. At the last count, 61 Circuit judges were former solicitors – about 12 per cent.

A Circuit judge has the title His Honour Judge Smith or Her Honour Judge Smith; they are normally addressed in court as 'Your Honour'.[141] Once retired, they are no longer entitled to be called 'Judge' but they retain their 'Honour'.

Curiously, those Circuit judges who were Queen's Counsel keep the letters 'QC' after their names even though by convention they do not return to practise as barristers. High Court judges are never called 'QC'. The official reason for this is said to be that High Court judges are appointed by letters patent and these replace the silks' letters patent; while Circuit judges are appointed by warrant, leaving their patents unaffected. A more plausible reason is that those Circuit judges who were Queen's Counsel wish to retain their former seniority: almost all High Court judges were formerly QCs but the same is certainly not true of the Circuit bench.

Circuit judges sit in the Crown Court to try all but the most serious criminal cases and in the county courts where they handle most types of civil cases (apart from judicial review). Much of the work they do these days is on a par with work done by High Court judges and indeed they are deputising for High Court judges more and more often. But the pay and prestige are not as great: there is no escaping the conclusion that many of the lawyers who become Circuit judges would not have made it to the High Court. This issue is discussed more fully in chapter 2.

District judges

There are around 290 full-time District judges working in the county courts, handling minor judicial work which is not thought to need the expertise of a Circuit judge. Until 1990 they were called Registrars but this title did not indicate to most people that they served a judicial function. It was also realised that the job – which is not always easy to fill – could be made to sound much more impressive for no extra pay and it was retitled accordingly.[142] And now that the Registrars had become judges, it was felt that they could be given more responsible work to do.[143]

District judges are appointed from among those who have rights of audience in the county courts or magistrates' courts (which currently means barristers and solicitors). There are approximately 740 Deputy District judges who sit part-time.

Recorders and Assistant Recorders

Recorders and Assistant Recorders are part-time judges. The qualification for appointment is to have had rights of audience in the Crown Court or county courts for ten years (which means solicitors are eligible).[144] There are currently around 860 Recorders and 390 Assistant Recorders. Solicitors account for about 9 per cent of Recorders and about 17 per cent of Assistant Recorders.

It was only towards the end of 1990 that the Lord Chancellor made it clear that anyone wanting to become an Assistant Recorder would have to make a formal application. Until 1991 solicitors were required to apply, while barristers were approached by the Lord Chancellor's Department.[145]

In 1993 there were approximately 1,000 applications for Assistant Recordership on the books. The Lord Chancellor expected to make around 90 appointments during the year, which perhaps explains why some applicants have to wait a number of years for a decision. Applicants are interviewed by a panel of two people: a Recorder and an official from the Lord Chancellor's Department. Only the official sees the Lord Chancellor's secret file on the candidate.[146] Around 20 Recorders were recruited for the selection process: they are given no formal briefing on what qualities to look for.

An Assistant Recorder is authorised by the Lord Chancellor to sit part-time in the Crown Court and the county courts for a fixed period of approximately five years. He or she is required to sit for a minimum of 20 days per year: some of the most successful QCs have difficulty finding four clear weeks in a busy year. During that time the Assistant Recorder's work will be assessed, and 'it is expected that he or she will have progressed to a full Recordship after three to five years'. If not, the Assistant Recorder is not given a second chance.

Recorders are appointed by the Queen on the recommendation of the Lord Chancellor. The initial appointment is for approximately three years. Provided the Recorder's work is satisfactory, his or her appointment will be renewed at three-yearly intervals until the Recorder is 72 or becomes a full-time judge. Recorders sit for between 20 and 50 days a year.

Magistrates

The title Justice of the Peace first appeared in the year 1361 although Simon de Montfort had appointed 'Keepers of the Peace' as early as 1264.[147] The Justices of the Peace Act 1361 is still in force; it is used to 'bind over' people to be of good behaviour. Even people who have not committed offences can be bound over under this power. It seems absurd that the courts should still be relying on medieval statutes at the end of the twentieth century.

There are currently nearly 30,000 part-time lay magistrates (also called Justices of the Peace) together with some 85 full-time legally qualified stipendiaries. Most of them are appointed by the Lord Chancellor. However, magistrates in Greater Manchester, Merseyside and Lancashire are appointed instead by the Chancellor of the Duchy of Lancaster, a government minister who usually has no interest in legal matters: even though he invariably acts on advice, there can be no possible justification for maintaining this anomaly.

Magistrates must live within 15 miles of the county in which they sit. They must be under the age of 60 on appointment, and of good character. Their occupation must not conflict with their judicial role.

Magistrates are recommended for appointment by local advisory committees, of which there are more than a hundred in all. When vacancies arise, these committees can seek nominations from local organisations and political parties; or individuals may put their own names forward. The secretary of the local advisory committee can be contacted through the magistrates' clerk: many committee members are themselves magistrates. Most advisory committees used to keep their membership secret to avoid 'possible subjection to undesirable or unwanted influences',[148] which presumably meant people lobbying for or against particular candidates. But to 'remove the aura of unnecessary secrecy' Lord Mackay decided that from the beginning of 1993 all advisory committees would publish the names of their members.[149]

Magistrates may be sacked by the Lord Chancellor. A magistrate will be expected to resign if he or she is convicted of an offence of dishonesty, although magistrates who are found guilty of drink-driving offences may simply be suspended during the period of disqualification and those convicted of other motoring offences sometimes receive no more than a reprimand (in addition to whatever penalty the court may impose). There is a strong argument for saying that a person convicted of drunken driving is no longer fit to serve as a magistrate.

Local authorities pay 20 per cent of the cost of running their magistrates' courts while the government makes available the remaining 80 per cent – £303 million in 1992–3. In 1992 the Home Office introduced new restrictions on the way it allocated this money. Courts would be assessed on how many cases they handled, how efficiently they enforced the fines they imposed and, to a much lesser extent, on the speed and quality of their work. The more cases they dealt with and the more fines they collected, the more money they would receive to run their courts.

When this remarkable pay-by-results scheme was announced in 1991 the chairman of the Bar, Anthony Scrivener QC, condemned it as 'one which would be entirely appropriate for a meat packaging factory'. He pointed out that a case would attract the same level of government grant whether the defendant pleaded guilty or insisted on a long-drawn-out trial. With this in mind Mr Scrivener predicted that a good magistrates' clerk would make sure his court got all the drunk and disorderly cases. 'An afternoon of motoring pleas will be like a day at the sales,' he suggested.[150]

Mr Scrivener's predictions proved right. Speaking in the summer of 1993 the clerk to the Liverpool magistrates, Malcolm Marsh, said that he could make a lot of money out of people who had not bought their television licences:

> TV licence cases can be dealt with very quickly in court: sometimes we may list as many as 100 to be dealt with in two and a half hours. Each case generates in excess of £25, so that court can generate a tremendous amount of income. If you go on to have those people fined and they all pay without much enforcement, then each payment generates between £16 and £20 income for the court.[151]

Mr Marsh acknowledged that it was better to spend the time of his courts on the more serious cases brought by the police, but a contested case could last two or three days. 'That just takes up time in court, costs the court a lot of money, and in the end generates between £100 and £150 in income,' he said. Mr Marsh realised that his courts were part of the fight against crime. But he also had to balance his books.

Anthony Scrivener pointed out in 1993 that the new system of funding magistrates' courts was designed to save money rather than dispense justice. From that point of view, he said the most successful case was one where a defendant was denied legal representation (thus saving legal-aid costs), who was too inarticulate to speak (thus saving time in court) and who agreed to plead guilty (thus saving the costs of a trial). 'Now, to an economist that is a complete triumph,' said Mr Scrivener, 'but it doesn't mean to say you've necessarily got the right result.'[152]

The government argued that efficiency and justice were not enemies: they were to be found side by side. But how can it be just to reduce the charges in exchange for a cost-effective plea of guilty? And how can it be just to caution offenders simply because it is too expensive to prosecute them?

Under the new funding arrangements courts are given an incentive to crack down on offenders who do not pay their fines. In theory, this seems just: why should people get away with defaulting? But if an offender does not have the money, then enforcement means sending him to prison for non-payment. Far from benefiting anybody, this ends up costing the system more.

The drive to clear backlogs of unpaid fines produced some strange results. In September 1993 magistrates at Aylesbury in Buckinghamshire sent two offenders to police cells for the afternoon to clear unpaid fines of more than £1,000 each. The court had decided there was little or no prospect of these fines being paid: in one case they dated back to 1988. The local police protested that the men were 'earning' £300 an hour by sitting in the cells – 'It's the sort of money Michael Jackson gets,' said one astounded officer.[153] In fact, the magistrates had acted perfectly reasonably: they would have been penalised for keeping the outstanding fines on their books. True, the exchequer did not receive any money from the offenders – but there was little chance of that anyway. And the punishment imposed on the two men cost the system less than a single day in prison.

In 1955 the Lord Chancellor, Lord Kilmuir, said:

> Of all the duties of the Lord Chancellor, whether presenting a person to a living[154] or dealing with the affairs of a lunatic, there is nothing in a day's work which is of greater importance to the community as a whole – and, I would add, nothing which is liable to give him a greater headache – than his duties in relation to magistrates.[155]

Times have changed, but the organisation of magistrates' courts is still something of a headache for the Lord Chancellor. Since 1989 the government has been looking for an analgesic. However, as we shall discover in chapter 6, its latest prescription has produced some alarming side-effects.

An executive agency

In 1993 the government announced that the court service in England and Wales would become an executive agency from April 1995. This was in line with the government's policy of aiming to improve the way court staff were managed and it meant more delegated authority in operational matters. Lord Mackay said that agency status would provide court service management with 'a clearer focus on the job to be done, and greater flexibility to respond to the needs of court users'.

It was intended that the changes would apply to the county courts, the Crown Court, the High Court and the Court of Appeal. Staff would remain civil servants but they would report to a Chief Executive, who in turn would be answerable to the Lord Chancellor. In the almost meaningless jargon of the Lord Chancellor's Department there would be a change towards 'a more performance-oriented culture' with 'a greater sense of unity and corporate identity'. The government had, however, dismissed a similar plan for the magistrates' courts.[156]

The Lord Chief Justice said it was important that the independence of the judiciary should not be undermined by these changes. In Lord Taylor's view, agency status ought not to affect the judges and could lead to greater efficiency in the courts.[157] This sounded like wishful thinking.

It was perhaps surprising that there was so little opposition to the announcement of agency status for the court service. No longer would a cabinet minister be directly responsible for the men and women who administered the courts of justice. The old ideals of public service would be replaced with a new policy of making the courts pay their way. Nobody could seriously suppose that justice would prosper as a result.

2

What's Wrong with the Judiciary?

The politics of the judiciary

The judges have a unique role in our unwritten constitution. It has always been part of their job to make new law. As we shall see, that is inevitable: parliament cannot provide for every contingency. And increasingly the judges are having to hold the ring between the citizen and the state. That, too, is clearly part of their function. But what nobody predicted is that they would now be stepping into the empty shoes of the parliamentary opposition, shoes which are now more than a little scuffed after kicking ineffectually against the government for fourteen years and more.

Speaking in May 1993 Sir Thomas Bingham suggested that the constitutional balance was tilting towards the judiciary. 'The courts have reacted to the increase in the powers claimed by the government by being more active themselves,' he said, adding that this had become all the more important at a time of one-party government.[1]

Among those who have observed the judiciary in this new role is Robert Stevens, a distinguished lawyer and historian. In a lecture during the summer of 1993 Professor Stevens said that as a group the judges were more in touch with the nation than they had been and this made them feel frustrated by the apparent failings of the political leadership in Britain.[2]

Interviewed afterwards[3] Professor Stevens said the judiciary was much stronger than it had been twenty years earlier. He thought that this was a remarkable generation of English judges: 'extremely well educated, extremely bright, politically quite sophisticated. I suspect they are concerned when they see government appearing to flounder: they have moved into that vacuum as you would expect from people who are very talented, perhaps more talented than the other branches of government'. Towards the end of 1993 the judge who stepped most prominently into his new role was Lord Woolf. As we shall see later in this chapter, he did not find it a happy existence.

If the judiciary is going to enter the parliamentary vacuum created by such a long period of one-party government it is essential that we should have judges of the highest integrity. In this chapter we shall be looking at how the judges are selected, trained and kept under review. Are we really getting the best men and women for the job?

Judges as law-makers

There are two types of law: *statute law*, which is made by parliament, and the *common law*, made by the judges. At one time the judges used to pretend that they were not law-makers: they maintained that their job was simply to declare what had always been the law. It is unlikely that the judges ever believed this themselves; what has changed is that they no longer try to convince others of it.

As the great Scottish jurist Lord Reid said in a much-quoted lecture:

> There was a time when it was thought almost indecent to suggest that judges made law – they only declare it. Those with a taste for fairy tales seem to have thought that in some Aladdin's cave there is hidden the common law in all its splendour and on a judge's appointment there descends on him knowledge of the magic words Open Sesame. Bad decisions are given when the judge muddles the password and the wrong door opens. But we do not believe in fairy tales any more.[4]

Though charmingly put, this is no more than a statement of the obvious. Perhaps there are some people who think that by making the common law our judges are usurping the role of parliament; perhaps those people fear that the law can never be certain if it is being constructed afresh on a case-by-case basis. But parliament cannot legislate for every possible combination of human affairs, and it can be difficult to discover the will of parliament when the absence of legislation shows that parliament, as such, has given no thought to the point at issue. If there is a statute on the subject, the best that can be done is to interpret it in a way that seems to make sense of its declared intention. If there is not, then the courts must look for some old legal principle on which to base a new legal point. That, after all, is how the common law is created.[5]

Sometimes the judges seem to go further still. One distinguished law lord told the writer Marcel Berlins that the judiciary was becoming more honest about its role in making law:

> Up to now, we've been pushing the door a little apologetically. We've been pretending that we're still operating under the old system by which judges are not supposed to be law-makers, only law-interpreters. I think we can be more forthright now and come clean. It's not always easy. There are still decisions which only parliament or the executive should take. We must always keep in mind that no one has elected us.[6]

A good example of that process at work was the case of *Barclays Bank Plc v. O'Brien*, decided by the House of Lords in October 1993.[7] It was the first time the law lords had considered the phenomenon of 'sexually transmitted debt'.[8] Bridget O'Brien agreed to mortgage her family home in Slough after her husband Nicholas told her she would be guaranteeing a business debt of £60,000 for a few weeks. In fact, Mr O'Brien's company soon owed Barclays Bank more than £150,000 and Mrs O'Brien then realised she had pledged the house, which was in joint names, to cover the whole of her husband's overdraft. Nobody had advised her to seek legal advice before signing the mortgage, although the bank had intended to warn her of the risks. Barclays then sought to sell her home to recover the money it was owed.

The law lords' judgment was given by Lord Browne-Wilkinson. As a former Chancery judge he was perhaps more used to channelling the streams of equity into deserts which the common law had left parched and barren; he certainly had no hesitation in shaping the law to fit what he saw as the needs of modern society.

Lord Browne-Wilkinson began bluntly enough by outlining the 'policy considerations' which lay behind his decision. The concept of the ignorant wife leaving all financial decisions to her husband was outmoded, he said, but the practice did not yet coincide with the ideal. In many marriages it was still the husband who had the business experience and the wife who was willing to follow his advice. Such wives could reasonably look to the law for some protection when their husbands had abused the trust put in them. On the other hand, it was easy to allow sympathy for a wife who was threatened with the loss of her home at the suit of a rich bank to obscure the important public interest: if small businesses were to grow bigger, banks should be able to lend safely on the security of the matrimonial home.

The whole of the modern law on this subject had been derived from a decision in 1902 which Lord Browne-Wilkinson decided was built on unsure and possibly mistaken foundations. He concluded that the law lords should 'seek to restate the law in a form which is principled, reflects the current requirements of society and provides as much certainty as possible'. In his view, if a woman offered to guarantee her husband's debts, the bank should warn her – in person and without her husband present – of the risks she was taking on. That principle would apply to all couples, married or single, heterosexual or homosexual, whenever there was a risk that one party had been guilty of undue influence or misrepresentation.[9] The law lords agreed, and that became the law.

It is an essential requirement of our system that the judges should create law: 'all rules have a penumbra of uncertainty where the judge must choose between alternatives.'[10] Sometimes that choice may be very wide indeed. In reaching their decisions judges are bound to be influenced by their view of the world and by the needs, as they see them, of society.

The first academic to write about these issues was John Griffith, who taught at the London School of Economics from 1948 to 1984. In 1977 Professor Griffith first published his famous thesis that 'the judiciary, under our constitution, cannot act neutrally but must act politically'.[11] By this he meant that judges make choices. 'If the judicial function were wholly automatic, then . . . it would not be necessary to recruit highly trained and intellectually able men and women to serve as judges.'[12] In reaching their decisions the judges themselves are making law – without any intervention by parliament.

Put like that, Professor Griffith's argument is irrefutable. There are, of course, many cases where the outcome is so clear-cut that little judicial creativity is required. But even at the lowest level in the judicial hierarchy there can be scope for a novel interpretation which – if upheld on appeal – can have a profound influence on future cases.

A more interesting question is how the judges reach their decisions: what it is that influences them. Is it party politics? Professor Griffith says the judges have 'a unifying attitude of mind, a political position, which is primarily concerned to protect and conserve certain values and institutions . . . They do not regard their role as radical or even reformist.'[13]

This may have been true when John Griffith wrote it. It is harder to justify today. We saw in chapter 1 how a new generation of judges has moved into the most senior judicial posts. They have shown little hesitation in attacking the policies pursued by Margaret Thatcher and John Major.

Those policies involved doing away with the barristers' advocacy monopoly and legal aid for people of moderate means – which Professor Griffith would no doubt include among his 'values and institutions'. In opposing their abolition, the judges were clearly 'concerned to protect and conserve' these values and institutions. But fighting the Conservative government was a radical step for a bench of men and women whose heads were, until recently, kept well below the parapet. In the new judicial order it is the judges who are standing up for radicalism, for the rights of the individual, while the government does its best – as the judges would see it – to wreck the system.

Party politics
It is hard to keep politics out of the courts when the Lord Chancellor, the judge at the very top of the legal pyramid, is himself a member of the cabinet. But in general, judges should steer well clear of party politics. Being known as a supporter of one party or another can only make a judge's role more difficult. Rightly or wrongly, a litigant who happens to vote Conservative is unlikely to have much confidence in any judge known to be an active member of the Labour Party; similarly, a working-class defendant will not welcome the prospect of being sentenced by someone who declares himself to be a member of the Conservative far right.

It is therefore surprising that politics and the judiciary should be so closely linked. The connections can be seen at the lowest level. Everyone applying for appointment as a lay magistrate must complete an application form. One of the questions asks: 'Do you usually vote at General Elections?' Those who answer Yes are asked 'For which political party?'

There is nothing in the way the question is phrased to suggest that an answer is optional. Yet clearly the Lord Chancellor's Department feels some explanation is needed; a note tells candidates that their political views are neither a qualification nor a disqualification for appointment. It reads: 'This information is required only to avoid the appointment of a disproportionate number of justices supporting any one political party.'

The Lord Chancellor's Department explained in 1992 that a bench of magistrates was required to reflect a cross-section of the local community. The political affiliation question was asked alongside many others with a view to providing a balanced bench. A spokesman said that if an applicant acknowledged a political party preference which already had a heavy majority on the bench, the candidate would be given the choice of reapplying later or waiting for a suitable gap.[14]

There would be a public outcry if it became known that High Court judges were being selected or rejected on political grounds. It is no longer the case that MPs are regularly appointed to the bench as they were during the nineteenth century.[15] And it is no longer the case, as it was until the Second World War, that a retiring Attorney General can expect appointment as Lord Chief Justice or some other high judicial office when a vacancy next arises.[16] However, it is still possible for a defendant to find himself appearing in court before someone with declared political views: a number of MPs sit from time to time as Recorders of the Crown Court. Indeed, there is always a chance that the part-time judge called upon to interpret an unintelligible provision in the latest Criminal Justice Act was the MP who helped fashion it.

Perhaps the most striking overlap between politics and the judiciary can be found in the House of Lords. There is no particular reason why our most senior judges should become members of the legislature. It is said to astonish foreigners. But the law lords are of course members of the upper house; so too are the Chief Justice (from the date of appointment) and the Master of the Rolls (after a decent interval). Does this mean they are free to take part in political debate? That can surely never have been intended but it may be difficult to persuade someone who has just been given a seat in the House of Lords that he should never rise from it to speak his mind.

It was once a convention of the constitution that the judges did not take sides on matters of dispute between the political parties. This was taken to mean that they might help out if an obscure legal topic was under debate, or even pilot an uncontroversial Law Commission bill through the House of Lords,[17] but they would never express a view on issues of public controversy. That convention no longer exists.

Speaking their minds

Early in 1985 two judges overstepped what was then considered to be the mark. At the end of the previous year, just a day before parliament was to rise for the Christmas recess, the government had published its Administration of Justice Bill. Hidden away towards the end, unmentioned in the government's press release, was a clause dealing with applications for judicial review.[18] The law says that anyone who wants to challenge an administrative decision by way of judicial review must first ask the High Court for permission to start proceedings. If an applicant is refused leave by the High Court he can try again in the Court of Appeal. Clause 43 of the government's bill would have taken away that right to 'renew' an application for leave before the Court of Appeal. So if the High Court were to refuse leave, an action would have been over before it had started.

In support of its proposals, the government argued that leave to apply for judicial review was almost always granted if there was a case worth answering and that renewed applications to the Court of Appeal therefore wasted a large amount of judicial time. However, in January 1985 a taxpayer who had been refused permission by the High Court to challenge the decision of an Inland Revenue Special Commissioner tried again in the Court of Appeal and was granted leave by Lord Justice Ackner and Lord Justice Purchas. The two judges said in court that they were 'troubled' to find that the Administration of Justice Bill would take away the right to bring a case like the one before them. Although the case was unusual, the judges said it demonstrated very strongly the merits of the existing rule in an area where so much of the legislation was directed towards preventing alleged abuses of power.[19]

As Lord Chancellor, Lord Hailsham was far from pleased with this demonstration of judicial independence. It seemed to him 'a clear breach of the constitutional rules and conventions about the separation of powers'. Lord Hailsham 'sought and obtained apologies' from the two judges.[20] He told parliament that while it was perfectly legitimate for the judiciary to criticise the law as it stood, it was 'utterly improper for a Court of Appeal judge or any other judge speaking on the bench to criticise matters passing through parliament'.[21] They had ample means 'to make their views known in the proper quarter. This could be done quite easily by approaching the Lord Chancellor privately, or in public on the floor of the House of Lords through the mouth of one or more of the law lords.'[22]

There is no reason why a judge who makes a comment in the Court of Appeal should be publicly humiliated by a Lord Chancellor, especially by one who believes that same judge may say what he likes if he becomes a member of the House of Lords (as Lord Justice Ackner subsequently did). And there is no logical reason why a judge should be allowed to *criticise* the existing law – which Lord Hailsham permitted – if the same judge was not allowed to *support* the present law, which was what the two appeal judges had done. However, the judges had the last laugh. Despite offering a number of concessions the government was defeated on a vote in the House of Lords and the clause disappeared for good.

The two judges had not even broken the Kilmuir rules, which were meant to stop the judiciary speaking to the media.[23] These so-called rules were in fact no more than a letter, written in 1955 by the then Lord Chancellor to the Director General of the BBC, in which Lord Kilmuir said that as a general rule it was 'undesirable for members of the judiciary to broadcast on the wireless or to appear on television'. Lord Hailsham supported the rules ('public indulgence in publicity off the bench is in my view quite incompatible with proper performance of the judicial office'[24]) while maintaining that he was only keeping them because 'an overwhelming majority' of the judges did not want them altered.

Nevertheless, Lord Hailsham seems to have rewritten the Kilmuir rules so as to exclude law lords (and former law lords like Lord Denning) from their strictures. It was inconsistencies like these which encouraged Lord Mackay to abolish the Kilmuir rules as one of his first acts after taking office in 1987.[25] The judges certainly did not try to persuade him to leave the rules unchanged.[26]

At first, the judges behaved cautiously. Now, even quite junior judges express their disagreement with government policies. Mr Justice Laws, for example, has spoken publicly in support of incorporating the European Convention of Human Rights into the legal systems of the United Kingdom, contrary to the views of successive Conservative governments.[27] And the law lords have shown no hesitation in biting the hand of the very government which appointed them: some of them are already coming to be seen as supporters of the opposition parties. One law lord said:

What really caused me surprise was that a Labour shadow minister in the Lords asked me: 'When are you going to make another fiery speech?' I thought that was unfortunate. And I was actually approached by the Whips to the Labour peers saying: 'We're going to have a vote on this clause tomorrow night – let the boys know!' I thought that was really very undesirable. But it illustrates the dangers.[28]

As Lord Chief Justice, Lord Lane spoke out in blunt terms against Lord Mackay's proposal to reform the legal profession; he also criticised the government's insistence on keeping the mandatory sentence of life imprisonment for murder. And in January 1993, within a week of making his maiden speech, Lord Woolf was to be found on his feet in the House of Lords, criticising a provision in the government's Asylum Bill which was designed to take away a right of appeal that had existed for twenty-one years.[29] The proposal was unjustified, he explained, and it was bound to lead to many more applications for judicial review at a time when there were not enough judges to deal with existing cases. Lord Woolf went on to say that the Lord Chief Justice, Lord Taylor, shared his views.[30]

Two months later Lord Taylor himself roundly attacked the Criminal Justice Act 1991, introduced by the Conservative government with the aim of restricting prison sentences to those offenders who really deserved them. Lord Taylor referred to two sections in particular 'which many people feel run counter to all the principles of good sentencing policy . . . and in fact defy common sense'. He hoped that 'very soon it may be reviewed and sanity restored'. In a speech to Scottish solicitors Lord Taylor said: 'the fundamental error underlying the Act was a misconceived notion that sentencing should be programmed in detail so as to restrict the discretion of the sentencing judge. The laudable desire to reduce and confine custodial sentencing to cases where it is really necessary has led to restrictive provisions forcing the judge into an ill-fitting strait-jacket.'[31]

The substance of Lord Taylor's remarks will be discussed in chapter 6. The question here is whether he should have spoken out at all. It is true that many people were worried about how the Criminal Justice Act was working. And no doubt the judges were in a better position than almost anyone else to see what was going wrong. Lord Taylor was also vindicated by events: within six months the legislation had been repealed.

And yet: we are still a parliamentary democracy, are we not? If parliament passes legislation, is it not the job of the judges to implement it to the best of their ability? Clearly, the judges would accept that it is. Should they at the same time be trying to get that legislation overturned if they happen to think it is misguided? They would say that in a democracy they are entitled to be heard, particularly when they speak with special knowledge. But are they really in a better position than parliament to decide sentencing policy? If parliament has recently concluded that the courts are sending too many people to prison for too long, surely the judges should accept the view of the people?

In reply, the judges would no doubt say that it was parliament – not the judiciary – which repealed the legislation it had passed earlier; the judges' role had simply been to lobby parliament. Lord Woolf's answer[32] was that the judges were not criticising the policy of the government as such: in commenting on the sentencing provisions of the Criminal Justice Act the Lord Chief Justice was in effect saying that parliament had given the judges a piece of machinery which was not working. Lord Woolf thought there should be a system for examining legislation before it was implemented. He pointed to France, where a section of the Conseil d'État – the court dealing with administrative law – has responsibility for looking at draft legislation and advising on whether it complies with the French constitution. Lord Woolf also suggested[33] that there should be closer links between the different arms of the criminal justice system: he hoped that the Criminal Justice Consultative Council set up under the chairmanship of Lord Justice Farquharson might develop a similar role in due course. An alternative sponsor might be the Law Commission. Lord Woolf accepted that such a committee should be carefully structured to avoid the judiciary being sucked into politics.

Alas, that was precisely the fate that was to befall Lord Woolf himself just a few months after he made those remarks. As Lord Justice Woolf, he had been appointed to head the inquiry into the series of disturbances which began at Strangeways Prison in Manchester in April 1990. The 600-page report he published in February 1991[34] was a major document outlining a comprehensive package of reforms. For most of the following two and a half years he had been pleased with the progress that was being made. He believed the Home Office and prison staff were making efforts to ensure that prison would no longer be 'a wholly negative experience' for the vast majority of those who were sent there.[35]

By the summer of 1993, however, the political climate had

changed. The government was no longer encouraging the courts to make use of alternatives to prison; indeed, the reverse seemed true. And the prison population was rising at an alarming rate: it grew from well under 41,000 at the beginning of 1993 to more than 47,000 by November, an increase of some 6,500 prisoners in just ten months.

Unlike some judges who write reports and then forget about them, Lord Woolf was determined to speak out about the looming crisis in Britain's prisons. He gave an interview to the Press Association news agency in which he said it would be 'short-sighted' to respond to fears about law and order by trying to force more people into the prison system than it could hold. 'All the experience shows that imprisonment is not a cure,' he said.

Perhaps surprisingly, Lord Woolf's remarks received little coverage except in *The Times*.[36] His interview was available to the whole of Fleet Street but that made it less attractive to each individual newspaper than an exclusive of their own. Perhaps dispirited or perhaps emboldened by the muted response to his Press Association interview, Lord Woolf became even more determined to speak his mind. Several months earlier he had accepted an invitation to deliver a public lecture in October 1993 with the title 'Crime, Punishment and Rehabilitation'.[37] This time the impact of his remarks was profound.

Lord Woolf's speech came less than a week after the Home Secretary had assured his party conference in Blackpool that 'prison works'. Now here was a law lord saying exactly the opposite: prison does not work, Lord Woolf argued, if it means an offender becomes more likely to commit further offences as a result. In a clear reference to the Home Secretary, Lord Woolf said:

> Statements are being made that, having tried the soft option and that having failed, now is the time to get tough on crime. Such talk is short-sighted and irresponsible. The easy option which has a miserable record of failure is to send more and more people to prison regardless of the consequences, including the shocking waste of resources which could be spent elsewhere. The difficult option is to try to identify the underlying causes of criminal conduct and then to set about tackling those causes.

Michael Howard was not amused. In a speech two days later, he responded: 'The fact is that prison does work. Thousands of dangerous criminals are prevented from attacking the community while they're inside. And many who might commit crime are deterred from doing so.'[38] The Home Secretary was clearly stung by Lord Woolf's remarks. It seemed to Mr Howard that Lord Woolf was deliberately attacking policies which he had launched barely a week earlier. Any hopes the government may have had that Lord Woolf was speaking only for himself were soon dashed when the *Observer* persuaded seven other judges to declare their broad support for Lord Woolf's views.[39]

However, Lord Woolf's speech did not display the level of political sophistication Professor Stevens might have hoped for. He included a passing comment which enabled his critics to divert attention from its central message. In his speech Lord Woolf suggested channelling some of the money currently spent on prisons into crime prevention, 'ensuring that cars can be immobilised and then, just as we can be fined for not protecting ourselves by wearing seat belts, so we could be fined if we do not take steps to lock our cars and protect our property'.

The Home Secretary immediately poured scorn on that idea. 'Can it seriously be suggested,' he asked, 'that the most effective way we can find to fight burglary is to fine the victims? We need to help victims, not punish them.'[40] Newspapers printed pictures of Lord Woolf's house, suggesting that he himself could be fined because burglars could have climbed in from some scaffolding next door. A Home Office minister stepped up the pressure. David Maclean said he strongly supported crime prevention, 'but if you start fining victims who have not locked their doors or turned on the burglar alarm it is only a short step before you start suggesting that attractive women are at fault because their appearance entices the attacker'. Mr Maclean promised victims they would never be blamed because they had not turned their homes into a Fort Knox or their bodies into an Arnold Schwarzenegger.[41]

These flights of fancy had considerably more impact than Lord Woolf's somewhat restrained reply a week later, in a letter to *The Times*.[42] 'My remarks', he said, 'were directed not at house owners, as has been widely suggested, but at car owners. They were so directed because joy riding, as it is misdescribed . . . involves mainly teenagers; it can be their introduction to crime; it is different to the majority of offences since, while it is distressing to the owner of the car, it can have disastrous consequences to other road users.'

The next day Lord Woolf was due to give another public lecture.[43] He had thought of cancelling it but decided, rightly, to go ahead. This time it was an older, wiser law lord who spoke. He explained that he had never imagined for a moment that his previous talk would receive the attention it had. While he stood by what he had said, he thought it would have been better if he, as a judge, had not been drawn so overtly into controversy.

Even so, Lord Woolf did not want to go back to the days of the Kilmuir rules. It was essential, he thought, that the Heads of Division – the four most senior judges[44] – should 'explain the steps which are being taken to fulfil the judicial programme' and talk about 'matters which are of interest to the public on which they are in a special position to speak with authority because of the offices which they hold'.

Lord Woolf then offered his own advice to the judges. It betrayed all the inner torment of someone who was trying to have his cake and eat it. Apart from the Heads of Division (and, presumably, the law lords) judges 'should exercise more circumspection before speaking in public'. So far, so good. But then came the exceptions:

> Judges are constantly in demand to give public lectures and they cannot avoid doing so from time to time. In addition, there are programmes on the media with which judges need to become involved so the public can understand how the judiciary works. There can also be situations where they are in a special position to make a contribution to a debate and then they should do so. They should however still avoid, so far as is possible, being involved in controversy because to do so can undermine the rule of law.

That view was shared by the Lord Chief Justice although it seemed he favoured fewer exceptions. His public position was to accuse the media of magnifying differences of view between Lord Woolf and the Home Secretary by reporting them in extreme terms. More privately, he wrote to all High Court judges reminding them, in effect, to think twice before speaking to the media.[45] Perhaps Lord Taylor had in mind the justification Lord Kilmuir had given for his so-called rules nearly forty years earlier:[46] 'So long as a judge keeps silent his reputation for wisdom and impartiality remains unassailable: but every utterance which he makes in public, except in the course of the actual performance of his judicial duties, must necessarily bring him within the focus of criticism.'

This is clearly true. But the newly written Taylor rules did not seem to apply to the senior judiciary. In February 1993 Lord Taylor himself had spoken out against the government's plans to cut eligibility for legal aid: they were 'draconian cuts', he said, and 'wrong in principle'. Lord Taylor urged the Lord Chancellor to think again.[47] This was not the first time Lord Taylor had attacked the government on legal aid. It was a subject with which he was closely concerned and it may have seemed to him entirely reasonable to express what were undoubtedly the views of his fellow judges.

But the more the judges declare their views in public – whether on legal aid or anything else – the more difficult it is for them to do their job. That is why they have previously refused press interviews or appearances on programmes like *Question Time*;[48] that is why they never comment outside the courtroom on specific cases. Once they have declared a view on a particular topic it is very hard for them to deal with the same subject from the bench while still maintaining the confidence of both sides.

The issue of legal aid did indeed come before the courts. In the spring of 1993 the Law Society sought judicial review of the Lord Chancellor's proposals to cut legal aid eligibility, as well as his plans to introduce standard fees for criminal legal aid work in the magistrates' courts. Could the government have been confident of getting a fair hearing when judges had already declared their opposition to the proposed changes? In practice, the answer was clearly Yes[49] but it may not have looked that way to an outside observer. Lord Taylor's intervention debarred him from hearing either of the Law Society's applications, or the subsequent appeal, although he had expressed a wish to hear more applications for judicial review and might reasonably have thought a case brought against the Lord Chancellor sufficiently important to justify his presence on the bench.

Asked[50] whether it was proper for the Lord Chief Justice to criticise the policies of an elected government, in particular when those policies might have to be reviewed by the courts, Lord Taylor conceded that it was difficult to say how far a judge, even a senior judge, should become involved in such matters. But, he continued:

whilst a judge must obviously be entirely independent of party politics, and indeed political issues which don't concern the law, I think that the

Lord Chief Justice and the Master of the Rolls ought to have views and ought to make them known on matters which affect the administration of justice. Accordingly, I think it is right that I should be able to express a view for example on legal aid: what is clear is that having expressed one it would be quite wrong for me to sit on the case which is now before the courts. If you are asking: am I becoming political by addressing these issues, I see my membership of the House of Lords as being precisely for the purpose of enabling me to go and speak in the Lords on a debate which affects the administration of justice.

Both Lord Taylor and Sir Thomas Bingham have spoken in favour of incorporating the European Convention on Human Rights into the legal systems of the United Kingdom. As we shall see in chapter 4, that would make the judges very much more powerful. Professor Robert Stevens believes the judges may not have thought through many of the implications of such a dramatic change. He argued that they were not fully conscious of the politicisation of the judiciary that would follow if they were to have to make vital decisions about fundamental civil liberties: 'A more political judiciary requires an intellectual framework . . . In England, the creative role of the judiciary is too recent to allow a sophisticated literature about judicial activism and judicial restraint.'

It is encouraging to hear the judges speaking frankly on matters of public controversy, particularly if one happens to support their views, but where to draw the line between party politics and the administration of justice must be a matter of fine judgment. It would be easy enough for a journalist to argue that all judges should say whatever they like whenever they choose. No reporter wants to hear silence at the other end of the telephone. However, Lord Woolf's experiences in the autumn of 1993 demonstrate what happens when judges start playing with fire.

Lord Woolf speaks with great authority on prisons. But his report is there for everyone to see: there are others who can equally well point out the government's failure to implement his recommendations. Lord Woolf and his brethren have a more important role to play in the field of public law.

We do not pay judges to pronounce government policy unwise. We pay them to decide whether it is unlawful. If it is, they must strike it down. They can only do so if they are independent and impartial arbiters. That impartiality is put at risk by the politicisation of the judiciary. The judges should indeed think twice before opening their mouths, and that rule should apply just as much to a law lord as to any other judge.

There are times when silence is necessary in the wider public interest. There are also times when to keep quiet would be an abdication of the judges' responsibilities. The answer to the judges' dilemma is as simple to express as it is difficult to implement. The judges should do what they are paid to do: use their judgment.

Perhaps inevitably, money lies at the heart of the problem. Asked how far judges should enter the public debate, one loyal civil servant said he flinched whenever he saw 'pound signs'. By that he meant it was acceptable for the judges to speak in general terms but wrong for them to advocate the spending of taxpayers' money since – unlike the Lord Chancellor – they were not accountable to parliament.[51]

The first judge to identify this as an issue was Lord Browne-Wilkinson who, as Sir Nicolas Browne-Wilkinson, was Vice-Chancellor of the Chancery Division. Speaking in 1987 Sir Nicolas said that government control of judicial finance and administration was a threat to the independence of the judiciary as a whole.[52] He pointed out that although judges' salaries were paid direct from the Consolidated Fund the legal system as a whole was funded by money voted by parliament. That meant the courts having to satisfy the Treasury that they were providing value for money. But, said Sir Nicolas, 'justice is not capable of being measured out by an accountant's computer'.

Sir Nicolas went on to say that there were increasing stresses in the relationship between the Lord Chancellor's Department and the judiciary, the former being forced by demands for financial economy into areas which the judges considered their exclusive territory:

> Some in the Lord Chancellor's Department think, wrongly, that the judges are incorrigibly concerned only with their personal status and privileges rather than with the administration of justice, indifferent to the need for improvements and economies and blocking all attempts at change however well directed. On the other side, a number of judges consider there is some form of civil service conspiracy designed to erode the independence of the judiciary and their powers.

Sir Nicolas did not share the latter view but he accurately depicted the atmosphere of mutual suspicion which was to erupt a year or so later into open warfare between the judges and the Lord Chancellor.

The 'Judges' Strike'

The most dramatic intervention in party politics by the judges arose from the Lord Chancellor's 'Green Papers' on the future of the legal profession. These plans, published in January 1989, will be discussed more fully in chapter 3; for the moment it is sufficient to note that the judges were more than a little concerned by them. They decided to discuss their response at what amounted to a shop-floor meeting, and a date was agreed in the middle of April 1989.

With ten days to go before the planned meeting, a debate was held in the House of Lords. More than fifty peers put their names down to speak – an unprecedented number for a Friday – and the debate lasted for nearly thirteen hours. The Lord Chief Justice, Lord Lane, argued that letting the government decide who should have rights of audience in the courts would lead to 'control by the executive of the principal means available to the ordinary citizen of controlling that same executive'. Then, in a much quoted phrase, Lord Lane added: 'Loss of freedom seldom happens overnight . . . Oppression does not stand on the doorstep with a toothbrush moustache and a swastika armband. It creeps up insidiously; it creeps up step by step; and all of a sudden the unfortunate citizen realises that it has gone.'[53]

With judicial invective at this level it was perhaps not surprising that the judges' works meeting – planned for later in the month – should have been interpreted by some observers as a calculated snub to the Lord Chancellor. The newspapers described it as the 'Judges' Strike'. In vain did the judges protest that 'their meeting is not intended to be nor is it a protest of any sort'.[54] They pointed out that they had regular meetings at the start of every term; this one had to be arranged at short notice to meet the Lord Chancellor's deadline. Either the judges were being disingenuous or – much more likely – they were guilty of culpable naïvety.

The High Court judges do indeed meet once a term. The meeting is chaired by the Lord Chief Justice and its main purpose is to give the judges the opportunity to select the circuits to which they will travel during the following term. It also allows the judges the chance to agree a common approach on contentious issues, although much of the decision-making is done by the presiding judges of each circuit who meet three times a term.

In addition there is an informal body known as the Judges' Council. As an organisation it was moribund for many years; it certainly did not exist in November 1987 when Sir Nicolas Browne-

Wilkinson said, 'There is no body which can speak for the judges as a whole . . . let alone take decisions.'[55] The Judges' Council regenerated itself in 1988 when the judges wanted to submit evidence as a collegiate body to Lady Marre's committee on the legal profession.[56] By 1989 it comprised the four Heads of Division, the Deputy Chief Justice and two High Court judges: it seemed to operate as a committee or steering group, working on behalf of the judiciary as a whole.[57]

When the Lord Chancellor's Green Papers were published early in 1989 the Judges' Council set up a working party to draft the judiciary's response. It was this response that all the judges of the High Court and the Court of Appeal, numbering more than a hundred, wanted to discuss at the meeting arranged for 17 April 1989 – a Monday. That meant they would not sit to hear cases in the normal way: for the first time during the legal term the courts would have been at a standstill. It was hardly surprising, in the climate of the times, that this should have been seen as a strike.

In the end a compromise was reached. The Lord Chancellor agreed to extend his consultation period by four weeks and the judges rearranged their meeting for a Saturday in May. A few days afterwards they published their response. The accompanying press release[58] – itself an innovation for the English judiciary – said the judges regarded independence from the government as fundamental to the rule of law. They made some pertinent criticisms of the government's plans to extend rights of audience[59] and concluded that it would be 'disastrous if safeguards essential to the administration of justice in the higher courts[60] were to be discarded for no clearly discernible advantage'.

In the event, the government went ahead with its plans to extend rights of audience although they were slightly modified to take account of the judges' concerns. As we shall see, progress towards greater rights of audience for solicitors has been painfully slow. And, since the Judges' Strike and the campaign it marked, the judges have no longer been able to masquerade as totally apolitical – even in the eyes of the public at large.

Judging who shall judge

The mechanics of appointing the judiciary are now well understood but the reality is still shrouded in secrecy. Appointments to the High

Court are not advertised.[61] There is no application form, no structured interview process.[62] There is not even a job description at present although the Lord Chancellor is working on one.[63] And while there is no formal veto, the four most senior judges – the Heads of Division[64] – have a major say in senior appointments. There is now a process of consultation with the chairman of the Bar but not with the Law Society:[65] in any case, it has done little to open up the process.

In 1986 the then Lord Chancellor, Lord Hailsham, thought he could 'dispel any lingering sense of mystery or obscurity' about judicial appointments by publishing a guide to his policies and procedures.[66] In 1990, following new legislation, his successor Lord Mackay felt the need to publish a revised edition of the booklet so as 'to give more information about some aspects of the system which may still give rise to uncertainty or misunderstanding'.[67] More light was subsequently cast on the darkness in a report on the judiciary published by JUSTICE in 1992.[68] But the more we are told *how*, the more we should ask *why*. As David Pannick QC says:[69]

> Grateful as one is for any information about the working practices of the Lord Chancellor's Department, it is unlikely that the published guide will satisfy the growing number of people concerned about, first, the extent of patronage in the hands of the Lord Chancellor and, secondly, the absence of mechanisms to ensure that decisions are made on adequate information and proper criteria.[70]

In appointing judges the Lord Chancellor looks for 'professional ability, experience, standing, integrity, a sound temperament and the physical ability to carry out the duties of the post'.[71] A leading solicitor described these criteria as 'strikingly vague and subjective'.[72] 'Professional ability' seems fair enough but 'experience' is far from clear: does it mean experience of life, experience of sitting as a part-time judge or simply experience as an advocate? 'A sound temperament' and 'standing' are also elusive qualities; they could be used to exclude people who do not fit into the Establishment mould. 'Standing' probably means success as a lawyer, judged largely on how much money the applicant is making; but that may not, of itself, indicate potential as a judge. 'Integrity' is an acceptable requirement, and so is 'physical health' although certain types of physical disability should not necessarily disqualify applicants. The Lord Chancellor's booklet also points out helpfully that 'checks are made to confirm that candidates for full-time judicial office do not have criminal records'.

We are told in the booklet that both High Court judges and Circuit judges are appointed by the Queen on the recommendation of the Lord Chancellor. It is clear that High Court judges are superior creatures: they are 'selected from the most eminent and able members of the profession' while would-be Circuit judges need only have 'attained a high standard of professional ability'.[73] But we are not told what qualities make one lawyer good enough for appointment to the High Court while others have to make do with the Circuit bench. How does the Lord Chancellor judge the judges?

Perhaps he lets them judge themselves. 'In general it is necessary for those interested to apply for appointment' as a Circuit judge.[74] For those wanting to be High Court judges, 'each appointment is made by invitation to fill particular vacancies, so it is not appropriate to apply'.[75] This suggests that anyone who thinks he or she is High Court material should sit tight and wait to be approached. Of course, the letter may never come; and whenever lawyers apply for a judicial post they are effectively telling the Lord Chancellor that they do not see themselves as top grade.

In the real world this is not something the Lord Chancellor would hold against them. 'If I thought that person was High Court judge material,' said Lord Mackay, 'that would not stop me inviting him to become a High Court judge. Some people are modest and underrate their own talent.' Indeed, some candidates now ask about their chances of becoming High Court judges. That used to be thought not quite the done thing but Lord Mackay made it clear that as far as he was concerned anyone could ask about their prospects at any time.

Lord Mackay explained that High Court judges generally have a higher public profile than Circuit judges. 'They are required to deal with the most important cases. And therefore I wish to have people with the highest talent and the widest experience.' Those with 'not quite so high talent and perhaps not quite such wide experience' would be suitable for the Circuit bench. Lord Mackay pointed out that Circuit judges were invited to sit in the High Court from time to time.[76]

Prospective judges who are not sure whether their talent is of the highest or not quite so high can take up the Lord Chancellor's open invitation to drop in for a chat with the head of his Judicial

Appointments Group.[77] The Lord Chancellor insists that his officials 'are ready at any time to discuss with individuals their prospects of appointment and no one need feel inhibited about asking. It is not held against someone if they do.'[78] However, prospective judges should be aware that anything they say will be written down and may be used in evidence against them.[79]

Officials from the Lord Chancellor's Department spend a fair amount of time collecting views on candidates from judges and senior members of the profession. The Lord Chancellor realises 'this sometimes gives rise to anxiety that there is an undisclosed black mark against the candidate' but we are assured that 'this is hardly ever the case'. And a member of the appointments team is always willing to tell the candidate if there is a black mark – provided this can be done without revealing who put it there.[80] The Lord Chancellor's officials said that in an increasingly competitive situation it was 'a myth' for barristers to suppose there was a black mark against everybody who had not been successful in achieving promotion. This sounds plausible although there is no way of knowing if it is true.

It is well known that the information collected on each candidate finds its way into the Lord Chancellor's secret files. In October 1990 the BBC was allowed to film the windowless room in the House of Lords where the files were kept.[81] It all looked charmingly amateur. A wooden cage had been constructed inside the room and within it some 11,000 dog-eared manilla folders bulging with flimsy papers could be seen sitting on shelves of bare wood. The door to the cage was secured with a sturdy padlock but the whole construction was protected by nothing stronger than chicken wire. It faintly resembled a garden shed.[82] Officials insisted that the area was perfectly secure; the main door was kept locked when the room was not in use. There are not many lawyers who would have turned down the chance of a sneak glance at their file if they happened to be walking past. In it they could expect to find comments from senior colleagues and judges, notes of meetings and interviews, occasional letters from jurors and other members of the public, articles and profiles cut out of local newspapers – as well as who knows what else. Staff admitted that they retained anything sent to them which was likely to help the Lord Chancellor consider any application in respect of that individual.

A summary of this priceless information is kept in a series of huge ledgers. Notes of the main facts and opinions about each candidate are written on pink slips and bound into these volumes which are held in a nearby office for easy reference.

Officials responsible for the appointments system said they tried to be fair on candidates, but the men and women who were appointed would be sitting in judgment on their fellow citizens: it was the interests of the litigants which were paramount rather than the interests of candidates. In a careers system with no line management structure it was essential to rely on references, and those references would only be given if strict confidentiality could be assured.

Lord Williams of Mostyn QC, chairman of the Bar in 1992, was scathing about the system in a speech to solicitors:[83] 'You apply to become an Assistant Recorder. A secret file is then opened on you. You do not know what is in it. You do not know which of your dear friends has contributed to it. The cruellest error may be contained in it. You cannot put it right. It is kept under lock and key by a graduate from the Franz Kafka School of Business Management.' Lord Williams said he had recently suggested to the Lord Chancellor's Department that anyone with a complaint about what might be on his file should be entitled to an independent review by the current chairman of the Bar. After some thought, the suggestion had been rejected which, in the opinion of Lord Williams, was 'intolerable'. Staff in the Lord Chancellor's Department believe that most candidates would prefer a government official to tell them how they were regarded rather than the chairman of the Bar.

What remedy is there for a would-be judge whose advancement never comes? One possibility would be an application to the High Court for judicial review. The courts might be willing to step in if it could be shown that the Lord Chancellor had acted capriciously or unfairly. Even asking for leave to bring proceedings might force the Lord Chancellor to explain the basis for his decision. But there can be little doubt that a court would be very reluctant to substitute its own judgment for that of the Lord Chancellor. And a rush of litigants seems improbable. Anyone who sues the Lord Chancellor is not likely to be seen as a suitable candidate for judicial office.

How to choose the judges
David Pannick QC once wrote that 'judges are appointed by a process that resembles a pre-1965 Conservative Party leadership contest or a Papal Conclave rather than the choice of law-makers in a

modern democracy'.[84] He argued for something resembling the United States system where federal judges must have their appointment confirmed by the Senate and judges nominated to the Supreme Court have to undergo a public examination.

While this idea may be superficially attractive it should not be taken too far. None of our courts has quite the same constitutional functions as the United States Supreme Court. Nobody would want to see judges selected by the Lord Chancellor because their political views were attractive, or rejected by parliament because they were not. And although not all our potential law lords have led such interesting lives as some US Supreme Court nominees, anything resembling some of the recent Senate Judiciary Committee hearings would do little to enhance public respect for our judiciary.

In 1987 Judge Robert Bork spent five long days in Washington being cross-examined about his views and his judicial record. According to *Newsweek*[85] he portrayed himself as a moderate judge rather than as the legal radical depicted by his opponents. That ordeal was as nothing compared with the committee's investigation of Judge Clarence Thomas in 1991. The country was transfixed by allegations of sexual harassment made by Anita Hill, a professor of law, who claimed that Judge Thomas had made lewd remarks about his anatomy after she refused to go out with him. The senators believed in his anatomy of the law rather than her anatomy of the lawyer, and at the age of 43 Clarence Thomas was given a job for life as a Supreme Court justice.

Lord Taylor was right to say that 'the candidature of Judge Bork and more horrendously of Judge Clarence Thomas gave us object lessons in how not to proceed'.[86] It was also a warning of what might happen if our own judges were nominated on political grounds.

A more British approach to the problem of judicial appointments would involve setting up a committee of the Great and the Good. In 1972 a sub-committee of the broadly-based and influential lawyers' group JUSTICE called for a Judicial Appointments Committee to advise the Lord Chancellor on selecting judges. This proposal was considered too controversial and the sub-committee's recommendations were not approved by JUSTICE as a whole.[87]

In 1992 JUSTICE published another report, *The Judiciary in England and Wales*, this time calling for a Judicial Commission with a broader range of responsibilities. On this occasion the proposals were 'supported in principle by a large majority' of JUSTICE council members.[88] As envisaged by JUSTICE, the Judicial Commission would be responsible for all judicial appointments, judicial training, complaints against judges and the career development of all judges below High Court level. However, the Judicial Commission would not have the last word on appointments: it would provide the Lord Chancellor with a shortlist of names and he would make the final selection.[89]

This proposal bears all the signs of a compromise: some members of JUSTICE would clearly have wanted the Judicial Commission to take on full responsibility for appointments and they had to content themselves with what was seen as the first step down that road.

The Lord Chancellor responded to this suggestion in a speech in March 1993.[90] Lord Mackay said he did not favour the idea of a Judicial Appointments Commission: 'I make or recommend appointments personally. If appointments continue to be made on merit alone – as I believe they should – it is difficult to see how a commission would be better placed to reach decisions . . . I fear too a risk that it could lead to external pressures or lobbying in the appointments process.' The Lord Chancellor also doubted whether a Judicial Appointments Commission would make the system any more open. He stressed that, as a rule, he made full-time appointments from those who sat part-time. This they did in full public view. 'All parts of the current system are open,' he said, 'apart from the references given by others on the qualities of the candidate. These are given in confidence and this confidentiality encourages referees to give their comments fully.'

Speaking in July 1993 Lord Mackay again stressed the personal accountability he had for judicial appointments: he said he believed an appointments commission could, and probably would, impair his direct accountability to parliament, which he believed was essential to good administration. Of course, he took advice from the judiciary and the practising profession but the ultimate decision was his alone.[91]

That may be all very well but there is no point in holding the Lord Chancellor to account in parliament if there *is* a bad appointment: it would be too late to do anything about it by then. It must surely be better to avoid bad appointments in the first place. As Professor Robert Stevens said: 'The higher judiciary should not be chosen – or vetoed – by the four senior judges, a member of the cabinet and the senior civil servants in his department without considerable input from a wider group of the profession with a strong lay element.'[92]

There may be dangers in this approach. In Israel the judiciary started out on the English model, detached from politics; the judges posed more and more challenges to government; judicial appointments passed from the Attorney General to a commission; and by 1993 the Israeli parliament, the Knesset, was trying to get seats on the appointments commission. The moral of this story is that judges should distance themselves from politics, not that a politician should appoint the judges.

Delivering the Dimbleby Lecture at the end of 1992, Lord Taylor did not hesitate to attack the Lord Chancellor over what was then a shortage of judges. But turning to the way in which judges were appointed, the Lord Chief Justice was broadly happy with the status quo: 'It is said the Lord Chancellor wields too much power over judicial appointments. However, he does not sit in isolation and simply scan the Law List before appointing a new judge. He receives a great deal of information about all those eligible to step on even the first rung of the judicial ladder as Assistant Recorder.'[93]

Lord Taylor rejected the idea of an appointments commission. 'The lay members', he said, 'would have little direct knowledge of the candidates, and interview by such a commission would be a poor and perfunctory substitute for the present system of screening and selection.' However, the Lord Chief Justice said he was aware that there were worries about the lack of non-lawyers in the judicial appointments process. He believed 'it would be beneficial and it would certainly reinforce public confidence if a lay observer were included in the consultations leading to the Lord Chancellor's choice or recommendation'.

The last time a 'lay observer' was appointed, in 1974, his job was to supervise complaints against solicitors.[94] By limiting his powers Whitehall ensured that the solicitors' Lay Observer was almost totally ineffectual. He was not allowed to identify individual cases or to award compensation. Few people knew the Lay Observer existed and successive office-holders did little to disabuse the public of this notion. Even fewer noticed his passing.[95] Lord Taylor's lay observer is unlikely to have a greater impact than others long since forgotten. It would be far better to create an appointments panel along the lines of a civil service selection board.

By the summer of 1993 Lord Mackay was clearly getting tired of criticism of the sort reflected in this section. 'I have now worked with the existing procedures for some six years,' he said, 'and I have changed them and improved them at various points. In my view the merits of this reformed system are too little appreciated by its critics.' He had a blunt message for those who criticised the existing appointments system. 'Judge it by its product,' he said. 'It gives the country the services of fair-minded, robust and independent judges of the highest quality and integrity.'[96]

Even so, Lord Mackay was well aware that more needed to be done. In July 1993 he announced:

- the devising of more specific descriptions of the work of the judicial posts to be filled and of the qualities required;

- the progressive introduction of open advertisements for some judicial vacancies;

- the holding of specific competitions;

- such further measures as may seem appropriate to encourage applications by women and black and Asian practitioners; and

- a further look at the scope for involving suitable lay people in the selection process.[97]

More details of the Lord Chancellor's plans were revealed in May 1994.[98] The only jobs he planned to advertise were Circuit judges and District judges: there would be no change in the appointment of High Court judges. Advertisements would begin to appear in October 1994 and the Lord Chancellor's Department would then start holding annual competitions for appointments in 1995. For the first time, non-lawyers would have a part to play in the selection process. Applicants would be interviewed by a panel of three: a member of the judiciary, an official from the Lord Chancellor's Department, and a lay person familiar with the judicial system. However, the Lord Chancellor would be free to ignore the advice of the panel; in reaching decisions he will still take account of the information built up in his secret files. Lord Mackay outlined the qualities applicants would have to meet. These include the capacity to concentrate for long periods of time as well as the ability to maintain discipline in court 'without appearing pompous, arrogant or overbearing'. Judges are told they need intellectual ability, sound judgment, and communication skills. They must be 'firm and decisive while remaining patient, tolerant, good-humoured and even-tempered'.

As we saw in chapter 1, Lord Mackay made some excellent judicial appointments. That approach did something to deflect criticism of the judicial appointments system over which he presided. Since the Lord Chancellor was acting with such transparent integrity it might have seemed that there was little need to change the system. But the fact remained that Lord Mackay was carrying the whole system of judicial appointments single-handedly. He would not be Lord Chancellor for ever, and his successors[99] might turn out to command rather less respect. The clamour for reform of the judicial appointments system will not easily be silenced.

Who should be a judge?

The great majority of judges started life as barristers. Solicitors have been eligible for appointment as Circuit judges since the mid-1970s but almost 90 per cent of the current Circuit judges are former members of the Bar.[100] All High Court judges appointed before 1993 had previously been barristers.

There are two routes to the High Court bench for solicitors. They can either become Circuit judges and hope for promotion to the High Court after at least two years' service. But at the last count there were fewer than sixty 'solicitor' Circuit judges; and by the end of 1993 only one of them had been moved up to the High Court.[101] Solicitors will also be eligible for appointment direct to the High Court bench – although not until they have gained ten years' High Court advocacy experience,[102] which means the year 2004 at the earliest. So for the time being the High Court will be composed almost entirely of former barristers. No solicitor has ever been appointed to the Court of Appeal or the House of Lords without first requalifying as a barrister.

In reality, the pool from which High Court judges are selected is narrower still. Virtually all candidates are leading counsel in private practice at the bar. The JUSTICE report proposed that appointments should be made from a much broader pool, comprising 'all qualified barristers and solicitors, whether in private practice or employed in commerce, industry, the unions, in central and local government and elsewhere'.[103] In theory, that is already the case: the Lord Chancellor's booklet on judicial appointments says that although 'presiding over a court will, generally, come more easily to those who spend their working lives in court in other capacities . . . it should not be assumed that those who do not appear regularly in court are thereby ruled out'. Indeed, we are told that 'some years ago' the Lord Chancellor appointed a number of academics as Assistant Recorders (the most junior type of part-time judge) and some of them have now become full-time judges.[104]

There was no indication of who these academics were or what sort of judges they turned out to be. In any event, this daring experiment seems not to have been repeated. Officials in the Lord Chancellor's Department commented tartly that the Lord Chancellor would want to make sure that any academic seeking a judicial appointment was looking for a genuine career move rather than attempting to collect material for a university thesis. An academic who wants to be a judge is normally expected to practise at the Bar and sit as a part-time judge first before being considered for appointment to the High Court. This was the case with Mr Justice Buxton who sandwiched a successful practice at the Bar between his first career as an Oxford don and his third career as a Law Commissioner; he was given a seat on the High Court bench at the beginning of 1994. His former colleague at the Law Commission, Mrs Justice Hale, became a judge at the same time. Professor Brenda Hoggett QC had been called to the Bar some twenty-five years earlier but then became a university lecturer. She had sat part-time since 1989 but was the first High Court judge not to have made her career as a practitioner.

Former academics apart, not many of Her Majesty's judges would consider themselves great legal scholars. Academic lawyers would make a useful addition to the strength of the judiciary, especially in the Chancery Division. There is even a case for appointing them straight to the Court of Appeal or the House of Lords where they would invariably sit as part of a team. That would avoid the need for them to preside over trials, where the academic's lack of day-to-day court experience could be something of a handicap. But it would undoubtedly annoy High Court judges who might feel their chances of promotion were being thwarted by people with no practical experience of handling a court.

There are bound to be many suitable academics who feel excluded from consideration. They are not likely to be convinced by the grudging remarks in the Lord Chancellor's booklet. Professor Michael Zander lists 'outstanding judges in other common law jurisdictions who came to the bench from the university law school – including Oliver Wendell Holmes, Benjamin Cardozo, William O. Douglas and Felix Frankfurter in the United States and Chief Justice

Bora Laskin in Canada'.[105] He modestly does not include his own name in such exalted company but there seems little doubt that he would accept the call if it were ever to come.

It is also worth considering fixed-term appointments to the judiciary. These have never been contemplated in England and Wales because of the convention that a full-time judge may never return to practise at the Bar. The JUSTICE report recommended, by a majority, that judges should be appointed, at all levels, for a limited term of perhaps five years. This would bring to the bench distinguished lawyers in their early fifties who might not want to commit their lives to judging but who would nevertheless have a valuable contribution to make – perhaps in areas where the full-time judiciary is lacking in expertise. It would also be an option for lawyers in their sixties who, until then, had declined a judicial appointment.

JUSTICE was told that one of the problems was whether these short-term judges should get knighthoods.[106] To refuse them the honour would be to make them appear inferior to the long-term judiciary; on the other hand, to allow them knighthoods might devalue the currency and annoy the permanent judges. The latter argument does not bear scrutiny: a judge receives his knighthood at the start of his appointment, not the end; he keeps it even if he chooses to retire early.[107] Few people take a judicial appointment for the title, and those that do are hardly likely to begrudge it to others.

A more serious objection is that short-term judges would be dependent on the executive for the renewal of their appointment (if they liked the job and wanted to stay). The real problem, however, is whether these judges should be allowed to return to practise as lawyers. There is no law against it but those appointed in England and Wales are asked by the Lord Chancellor to promise that they will not return to legal practice. Judges in Scotland may return to the Bar; so do judges in other common law countries.

There is presumably a feeling that a judge who returns to practice will have some unfair advantage over his fellows, that he will have seen life from the other side and be on friendly terms with the judges he will be addressing in court. But this is already the case. Most practising barristers of any seniority will have sat as Recorders or Assistant Recorders. Some may sit as Deputy High Court judges. They will certainly be on first-name terms with those of their contemporaries who have made it to the bench. If it is considered acceptable for a lawyer to step down from the bench several times a year when he finishes his stints as a member of the part-time judiciary, why should he not step down when he finishes his contract as a fixed-term judge?

It must surely be right to search for judges among the widest possible pool of talent. This is particularly important at a time when it may not be easy to get the best people to serve as High Court judges.

Minorities on the bench

The Lord Chancellor says he appoints to each judicial post the person who appears to him to be best qualified to fill it, whatever the candidate's background. Lord Mackay declared himself 'opposed to any form of discrimination on the grounds of ethnic origin, gender, marital status, political affiliation, religion or physical disability'.[108] Despite that admirable policy there is increasing concern over the fact that women, though not a minority in society, are still a minority on the bench.

By the summer of 1994 there were six women on the High Court bench. They were Mrs Justice Bracewell, Mrs Justice Ebsworth, Mrs Justice Smith, Mrs Justice Arden, Mrs Justice Steel and Mrs Justice Hale. Mrs Justice Ebsworth was the first woman appointed to sit in the Queen's Bench Division (in 1992); she was followed by Mrs Justice Smith and Mrs Justice Steel. Previously all the women in the High Court had been family judges. Mrs Justice Arden was the first woman appointed to the Chancery Division (in 1993).[109] In 1990 a woman was appointed as a Deputy Judge Advocate for the first time.[110] In 1993 the first black woman was appointed to chair an industrial tribunal.[111]

Lady Justice Butler-Sloss was the only woman among 29 judges in the Court of Appeal. There seems no immediate prospect of a woman becoming one of the ten law lords.

At the last count there were 29 women out of a total of 510 Circuit judges. Three of them were formerly solicitors. Among the part-time judiciary there were 41 women Recorders out of a total of 866 and 60 women Assistant Recorders out of a total of 394.

A report commissioned jointly by the Bar Council and the Lord Chancellor's Department concluded that 'gender discrimination appears to be institutionally present within the Bar and the judiciary'.[112] On the basis of a survey of barristers and judges[113] the report's authors said that the Lord Chancellor's procedures for selecting judges amounted to 'a closed system of selection by peers and superiors which is free from scrutiny and largely free from challenge or redress'. The researchers believed there were a number of factors which discouraged women from applying for a judicial appointment:

- The secrecy of the selection procedure and its reliance on comment from a majority male group.

- A lack of confidence that women have the qualities which are being looked for, coupled with a lack of information about selection criteria.

- The low representation of women on the bench and the consequent lack of role models.

- Less opportunity to appear in high-profile cases because of problems of work allocation.

- The perception of QC status as a selection criterion for judicial appointment.

- Possible experience of discrimination and patronising treatment from some male judges who will determine selection.

- A professional culture which finds stereotypical and discriminatory remarks acceptable.

- The knowledge that someone who does not specialise in criminal law will be expected to sit in a criminal court if appointed as an Assistant Recorder.

- The lengthy selection process.

- The requirement, especially difficult for those responsible for child care, to be away from home overnight on circuit.

The researchers found there was dissatisfaction with the system of performance appraisal for part-time judges and recommended that the procedure of informal soundings should be replaced by a more objective approach related to the requirements of the job. 'There was concern that there were no clear guidelines about performance appraisal and that a judge's performance could be appraised by a court official. Individuals have no access to their files, and this prompted much concerned comment in the surveys. Whatever the reality, the perception is one of opportunity for unfair comment . . . The system depends on patronage, being noticed, and being known.'

A number of the report's recommendations would – if implemented – benefit all potential judges, not just women. The report suggested a series of one-day conferences where candidates could discuss the skills needed for judicial work and the selection criteria. Such conferences would give candidates the chance to reflect on how they needed to develop their personal skills before they applied for a judicial appointment.

The dearth of ethnic minority judges is even more striking than the shortage of women on the bench. When this book went to press, there were no black or Asian judges in the High Court. Nor were there any Afro-Caribbean High Court or Circuit judges, although there were four members of the Circuit bench who described themselves as members of ethnic minorities. These were Judge Mota Singh QC, Judge Cooray, Judge Cotran and Judge Pearce (the first woman to be appointed). According to Law Society figures, there were six Recorders and six Assistant Recorders from the ethnic minorities in 1991. The first black QCs practising at the English Bar were appointed by Lord Mackay in 1988: they were Leonard Woodley QC and John Roberts QC.

It is clear that the Lord Chancellor would like to appoint more women and black people to the judiciary. The same goes for Queen's Counsel: Lord Mackay says he particularly wishes to encourage applications from suitably qualified women and members of ethnic minorities because today's QCs are tomorrow's judges. At the QCs' admission ceremony in May 1992 Lord Mackay said he had long been 'concerned that relatively fewer women feel able to put themselves forward, whether as applicants for Queen's Counsel or for judicial posts'. In the official booklet he says he is 'anxious to extend the range of candidates from which appointments are made and to include more women, more solicitors, and more individuals from ethnic minorities'. In 1991 he appointed Patricia Scotland as the first black woman QC – even though at the extremely young age of 35 not even she considered herself ready for such seniority.[114] Lord Mackay thought she was well up to the job, however, and he considers that the way she has handled matters since her appointment has justified that view.[115] Come the millennium, Mrs Justice Scotland is likely to be the first black woman High Court judge.

Tony Holland, a former president of the Law Society, made the point that if more solicitors had been appointed as Circuit judges when they first became eligible there would now be a greater number of women and members of the ethnic minorities sitting because the solicitors' branch of the profession is so much larger than the Bar.[116] The Lord Chancellor's response was that even the solicitors could not supply enough women of sufficient seniority. Drawing on the Law Society's figures he accepted that the number of women in partnership was 'an appreciable, if not large, proportion of the total for the first nine years of practice. [But] after 10 years of practice the proportion of women starts to dwindle rapidly to only 13 per cent of the total. At 15 years, when candidates for part-time judicial office can expect to be under active consideration, the proportion of women falls again to only 6 per cent, and at 20 years drops once more to 4 per cent.'

The Lord Chancellor reluctantly introduced a system of ethnic monitoring in October 1991 to see whether the proportion of people from the ethnic minorities applying for judicial appointments was in line with their representation in the legal system as a whole. 'I'm not personally keen on "ethnic monitoring" or "ethnic origins",' he said. 'I like to treat everyone as a person. Their ethnic background is part of their personality like everything else. We don't keep a register of people's heights, for example. But people want it now, they want to be sure I'm giving fair treatment to candidates.'[117] He said he made allowances for some of the factors which would otherwise discriminate against women. 'For example', he explained, 'we are careful to take account of career breaks in assessing comparative incomes and weight of practices, and on a number of occasions we have made age exceptions so as to be able to appoint a promising female candidate.'[118] But he also said that 'nothing would be worse for the reputation of the judiciary in this country than for me to lower the standards for appointment to the judiciary simply to ensure a different racial or sexual mix.'

The Lord Chancellor could still be doing more. It would be naïve to suppose that those who recommend candidates for the judiciary are never guilty of improper discrimination. More could surely be done to offset this without lowering standards.

The main problem facing women solicitors is lack of training. According to Amanda Royce, chairman of the Association of Women Solicitors, 'Many women in the City law firms want to apply for the bench but they say: how do I get experience as an advocate?'[119] What is required is a major training programme for judges who have little experience of courtroom work. How the judges should be trained is a topic which will be considered later in this chapter.

Who would be a judge?

From the outside it looks an ideal job. An appointment to the High Court means an automatic knighthood or a DBE, a clerk to look after you and the power to make decisions yourself instead of trying to persuade others. What's more, from time to time you will spend several weeks out 'on circuit' in fine old English or Welsh market towns and cities where you will try the most serious cases in the criminal calendar. Instead of going to work on the Underground, or walking to court from your flat in the Temple, or even cycling as some judges do, you will ride there in a black Daimler with police outriders to stop the traffic[120] and you will live in the Judge's Lodgings with a cook and butler to wait on you.

From the inside it may seem less tempting. As we move towards a classless society a title may produce derision rather than deference. While a clerk may be useful, an assistant with legal training might be of more help. Many lawyers do not find crime intellectually stimulating. It is hard to maintain your dignity while wearing an eighteenth-century wig and something resembling a red dressing-gown. And having to spend about half the year living away from your family – often at a time when your children are growing up – is something which not many men, and even fewer women, willingly accept these days.

It is this last factor which makes being a Circuit judge so attractive: just as county courts have nothing to do with counties, Circuit judges do not go out on circuit.[121] Neither do judges of the High Court Chancery Division, which is one of the reasons why the job is so highly favoured. Being able to sleep in one's own bed for most nights in the year has its advantages. There is an argument for appointing some Queen's Bench judges who would not have to go out on circuit and indeed Lord Mackay thought that might well be possible.[122] It would certainly make the job more appealing for those who still had their children living at home.

Who would then try the most serious cases outside London? The Lord Chancellor seemed to think Circuit judges should hear virtually all criminal cases anyway, but it should not be impossible to find

High Court judges who would make their homes outside London and sit at the local Crown Court. To avoid becoming too isolated they would come to London from time to time and sit in the Court of Appeal.

That in turn might cause other problems. One advantage of the present circuit arrangements is that a peripatetic High Court judge does not get too close to the local dignitaries. There is a risk that the Circuit judge, living near his local courts, can become too friendly with the local chief constable, the local Chief Crown Prosecutor, even the local solicitors and barristers. And that can make it more difficult for the judge to do justice. Despite the attractions of making their homes on circuit many High Court judges are firmly against the idea.

Even so, something needs to be done to make the bench more attractive. There are plenty of leading barristers these days who have spurned a judicial appointment, and having to try criminal cases on circuit is a powerful disincentive for many of them.

It was previously thought that the chairman of the Bar – invariably a leading QC – is invited to take a seat on the bench at the end of his year of office. But several recent Bar chairmen have not become judges: among them Richard du Cann QC (chairman in 1980–81), Sir David Calcutt QC (1984–5), Lord Alexander of Weedon QC (1985–6), Peter Scott QC (1987), Anthony Scrivener QC (1991) and Lord Williams of Mostyn QC (1992). Those who stayed at the Bar continued to enjoy practising the profession to which they had devoted their working lives. Those who left, to head a Cambridge college or a clearing bank, did not do too badly either. Some leading counsel make no secret of their reluctance to take a judicial appointment, but that may of course be because they know that an appointment will never be offered to them.

For Anthony Scrivener QC[123] the main reason for not wanting a red gown was the loss of freedom and independence that went with it. Asked to what extent money had influenced his decision he confirmed that a highly successful QC would make 'a considerable sacrifice' by joining the judiciary. One judge, he said, had to remortgage his house to pay his back tax. And because barristers now make their own pension arrangements there is no need for them to join the judiciary simply to provide for their old age.

The consequences of this judicial reticence are clear to see. For much of 1992 the Commercial Court (part of the High Court

Queen's Bench Division) was operating at reduced strength. Pressed in the House of Lords to explain why judicial vacancies remained unfilled Lord Mackay explained that cases there lasted longer and it therefore took more time for commercial barristers to wind down their commitments. Asked whether barristers had turned down an appointment to the Commercial Court he confirmed, somewhat delphically, that from time to time he had approached people 'who have had particular circumstances in a situation which have made it impossible for them to accept appointment at that time'. Suspecting, perhaps, that he had not made himself entirely clear the Lord Chancellor tried again: 'The only reasons that have ever been advanced to me for anyone not accepting a proffered appointment to the High Court bench,' he explained, 'have been personal circumstances relating to a present situation.' In none of these cases had 'remuneration, pension or anything of that kind been the reason for the refusal'.

One suspects that these barristers were being less than frank. The average net annual income of Queen's Counsel in England and Wales in 1991 was £183,500.[124] Queen's Counsel at the commercial Bar can now make £500,000 a year or more: several earn as much as £1,000,000 a year before expenses. Such people are hardly going to rush into a job paying an annual salary of £90,000. The consequence was a court which in 1992 was in 'complete disarray'. Mr Justice Saville, the senior judge of the Commercial Court, admitted that the decision to reduce the number of judges in his court to below six, the minimum number required, had caused 'immediate and grave injustice'. Speaking from the bench in December 1992 Mr Justice Saville said there would still only be five High Court commercial judges available at the beginning of 1993 instead of the six required. This state of disarray would continue and cases would have to be postponed.

The situation was ironic because the Commercial Court had been set up in 1895 after the business world had become dissatisfied with the services provided by the ordinary courts. Mr Justice Saville said it was sad that 'a hundred years on, the court designed to provide the commercial community with a proper service should be allowed to suffer from the defects that brought it into existence in the first place'.[125] And the Commercial Court was not alone in this. By the beginning of 1993 the shortage of High Court judges had reached crisis point.

Judicial numbers

Delivering the BBC's annual Richard Dimbleby Lecture in November 1992 the Lord Chief Justice said that the 'persistent failure to appoint enough High Court judges had caused backlogs to reach unacceptable proportions'. Lord Taylor told the Lord Chancellor that unless more judges were appointed soon the arrears would become 'a national disgrace'.

It was the first public sign of a growing crisis. In October 1992 Lord Mackay had set up a working party of senior judges and officials to see how many judges were really needed in the High Court. It was chaired by an appeal judge, Lord Justice Kennedy.

One member of the Kennedy working party, Mr Justice Macpherson of Cluny, told his colleagues that despite the transfer of work from the High Court to the county courts there was 'nothing like enough High Court Queen's Bench judge power'. As a result, he said, it had been necessary 'to continue the highly undesirable practice of large-scale use of Deputy High Court judges'.[126]

Parliament intended Deputy judges to help out in times of crisis.[127] It is also reasonable for the Lord Chancellor to try people out as Deputies before deciding whether they should be given a permanent appointment. But most of the Deputies are not up-and-coming QCs. Mr Justice Macpherson said that was hardly surprising when they could be earning 'refreshers' of £2,000 *a day* at the Bar.[128] Most Deputies, he continued, were in fact 'warhorses', people in their mid- to late sixties. They were 'full of experience in the past, but not appropriate regular tribunals for 1992'.

Lord Justice Kennedy's working party concluded that the High Court needed ten to thirteen more judges: four in the Chancery Division, one in the Family Division and five to eight in the Queen's Bench Division. Even then, it said, 'far too many criminal and civil trials which are properly classified as cases to be heard by a High Court judge would still be heard by a Deputy'.

Rather to their surprise the judges got what they asked for. The Lord Chancellor announced in March 1993[129] that parliament would be asked to raise the statutory maximum number of High Court judges by 13 (to 98); he promised that ten additional judges would be appointed during 1993. In the event, most of them were absorbed by the Criminal Division of the Court of Appeal: as Lord Justice Kennedy had predicted, there were still too many civil cases being heard in the High Court by Circuit judges – sometimes with embarrassing results.[130]

The Lord Chief Justice welcomed the Lord Chancellor's decision to appoint more judges, and relations between the two men immediately improved.[131] But it seemed strange that this lengthy and unseemly public wrangling should have been necessary to produce a result which would undoubtedly save public money in the long run. Officials in the Lord Chancellor's Department thought the judges were naïve if they expected that the Treasury would sanction an increase in spending without proof that it was really necessary, but the judges felt that a more sympathetic Lord Chancellor would have acted on the Lord Chief Justice's request without further ado.

Judges' pay

For the best part of two hundred years judges' salaries could only be changed by Act of Parliament. This was considered essential to preserve their independence from the government of the day. In 1965 parliament agreed that judges' pay could be increased by a ministerial Order in Council, which still required the agreement of both Houses of Parliament.[132] Then in 1973 even that safeguard was abolished.[133] Instead, it was agreed that the Top Salaries Review Body would recommend pay rises which the government would then implement.

Or so it seemed. In 1992 the government decided, for the first time, that it would not accept the recommended increases for judges. In July 1992 the Top Salaries Review Body recommended pay rises for judges of 20 to 30 per cent.[134] The government decided on a rise of 4 per cent (from April 1992) with a promise of more to come in 1993 and 1994. That took the pay of a Circuit judge by 1994 to £69,497; the earnings of a High Court judge to £95,051; the income of a Lord Justice of Appeal to £104,922; the salary of a law lord to £109,435; and the emoluments of the Lord Chief Justice to £118,179.

The review body had pointed out that most lawyers who were appointed to the Bench had their income halved: 'median pre-appointment earnings of those appointed to the High Court in recent years were about twice the judicial salary,' it said.[135] However, it added, 'as yet, there have been no refusals of a formal offer of appointment'. But, of course, nobody gets a formal offer if it is known they will refuse: indeed, the review body was told that 'some candidates for the High Court bench had asked for a deferment because of their current financial commitments'.

This was the start of an alarming trend. In the three years from April 1988 to April 1991 nobody turned down the offer of a High Court appointment. In the financial year 1991–2 one person declined to allow his name to be recommended to the Queen for immediate appointment to the High Court bench (while seven accepted the appointment). In the following year six declined although nineteen people were appointed. In the second quarter of 1993 eight people were appointed and two declined. Eight of the nine people who declined appointments during the two-year period said politely that they would like to be reconsidered for appointment in the future; one was not interested at all.[136] Lord Mackay maintained that the candidate's decision had nothing whatever to do with money; he refused to say why the appointment had been turned down in case this identified the lawyer concerned.[137]

Lord Justice Parker drew attention to the findings of the Review Body on Top Salaries in a speech he made to mark his retirement from the Court of Appeal in July 1992. He noted that since 1985 'the salaries of the top groups within the review body's remit, which include the judiciary, have in real terms fallen by 3 per cent, whilst at the same time . . . average earnings in Great Britain have risen by 22 per cent in real terms and the earnings of equivalent groups in the private sector have risen by 41 per cent.'

Interviewed subsequently, the judge admitted that appointment to the bench meant such a significant drop in earnings for the successful lawyer that some would inevitably decline the job, with adverse effects on the quality of the judiciary: 'if you pay peanuts, you get monkeys,' he added somewhat unoriginally.[138] David Pannick QC, supporting the judges' call for increased earnings, said, 'Pay rates for an independent judiciary should not be set by the executive, the most frequent client of the courts'.[139] And Lord Williams of Mostyn QC agreed that judges' pay should be fixed by a properly independent review body. It was pointless and, he believed, 'dangerous to have an allegedly independent body which is then overruled by politicians'.[140]

The Top Salaries Review Body said that judges accepted the principle of a pay cut on appointment 'in the light of the status and security of judicial office, with its prospect of continuing in paid, rewarding and pensionable employment to a later age than is possible in most walks of life'. But, the government's advisers concluded, 'the discount . . . has now become too great'.[141]

Even so, 1992 was a time of pay restraint. Inflation was low, the recession was biting and many thousands of workers were losing their jobs. The money judges receive may not be nearly as much as they could earn at the Bar, it may not be as much as successful industrialists receive, it may not even be as much as the executives who run government agencies like the prison service are paid, but it is hardly a pittance. People who say they cannot keep a family on £90,000 a year cannot expect much public sympathy. The real problem is not that judges earn too little but that lawyers earn too much.

Lord Taylor said that if it was purely a question of money nobody who was doing well at the Bar would join the bench. Those who became judges considered it to be the 'natural culmination' of a career in the law; they did it as a matter of duty and because they thought the work was worthwhile.[142]

But when duty calls, some leading barristers find themselves rather hard of hearing. Low pay is not the only reason.

Judges' pensions

Barristers are self-employed: that means they have to pay for their own pensions. One of the main attractions of being a Circuit judge or a High Court judge was being able to retire on half-pay after 15 years' service. This arrangement had been unchanged for nearly two hundred years when the Judicial Pensions and Retirement Act 1993[143] raised the period of service required for a full pension from 15 to 20 years.[144] The Lord Chancellor said he was simply bringing the senior judges into line with other judicial officers and judicial pensions into line with modern pensions law. The judges argued that this meant an effective pay cut of 7.5 per cent. Lord Taylor, the Lord Chief Justice, spoke of the 'unfairnesses and meannesses' contained in the legislation.[145] Other judges described it as 'mean and penny-pinching'. Paradoxically the Judicial Pensions Act also lowered the retirement age to 70 (but only for judges appointed after the Act came into force).[146] This means judges must now be appointed by the time they are 50 in order to qualify for a full pension. In the past, most were not.[147]

A younger judiciary is certainly a good thing. If other public servants must retire at 60, why not the judiciary? As we have seen, it can be hard to get good people to become judges. It will be even harder if they are expected to accept the inevitable drop in earnings several years earlier than they do already. Not many good barristers will be queuing up for a judicial appointment as they approach the age of 50.

The fact that people joining the judiciary in their early fifties will get a smaller pension than they would have received before the Act took effect was no doubt the Treasury's aim. But what of the consequences? When the legislation was going through parliament Lord Simon of Glaisdale, a former Conservative MP who later became a law lord, said it would 'do great damage to the judiciary of the future and . . . therefore to the rule of law and the liberty of the citizen who depends on the rule of law'.

Needless to say, the Lord Chancellor did not share this view. According to Lord Mackay, there was no reason to think that the high standard of the judiciary would not continue. His junior minister, John Taylor, said in the Commons: 'There is very little evidence that people accept judicial appointment because of the pension arrangements or that they are deterred from accepting by the pension arrangements.' Sir Ivan Lawrence QC, a Conservative MP and chairman of the Commons Home Affairs Committee, disagreed. 'Fewer of the better and more successful practitioners will want to become judges,' he maintained, 'and fewer women will want to become judges.'

The retirement age of 70 does not apply to the Lord Chancellor.

Judges' hours
High Court judges are required to sit for just 189 days a year: about 38 weeks. But no judge takes 14 weeks' holiday. Lord Taylor said the time a judge spent in court was merely the tip of the iceberg:

> People sometimes imagine we come in at 10.30 straight from the breakfast table and leave at 4.30 for tea, and that's the day's work. But there's a great deal to read beforehand, there's the writing of judgments, there's keeping up to date with the law, there's duties on the Parole Board and the Judicial Studies Board and seminars and so on. So judges really do work very hard, and usually at nights and weekends during term time.[148]

There is no doubt that the judges work long hours when they are sitting. But could they make do with less time off? The Lord Chief Justice suggested in the same interview that the judges could consider taking slightly less leave during the Long Vacation (which runs from the beginning of August to the end of September). However, the suggestion that they should sit for an extra ten days each year had just been rejected by the judges themselves. The working party chaired by Lord Justice Kennedy reported that 'such a proposal would be unlikely to find much favour with the judiciary who, having recently been awarded a pay increase below the rate of inflation and far below the level recommended by the Top Salaries Review Board, are bound to regard the vacations as one of the few remaining attractions of the job.'[149] This passage provides a remarkable insight into the state of the English judiciary in 1993. Five appeal judges and three High Court judges[150] were saying, in effect, that the best thing about being a judge was the time off. They were not prepared to ease the judicial backlog by spending more time in court.

Who could blame them? They had made a financial sacrifice by joining the judiciary. Now Lord Mackay was demanding a further financial sacrifice from them – as well as cutting their pension rights. They could hardly have been blamed for sounding bitter. But the Lord Chancellor could certainly be blamed for inspiring that sense of bitterness in his fellow judges.

Answering for themselves

In his book *Judging Judges* Simon Lee proposed that the law lords 'should call press conferences when issuing their judgments in cases of great public interest instead of allowing their reasons to be lost in a welter of ill-informed criticism'.[151] It was one of the conclusions he drew from examining the way in which the House of Lords had handled the *Spycatcher* case in the summer of 1987, when the British government asked for a temporary ban on reporting the allegations in Peter Wright's M15 memoirs even though the information he had disclosed was already in the public domain. The law lords' decision to grant the temporary injunction – by a majority of three judges to two – was reported by the *Daily Mirror* in dramatic terms. On its front page it printed pictures of Lord Ackner, Lord Brandon and Lord Templeman – upside down. Taking up half the page was the comment: 'You Fools'.[152]

Professor Lee's book was published in 1988. In the paperback edition a year later he added, perhaps a little self-indulgently, an imaginary dialogue between two (black, female) judges who had supposedly been reading his book.[153] One says it would be 'silly' for judges to hold press conferences after they give judgment. The other helpfully explains what Professor Lee is getting at:

'He's thinking of *Spycatcher* and the way in which the media fastened on the dissents, ignoring the majority's explanations. Surely it's got to be a good idea to think about communicating reasons in such a way that they will be understood by the public. [Lee] doesn't mean a press conference like the ones Bobby Robson has to suffer after a disappointing England soccer game. He means Joshua Rozenberg or some other . . . legal journalist asking the presiding judge to explain, in a nutshell, why the decision was reached.'
'I don't write my judgments for the *Nine O'Clock News*, you know.'
'Who do you write them for?'
'The litigants, their lawyers, future lawyers.'
'And the public doesn't matter?'
'Of course the public matters but they can read it in the *Times* Law Report.'
'But people take their news from television nowadays and, even if we stick to newspapers, the widely read papers don't have a law report. Doesn't the majority of the public count?'

When Simon Lee first put forward the notion that judges should explain their judgments on the television news the idea seemed laughable – and not only to the judges. Five or six years on, it seems much closer to the realms of possibility.

In 1988 the judges were making few concessions to the press. At the beginning of that year Lord Lane, then Lord Chief Justice, delivered a judgment of immense public interest. In it he explained why the Court of Appeal had dismissed an appeal by the Birmingham Six.[154] The judgment ran to more than 160 typed pages and took the three appeal judges, speaking in turn, most of the day to read. But there was not a single copy available for the press. Without one, even a journalist with perfect shorthand could hardly have been expected to report accurately a judgment of such length and complexity for the following day's papers. And there had been no attempt to tailor the judgment for a listening audience by including brief summaries or oral signposts.

Lord Lane was disappointed that little of his carefully written attempt to justify the court's decision was ever reported in the press. He did not understand why this was so, and at that time no journalist was close enough to the Lord Chief Justice to tell him. All he needed to do was provide copies for reporters.

Nowadays some courts do arrange for copies of a judgment to be handed to the media immediately after it has been read aloud in court. But that still involves a vast amount of public money going to pay judges to read – and lawyers to listen to – words which could be absorbed more quickly and effectively from the printed page. Why bother to read them out at all?

One well-meaning judge who had just spent more than four hours of valuable court time reading out his judgment said he had thought it was important for the plaintiff – an elderly lady – to understand in detail why her case had been dismissed.[155] But the lady and her legal advisers would have understood the judgment just as well – if not better – from the printed page; and they would not have had to wait until the middle of the afternoon to find out who had won the case.

In the House of Lords and the Civil Division of the Court of Appeal the judges do not generally read out their rulings; for some years they have handed down typed copies of their judgments instead.[156] That might seem unsatisfactory in a criminal appeal, where those most affected by the outcome do not always have the literacy skills to match those of a Lord Justice of Appeal. The answer must surely be a compromise. While the appellants are present the judges should read out a short summary of their judgments, stressing the key factors which have led them to allow or dismiss the appeal. That summary, together with the facts of the case, the legal precedents and the detailed reasoning should then immediately be made available in writing to everyone in court. The same course should be followed by every court which takes time to prepare a written judgment.

This, in essence, is what happens at the European Court of Justice in Luxembourg and the Human Rights Court in Strasbourg. A useful refinement at those courts is that a summary of the entire judgment is generally made available in the form of a press release and faxed immediately to those who need it.[157]

Since Simon Lee first proposed that judges should be interviewed about their decisions there has been progress on two fronts. In 1991, when the Court of Appeal gave its reasons for freeing the Birmingham Six, the judges arranged for more than a hundred copies to be printed and made available to reporters outside the court.[158] And judges do now give press conferences, though so far not on specific cases. In November 1992, within the space of a week, Mr Justice

Brooke, Mrs Justice Booth, and the President of the Family Division, Sir Stephen Brown, all answered questions from the media about reports for which they were responsible. Lord Taylor, the Lord Chief Justice, agreed to meet journalists every six months or so – although in practice meetings were less frequent.[159]

That is about as far as it goes. Judges are now much more willing to appear on television – so long as the discussion does not move beyond general issues. Individual judges are more relaxed about talking privately to selected legal correspondents, even over dinner.[160] Now and again a judge will tip off a trusted reporter about the date of a forthcoming judgment – without, of course, revealing the result. Judges sometimes agree to give judgment in open court or release written copies of their decision after a hearing in private; occasionally a judge will call reporters in to brief them after a hearing even if there is no judgment to report.[161] In 1987 Judge Lymbery QC told the Press Association news agency why he had granted bail on a murder charge to a man who was then accused of committing a second murder during his period of bail.[162] At the end of 1992 an appeal judge issued a four-page summary of a lengthy judgment 'for those who might not get copies of the full decision', the first recorded example of a judicial press release in an English case.[163] In November 1993 Mr Justice Morland held a briefing at Preston Crown Court for reporters attending the trial of two boys, both aged 11, who were subsequently convicted of murdering two-year-old James Bulger: the judge outlined the reporting restrictions he would be imposing and even offered a few hints on English courtroom procedure for the benefit of foreign journalists. It is not unknown for the law lords to help a reporter understand a particularly complicated split decision by privately indicating which speech best expresses the majority view. And when judges find they have been misunderstood by the press, they sometimes make an opportunity to return to the point in a later judgment[164] or even call in the media to explain.[165] However, our judges have never agreed to be questioned in public about their judicial decisions; their view is that a judgment must speak for itself.

This approach lends certainty to the law but does little to enhance public understanding of the decision or the decision-making process. For more than two hundred years the judges took the view that they should not look at Hansard to see what parliament meant by a piece of legislation which they had found obscure. The law lords abolished that rule in 1992: if the meaning is not clear there are circumstances in which they can 'ask' the minister – by looking at Hansard – what he intended the words to mean.[166] The judges should apply the same rule to their own decisions and let the media ask them what was meant by an obscure judgment.

They might raise three possible objections to this. First, that what the judges say out of court may confuse or contradict what they said in their formal judgments. That should not be a problem. The law is what the judges declare it to be in court. What they say outside the court would have no greater force than remarks made during the course of legal argument.

The second objection is that the judges would lose some of their independence by allowing themselves to be cross-examined; moreover, they may even be led into saying something they might regret. The answer here is that the judges are well able to look after themselves.

The third objection is that broadcasters could distort an interview by selective editing. There is already a risk that the media will misrepresent a written judgment; indeed, the judges often complain about misleading reporting when the media have only had a short news-agency version of a judgment available. By giving a broadcast interview the judge is less likely to be misunderstood by the reporter or producer responsible and so more likely to get his meaning across to the audience.

As things stand, the judges can only look on in anguish. In 1991 Mr Justice Rougier said that if the *Times* columnist Bernard Levin could change places with a judge he would find himself

dismayed by the continual misreporting of any proceedings in his court which were of topical interest. Crucial facts will be omitted from the report. Special circumstances which called for unusual treatment will be ignored, leaving only an apparently peculiar decision for the public to contemplate. He would also find that insulting comments from those whose only knowledge of the matter stemmed from those distorted accounts will be given far greater coverage than his painstaking and doubtless well-expressed reasoning.[167]

The judges may take the view that it is for journalists to explain judicial rulings to the public as a whole. How much better it would be to have the explanation from the judges themselves. Simon Lee is right. From time to time presiding judges should explain, on camera, why a particular decision was reached.

Spreading the judicial word
In recent years the judges have begun to worry about what they have learned to call their public image. Every time the BBC shows the traditional pictures of the judiciary in procession from Westminster Abbey to Westminster Hall at the start of the judicial year, a collective groan goes up from those judges who do not want to be seen in ear-flapping wigs, black tights and red dressing-gowns: like Father Christmas in drag, as somebody once said.[168]

In 1990 Lord Justice Glidewell, one of the more thoughtful of our appeal judges, said it was ironic that the judges should be criticised so much more than they had been ten or twenty years earlier. In his view the judiciary was now far more professional and it got 'the right answer' more frequently than it had in the past. But he conceded that the public did not realise this. Was that the judges' fault? 'It's our fault if what we're doing is misunderstood,' he said. 'If we ought to publicise what we're doing more then perhaps it is our fault.'[169]

Traditionally the judges have been quite unable to cope with the vexed issue of their own public relations. Not long ago a distinguished Lord Justice of Appeal was disturbed to find that his after-dinner speech to the High Court Journalists' Association had gone largely unreported. There were several reasons for this: the occasion was traditionally considered off the record and it was thought unlikely that the judge would say anything worth reporting; an after-dinner speech is usually too late for the morning newspapers unless a text has been circulated in advance; and journalists are not renowned for their sobriety during the latter part of the evening. Any competent press officer would have explained this to the judge, but the judges were then one of the few organised associations of men and women in British society without anyone to advise them on their public relations.

At the same time the Lord Chancellor was becoming increasingly concerned about the bad press some judges were receiving. In 1990 Lord Mackay revealed that he was thinking of offering the judiciary the assistance of his own press office to publicise their judgments. 'It's not that anything private would be disclosed,' he said, 'but I think that sometimes it might be helpful if it was possible to draw attention to some of the facts which haven't been fully appreciated.'

All journalists are wary of press officers. A press officer is appointed to serve his or her employer, not the media: press officers are responsible for keeping journalists away from their sources of information, at least until the source is ready to speak. Even so, press officers have their uses. A good press officer will provide a journalist with speedy access to information once those in authority are willing to reveal it. He or she may even be able to persuade their employer that a journalist may be trusted.

It was in this sense that the idea of a judicial press officer was a good one. The idea of the judges' press officer also working directly for the Lord Chancellor was not. However, Lord Mackay took a different view; he was a judge himself, he said, and all the court staff worked for his department anyway.[170]

At first the notion of a judges' press officer seemed to flourish. Sheila Thompson, the Lord Chancellor's head of information, organised the press conferences given by Lord Taylor on his appointment[171] and during his first year in office. However, there was a clear conflict of interest. The judges are constantly criticising government policy on everything from legal aid to the organisation of the magistrates' courts. Relations between the judges and the Lord Chancellor are not always cordial: what Lord Lane, the former Lord Chief Justice, thought of Lord Mackay was virtually unprintable.[172] His successor has a better relationship with the Lord Chancellor but Lord Taylor has not hesitated to criticise the government's policies in front of a mass television audience. Furthermore, it is common for the courts to have to rule on legal actions against the Lord Chancellor: these have included applications for judicial review of his policy on legal aid and on one occasion a claim that he had acted unfairly in allocating contracts to court shorthand writers.[173]

The most telling objection to the present arrangements is that the Lord Chancellor's head of information owes his or her first duty to the Lord Chancellor. If the interests of the Lord Chancellor are in conflict with the interests of the judges, the civil servant's duty is clear: officials must have no secrets from their ministers. They owe no such duty to the judges.

One consequence of this policy was that journalists were not told when the Lord Chief Justice was about to make a major anti-government speech, either in the House of Lords or outside. On at least two occasions in the spring of 1993 these broadsides did not receive the coverage they deserved. There was also a 'misunderstanding' over who was meant to distribute a speech on the Criminal Justice Act made by Lord Taylor to Scottish solicitors.[174] As a result, nobody from the London-based media even knew that the Lord Chief Justice of England was in Scotland. Lord Taylor said subsequently that he had no complaints about the way the Lord Chancellor's press office had worked for him although he could see there was a greater immediacy in having press relations handled by somebody in the next room rather than in a different building.

Another consequence was the embarrassment suffered by Lord Woolf after his speech on prisons in October 1993.[175] A competent press officer would have warned him of what he could expect.

Even so, the idea of giving judges their own press officer was rejected. The Lord Chancellor's press office continued to distribute speeches whenever it was asked to do so by the judiciary. It was also agreed that from July 1993 the Lord Chief Justice would have a private secretary, just as a government minister has. The first holder of that office was Edward Adams, a 33-year-old high-flyer who had joined the Lord Chancellor's Department as an administrative trainee some eight years earlier. It was announced that he would support the Lord Chief Justice in all his non-court work and provide a link between the Lord Chief Justice, government departments and the judiciary.[176] In addition he was also to serve as secretary to the Judges' Council.[177]

Mr Adams should also be responsible for alerting the media to forthcoming guideline judgments and handling press relations for the senior judiciary. It should be made clear that the private secretary owes his first duty to the Lord Chief Justice, not the Lord Chancellor – even though, like a ministerial private secretary, he relies on his parent department for promotion.[178]

Meanwhile, the judges have discovered that they have an even more powerful weapon at their disposal: the libel writ. It was not so long ago that they would shrug off inaccurate press reports: journalists tended to assume, somewhat rashly, that judges were not allowed to sue in the courts where they themselves sat. But after receiving a solicitor's letter in 1991 the *Sunday Telegraph* 'unreservedly' apologised to Mr Justice Tudor Evans for a 'serious and untrue allegation' that he had given an improper direction to the jury in a murder trial four years earlier.[179] And Mr Justice Popplewell was subsequently awarded damages against newspapers which wrongly accused him of falling asleep during a trial.

Training judges to judge

Training judges to judge is a new idea.[180] Until the 1970s judges resented the implication that they needed training: some thought that being trained could be positively harmful.[181] That attitude is reflected in the name of the body set up in 1979 to train the judiciary: 'Judicial Studies Board' is a euphemism which fools nobody.

The idea of disguising judicial training as judicial studies came from a working party chaired by Lord Justice Bridge (as he then was). Following its appointment in 1975 the Bridge committee spent a leisurely three years looking at the existing pattern of sentencing seminars before recommending a more centralised structure based at one of the universities.[182] That plan was rejected by the government on grounds of cost but the board was allowed to appoint a Studies Consultant to help plan courses of study and to prepare written study material. The job went to Dr David Thomas of Cambridge, the author of standard works on sentencing.[183] He continues to hold it: the board decided in 1991 that it did not want to replace him with a full-time Director of Studies. That was because the judges feel it is important to run their own show in their own way. The Judicial Studies Board was created by the judges and its work is still controlled and conducted by them. However, in 1988 an Administrator, Philip Taylor, was recruited to help run the board and its staff.

When it started life in 1979 the Judicial Studies Board was only concerned with criminal work. It provided training, instruction and information for full-time and part-time judges in the Crown Court – with the ultimate aim of reducing inconsistencies in sentencing. The board began by organising induction courses for new Assistant Recorders. In addition, it arranged refresher seminars for Recorders and Circuit judges covering topical problems in criminal law and procedure as well as the proper conduct of criminal trials.[184]

In 1985 there was a major expansion of the board's responsibilities. For the first time there was to be training for judges in civil and family work; the board also became responsible for supervising the training of magistrates and tribunal members. There is now a 'main board' which deals with policy and planning. It is chaired by an appeal judge, currently Lord Justice Henry, and among its members is the senior Home Office official dealing with criminal justice policy. The main board works through five committees. The Criminal Committee is now also chaired by an appeal judge (currently Lord Justice Kennedy) and is responsible for training those who sit in the Crown Court. The Civil and Family Committee is jointly chaired by High Court judges from the Queen's Bench Division (Mr Justice Tuckey) and the Family Division (Mr Justice Kirkwood); it trains the judges who deal with these areas of work, and it had the major task of teaching the judiciary how to implement the far-reaching changes of the Children Act 1989. There is also a Magisterial Committee, chaired by a senior Circuit judge, to advise the Lord Chancellor on the training of magistrates. And there is a Tribunals Committee to advise on the training of those who serve on tribunals.

The fifth committee to be established – in July 1991 – was the Ethnic Minorities Advisory Committee. It too is chaired by a High Court judge, Mr Justice Dyson, who took over from the first chairman, Mr Justice Brooke. Its aim is to ensure that judges and magistrates are given the information and understanding they need in order to avoid discrimination on racial grounds.[185] The committee believes there is no point in trying to change people's personal attitudes towards issues of race: people 'with strong feelings of antagonism against people of a different culture' should not be appointed to a judicial post in the first place. Instead the committee saw its role as changing people's behaviour 'so they no longer, consciously or unconsciously, say or do things which understandably give offence to people from ethnic minorities or lead to discriminatory treatment'.

The chairman of the Ethnic Minorities Advisory Committee gives talks at training seminars on such diverse topics as body language and the oath taken by witnesses in court. These talks are generally well received. The committee's detailed paper on oath-taking[186] makes fascinating reading. It says, for example, that there are a number of holy books such as the Gita (Hindu), the Adi Granth (Sikh) and the Koran (Muslim) which ought to remain covered except when they are being touched by the witness taking the oath. They should not be handled by an usher who has not washed his hands. In the past, court staff have been told to administer a form of declaration to Chinese witnesses in a ceremony which involves breaking a saucer. The committee says they should no longer do so; the only people who practise this ceremony today are the Triads.

The board's induction seminars last three and a half days.[187] There are two types: criminal courses for newly appointed Assistant

Recorders, and training in civil and family work for Recorders, Assistant Recorders and Circuit judges who have limited experience of civil cases.

There are four criminal induction seminars a year attended by an average of 120 lawyers, some of whom have never even conducted a case in the criminal courts. On the first day they are given an introductory talk by a High Court judge, covering such topics as how to prepare for and conduct a trial, and how to sum up to a jury.

Day two is the highlight of the course – a mock trial in which the novice judges play almost all the roles including defendants, counsel, jurors and witnesses. Ironically, the one role the trainees do not play is that of the judge: that part is taken by a real one, usually a Circuit judge. He throws in the odd deliberate mistake to see how many people pick it up. The High Court judge in charge of the seminar acts as an impresario, stopping the action from time to time and asking some unfortunate lawyer what he would do next.

Actual cases are used as the basis of the mock trials, with variations added to make them more interesting. According to the Judicial Study Board's chairman, Lord Justice Farquharson, 'The idea is to have them on the edge of their chairs all the time, being required – as they have to when they sit in court – to make decisions very suddenly.'[188] Sometimes a novice judge will be primed to act as a heckler; he will shout obscenities from the public seats, or throw something at the judge. The action is stopped, and the trainees are asked what to do next. 'You mustn't overreact,' said Lord Justice Farquharson, 'or the press will headline you as imprisoning a chap who's just a bit silly, rather than somebody who's evil. Equally, you can't allow the court to be interrupted in that way; you've got to take some effective action.' His advice was that judges should normally act with great caution. 'It's that kind of management of the trial that is now in my judgment one of the most important aspects of the training.'

These days it is not unknown for the public gallery to break into cheers when spectators hear the verdict they have been waiting for. Lord Justice Farquharson was asked how a judge should react to such an outburst. He adopted his sternest tone. 'Stop that noise,' he demanded, 'or I shall clear the court!' That normally worked, he explained; otherwise he would adjourn the court, retire to his room and order the miscreants to be removed.[189]

During their training the would-be judges attend lectures given by visiting academics; they also hear from others involved in the criminal justice system such as probation officers and prison governors. The rest of the course is devoted to sentencing exercises. Much of the work is now done in groups of five or six pupils, each with its own tutor judge.

As homework the trainees are given examples of real cases and asked what sentences they would impose. These are marked and compared with the actual sentences approved by the Court of Appeal. There are normally huge variations in the sentences passed by the would-be judges. In particular, it seems some trainees are reluctant to send people to prison. Indeed they should be, but they should remember what the public requires of them. If serious and violent criminals are not sentenced in accordance with the law, the victims of crime will rightly complain that justice has not been done.

The Judicial Studies Board also offers lessons in how to sum up to a jury: the trainee judges are given a pile of evidence and asked to write and deliver a summing-up the next day. There are standard precedents they are expected to follow. Other members of the group are then invited to make critical comments.

And that's it. The trainee judges get a week or two sitting in with an experienced judge in the Crown Court before they are let loose on real criminals. Even the most experienced criminal lawyers find it a daunting prospect. However, many of those on the course normally practise as commercial or family lawyers. Certainly those who have not practised in the criminal courts will still find themselves largely ill-prepared to sit as judges, even after three and a half days of intensive training.

If possible, the new Assistant Recorder will begin his judicial career sitting in the court where he gained his work experience. There is always a more senior judge sitting in a nearby court; if anything goes wrong Assistant Recorders are told to adjourn the case immediately so they can seek the advice of another judge. In July 1994, the Lord Chief Justice announced that the experienced judge in whose court the Assistant Recorder first sat will continue to monitor the trainee judge when he sets out alone. The senior judge, who is likely to sit at a corner of the bench, will tell the Assistant Recorder how he is doing, and report back to the Lord Chancellor if he's not up to scratch.

After sitting for five years Recorders and Circuit judges also get a three-and-a-half-day refresher course for each subject area in which they are involved – crime, civil actions and family work. Criminal refresher seminars include sentencing exercises and discussion sessions designed to ensure consistency of approach. There are talks by Home Office ministers and officials as well as representatives of the prison service, the probation service and the Law Commission. Civil and family refresher seminars are designed to bring judges up to date with new law.

There are no residential training courses for High Court judges or appeal judges. It is hard to see why this should be, and Lord Justice Farquharson revealed in 1993 that he was keen to introduce training for the higher judiciary. If the money could be made available he thought High Court judges should attend regular refresher seminars just as Circuit judges now do. He believed that even his fellow members of the Court of Appeal could benefit from training, if only to ensure consistency of approach.[190] In the meantime, members of the higher judiciary do attend occasional evening seminars to learn about developing areas of the law.[191] They also attended one-day seminars on new legislation such as the Children Act 1989 and the Criminal Justice Act 1991. High Court judges who try criminal cases are invited to criminal refresher seminars on appointment; they also receive written advice from the Judicial Studies Board on how to cope with problems that may arise during a trial. In addition, they are provided with specimen directions for giving to juries and sentencing guidelines approved by the Court of Appeal. New training sessions were being planned in 1993 to advise judges how best to make use of evidence from psychiatrists.

For many years the Judicial Studies Board refused requests from journalists for permission to watch training seminars. The main reason given was that it would be embarrassing and inhibiting for observers to see trainee judges passing inappropriate sentences or not knowing how to cope with problems at a trial. In rejecting such a request during the spring of 1993 Mr Justice Judge, until recently chairman of the board's Criminal Committee, said the work at these seminars 'is amply and publicly described in the reports of the board, the most recent of which has only just been published'.[192] This attitude was disappointing if not surprising, and it was impossible to reconcile with Lord Mackay's earlier decision to allow an independent film-maker, Amy Hardie, to film a mock trial and a sentencing seminar for a programme shown on BBC television in May 1993. The programme showed everything that Mr Justice Judge and his predecessors had been so keen to conceal from the public for so many years. The heavens did not fall in: on the contrary, the Lord Chief Justice regarded the programme as an example of the 'favourable coverage' the judges had received in 1993.[193]

Room for improvement

Judicial training in England and Wales has moved a long way in less than fifteen years. It is now fully accepted by the judges for whom it is compulsory; and it seems that even the most senior judges would be prepared to give it a try. The old taboos have gone for ever. Even so, there is clearly scope for very much more training, both on developments in the law and in ways of ensuring that court time is used as efficiently as possible.

For a start, the present training course is clearly not long enough. Tony Holland, a past president of the Law Society, scorned the notion that three and a half days offer the necessary skills to sentence a man to ten years in prison. 'Would anyone want to appear as a potential customer before a newly appointed Assistant Recorder – perhaps a Chancery practitioner with just three and a half days' training under his belt? Does the criminal law consumer have no rights?' he wondered.[194] David Pannick QC favoured a residential course of two to four weeks.[195] But time is money – not just for the Lord Chancellor's Department which has to pay for the courses but also for the lawyers who lose their normal earnings while they are in training. They are paid an allowance of £100 a day while attending residential courses, about half what they receive while sitting.

Many Assistant Recorders begrudge the 20 days a year they spend on the bench: the fees they earn sitting are not as high as the fees they earn on their feet. Some of them have no wish to become full-time judges; they become Assistant Recorders because they believe the Lord Chancellor will think better of them when the time comes to appoint the next batch of Queen's Counsel. His officials professed surprise that anyone should take such a cynical view, but barristers are convinced that a willingness to help out by sitting judicially is an essential qualification for promotion.

Lord Justice Farquharson wanted to hold refresher seminars more frequently than every five years. 'If you get an important new piece of legislation it's hopeless waiting five years for the last chap to come through the hoop,' he said. He thought every judge should attend a refresher seminar once every three years.[196] Others believe that once a year would be better still.

At present, a lawyer is made an Assistant Recorder or Deputy District Judge *before* he or she attends a training course. On this basis the Lord Chancellor cannot afford to appoint people who may not be up to the job. Once appointed, the part-time judge will soon be summing up to a real jury or let loose on real litigants. Reasonably enough, successive Lord Chancellors have taken the view that candidates for the bench – even for part-time appointments – must have experience of the courts or tribunals in which they will sit. That requirement rules out many people who could certainly be taught the skills needed.

Solicitors in the big commercial firms do virtually no advocacy work themselves: even litigation specialists have little experience of speaking on their feet because they still do not have rights of audience in the higher courts. How, then, can they show that they can do the job?

There should be a major new training programme for would-be judges. Suitable candidates could first be appointed as Justices of the Peace, perhaps for a limited period; they would then spend a year or so sitting part-time in the magistrates' courts. Although the role of a Crown Court judge is very different from that of a magistrate, this would at least give candidates some initial experience of the bench. After that they would attend a substantial residential training course, to be organised by the Judicial Studies Board. This would be an enlarged version of the board's induction courses for new Assistant Recorders. If such a training course ended with a practical examination, like the tests pupil barristers now have to pass, then the Lord Chancellor could afford to try out lawyers with no courtroom experience; those who did not make the grade would not be offered paid judicial posts (although they might still have a useful role to play as magistrates).

The writer Marcel Berlins has suggested that lawyers who have no interest in crime ought to be able to serve on the bench without having to be a criminal judge first.[197] But Circuit judges who do no criminal work – and there are already a number of these – are never going to be promoted to the High Court or above. It must be undesirable to create a caste of second-class judges who cannot handle one of the judiciary's greatest responsibilities.

The Royal Commission on Criminal Justice concluded in July 1993 that 'substantially more resources need to be allocated to judicial training than at present'.[198] The commission had been set up two years earlier to examine the effectiveness of the criminal justice system following a series of miscarriages of justice which culminated in the release of the Birmingham Six. The report also expressed concern that trainee judges were not told how well or how badly they had done on their courses. The commissioners agreed that intervals between refresher courses were too long: they thought Assistant Recorders in particular should be recalled for their first refresher training after two years, not three and a half years. The commission was sure that additional investment in training would be cost-effective: there would be fewer expensive appeals if judges made fewer mistakes during trials.

Judging the judges

If a judge goes astray there is not much that anyone can do about it. All judges of the High Court and above hold office 'during good behaviour, subject to a power of removal by Her Majesty on an address presented to Her by both Houses of Parliament'.[199] That power has never been exercised in the case of an English judge although Sir Jonah Barrington, a judge of the High Court of Admiralty in Ireland, was removed with immense difficulty in 1830 for helping himself to money which suitors had paid into court. Anthony Sampson noted in 1992 that 'at least one current High Court judge is considered seriously unstable, if not mad, by his colleagues: but he cannot be fired'.[200] In fact, if he really *were* mad he *could* be fired: provided there was medical evidence of 'permanent infirmity' then the Lord Chancellor could declare the judge's office to have been vacated.[201]

Circuit judges are vulnerable even if sane: they can be sacked by the Lord Chancellor 'on the ground of incapacity or misbehaviour'.[202] That has happened once, but in practice it seems to be a power which can be used only if the judge is prepared to put up his hands and go quietly. In 1983 Judge Bruce Campbell was dismissed after being caught smuggling 125 litres of whisky and 9,000 cigarettes into Britain in his yacht.[203] He offered his resignation, and Lord Hailsham, the Lord Chancellor, naturally wanted to accept it; but that would have meant Judge Campbell losing the pension which, in Lord Hailsham's view, he had earned by the proper performance of his judicial duties. However, a judge who is dismissed for conduct which does not arise out of his office can keep his accrued pension at the discretion of the Crown. So Lord Hailsham sacked Judge Campbell.[204]

The case of James Pickles was very different. It began in 1985 when Judge Pickles, a Circuit judge from Halifax, wrote an article for the *Daily Telegraph* calling for tougher punishments and criticising what he saw as government pressure on the judiciary to keep people out of prison.[205] Looking back at the incident, it is almost impossible to believe what happened next. The Lord Chancellor's Permanent Secretary, Sir Derek Oulton, immediately wrote to warn Judge Pickles that Lord Hailsham considered his article, at first sight, amounted to 'judicial misbehaviour'.[206] A subsequent letter confirmed that Lord Hailsham was thinking of using his powers to dismiss the judge: Sir Derek Oulton told him the Lord Chancellor would shortly 'consider your future on the circuit bench'.[207]

The accusation against Judge Pickles was that he had failed to comply with the Kilmuir rules. (As we have seen, these restrictions on judges' freedom of speech were subsequently abolished by Lord Mackay during his first press conference as Lord Chancellor. Judge Pickles claimed the credit for 'single-handedly' getting the judiciary 'freed from the Kilmuir gag';[208] but this seems a little implausible.)

Judge Pickles's response to his threatened dismissal was typically robust. He called Lord Hailsham's bluff, saying he was prepared to go public on the affair. He also threatened to seek judicial review of the Lord Chancellor's decision.

In the event, it did not come to that. Instead it was arranged that the Lord Chief Justice, Lord Lane, would have a quiet word with Judge Pickles. For a while that seemed to do the trick; but James Pickles felt he still had things to say and he wrote another newspaper article, this time for the *Guardian*.[209] Following that, he threw all caution to the winds and agreed to be interviewed for the BBC Radio programme *Law in Action*.[210] He drew the line at television, but there was clearly no going back. In the months that followed he was to appear – three times – on *Wogan*.[211]

There were even more serious lapses of judgment to come. In March 1989 Judge Pickles sentenced a young woman to seven days' imprisonment for contempt of court. Michelle Renshaw had refused to give evidence against her former boyfriend – who had been accused of assaulting her – because she had received threatening telephone calls. The case caused an uproar and Judge Pickles agreed to explain his decision on the television news.[212] Lord Mackay, by then Lord Chancellor, asked the judge for an explanation, suggesting that his behaviour was improper at a time when Miss Renshaw's appeal was pending.

James Pickles backed down. He wrote in reply: 'I give you my undertaking that in the relatively short period prior to my retirement, I will not comment publicly on any judicial decision of mine, in a manner which identifies the case concerned.'[213]

That was in October 1989. A few months later came the case of Tracey Scott. She was a 20-year-old single mother who had pleaded guilty to the theft of more than £4,000-worth of goods from the supermarket where she worked as a checkout operator. The court heard that she had simply waved her friends past the till, including one who wheeled out a brand-new bicycle.

Although she had a young baby by the time she came before Judge Pickles for sentencing, Tracey Scott had not been pregnant at the time of the offences. In court the judge suggested young women might think that one way of avoiding prison would be to become pregnant between committing a crime and being sentenced. He sent Tracey Scott (and her baby) to prison for six months. Soon afterwards the Court of Appeal criticised Judge Pickles's decision and substituted a probation order.

James Pickles was besieged by the press. He made a decision 'which with hindsight was unwise'.[214] He decided to hold a press conference at lunchtime that day, to correct a point which he thought had been inaccurately reported: 'Obviously I could not invite the press into the Crown Court building where I was sitting. So I rang the licensee of the adjoining aptly-named Inns of Court pub, where I sometimes had lunch . . . I corrected the misunderstanding and what I said was duly reported. I also called the Lord Chief Justice "an ancient dinosaur living in the wrong age". I should not have said that . . .'[215]

The Lord Chancellor said he had been advised that the judge's latest actions amounted, in law, to misbehaviour. Lord Mackay asked Judge Pickles why he had broken the undertaking he had given not to comment publicly on his own cases.

After dragging out the correspondence for as long as possible Judge Pickles responded by once again threatening to go public in his own defence, and he again mentioned judicial review. He also raised a point of some substance. He noticed that the Lord Chancellor had the power to dismiss a judge but not to discipline him.[216] Judge Pickles thought that power had been deliberately omitted from the Courts Act 1971 because it might be seen as interference with the judiciary by the executive. 'What sort of disciplinary code is it,' he asked, 'which provides for dismissal but nothing less than that? What criminal code in any civilised country would provide the death penalty and nothing less?'

Lord Mackay's response was to outline his plans for what would have been the first trial of a judge in modern times. In James Pickles's words: 'The Head of the Judicial Appointments Group – I do not suppose they have a group for dismissing judges – wrote stating that the hearing would be in a committee room in the House of Lords at noon. "The Lord Chancellor would like you to put your case in the way you wish with the minimum of preliminaries and interruption." ' This would have made a great spectacle if it had ever happened but Judge Pickles, not unreasonably, declined to attend a hearing which he judged 'would not accord with the rules of natural justice'.

Lord Mackay backed down. He agreed to see Judge Pickles informally, at a meeting in November 1990. At the meeting Judge Pickles agreed not to accept fees for broadcasts, articles or appearances while serving as a judge. He also had to accept a 'serious rebuke' from the Lord Chancellor.[217]

It is clear from the account Judge Pickles gives of this meeting[218] that Lord Mackay used his undoubted courtesy and charm to disarm Judge Pickles and defuse a difficult situation. As a result, the judge caused no more trouble for the few remaining months he had to serve in order to qualify for his pension. It seems there is little else the Lord Chancellor could have done. Any attempt to sack Judge Pickles could well have left the Lord Chancellor facing lengthy and embarrassing legal proceedings.

The Pickles affair raises two key questions. First, just what is judicial misbehaviour? Second, is the so-called power to dismiss a Circuit judge any more than an empty threat?

Misbehaviour is not defined in the Courts Act and no procedure is provided for dismissing a judge. However, Lord Hailsham seemed sure that Judge Pickles was guilty of it. In what is clearly a reference to Judge Pickles, Lord Hailsham wrote in his memoirs: 'I was strongly advised by two of the most respected members of the senior judiciary and by my own office that a particular judge had . . . been guilty of misbehaviour within the meaning of the Act and should be removed.'[219]

But Judge Pickles was not removed. Lord Hailsham explained why.[220] The judge had made what Lord Hailsham thought were 'quite unjustified and scurrilous criticisms' of him. This put Lord Hailsham in an awkward position: 'The principle that justice should be seen to be done meant that I could not act as victim, prosecutor, judge and jury in the same proceedings.'

So it may have been the threat of judicial review which saved Judge Pickles his job. Lord Hailsham was in no doubt that a decision to sack a judge would have been reviewable by the courts as well as by parliament.[221] It is unlikely that the courts would have over-turned his dismissal but any litigation would have proved extremely embarrassing for the judiciary. The prospect of one judge asking another judge to decide whether the most senior judge of all had acted fairly was not one which endeared itself to successive Lord Chancellors.[222]

Whether Judge Pickles would have got very far with an application for judicial review is a moot point.[223] His best argument was that, as he saw it, the Lord Chancellor was 'complainant, prosecutor, judge and jury'.[224] It is hard to see how this is consistent with the rules of natural justice but counsel for the Lord Chancellor would no doubt have argued that it was consistent with the terms of the Courts Act. If parliament had wanted another legal mechanism it could have provided one.

Lord Hailsham certainly wanted something different. He regarded the system of dismissing Circuit judges as 'wholly wrong in principle'.[225] But his behind-the-scenes pressure for reform had been frustrated by 'opposition from within the judiciary'. Lord Hailsham said other countries had much better procedures: 'To name only three examples, Scotland, Canada and Australia have a different and more satisfactory provision by which the indispensable act of removal is preceded by a quasi-judicial hearing of a disciplinary panel of a judge's peers.'

The Master of the Rolls, Lord Donaldson, had also been worried about the Lord Chancellor's power to sack Circuit judges for misbehaviour. Some years earlier, in 1987, he suggested that this power should not be used without the agreement of four leading judges, the Heads of Division. At the same time Lord Donaldson was in favour of abolishing the power of a dismissed judge to seek judicial review, which he thought was 'both unseemly and damaging to the rule of law as a whole'. Lord Donaldson said the new procedure would bring two benefits. 'First, it would underline the independence of the Circuit judiciary, politically and in every other sense. Second, it would enable the Lord Chancellor to demonstrate that he was not acting politically if ever a Circuit judge had to be removed from office for incapacity or misbehaviour.'[226]

Lord Donaldson was surely right to question the desirability of a Lord Chancellor acting alone to sack a Circuit judge. As Lord Hailsham said, it is wrong for anybody, even the Lord Chancellor, to be victim, prosecutor, judge and jury. If the issue should arise again, as no doubt it will, the Lord Chancellor would be well advised to set up a disciplinary panel from the senior judiciary to hear what the errant Circuit judge may have to say. By statute, the final decision would be one for the Lord Chancellor, but there is nothing in the statute to say he should not take the advice of his fellow judges before making up his mind.

Judicial misbehaviour of a very different kind took place in Newcastle-upon-Tyne in the autumn of 1992. Judge William Crawford QC had been accused of what the Lord Chancellor's press release described as 'over-familiarity towards female court staff'.[227] Newspapers reported that he had kissed a 25-year-old court usher on both cheeks and put his hands on her waist: she was in tears over what had happened. After considering a report from one of the senior judges on the North-Eastern Circuit Lord Mackay called Judge Crawford in and told him that he 'took an extremely serious view of his conduct'. The judge had 'behaved in a quite unacceptable way'. Judge Crawford apologised and promised not to do so again. The Lord Chancellor allowed him to return to work but told the judge it was his duty to rebuke him and make public that he had done so. He warned the judge that if there were to be any substantiated future complaint of a similar nature he would be obliged seriously to consider the exercise of the powers available to him under section 17(4) of the Courts Act, under which he can remove a Circuit judge from office on the grounds of misbehaviour.[228]

Is sexual harassment of this kind really 'misbehaviour' within the meaning of the Act? If it amounts to a criminal assault then the answer is probably Yes. Nobody would condone what the judge did: it was, in Lord Mackay's words, 'wholly inconsistent with the behaviour expected of a judge'. However, it would be worrying if a future Lord Chancellor could sack a Circuit judge for non-criminal misbehaviour not directly connected with his competence on the bench.

What if a judge acquires a criminal record? In April 1993 James MacArthur, a District judge based at Peterborough County Court, was convicted of driving with excess alcohol, having been convicted of a similar offence in 1985. He was disqualified for two years and fined £3,000.

The Lord Chancellor told District Judge MacArthur that he expected members of the judiciary to observe standards of behaviour which would not undermine public confidence in them, and added that he viewed a conviction for drink-driving as a justification for exercising his power to dismiss a District judge on grounds of misbehaviour.[229] On this occasion, however, he decided to let District Judge MacArthur off with a public reprimand.[230]

Was this the right decision? It was in line with precedent: at least half a dozen members of the judiciary have kept their jobs after being convicted of driving with excess alcohol, including a High Court judge in 1975 and a Lord Justice of Appeal in 1969. It may well be that some motoring or parking offences would be too trivial to be considered 'misbehaviour' but there can be no doubt that a conviction for drunken driving is grounds for dismissal. It is clearly a very serious offence: somebody might have been killed.

In July 1994, the Lord Chancellor accepted the force of these arguments. Lord Mackay sent every judge (by recorded delivery) a letter saying he regarded a conviction for driving under the influence of alcohol or drugs so grave as to amount, at first sight, to judicial misbehaviour. The message was clear enough: the next Circuit judge found guilty of drink-driving could expect the sack. In future, judges could no longer have a 'legitimate expectation' of lenient treatment. Discussing the letter at a news conference, the Lord Chief Justice said that a High Court judge in that position 'might feel he ought to go'. Otherwise, he thought, 'the whole clanking machinery of an address of both Houses of Parliament could be brought into operation'.

Judiciary review
As we have seen, the power to dismiss a Circuit judge amounts to 'all or nothing'. What if a judge's behaviour simply falls short of the standards we might reasonably expect? What if he is rude to the witnesses, reserves judgment for too long or is simply lazy or

insensitive? The Lord Chancellor has not hesitated, where he has seen fit, to issue public rebukes and reprimands (it is not clear which is the more serious). But is that sufficient? Should there not be some sort of 'judiciary review' to keep an eye on the judges?

The idea of a judicial ombudsman was put forward by Lord Williams of Mostyn QC, then chairman of the Bar, at the barristers' annual conference in 1992.[231] Lord Williams proposed a panel of judges, lawyers and laymen to investigate complaints about the judiciary. He suggested that in less serious cases the panel might have a quiet word with the judge concerned. If things did not get any better the panel would advise the Lord Chancellor that action was needed. However, Lord Williams stressed that there would be no interference with decisions made by the judges in court.

There was a swift and predictable response from the judiciary. Speaking at the first news conference ever given by a serving Lord Chief Justice, Lord Taylor expressed the view that such a watchdog would undermine judicial independence. 'I don't think there's any particular advantage in pillorying judges in public,' he said; it would only diminish confidence in the judge concerned. He thought the existing safeguards – where a judge was 'spoken to' in private by senior colleagues or the Lord Chancellor – were satisfactory. And if confidence in a Circuit judge had been diminished to a point where he really should not be sitting, the Lord Chancellor had power to dismiss him.[232]

Within a month Lord Williams hit back.[233] Judges were not 'God's representatives here on earth'. There was nobody who would not benefit from a system of advice and monitoring. 'If it came from a body such as an expanded Judicial Studies Board, nothing but benefit would follow.' Few judges agreed with him, he said, but his postbag had been full of letters of support, from lay people, witnesses, barristers and solicitors.

The idea of keeping an eye on the judiciary was discussed in 1987 by David Pannick QC in his book *Judges*.[234] Drawing on the experience of other countries, where there are powers to investigate whether a judge has acted injudiciously, Mr Pannick proposed the creation of a Judicial Performance Commission. He anticipated the response of the English judges – that it would be an attack on their independence – by asserting that the judges would not allow the fear of complaints to influence their decisions.

The JUSTICE report mentioned earlier in this chapter[235] which called for a Judicial Commission also proposed the idea of a Judicial Standards Committee which would report to it. 'The committee's function would be to provide an independent mechanism for reviewing the professional conduct of judges.'[236] If there were serious allegations against a judge they would be presented, independently, to a tribunal. In extreme cases the tribunal would be able to recommend to the Lord Chancellor that a judge should be suspended or dismissed.

There was unexpected support for these ideas in July 1993 from the Royal Commission on Criminal Justice. In its report[237] the commission recommended that 'the judiciary as a profession should have in place an effective formal system of performance appraisal'. The commission said that 'where serious inefficiency among judges occurs' it must be possible to have a judge removed 'in view of the damage that he or she may do'. It was satisfied 'that the Lord Chancellor can use, and on occasion has used, the threat of exercising these powers to procure the resignation of judges whose continuance in office would prejudice the interests of justice' but 'less satisfied that adequate monitoring arrangements are in place'.

Members of the Royal Commission had been surprised that senior judges never watched trials conducted by their more junior colleagues. 'We would like to see time found for resident judges[238] to attend trials so they can assess the performance of judges in their courts,' they concluded. The commission also called for systematic procedures so that members of the Bar (though apparently not solicitors) could make their views known on the performance of individual judges. These comments would be channelled through the leaders of the profession and the resident or presiding judge to the judge concerned.

Clearly the Royal Commission on Criminal Justice was concerned only with criminal trials, and it seems from the context that the commissioners were concerned about errant Circuit judges rather than High Court judges. The fact that there was no such limitation on the commission's recommendations drew a predictable response from the judiciary. Lord Taylor said that senior judges already received information about the conduct and capacity of judges in their areas; 'where appropriate, they bring such comments or criticisms to a judge's attention.' In the Lord Chief Justice's view, 'To introduce formal performance appraisal such as may be appropriate in industry or the civil service would clearly endanger the fundamental independence of individual judges, not only from the executive but also from each other.'[239]

There was a time when nobody could imagine a need to keep judges' behaviour under review. But that was the very time when some particularly disturbing things were happening – quite unknown to the public at large. Lord Widgery, Lord Chief Justice from 1971 to 1980, was seriously ill towards the end of his judicial career. He was suffering from the early stages of a degenerative nervous disease which got so bad that he could no longer cope with his judicial work. He spoke in a barely audible voice and fell asleep in court. For a year or more, lawyers and fellow judges closed ranks to protect him. Sometimes the judges he was sitting with had to write his judgments for him. For some considerable time before he resigned in 1980 he was – in the words of one leading academic – 'visibly and distressingly half-senile'.[240] But he remained in his job.

More recently, in November 1988, Judge Sir Harold Cassel put a child molester on probation for two years. The 30-year-old man had indecently assaulted his stepdaughter three times, twice when she was twelve and once after her thirteenth birthday. There were extenuating circumstances which in the judge's view justified such a lenient sentence but what outraged people were Judge Cassel's remarks in court. He told the man that his wife's pregnancy had led to her 'lack of sexual appetite'. It had caused considerable problems for a healthy young husband. The judge said: 'This is a time when ladies are naturally not very receptive to their husbands.'

Shortly afterwards the Lord Chancellor announced that Judge Cassel was 'to retire on medical grounds forthwith'. It was reported that he had suffered a slight stroke some months earlier. The official announcement maintained that the Circuit judge, who was 72, had tendered his resignation on grounds of ill-health the day before he made his controversial remarks in court. The Lord Chancellor expressed his own disapproval of those comments. 'It is regrettable,' said Lord Mackay, 'that a judge should have expressed himself in a way that suggested that there are any circumstances that can excuse or condone indecent assaults on children.'

The Lord Chancellor moved quickly to accept Judge Cassel's resignation: he left the bench that day. But it is likely that signs of the judge's impending 'ill-health' would have been spotted in advance if there had been a proper way of monitoring odd behaviour.

More recently still, the behaviour of another prominent judge caused serious concern to his colleagues, and again nothing was done about it. He was the most senior judge at the Old Bailey, the Recorder of London, Sir James Miskin. He may have been suffering at the time from the early stages of Alzheimer's disease, from which he was to die in November 1993.[241] The public was completely unaware that there was anything wrong until the judge spoke to an unwitting reporter from the BBC's *Newsroom South-East* programme on the day before he retired in 1990. In the interview Sir James observed that it had been 'a mad decision' to free the Guildford Four a year earlier. Referring to the Court of Appeal judges he said, 'They didn't give any thought to the fact that three years after [the men were convicted] there was a full appeal, and there was no suggestion from any source that police documentation showed the confessions had been cooked up.' Sir James went on to criticise the Court of Appeal for being too lenient and blamed the government for letting people with criminal convictions sit on juries.[242] A year earlier, in an after-dinner speech, he had called black men 'nig-nogs'.[243] On another occasion he referred to men involved in one of his cases as 'murderous Sikhs'. His colleagues were well aware of his views, if not his illness, but they allowed him to remain a judge until he was ready to retire.

Lord Mackay saw no need for any changes in the system. He said he looked into all the complaints he received, and if anyone was to monitor the judges' performance, he thought it should be the Lord Chancellor rather than some sort of executive agency. However, if the Lord Chancellor's officials have shown themselves unaware that prominent judges have been suffering from serious illnesses which affected their judgment, how can they be relied upon to keep an eye on nearly 130 judges in the High Court and the Court of Appeal, not to mention more than 500 Circuit judges, many of them over the age at which most people now retire?

An early-warning system is needed to spot problems while there is time to put matters right. This would be no threat to the bench as a whole: on the contrary, it should enhance the reputation of the judiciary by identifying the judges who are likely to bring the system into disrepute. Competent and fair judges should have nothing to fear from a system of judicial monitoring.

3

Lawyers and the Courts

An anatomy of the courts
Viewed from the outside, lawyers and the courts must seem timeless and unchanging. On television we see men and women dressed in ancient costume emerging from ancient buildings and speaking an ancient language. We may imagine that this is how they have been for centuries; but things are not always what they seem, especially on television. The wigs date from 1822 (although their origins can be traced back a hundred years earlier), while the law courts in London date from 1882. By legal standards neither is particularly old.

Behind the scenes, things are changing rapidly – and not always for the better. Money must be saved above almost everything else. There is constant pressure to move legal cases down the system, to have them heard in the cheapest available way and with as few lawyers involved as possible. What effect has this had on the search for justice? This chapter begins with a look at the organisation of the courts in England and Wales. This will be followed by an assessment of the legal profession and the Lord Chancellor's attempts at reform.

The civil courts
It is customary to divide the courts into civil and criminal – although there is some overlap between the two structures and they meet at the top. The civil courts deal with disputes between individuals. In this sense the definition of an individual is wide enough to include private citizens, small firms, large companies and government departments. Even the Sovereign can bring a case but because they are 'her' courts a civil action by the Queen is taken in the name of Her Majesty's Attorney General, a member of the government.

123

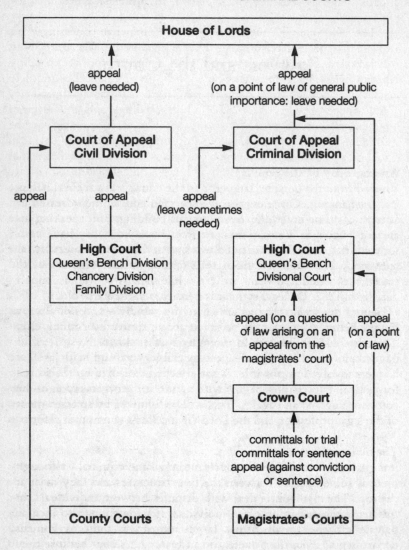

CIVIL COURTS   **CRIMINAL COURTS**

House of Lords

appeal
(leave needed)

appeal
(on a point of law of general public
importance: leave needed)

**Court of Appeal
Civil Division**

**Court of Appeal
Criminal Division**

appeal

appeal

appeal
(leave sometimes
needed)

High Court
Queen's Bench Division
Chancery Division
Family Division

High Court
Queen's Bench
Divisional Court

appeal (on a question
of law arising on an
appeal from the
magistrates' court)

appeal
(on a point
of law)

Crown Court

committals for trial
committals for sentence
appeal (against conviction
or sentence)

County Courts

Magistrates' Courts

Simplified diagram of the English Courts

The person who brings the case is usually called the *plaintiff* (or *claimant*). He or she *sues* the *defendant*. If there is an appeal, the losing party is renamed the *appellant*; the other side becomes the *respondent*.

The lowest civil courts are known, somewhat confusingly, as *county courts*: they have nothing to do with counties. There are about 270 county courts in England and Wales and their work is expanding in line with government policy. It is the Lord Chancellor's aim to achieve 'a closer match between the worth (substance, complexity and value) of what is at stake in proceedings and the level of judiciary, type of procedures and the resources devoted to the conduct of those proceedings.'[1] Put simply, this seems to mean spending as little as possible on a court case. In practice, it means that many cases which were heard by a High Court judge until 1991 are now handled by a Circuit judge, who of course is paid less. Before July 1991 the county courts could only hear a case if the amount in dispute was no more than £5,000 (or £30,000 in housing and probate cases). Those financial limits have been replaced with new, flexible criteria for allocating proceedings between the county courts and the High Court. Personal injury cases worth up to £50,000 must start in a county court.[2]

Nearly 3,000,000 cases were started in the county courts in 1993. That figure was 15 per cent down on the year before, which is rather surprising. Nine claims out of ten were for money and the remainder were mostly for the recovery of residential premises.[3]

Small claims (which now means those worth up to £1,000) are automatically sent for arbitration by the District judge. This is an informal, private procedure and litigants are encouraged to appear without lawyers. In 1993 more than 105,000 arbitrations were heard in the county courts. We shall be looking at small claims in chapter 4.

In August 1994 the Lord Chancellor abandoned plans to extend the scope of the small claims arbitration procedure. A discussion paper issued in October 1993 looked at cases where the value of the claim is decided by the court rather than specified by the claimant. These include personal injury claims. In the past, such cases were not referred to arbitration unless the claimant was claiming less than £1,000. The discussion paper had proposed that these claims should always go to arbitration unless the claimant said his case was worth *more* than £1,000.[4]

Most divorces are granted by designated county courts. The newspapers still talk about 'quickie' divorces as if they were something special: under a procedure first introduced in 1973 all but a tiny handful of divorces are now granted without the need for either party to attend court.

Above the county courts is the *High Court*, which sits in London and also at some 25 regional centres. In London the High Court is to be found at the Royal Courts of Justice in the Strand, a magnificent Gothic building designed by George Edmund Street RA and opened by Queen Victoria in 1882. The building, known more simply as 'the law courts', also houses the Court of Appeal. It stands on a six-acre site and 450 houses had to be demolished for work to start in 1873. The building costs were met by £700,000 which had accumulated in court from the estates of people who had died intestate. Another £70,000 went to pay for the elaborate oak carving and panelling.

Each of the original courtrooms has a unique interior: they were designed by different architects. The carved Royal Coat of Arms in Court 4, the Lord Chief Justice's court, is particularly fine. The Great Hall is a magnificent folly; measuring 230 foot long, 48 foot wide and 82 foot high, it is used by court staff for badminton matches in the evenings.

In the crypt area near the coffee shop there are several ornately decorated stone pillars. These were carved by foreign stonemasons – mostly Germans – who were living on site at the time: they had been brought in after English masons had gone on strike. It seems that the foreign workmen started the carvings to amuse themselves or improve the columns: they were asked to stop once it was realised that the decorations were not part of the architect's designs. Nearby, behind the northern entrance to the Great Hall, a pillar has been left incomplete because George Street believed – in line with contemporary thinking – that only the Great Architect in heaven could create a perfect building.[5]

The High Court is split into three divisions: Queen's Bench, Chancery and Family. The *Queen's Bench Division* is the largest and handles personal injury cases, breach of contract, debt and the like. The most senior of the 63 Queen's Bench judges can effectively pick their own cases: they generally go for defamation work, which is usually more interesting than the staple diet of personal injury and medical negligence.

The Queen's Bench Division has an important supervisory role, hearing applications for judicial review.[6] For these purposes, the court sits in what is known as a *Divisional Court*. The High Court department dealing with judicial review cases is called the *Crown Office* and the cases themselves are allocated to the *Crown Office List*. It would make sense to rename it the Administrative Court[7] or even the Judicial Review Court.

Between 1991 and 1992 the number of new legal actions in the High Court fell by a quarter, while the number of judgments fell by one-third – no doubt mainly because cases were being heard in the county courts instead.[8]

For the past hundred years the Queen's Bench Division has employed specialist judges to deal with major commercial cases. Since 1970 there has been a *Commercial Court* to deal with cases 'arising out of the ordinary transactions of merchants and traders'. As a result of a willingness to innovate and a high level of responsiveness to the needs of its users, the Commercial Court has become an international success, attracting litigants who would otherwise take their disputes to other jurisdictions or to private arbitration. The senior judge, Mr Justice Saville, said that 'the Commercial Court is a very substantial earner indeed of foreign exchange in the form of invisible earnings'. He said this could probably be measured 'in hundreds of millions of pounds'.[9]

As long ago as the mid-fourteenth century there was a specialised court to deal with maritime matters; the *Admiralty Court* has been part of the Queen's Bench Division since 1970. It supports a number of apparently arcane practices of which the best known is the power to take proceedings against a 'thing' – a ship or a cargo – as well as against a person or company. Traditionally a plaintiff started a legal action against a ship by nailing a writ to the mainmast. Now that wooden masts are less common this has become impractical and writs are fixed to the window of the bridge house with adhesive tape, rather in the fashion of a parking ticket.[10]

As well as including a Commercial Court and an Admiralty Court, the Queen's Bench Division is also responsible for administering the eleven strangely named *Official Referees*. These are Circuit judges who hear lengthy technical cases such as construction disputes and others involving prolonged examination of documents or accounts. A recent case required the judge to master the computer systems of bank 'hole in the wall' cash machines so that he could consider claims by customers who said their accounts had been wrongly debited.

Most of the Official Referees sit in London, at courts in an unattractive modern office block a couple of streets away from the main buildings. This back-street justice symbolises the low status of the Official Referees. It is entirely unjustified: they are required to do work which is just as demanding and important as that of a High Court judge, but for less pay. Often huge sums are at stake. They should be given the same status and title as their fellow judges in the High Court.

The *Chancery Division* of the High Court inherited the jurisdiction of the old High Court of Chancery and with it some of the fog that settled round the case of *Jarndyce and Jarndyce*[11] in Dickens's *Bleak House.* The Chancery Division is mainly concerned with land and property: wills, trusts, tax, partnerships and other financial matters which hit the headlines only occasionally but often in spectacular fashion.[12] Though some would find this type of work dull it is often where the money is to be made and it attracts the finest legal brains at the Bar. There are 17 Chancery judges in addition to the Vice-Chancellor.

The *Family Division* of the High Court has 15 judges apart from the President. Under the Children Act 1989 cases are heard at the most appropriate level in the court structure; the High Court Family Division hears the most difficult and important cases. These include wardship cases where the court assumes responsibility for the welfare of a child. However, the intention of the Children Act was to reduce the number of children being made wards of court.

Appeals from both the county courts and the High Court generally go to the Civil Division of the *Court of Appeal*. The division handled some 870 final appeals in 1993, 8 per cent more than in 1992, while the number of outstanding interlocutory (preliminary) cases was up by 6 per cent. In 1992 the Master of the Rolls, Sir Thomas Bingham, said the outlook for the Court of Appeal civil division was 'bleak'. He explained that 'far from eating into its backlog of cases, the court is losing ground and the backlog is growing, with the inevitable consequence of increased delay for litigants'. In his view, there were three possible solutions: reducing the time spent on each case; increasing the number of cases where an appeal could only be brought with the permission of the court; and increasing the number of judges. Sir Thomas suspected that a combination of all three would be required.[13]

His words were duly heeded. As well as increasing the number of judges Lord Mackay announced plans to reduce the number of civil appeals. Since October 1993 leave to appeal has been required in certain types of case. These include applications for judicial review (with the exception of immigration and nationality cases).[14] Lord Mackay, like Lord Donaldson before him, thought it wrong to waste everybody's time on hopeless appeals.

It is possible to appeal once more, to the *House of Lords*, against a decision of the Court of Appeal – but only with the leave of the Court of Appeal or the law lords themselves. From time to time cases come before the Court of Appeal which are clearly destined for the House of Lords;[15] in such cases the Lords Justices of Appeal willingly grant the unsuccessful party permission to challenge their decision on appeal. However, it is more usual for the Court of Appeal to refuse leave, which means the law lords themselves can decide whether they want to hear the appeal. They delegate this function to an *Appeal Committee* of three law lords (not to be confused with the *Appellate Committee*, which is the formal name given to the law lords sitting judicially).

The criminal courts

The criminal courts deal with disputes between an individual and his fellow citizens. Most criminal cases in England and Wales are brought to court by the Crown Prosecution Service although it is possible for public authorities (such as HM Customs and Excise), private companies and even individuals to start proceedings. In criminal proceedings the person who brings the case is *the prosecutor* or *the prosecution*. The Crown (or any other prosecutor) *prosecutes* a defendant.

The vast majority of criminal cases – more than 93 per cent[16] – are heard in some 600 *magistrates' courts* throughout England and Wales. There are no juries. Lay magistrates normally sit in benches of two or three while stipendiaries always sit alone. Although there are limits to the sentence that magistrates may pass, they are the sole judges of fact and law; in that sense, a single stipendiary has greater powers than a High Court judge (who is bound by the jury's verdict on questions of fact) or an appeal judge (who may be outvoted by his or her colleagues).

Although most criminal cases are dealt with by the magistrates there are some which are considered too serious for lay justices to handle.[17] These are tried in the *Crown Court*. Crimes which must be tried in the magistrates' court are called *summary* offences; those that can be tried by a judge and jury in the Crown Court are called *indictable* offences. Some of these indictable offences – the most serious – must always be tried in the Crown Court. The remainder are triable *either way* – which means either in the magistrates' courts or in the Crown Court. In these middle-ranking cases the defendant can insist on trial by jury even if the magistrates would have preferred to hear the case themselves. But if the magistrates decide to send the case for trial in the Crown Court the defendant cannot demand a summary hearing. In what was seen as its most controversial recommendation, the Royal Commission on Criminal Justice said the magistrates should ultimately decide where a case of this nature should be heard, depriving a defendant of his right to insist on trial by jury. These and other related proposals are discussed in chapter 8.

Under the present arrangements a defendant who is to be tried in the Crown Court must first be 'committed' (or sent) there by the magistrates.[18] They will only do this if they consider that there is 'a case to answer'. To decide whether there is enough evidence to justify a case going to trial they may sit as *examining magistrates*. This used to be much more common than it is now. As each witness spoke a clerk would type up his replies; then the witness would read over and sign what was known as a *deposition*. These days the clerk would be more likely to whisper the substance of the witnesses' replies into a dictating machine; then the tape would immediately be transcribed. Either way, the depositions would form the evidence at the subsequent trial.

From the defendant's point of view this can be a useful way of testing the evidence but it is very time-consuming and has fortunately become rare:[19] it is known as a *full* or *old-style* committal to distinguish it from the more modern version, the so-called *paper committal*, introduced in 1967. Here the evidence is given in writing and, if the defendant agrees, the magistrates do not have to read it before sending him for trial.

As the Royal Commission acknowledged, the system of paper committals has no useful purpose apart from providing time-limits.[20] The magistrates are not even allowed to acquit the defendant at this stage: if they decide there is no case to answer the prosecution can still bring a fresh charge or apply to a High Court judge for what is called *a voluntary bill of indictment*. This is a way of bypassing the magistrates completely; if the judge grants a voluntary bill the case goes straight to the Crown Court. It can be used at any stage in place of committal proceedings. However, it is considered unsporting and tends to be used only when the magistrates have behaved irrationally or there has been a procedural error. We shall be looking at the Royal Commission's proposals to do away with committal proceedings in chapter 8.

There are two different types of appeal against a decision of the magistrates' court. Clearly, a defendant who has pleaded guilty cannot appeal against conviction: he can only challenge his sentence. A defendant who pleaded not guilty can appeal to the *Crown Court* against his conviction or sentence or both. If it is an appeal on a point of fact then the evidence is heard afresh: there is a complete rehearing of the original case, with witnesses but without a jury. The Crown Court has wide powers: it can actually increase the defendant's sentence if it wishes.

If the defendant considers that the decision of the magistrates (or the Crown Court) was wrong in law he can appeal instead to the *High Court*. Unusually, the prosecution can also appeal to the High Court on a point of law. This is an exception to the rule against double jeopardy which says that a defendant should not be put at risk of conviction twice for an offence arising from the same facts.

Appeals to the High Court are heard by a Divisional Court of two or three judges. They are *by way of case stated*, which means the magistrates are asked to state on paper the question to be decided by the High Court. An appeal to the High Court is not a rehearing. The case is decided on the basis of documents after the High Court has listened to legal arguments from both sides.

The Crown Court, which hears the most serious criminal cases, replaced the ancient Assizes and Quarter Sessions in 1971. The Crown Court sits in some 90 different places in England and Wales – mostly the big towns and cities. Cases are normally heard by Circuit judges, Recorders or Assistant Recorders but High Court judges sit at the larger courts to deal with cases such as murder, manslaughter and rape. The Old Bailey (or, more formally, the Central Criminal Court) is uniquely owned and run by the City of London but in practice it is treated as another branch of the Crown Court.

Cases in the Crown Court are tried by judge and jury. During

1992 just over 100,000 cases were received for trial at the Crown Court, down 4 per cent on the figure for 1991. More than half the defendants who pleaded not guilty to all charges were acquitted.[21]

Appeals from the Crown Court against conviction or sentence go to the Criminal Division of the *Court of Appeal*. Unless the appeal is purely on a point of law the appellant generally needs the leave of the court before his appeal can be heard. That means the papers supporting his application for leave to appeal will be read by a single judge and the appeal will go no further unless the judge – or, if necessary, the court itself – decides that there is an arguable case.

In 1993 the Court of Appeal received just under 7,000 applications for leave to appeal, mostly against the sentence imposed. In some cases a defendant may seek to appeal against conviction even if he pleaded guilty in the Crown Court.[22] Although the Court of Appeal cannot increase a sentence on *an appeal by the defendant*, the court can order a defendant to serve a few months more by directing that the time he has served in prison waiting for his appeal to be heard should not count towards his sentence.

This power is not often used and so an appeal poses no major risk to the defendant. What he does need to worry about is the risk that the sentence will be regarded by the prosecution as too light. In certain serious cases the Attorney General can invite the Court of Appeal to increase a sentence if he considers it 'unduly lenient'.[23] The Court of Appeal judges will not increase the sentence unless they think it was way out of line, even if they would have passed a somewhat higher sentence themselves. For the court to intervene there has to be an error of principle in the judge's sentence which would damage public confidence if it were not corrected.

Before this provision came into effect in February 1989 the government had not thought the Court of Appeal would pass custodial sentences on defendants who had previously been fined or given probation by the Crown Court judge and so no procedure was provided for taking these people into custody. In fact, the Court of Appeal regularly imprisons defendants who received non-custodial sentences in the Crown Court. Some of them turn up at the hearing and listen to the proceedings from the public benches: if a prison sentence is imposed they simply walk into the dock and down to the cells. Others choose not to attend the Court of Appeal: they presumably sit at home and wait for a knock at the door. And no doubt there are one or two defendants who don't hang around to hear the verdict of the Court of Appeal.

Unlike an appeal from the magistrates' court to the Crown Court, an appeal from the Crown Court to the Court of Appeal does not involve a rehearing of the case. To succeed, the appellant must show that something was wrong with the original trial:

- that under all the circumstances of the case the verdict is unsafe or unsatisfactory; or

- that at the trial there was a wrong decision of a question of law; or

- that there was a material irregularity in the course of the trial.

The chances of success are generally low, to some extent because of what criminal lawyers call *the proviso*. This is a provision in section 2(1) of the Criminal Appeal Act 1968 which says that even if the court thinks that the point raised in the appeal might be decided in favour of the appellant, it may dismiss the appeal if it considers that no miscarriage of justice has actually occurred.

The defendant is only allowed one appeal himself, even if fresh evidence subsequently comes to light. However, under section 17 of the Criminal Appeal Act 1968 the Home Secretary can refer a case to the Court of Appeal at any time if he believes one of the above-mentioned grounds is applicable. The case is then treated as if it had been a normal appeal. Defendants who believe they have been the victims of miscarriages of justice regularly try to persuade the Home Office to refer their cases to the Court of Appeal under this provision. It is because these arrangements have been found wanting that the Royal Commission has recommended new procedures to deal with miscarriages of justice.[24]

The prosecution has no right of appeal against an acquittal in the Crown Court, however perverse the jury's verdict may have been. However, if the prosecution believes that the Crown Court judge got the law wrong in such a case, the Attorney General can refer the point to the Court of Appeal for an authoritative ruling.[25] The defendant must not be identified and his acquittal is not affected.

There may be one further appeal to the House of Lords which gets through about 80 cases a year. The law lords hear criminal appeals from the Court of Appeal and the High Court (the Divisional Court). However, there are certain restrictions. First the lower court must certify that the case involves a point of law of general public importance. If it does not, there can be no further progress. Second, either the lower court or an Appeal Committee of three law lords must grant leave to appeal.

Remarkably, the prosecution has a right of appeal from the Divisional Court or the Court of Appeal to the House of Lords. So it is possible for the Court of Appeal to quash a conviction on a point of law and for the House of Lords to reinstate it.

Until 1948[26] a member of the House of Lords who was charged with a serious criminal offence was entitled – or, rather, obliged – to be tried by his peers. That had been the law for more than seven hundred years. The last peer to face this remarkable form of trial was the twenty-sixth Lord de Clifford, whose Lancia saloon had collided with a Frazer-Nash open touring car on the Kingston bypass in August 1935 at three o'clock in the morning. Unfortunately the other driver was killed and the inquest unexpectedly returned a verdict of manslaughter. That charge had to be tried. In December 1935 more than 80 peers (including a bishop) assembled in the Royal Gallery of the House of Lords. Lord de Clifford pleaded 'Not guilty' and demanded to be tried 'by God and my Peers'. The trial was presided over by the Lord Chancellor, the first Viscount Hailsham, who, in true Gilbertian style, had been appointed His Majesty's Lord High Steward especially for the occasion. After hearing evidence by police officers Lord de Clifford's counsel submitted that there was no proof of negligence. The peers, judges of law as well as of fact, retired to consider this submission. Having taken advice from four High Court judges who had been brought in specially for the purpose, they agreed there was no case to answer. Asked for their verdicts 85 peers stood up, in order of precedence, and each pronounced the prisoner 'Not guilty, upon my honour'.[27]

One remaining appellate court in London is of waning importance but its decisions may still be a matter of life and death for those involved. The *Judicial Committee of the Privy Council* is the final court of appeal for some sixteen Commonwealth territories which have chosen to retain the right of appeal to the Queen in Council. These include New Zealand, a number of Caribbean islands including Jamaica, Barbados and the Bahamas and dependent territories such as Hong Kong. An appeal also lies from Trinidad and Tobago, Mauritius, the Gambia and (in some cases) Singapore, all of which are independent republics within the Commonwealth.

The Judicial Committee of the Privy Council is generally manned by law lords although the occasional retired Commonwealth Chief

Justice may be found sitting as well. All law lords are privy counsellors, as indeed are members of the Court of Appeal, but the Judicial Committee draws its moral authority from its ability to call upon the most senior judges in the United Kingdom.

The Committee derives its statutory powers from the Judicial Committee Act 1833 but its history goes back to medieval times when the king sought his Privy Council's advice on disputes in the Channel Islands (from where an appeal still lies). Fifty appeals were lodged in 1992, together with another thirteen appeals by doctors against decisions of their disciplinary bodies (which also come within the Judicial Committee's responsibilities).

The Judicial Committee has both criminal and civil jurisdiction but its cases tend to be very different from those the law lords would normally have to decide. First, they may turn on the interpretation of a written constitution, something which judges have little experience of in the United Kingdom. Second, rather more may be at stake.

In November 1993 the Judicial Committee of the Privy Council allowed an appeal by two prisoners, Earl Pratt and Ivan Morgan, who had been under sentence of death in Jamaica since 1979.[28] The two men, and more than a hundred others facing the death penalty, were expected to have their sentences commuted to life imprisonment because of the length of time they had spent awaiting trial. Seven law lords instead of the usual five sat for the first time since 1949, overturning a decision the Privy Council had reached in 1983. They decided that in any case where an execution was to take place more than five years after the death sentence was passed, there would be strong grounds for believing that the delay constituted inhuman or degrading punishment, contrary to the Jamaican constitution.

The case had important implications. There was little doubt that it would be cited in the United States of America where it is sadly not uncommon for prisoners to wait on 'death row' for more than five years. Though the decision could not bind the United States courts it would certainly have persuasive authority. In London, Foreign Office sources thought that the decision would virtually oblige the British ambassador in Washington to make representations if it appeared that the Americans were preparing to carry out the death penalty on someone who had been held in custody for five years or more.

Solicitors

To anyone brought up in a class-based society it seems perfectly natural to find the legal profession divided into gentlemen and players. It is only when someone asks 'Are Two Legal Professions Necessary?'[29] that one begins to wonder why a practising lawyer in England and Wales can either be a solicitor or a barrister – but never both.[30]

Solicitors have always been the junior branch of the profession. Every year a number of barristers are knighted by the Queen when they become High Court judges. Until recently just one solicitor a year was guaranteed a knighthood – the president of the Law Society. Now even that perk has been abolished. However, there are signs of progress. There is a knighthood waiting for any solicitor appointed to the High Court bench. By August 1994 there had been only one such appointment.

In the remainder of this chapter we shall explore the differences between the two branches of the legal profession, while tracing the Lord Chancellor's attempts to eliminate them. Breaking down the barriers between solicitors and barristers has proved harder than many people would have expected. We shall also examine the problems faced by students seeking to join the profession, and by judges seeking to doff their wigs and gowns.

The inferior status of solicitors goes back to their origins in the late sixteenth century. The old courts of King's Bench had 'attorneys' attached to them who could represent clients. These men had some legal knowledge but they were less skilled than the barristers. Their opposite numbers in the new Court of Chancery were the 'solicitors', men whose job it was to 'solicit' (worry or bribe) officials so that the customary delays of the Chancery proceedings could be reduced as much as possible. In the fifteenth century the attorneys had often been housed in the Inns of Court where the barristers worked but in the later sixteenth century the barristers evicted them. Even so, the attorneys prospered and eventually, in 1739, they and the solicitors founded the Society of Gentlemen Practisers in the Courts of Law and Equity. The term 'attorney' went out of use in England and the solicitors' society became the Law Society in 1831.[31]

The Law Society has two distinct roles. On the one hand, it is the solicitors' professional body for England and Wales. It admits solicitors to the roll and can strike them off if they break the rules of professional conduct. Every solicitor is bound by those rules.

On the other hand, it is the solicitors' representative body. It has an elected council which negotiates with the government on behalf of the profession and does its best to further the solicitors' interests. Solicitors do not have to join the Law Society but most do. Their subscription buys them a weekly magazine (the *Gazette*) and entry to the Law Society's Hall, an imposing building in Chancery Lane which functions like a gentleman's club – except that ladies can become members. Those who use the Law Society as a club will find it is a place where nobody ever talks to anyone – which is why men prefer the Garrick.

When lay people refer to 'the Law Society' they generally mean the solicitors' representative body (and it is in that sense that the term is used in this book). More broadly, it can be used as a synonym for solicitors generally. There are local law societies up and down the country; and there are separate Law Societies in Scotland and Northern Ireland.

At the last count there were more than 76,000 solicitors in England and Wales. Of these more than 61,000 had paid the Law Society for certificates entitling them to practise their profession. More than 50,000 of them worked in private practice, for nearly 10,000 firms. Two per cent of solicitors were members of the ethnic minorities (compared with five per cent of the population as a whole). By 1993 more than a quarter of the 61,000 practising solicitors were women: the number of women practising as solicitors has trebled since 1983–4. There are more women solicitors under the age of 30 than men; and more women became solicitors than men during the year 1992–3, the first time that the majority of newly qualified solicitors were women. But Geraldine Cotton, chairman [*sic*] in 1992 of the Association of Women Solicitors, said that a woman was still less likely than a man to be made a partner in a firm of solicitors. She thought that until firms were prepared to be more open about their selection techniques women solicitors would continue to think that good candidates were being excluded simply because they were women.[32] The Law Society's Annual Statistical Report for 1993 confirmed that a higher proportion of men achieved partnership status in solicitors' firms than women.[33]

In all, some 4,400 trainees became solicitors during the year and 51 per cent of them were women, compared with 44 per cent in 1986. Nearly 13 per cent of newly qualified solicitors were from the ethnic minorities in 1992–3, slightly less than the year before:[34] twenty-three practising solicitors in every thousand were members of the ethnic minorities in 1992–3 compared with thirteen per thousand in 1990.

Barristers

Barristers can trace their history back to medieval times.[35] Legal life in London was centred on the four inns of court (Lincoln's Inn, Gray's Inn, the Inner Temple and the Middle Temple) and the nine or so inns of chancery. Each inn had a hall which was used for both meals and moots (a form of mock trial). The hypothetical pleadings in these moots were recited by 'inner barristers' and the arguments were conducted by 'utter barristers', so called because they spoke from outside the bar of the inn.

There are just over 7,700 barristers (or 'counsel') in England and Wales.[36] They still have to join one of the four inns of court (which 'call' students to the Bar). However, since 1987 barristers have been governed by the General Council of the Bar of England and Wales (which is generally known as the 'Bar Council'). Like the Law Society it is both a trade union and a watchdog.

Queen's Counsel

The most senior barristers are known as Queen's Counsel.[37] They were first appointed at the end of the sixteenth century in order to assist the law officers of the Crown. By the eighteenth century the appointment had come to be regarded as a mark of pre-eminence in the profession. Today QCs make up about a tenth of the practising Bar.[38]

A barrister who becomes one of Her Majesty's Counsel learned in the Law acquires no new rights: even the most junior barrister can appear before the highest courts in the land. The main difference is that QCs can charge considerably more than junior counsel. If a barrister becomes a QC at the right point in his career, he or she will get more money for doing less work. This system is defended on the basis of supply and demand: those who can afford it are prepared to pay as much as the market will bear in order to secure what is presumed to be the best legal advice and representation.

Queen's Counsel are known as 'silks' because they wear a gown which in a bad light could look as if it might possibly be made partly of silk. They are also called 'leading counsel' or 'leaders' because until

1977 they would not appear in court without a junior counsel sitting behind them.[39] Most silks still have juniors although clients are becoming increasingly reluctant to pay the fees of two counsel: they may now suggest that if their QC wants a junior to do his research, his fee should be reduced by the amount needed to pay the junior.

Barristers may apply once a year to become Queen's Counsel. Some no doubt apply year after year; others are successful the first time they ask. A few may even be encouraged to apply. The names of those appointed are announced on Maundy Thursday. They are sworn in at a splendid ceremony in the Royal Gallery of the House of Lords, usually held a week after Easter on the first day of the new legal term.[40] The names of those rejected are not published.[41]

Queen's Counsel are appointed by the Lord Chancellor on the advice of his Judicial Appointments Department. A certain level of seniority and experience is required which the most successful barristers will have acquired by their early forties; those who become QCs in their late thirties or even earlier are undoubtedly the stars of the Bar. Candidates have to show they are earning enough to demonstrate their success; the amount will vary according to the type of work done. The Lord Chancellor may bend this rule if there are other reasons for making a particular appointment: Lord Mackay was keen to appoint people from the ethnic minorities whose earnings might have been reduced by racial discrimination. To some extent QCs are appointed to fill perceived gaps in the market: a few years ago there were not many good Queen's Counsel willing to represent people charged with (or appealing against their convictions for) IRA terrorist offences and it is important that people facing serious charges should have a QC representing them.

In 1994, the Lord Chancellor appointed 77 new QCs. This was only a few more than in previous years although the number of applicants had risen rapidly from 410 in 1991 to 539 in 1994. In 1992, 1993 and 1994 there were between 11 and 14 applicants who described themselves as being from an ethnic minority background; on each occasion, just one of them was successful. There were nine women in the 1994 list – again, only slightly more than in recent years although the number of women applying for silk had risen from 24 in 1991 to 43 in 1994. It follows that it is becoming generally more difficult for women to become QCs although a woman still has a better statistical chance of success than a man.

It was only in 1992 that the Lord Chancellor's Department began announcing the ethnic origins of new QCs. Before then candidates had not been invited to say whether they were from the ethnic minorities. So, in 1991, the Lord Chancellor made no mention of the fact that he had appointed the first black woman QC – Patricia Scotland – even though the appointment did him (and, of course, her) much credit. Fortunately Miss Scotland's name was recognised by a journalist.

Barristers pride themselves on their independence from state control. Why then should they apply to a member of the Cabinet for a seal of approval at a crucial stage in their careers? As freelance lawyers, barristers trade on their reputations. Why should those reputations need inflating by ministerial endorsement?

Lord Mackay considered there were three advantages in keeping the current two-tier system of advocates:

- it enables lawyers and clients to identify the leading members of the profession and thus to exercise a more informed choice about the competence of the advocates they choose;

- it acts as an incentive for advocates to strive for the highest standards; and

- it helps the Lord Chancellor to identify those who are likely to become candidates for the High Court bench and for other duties like heading public inquiries.[42]

It would still be possible to keep the two-tier system while removing patronage from the Lord Chancellor and his officials. If the Bar really needs to identify its leading members to the solicitors and other professionals who instruct them, then barristers should be able to select senior counsel themselves. No other self-regulating profession would tolerate government interference in this way.

Even if leading counsel were selected by a panel of senior barristers it would still appear that the leaders of the profession were rewarding those who shared their own values. It would be preferable to abolish the rank of Queen's Counsel altogether. Other professions are not divided in this way. We do not talk of Queen's Accountants or Queen's Architects.

By the spring of 1993 there was growing pressure for reform. The Bar's magazine *Counsel*, said the existing arrangements did not preserve the profession's independence from the judiciary. In an unsigned leading article[43] the magazine noted that a barrister must be prepared to take a firm stand on behalf of his client, even in the face of some judicial disapproval. 'Yet it is predominantly the judges who advise the Lord Chancellor, himself the most senior judge as well as a government minister, on appointment to silk,' it said. 'There is sound reason to believe that deserving applicants for silk have been refused by reason of the animosity of a particular judge.'

At the same time an anonymous barrister was claiming in the *New Law Journal* that a single judge could delay or even prevent the appointment of a QC. In one well-known case, the author claimed:

> a judge threw obstacles in the path of a barrister who had the misfortune to share the judge's mistress. Although widely regarded as an excellent candidate for silk, his application was refused. It was only when the barrister went to the head of his division to tell his story that the wrong was rectified – the following year . . . Ultimately, success depends on whether you fit the mould the judiciary thinks is appropriate.

The author of this strikingly bitter piece said that barristers who practised away from London on one of the circuits could find their careers blocked if they did not meet with the approval of the presiding judge. In such a case the only way forward was to accept an appointment to the Circuit bench, if it was offered. Many Circuit judges resented the Lord Chancellor's Department, believing its officials had denied them the opportunity to make a living as a silk.

The writer continued:

> What may have been barely tolerable in a profession of 1,500 barristers is both ineffective and corrupt in its execution in a profession which has now expanded to 7,500. Any barrister who is concerned about his position and is invited by the Lord Chancellor's Department to go and 'talk about it' should refuse the invitation: many practitioners believe they are positively misled by the information they are given by officials during these informal talks.[44]

In *The Lawyer* there was concern, again expressed anonymously, that the majority of criminal silks came from Establishment chambers which did a lot of prosecution work. This was true enough but one of the new Queen's Counsel in 1993 was Patrick O'Connor, a member of the radical chambers headed by Michael Mansfield QC.

The chairman of the Bar in 1993, John Rowe QC, seemed happy enough with the existing arrangements. 'There is no doubt,' he asserted, 'that the Bar wants the silk system and wants to retain the rank and honour of Queen's Counsel.'[45] However, his predecessor,

Lord Williams of Mostyn QC, revealed that about twenty barristers had expressed their concern to him. 'They simply don't know where they are,' he said, 'whether there is a black mark against their name, or if their fee income isn't high enough.'[46]

Lord Mackay appeared stung by complaints that the selection process for silks was 'shrouded in secrecy'. He wrote an article for *Counsel* magazine to 'dispel some of the more commonly held misunderstandings'.[47] The Lord Chancellor insisted that the views of any one individual, however eminent, were not allowed to determine the outcome of any application.

Lord Mackay went on to explain the selection process in more detail than ever before. An alphabetical list of applicants for silk is drawn up every autumn and sent to the law lords, to every judge in the High Court and the Court of Appeal, and to certain senior Circuit judges. The list is also sent to the chairman of the Bar and the leaders of the barristers' circuits and specialist Bar associations. In all, 200 copies of the list are sent out. Lord Mackay said he asked recipients for views on as many of the candidates as possible and he encouraged them, where appropriate, to take 'discreet soundings' among other leading silks in their field. If adverse comments were made about a candidate, the Lord Chancellor asked for these to be backed up with examples. Although the Lord Chancellor does not encourage candidates to drum up support from their friends, any letters supporting an application will be considered.

Between November and January every year, staff in the Lord Chancellor's Department collate several thousand comments on the various candidates. Officials write 150 letters to people named on the application forms and they have about thirty-five meetings with judges and leading barristers to go through the lists in detail. The comments they gather are marshalled into a document more than 400 pages long, as big as a telephone directory. From this, Lord Mackay explained, he drew up a provisional list of successful candidates which he discussed with the four senior judges and the law officers. A copy is sent in confidence to the chairman of the Bar. The whole process must cost a fortune.

Lord Mackay said the qualities required for silk were not easy to define with precision:

Since practising silk is a working and functional rank within the profession, it is for the senior members of the Bar and the judiciary to be the main judges both of the qualities required and the degree to which each of the applicants possesses them . . . Silk is essentially awarded for advocacy . . . This, of course, is more than simply eloquence of expression. Advocacy skills include helpfulness to the court, cogency and brevity . . . It also goes without saying that successful applicants should be courteous and even-tempered, and should fulfil the legal and ethical requirements of the profession. I expect a successful applicant to display a very high level of legal, intellectual and professional ability; to command the respect of both the bench and the profession; and to have demonstrated both professional and personal maturity of judgment.

The Lord Chancellor then went on to unveil a few more secrets:

- Fee income is relevant but not decisive. The applicant is asked how much he or she earned over the past three years: this helps the Lord Chancellor form a view about the standing and, to some extent, the quality of the applicant's practice. The level of earnings could be a tie-breaker between evenly balanced candidates.

- The number of previous applications for silk does not affect the Lord Chancellor's decision either way. However, candidates who apply too early may be thought to lack good judgment.

- Some of those who do not take silk after two or three attempts fear there is some kind of 'black mark' against them. This is very rarely the case. More often it is simply that the strength and quality of support for others in their field is greater.

All this may be obvious enough, but it had never been spelled out in print before. It is difficult to see why this should have been so. In 1986 Lord Hailsham felt he had to let a brief shaft of daylight fall on the dusty files in his Judicial Appointments Department. Until then there had been no published information at all about the appointment of Queen's Counsel. In 1993 Lord Mackay opened the door wider still. But his critics have their feet firmly wedged in place and it will only be a matter of time before they heave the door off its hinges. Then, if silks survive at all, they will be selected by their fellow lawyers rather than by a member of the government.

Rodger Pannone, president of the Law Society, summed up the silks' issue very effectively.[48] When (as he assumed they would) solicitors had been granted rights of audience in the High Court, they would become eligible after ten years' experience for appointment as Queen's Counsel. Should solicitors apply for silk? Mr Pannone recognised that if senior advocates were still identified as such, solicitors should not be put at a disadvantage by being denied the possibility of advancement. He pointed out that the current practice was not led by consumer demand; there was no consultation with customers; applicants paid nothing although they stood to benefit; there were no published standards, let alone ones which were set objectively; and the restricted number of QCs forced consumers (and the public purse in legal aid cases) to pay inflated prices. 'I am far from convinced,' said Rodger Pannone, 'that this is a system I would want us to copy in our branch of the profession, given the dissatisfaction with it at the Bar. I am surprised that the Lord Chancellor is prepared to spend the significant public resources of time and money that the system costs.'

Political silks

It was once understood that any barrister elected to parliament could expect to become a QC. This is certainly not the case today. But a relic of the rule still remains: from time to time MPs become QCs without having to clock up the normal level of experience at the Bar.

The best-known political silk is David Mellor MP. He was called to the Bar in 1972 and practised as a barrister until he joined the government in 1981. David Mellor was still a minister at the age when some of his contemporaries were taking silk. Then one morning in 1987 a thick white envelope arrived from Lord Hailsham, a fellow member of the government, and a few days later he was David Mellor QC MP. In the Commons, Mr Mellor became the Right Honourable *and Learned* Member for Putney. Asked what he had done to deserve this honour Mr Mellor suggested that it was in recognition of his legal skills in piloting the Criminal Justice Bill through parliament. But it turned out to be a meaningless rank. When Mr Mellor resigned from the government in 1992 he took on a variety of part-time jobs. Practice at the Bar was not one of them.

At first sight Douglas Hogg MP[49] appeared to be another political silk: he joined the government in 1986 and became a QC in 1990. Clearly his appointment as a silk cannot have been based on his work at the Bar in the period immediately before he became a QC: he too was serving full-time in the government. But Mr Hogg had a strong practice at the Bar and there is no doubt he would have become a QC in the normal course of events if he had not become a minister.

It suits the government to have a pool of leading counsel in the House of Commons who could be made law officers if the need should arise. But there are other barristers who take time off to indulge in work of a legal nature; they are not usually made QCs in their thirties or forties. There should be no more political silks.

Honorary silks

In his White Paper on Legal Services[50] Lord Mackay announced that he would be extending the scope of 'honorary silks'. In the past that honour had been confined to barristers.[51] From 1991 solicitors would become eligible. So too would academic lawyers who were not solicitors or barristers. The only qualification for a Queen's Counsel *honoris causa* is to have given 'distinguished service to the law' in fields such as the public service or the academic world. It is a harmless enough gesture: honorary silks are not allowed to practise in the courts as Queen's Counsel and they must call themselves QC (Hon.) – rather than QC – if there is any risk of confusion with practising silks. Among the first practising solicitors to be appointed honorary silks were Lord Mishcon and Lord Goodman.

Rights of audience

For many years people who found themselves in court have wondered why they needed to pay for two lawyers. Their solicitor would tell them that he or she could not normally speak on their behalf in the High Court or the Crown Court: for that, he said, they needed a barrister. All right, they replied: next time we will go straight to the barrister. Sorry, the barrister's clerk would say, you have to start with a solicitor: barristers are not allowed to see members of the public unless a solicitor has been instructed first.

Even if the case was being heard in a court where solicitors had the right to be heard the client was often told he would be better off with a barrister. 'After all, they are the experts,' his solicitor would explain. The client would mutter darkly about double-manning and restrictive practices before paying up – as of course he had to do.

Since the early nineteenth century solicitors have had a right of audience – the right to be heard – in the magistrates' courts and the county courts. In addition they were able to appear for a client in the Crown Court on appeal or on a committal for sentence if their firm had already represented that client in the magistrates' court. For reasons of history and geography, solicitors also had broader rights of audience at five of the more remote Crown Courts in England and

Wales.[52] In the High Court they could appear before a judge in chambers but not in open court; the same rule applied in the Court of Appeal. Solicitors have always had rights of audience at the European Court of Justice and the European Court of Human Rights. Strangely enough, they could also appear before an Appeal Committee of the House of Lords.[53] That was as far as it went. Solicitors, however experienced, could not generally appear in the main criminal and civil courts to do the basic work of the serious advocate. The newest barrister, on the other hand, could appear in the highest courts from the day he or she was called to the Bar.

In 1976 it looked as if the government was willing to heed the chorus of complaints about restrictive practices in the legal profession. The prime minister, Harold Wilson, set up a Royal Commission on Legal Services chaired by the distinguished accountant Sir Henry Benson. Many people hoped the commission would recommend an end to the existing two-tier system. In the event, however, barristers managed to persuade the Royal Commission that the existing arrangements were ultimately in the public interest. The commission's report was published in 1979 and by early 1983 the government had come to the conclusion that no major changes were needed.

Then, quite by chance, things started falling apart. In November 1983 the Labour MP Austin Mitchell won a good position in the annual ballot for Private Members' Bills. Virtually all backbenchers go in for the ballot, whether they have a bill in mind or not; there is not a lot of point in picking a subject until you know you have done well in the ballot. Mr Mitchell put off making a decision until three hours before the deadline for filing a summary of his bill. He then telephoned the Consumers' Association and within ten minutes its legal adviser, David Tench, was in the House of Commons with a ready-made bill to abolish the solicitors' conveyancing monopoly. The bill was unexpectedly successful in its early parliamentary stages: on the last Friday of the session before Christmas, when the House is normally deserted, it mustered exactly the 100 votes it needed to survive. As a result, it received government support in February 1984.[54]

The solicitors were horrified at the potential loss of their lucrative monopoly. If they were going to lose conveyancing they needed to find other areas of work: barristers, they argued, would have to give up their exclusive rights of audience in the higher courts. It was no surprise to find that the Bar disagreed: already the battle lines were being drawn.

A year later the Liberal MP Cyril Smith put his considerable weight behind the solicitors' cause. Mr Smith had been sued for libel by 24 Labour MPs; he agreed to settle on the basis that his lawyer would apologise in front of a High Court judge. But Mr Smith's barrister wanted £150 to read out the apology: he said that even the most junior barrister in his chambers would charge a fee of £75. Cyril Smith's solicitor, Alistair Brett, said he would have been willing to read out the seven-line statement (which he had drafted anyway) for just £25. When Mr Smith asked the High Court to let Mr Brett read the apology, Mr Justice Leonard said he had no power to do so.

This surprised the government, which suddenly remembered that two years earlier it had accepted a proposal from the Royal Commission to allow solicitors rights of audience in 'formal or unopposed' proceedings like these. At the same time, the chairman of the Bar, Robert Alexander QC, questioned Mr Brett's proposed charge of £25. He said loftily: 'I would be surprised if one could get a plumber to do comparable work for the price at which Mr Brett appears to value his services.'[55]

Though true, this was an unfortunate remark. Cyril Smith replied: 'I am sorry that Mr Alexander chooses to deride the work of a plumber, which in itself is a professional skill – certainly as professional, though in a different way, as that of the chairman of the Bar.'[56] Mr Brett said £25 was 'a perfectly reasonable and realistic figure' based on his normal rate of £50 an hour.

Bar Wars

These were the opening salvos in what the newspapers would soon be calling 'Bar Wars'.[57] First blood went to the Law Society. Although the Court of Appeal agreed that Mr Justice Leonard had been right in refusing to hear Mr Brett,[58] the High Court judges held a meeting and announced the following summer that solicitors would indeed be allowed to appear there in 'formal or unopposed proceedings'.[59]

This was only a slight dent in the barristers' monopoly; solicitors were not going to get rich on reading out libel settlements. The Law Society was 'disappointed'; Mr Brett described the announcement as 'timid and pathetic'. The Bar, however, said it was 'glad the position has been tidied up'.[60]

But this was just a skirmish. Another had taken place earlier in 1986 when the Law Society published a discussion document which it modestly entitled *Lawyers and the Courts: Time for Some Changes*.[61] In it the solicitors said they were not claiming the right to appear as advocates in every case; nor were they saying that all solicitors wanted to be advocates. However, the Law Society insisted that 'the public interest requires the employment of no more lawyers than are necessary for the proper conduct of the case and the right of the client to choose the advocate'. It went on to suggest that all judicial appointments should be open to all lawyers.

In June 1986 the Bar issued a lengthy response. It recalled that the Benson Royal Commission had endorsed the present structure of the legal profession. 'That', said the Bar, 'should have been sufficient to lay such proposals to rest for the foreseeable future.' Not surprisingly, the Bar was totally opposed to the Law Society's proposals.

The Marre Report
By then the two sides in Bar Wars had agreed on a truce. As all governments know, the best way of buying time is to set up an inquiry. In April 1986 the Bar and the Law Society announced that they were establishing a Committee on the Future of the Legal Profession. It consisted of six leading barristers, six leading solicitors and six distinguished non-lawyers. The chairman was Lady Marre CBE, an indefatigable public figure who had a long record of public service on countless committees of the Great and the Good.

It had been the Bar's idea to set up the Marre committee although there was full support from the Law Society. No doubt the two branches of the legal profession were hoping to put an end to the increasingly acrimonious exchanges which were causing so much embarrassment to the lawyers and so much entertainment for everyone else.

Cynics maintained that Mary Marre and her committee were not meant to do anything except to sit for as long as possible. But Lady Marre said she would not have allowed herself to get involved if she had thought that would be the plan. She had been warned that lawyers might use her, that they might manipulate her, but she was determined to resist. 'Well, I'm not as clever as a lot of those people,' she claimed disarmingly, 'but I know when I'm being manipulated and I'm quite capable of being firm about the way the thing has to go.'[62]

Another theory about the Marre committee was that it was designed to persuade the government to leave the lawyers alone for a while. In the short term this had some success, but in the long term it was disastrous – as we shall see. In asking the Marre committee to decide whether solicitors should have rights of audience the Bar had forgotten the first rule of advocacy: never ask a question unless you know that the answer will help your own side.

As intended, the Marre committee deliberated for two years. In July 1988 it published a report running to more than two hundred pages.[63] There were a number of important recommendations, many of which were subsequently implemented to a greater or lesser extent – for example, that there should be a unified family court, that solicitors should be eligible for appointment as High Court judges, that there should be a select committee of MPs to monitor the legal aid system and that professionals other than solicitors should have direct access to barristers. But on the key issue – rights of audience – the committee was hopelessly divided along party lines. All the solicitors were in favour of a proposal to give properly trained solicitors rights of audience in the Crown Court[64] and all the barristers were against it.

So the lay members held the balance of power and it turned out that all but one of them had sided with the solicitors. That meant the recommendation of increased rights of audience for solicitors was supported by 13 votes to 6. Not surprisingly, the Bar rejected that proposal: indeed, the barristers had done so before Lady Marre's report had even been published. Robert Johnson QC, chairman of the Bar, said it would 'result in exactly what the committee apparently wishes to avoid: the erosion of a healthy, independent Bar.'[65] Not surprisingly, the Law Society disagreed; it gave Lady Marre's report a 'warm welcome'.

With the truce shot to pieces, both sides remained dug in along their 1986 trenches. The solicitors now had powerful reinforcements although the barristers believed there was nothing much to worry about: from where they were sitting, it seemed that the two sides could carry on sniping at each other for years.

Then the war moved into a new phase. An astute general might have seen it coming: the first sentence of Lady Marre's press release[66] had contained an ominous warning: 'The legal profession should be vigilant to initiate appropriate change, otherwise it will be forced upon them.'

But nobody was prepared for what happened next. At four o'clock on a quiet Monday afternoon in October 1988 legal correspondents were invited to a briefing by the Lord Chancellor. In a written parliamentary answer released that afternoon Lord Mackay said he had been considering the Marre Report published three months earlier. He continued:

> I have now decided it would be appropriate to publish my own proposals relating to the requirements for carrying out in the future the work presently conducted by the legal profession. I therefore intend to issue a Green Paper for consultation early in the New Year with a view to reaching decisions before the summer recess 1989. Separate consultation papers on contingency fees and corporate conveyancing will also be prepared with the intention of publication on a similar timescale to the proposed Green Paper.[67]

That was all. The briefing made it clear that everything was up for grabs. It became the lead story in the next day's papers: the Lord Chancellor was expected to make 'far-reaching proposals for sweeping away restrictive practices'; it was to be a 'speedy and wide ranging shake-up'; fundamental reforms were 'likely to mean the most far-reaching changes this century'.

The Law Society's president, Richard Gaskell, said he was surprised but not alarmed. The barristers' chairman, Robert Johnson QC, welcomed the announcement while maintaining that the Bar had no restrictive practices which were against the public interest anyway.

The Green Papers

As promised, the Lord Chancellor published his three Green Papers in January 1989. The most important one dealt with the legal profession.[68] In it the Lord Chancellor suggested, perhaps a trifle disingenuously, that he had only decided to review the provision of legal services in England and Wales because the lawyers themselves had set up the Marre committee.[69]

The government's aim, as stated in the discussion document on the legal profession, was to provide the public with the best possible access to legal services while at the same time ensuring that those services were of the right quality for the needs of the client. That meant the ideal of a free market had to be tempered with the reality of ensuring that those who provided legal services met certain minimum standards of competence and conduct.

And those providing certain legal services need not necessarily be lawyers. In future, said the Green Paper, 'rights of audience before particular courts should depend only upon whether advocates can demonstrate that they have the appropriate education, training and qualifications and are bound by appropriate codes of conduct'.[70] It would make no difference whether the advocate was a barrister or a solicitor, whether he or she was in private practice or employed by a company – or, indeed, by the Crown Prosecution Service.

To decide what level of education, training and qualifications were needed before an advocate was allowed to appear before a particular court, the Green Paper said that the Lord Chancellor would take advice from a new committee – to be called the Lord Chancellor's Advisory Committee on Legal Education and Conduct. He would also consult the judiciary. The Advisory Committee would be chaired by a judge but it would have a majority of laymen.

There was a great deal more in the Green Paper, but as far as rights of audience were concerned this was the beginning of the end for the Bar. The government was going even further than the Marre committee. Lady Marre had only proposed rights of audience for solicitors in the Crown Court. The government envisaged extending them to the High Court as well.

Under Lord Mackay's other proposals, the solicitors stood to lose what was left of their monopolies in conveyancing and probate. Even so, they gave the Green Papers a measured welcome. The Bar, on the other hand, raised the worst spectre it could summon: the risk of state control. Its new chairman, Desmond Fennell QC, said: 'The general public will be the loser and so will justice.' The Bar, he believed, would 'wither away' because the best barristers would be head-hunted by the big firms of City solicitors. That meant it would be more difficult for the High Street solicitor to find an independent barrister when his client needed one.

Mr Fennell was worried that the judges would lose the right to decide which advocates should appear before them. In his view, Lord Mackay's proposals would remove the control of justice from the judges and entrust it to the civil servants. 'The proposals for the licensing of advocates under government control,' he said, 'give rise to grave constitutional dangers.'[71]

So began a year in which the Bar fought for what it saw as its very existence. Desmond Fennell was not new to fighting for a cause: he had led the successful campaign from 1969 to 1971 which stopped the third London airport being built at Cublington – which happened to be near where he lived. Neither was he inexperienced in the ways of Whitehall: he had headed the inquiry into the King's Cross fire disaster of 1987. But despite the help of professional public relations advisers and a healthy fighting fund Mr Fennell and his campaign failed to persuade the public of the Bar's case.

It is not surprising that a profession founded on reason and logic should use those tools to fight its cause; but Mr Fennell's rhetoric failed to catch the public mood.[72] The Law Society's campaign was more subtle and therefore more effective.

The Courts and Legal Services Act

At the end of 1989 the government published a bill to implement the proposals outlined in the Green Papers. A year's campaigning by the barristers had come to naught: as far as rights of audience were concerned not much had changed.[73] Nor had the Bar's reaction: Mr Fennell was still saying that the bill's effect 'could be to deprive the public of their local lawyer and specialist advocate'.[74] In the view of the Law Society, the bill provided 'a modern statutory foundation for the legal profession of the future, in which outdated restrictions will have no part'. Understandably, though sadly all too prematurely, the Law Society said it was 'already developing plans for training solicitors who want to undertake advocacy in the higher courts'.[75]

In November 1990 the Courts and Legal Services Act received the Royal Assent. It looked as if rights of audience were finally just around the corner; but that was not to be.

The Bar's last hope was a highly complicated procedure laid down in the Act. It provided that any proposal to extend rights of audience needed the approval of the Lord Chancellor and four senior judges.[76] They would have to consider whether the proposals were compatible with the Act's stated 'statutory objective' and its 'general principle'.[77] The statutory objective of the legislation was to make provision for new or better ways of providing legal services (such as advocacy) and a wider choice of people to provide these services, while maintaining the proper administration of justice. The general principle behind the legislation was that the question of whether someone ought to have rights of audience should depend only on whether he was properly qualified and was bound by appropriate rules of conduct.

The legislation says that if, in the view of the Lord Chancellor and the four judges, any plan to extend rights of audience is not compatible with the objective and the principle, they must reject it. However, they cannot even begin to consider any proposed changes until they have taken advice from the Director General of Fair Trading and the Advisory Committee on Legal Education and Conduct.

The Advisory Committee on Legal Education and Conduct

When the Courts and Legal Services Act was passed it was announced that the new advisory committee would be chaired by Lord Griffiths, a law lord. But five months went by before the membership had been appointed and the advisory committee was able to start work. In April 1991 the committee members – eight lawyers and nine non-lawyers – were finally ready to receive the Law Society's application for increased rights of audience.

It came in two parts. First, the Law Society proposed that all solicitors should immediately be allowed to conduct non-jury cases in the Crown Court (guilty pleas, committals for sentence and appeals from magistrates' courts) as well as some preliminary matters in the High Court. Second, it was proposed that solicitors should acquire full rights of audience provided they had the necessary experience and had successfully completed an advocacy training course. Under the Law Society's plans, *all* solicitors would have been eligible for rights of audience, whether they were in private practice or employed in the areas of government and commerce.

The Bar's response to these proposals was predictably unenthusiastic. It was opposed to increased rights of audience for employed solicitors and especially those working for the Crown Prosecution Service. It said that extended rights of audience for solicitors in private practice should depend on a much greater level of training and experience than the Law Society had proposed. Indeed, the Bar suggested that solicitors should not be allowed to exercise their *existing* rights of audience without further training.[78]

The advisory committee took a whole year to consider the solicitors' application, much longer than anyone had expected. During that year the committee discreetly consulted the four senior judges who would have to approve any new rights of audience. Finally, in April 1992, it published its advice to the Law Society.

On the Law Society's first point, the committee rejected the proposal that all solicitors should immediately acquire additional rights of audience in the Crown Court (in non-jury cases) and the High Court (in preliminary hearings). This was because 'newly qualified solicitors will have little or no experience of advocacy'.[79] In the circumstances this was perhaps fair enough and the Law Society did not pursue the claim further.

On the Law Society's second point, the committee accepted the proposal that experienced solicitors who had successfully completed an advocacy training course should have rights of audience in the higher courts. However, it decided that this should apply only to solicitors in private practice, not to those employed in government and commerce.

The distinction reflected an existing rule in the Bar's Code of Conduct: employed barristers are not allowed to appear on behalf of their employers in most cases in the higher courts. It seems a strange rule – after all, surely the whole point of a company employing a barrister full-time is for that barrister to represent it whenever there are proceedings in court. But the Bar considered the restriction essential to ensure that litigants were represented by independent counsel; and the advisory committee, despite its lay majority, chose to extend the same restrictive practice to solicitors. The committee justified this decision by questioning the independence of employed lawyers: it suggested that 'lawyers in commerce and industry may hold senior positions in their firms and share responsibility for the company's actions and policies'.

Yet again the Law Society had been thwarted. Employed solicitors were rightly furious. A leading company solicitor, who at that time was one of the largest employers of lawyers outside government, rejected suggestions that employed lawyers might not exercise independent judgment because they had been involved in taking the decisions which had led to the litigation. He said it was more likely that solicitors in private practice would come under pressure from clients who threatened to withdraw their business. 'Since becoming an in-house lawyer,' he said, 'I have never had to compromise my integrity or independence.'[80]

The employed Bar was deeply offended at being told by the advisory committee that they could not 'demonstratively achieve the objectivity and impartiality needed by advocates in the higher courts'. Derek Wheatley QC, an employed barrister, said:

the supposed lack of objectivity and impartiality is accepted not to hinder the employed barrister who appears before magistrates and in the county court. The implication is that High Court judges and above are less able than their humbler colleagues to detect the supposed deficiencies. Such breathtaking illogicality will have enormous appeal from devotees of Lewis Carroll.[81]

It was not just the lawyers who were put out by the committee's advice. The government was equally unhappy. With exquisite irony the Government Legal Service[82] had put in its own application for increased rights of audience, only to have it rejected by the government's Advisory Committee on Legal Education and Conduct.

The problem was this. Government-employed lawyers – including those working for the Crown Prosecution Service – had no rights of audience in the Crown Court. If they were barristers that was because of the Bar's restrictions on employed barristers (explained above). If they were solicitors it was because they had no right to appear in the Crown Court anyway. And the Crown Prosecution Service desperately wanted their own lawyers to have the right to appear in the Crown Court. This was not because they wanted to present every prosecution themselves – far from it – but because an experienced Crown Prosecutor could handle short cases and guilty pleas from his or her own files much more efficiently and effectively than a newly qualified barrister who had probably picked up the papers the night before. The same went for other prosecuting lawyers in the Government Legal Service who worked for bodies such as the Serious Fraud Office, Inland Revenue and HM Customs and Excise.

There were also questions of prestige and status. It would be easier to recruit the best lawyers as Crown Prosecutors if they could also be offered the prospect of Crown Court advocacy. Barbara Mills QC, who subsequently became Director of Public Prosecutions, was 'disappointed, slighted and aggrieved' at being told that despite her years of experience and her unquestioned integrity she could no longer appear before a jury once she had been appointed head of the Crown Prosecution Service.

The advisory committee's reasons for refusing rights of audience in the Crown Court to government-employed lawyers were deeply unimpressive. First, the committee said, 'Government lawyers prosecuting on behalf of, for example, the Inland Revenue or the Department of Social Security will almost inevitably be identified . . . with the purposes and policies of their departments.' Second, it believed that it would be wrong to give rights of audience to people who only used them 'rarely'.

Since neither of these factors applied to lawyers working for the Crown Prosecution Service, another reason had to be found for denying them rights of audience. The committee therefore decided that the Crown Prosecution Service simply was not up to the job. It had to 'demonstrate a high standard of achievement in its present functions before an extension of rights of audience can be justified'.

Responding to the advisory committee's announcement David Gandy, who was acting Director of Public Prosecutions in April 1992, said that the Government Legal Service would 'pursue strenuously the case for all employed lawyers to receive rights of audience' in the higher courts: he believed the advisory committee had been 'mistaken' in its analysis of the role of prosecutors in the Crown Prosecution Service.

What were the solicitors to do? The Law Society could have accepted the offer of rights of audience for solicitors in private practice and ignored the wishes of employed lawyers, including those who worked for the Crown Prosecution Service. To its credit it did not. It accepted that there should be some restrictions on the type of advocacy work undertaken by an employed solicitor. It offered to keep an eye on the use of the new rights by government lawyers. But it maintained its application on behalf of all solicitors, including those in the prosecution service. The Law Society's revised application for increased rights of audience was formally submitted to the Lord Chancellor in November 1992. He, in turn, passed it to the advisory committee for advice.

Throughout the spring and early summer of 1993 there were further skirmishes between the Law Society and the advisory committee, with the solicitors offering a series of concessions to meet the committee's perceived requirements. In July 1993, however, the committee finally advised the Lord Chancellor not to approve the Law Society's application as it then stood.[83] The decision was greeted with justified howls of outrage from solicitors' leaders. More than two years after the Law Society had first asked for increased rights of audience and nearly five years after Lord Mackay had first outlined his plans for the future of the legal profession the barristers' monopoly was still firmly in place.

The advisory committee was satisfied with the Law Society's

highly detailed proposals to train and assess solicitor advocates, which had been drawn up after extensive consultation between the two bodies. The committee also gave its reluctant approval to the Law Society's proposed rules of conduct after being satisfied that clients would not be pressurised into having their own solicitor represent them in court whenever an outside barrister would be advisable.

Once again the question of employed solicitors proved to be the sticking point. The Law Society had devised a number of rules to ensure that employed solicitors who were allowed to appear as advocates would be treated as independent professionals by their employers rather than, for example, as company executives. The Law Society had also agreed that extended rights of audience should be confined to solicitors who worked for a separate legal department within their employer's organisation. But the two sides reached an impasse over whether the senior member of such a legal department needed to work exclusively as a lawyer.

The Law Society had not been willing to accept that restriction, which it said would significantly limit the work done by solicitors who were heads of their own legal departments. It pointed out that the head of a local authority's legal department was sometimes responsible for elections or administration, while senior solicitors in commerce often acted as company secretaries. That did not strike the Law Society as affecting the lawyer's professional autonomy. However, the advisory committee dug its heels in. The committee thought it essential that no lawyer should have 'potentially conflicting managerial or policy responsibilities', and so it advised the Lord Chancellor that the head of a legal department must be 'engaged full-time within it'. This was the only disagreement that stood between employed solicitors and rights of audience in the higher civil courts.

The criminal courts were a different matter. As far as the Crown Prosecution Service and the rest of the Government Legal Service were concerned, the committee was worried that 'even a limited extension of Crown lawyers' advocacy rights might be the thin end of the wedge, leading to a system where virtually all criminal advocacy in the higher courts was undertaken by lawyers employed by the Crown'.[84] The committee decided that the best way to resolve this particular problem would be by way of primary legislation in parliament, which would of course take years. And just in case this was not enough of an obstacle, the advisory committee set out two more requirements: it wanted further discussions with the Crown Prosecution Service to see whether standards were now at an acceptable level and it wanted to await the recommendations of the Royal Commission on Criminal Justice. The committee noted, with barely concealed delight, 'that these factors might lead to some delay in resolving the question of rights of audience by Crown Prosecution Service solicitors'.[85] But it had taken the advisory committee so long to come up with its own advice that there were only four more days to go before the Royal Commission published its final report.

By a curious logic the advisory committee went on to argue that if solicitors employed by the Crown Prosecution Service were not allowed extended rights of audience, then solicitors employed by local authorities and private companies should not have them either. The committee was worried that employers' commercial interests might lead to oppressive prosecutions. It overlooked the fact that companies can bring oppressive prosecutions already: their solicitors can happily appear for them in the magistrates' courts.

In the advisory committee's view, the Law Society's application was good only in parts. That meant the entire application had to be rejected. The committee concluded:

> The rules and regulations governing higher court rights of audience for solicitors in private practice could be approved; those governing employed solicitors require amendment and should for the present be limited to . . . civil cases. As the [Law Society's] application does not contain all the provisions relating to employed solicitors which the committee considers to be necessary, the committee must advise that it should not be approved in its present form.[86]

The Advisory Committee on Legal Education and Conduct had not been unanimous: the two barrister members – Nicholas Purnell QC and Peter Scott QC – and four other members wanted to go still further. They said solicitors should not get extended rights of audience at all unless they were prepared to accept the Bar's so-called 'cab rank rule' which in theory, and subject to many exceptions, obliges the barrister to accept any job that comes along. The committee was particularly worried that if solicitors were not bound by that rule barristers would not observe it either. Without conceding that the rule was honoured more in the breach than the observance, the barristers and their supporters argued that 'like speed limits, rules may not always be obeyed, but that does not make them undesirable or prevent them playing an important regulatory role'.

The two barristers also went further than most of their colleagues in arguing that even if the Law Society's rules were amended, employed lawyers should not have extended rights of audience for the time being. In any event, they said, employed solicitors should not have rights of audience in cases of judicial review. There was support for these views from a handful of the other members.

Although Mr Purnell and Mr Scott were lawyers of integrity who honestly believed they were acting in the best interests of justice, they seemed to be behaving like Japanese soldiers who could not believe the war had ended. Indeed, for them, the Bar Wars were not over: the barristers still had everything to play for. Responding to the advisory committee's announcement the chairman of the Bar, John Rowe QC, said the training requirements for solicitor advocates still did not go far enough. Not surprisingly, Mr Rowe supported the minority views of his fellow barristers while yet again insisting that prosecution work in the higher courts should be reserved for practising barristers.[87]

No less surprisingly, the president of the Law Society, Mark Sheldon, said on publication of the advisory committee's report that it was 'a depressing day for the profession and the public'. He accused the committee of sowing seeds of dissent within the profession: 'Many in the legal profession hoped that the committee would help heal the rift between the two branches . . . It has not only failed in this, it has opened up a potential new division between private practice and employed lawyers.'[88]

Sure enough, solicitors in private practice called the Law Society's all-or-nothing approach 'crazy'. David McIntosh, the outspoken senior partner of a large City litigation firm, said: 'We come across an opportunity for the vast minority of solicitors and the Law Society turns it down.'[89]

The Law Society's governing council had already given its views on the committee's advice when it had become known some two months earlier. Solicitors were understandably furious that a wedge was being driven ever more firmly into the profession. Philip Ely, a former president of the society, said the solicitors' application had been 'bogged down in a morass of unhelpful and destructive analysis' by the advisory committee. Much time had been wasted in 'futile discussions'.

The Law Society's response was to ignore Lord Griffiths's advice. It decided to ask Lord Mackay and the four senior judges to give all employed solicitors – including those in the Crown Prosecution Service and the Government Legal Service – the right to do advocacy work in the higher courts. This would be subject only to the conditions that there should be three lawyers in an in-house legal department and that the senior lawyer there should have direct access to management.

Some solicitors believed that if this was rejected the Law Society should not press ahead with its application on behalf of solicitors in private practice. According to Tony Holland, another former president of the Law Society, any further argument was demeaning for the profession; they should urge parliament to sort it out once and for all.[90] Mr Holland pointed out that the solicitors had made a 'perfectly reasonable application under the Courts and Legal Services Act' and then 'had to endure over two years of delay, irritation and aggravation'. The problems raised had nothing to do with the merits of the solicitors' case, he said; they were designed simply as 'delaying tactics' by some members of the advisory committee 'in order to frustrate, prevent or mitigate the effect of any solicitor having any rights of audience in the higher courts'.[91]

The solicitors' anger was heightened by the sight of twenty-four colleagues from north of the border who had just received rights of audience in the higher courts of Scotland. The first Scottish solicitor advocate was a civil servant employed by the Crown Office. In some ways the Scottish solicitors had an easier battle to fight than their English counterparts: solicitors in Scotland were already allowed to appear as advocates before juries in the sheriff courts.

In May 1993, two months before the committee's advice was published, Lord Griffiths had been asked why his committee was taking so long to reach its decisions. His answer was revealing. 'You are fundamentally altering a system that has existed for centuries,' he replied, 'and it may be very much better to move forward a little cautiously at this stage rather than jump in with both feet and make a hopeless mess of it.'[92]

But the Griffiths committee was not asked 'to move forward a little cautiously'. By passing the Courts and Legal Services Act, parliament had clearly indicated that it wanted solicitors to have rights of audience in the higher courts. It was not the committee's job to block the incoming tide for as long as possible. It should at the very least have found some way of severing the Law Society's application so that the main part of it could have been approved. Better still, the committee should have used the time at its disposal to work out realistic conditions for supporting the rights which were requested.

His work completed, Lord Griffiths retired in the summer of 1993. He was replaced by Lord Justice Steyn who had first practised as a barrister in his native South Africa before settling in England in the 1970s.

It was then up to Lord Mackay and his fellow judges to decide whether to accept the Law Society's application and reject the advisory committee's advice. The judges were also advised by the Director General of Fair Trading, Sir Bryan Carsberg, who thought the solicitors' proposal would widen choice for the consumer and could therefore be approved in its entirety.

In December 1993 Lord Mackay and the judges announced that the application for rights of audience in the higher courts for solicitors in private practice would be approved after all. The Lord Chancellor said that a decision on *employed* solicitors had been deferred: he and the judges had asked the advisory committee to look again at whether solicitors in government, commerce, industry and other employment should have rights of audience in criminal proceedings.[93]

The barristers' monopoly had finally been broken. Suitably qualified solicitors would have unrestricted rights of audience in the Crown Court, the High Court, the Court of Appeal and the House of Lords. Some seventy solicitors who were already experienced advocates were allowed to appear in these courts as early as the spring of 1994; for others, training courses started later that year. Rodger Pannone, the Law Society's president, welcomed the increased choice for clients: they would no longer be forced to employ two lawyers and in some cases costs would come down. He was, however, 'disappointed' that there was no decision on employed solicitors.

The Crown Prosecution Service was reasonably happy with the announcement: prosecuting lawyers thought it would be only a matter of time before they would be able to appear in the Crown Court. Barristers tried to put a brave face on the loss of their exclusive rights: Peter Goldsmith QC, vice-chairman elect of the Bar Council, said his branch of the profession had accepted for some time that solicitors in private practice would be able to become advocates in the higher courts. Barristers were ready and willing to face increased competition, said Mr Goldsmith: they remained the 'pre-eminent advocates' because only they would have full training in advocacy and only they were likely to practise it full-time.

The Lord Chancellor's announcement of December 1993 was an unexpected victory for the solicitors. Lord Mackay had found himself able to sever the good parts of the Law Society's application: even those parts which appeared tainted were still on the table. This was also a victory for the Lord Chancellor. It cannot have been easy for him to persuade the four designated judges to grant rights of audience to solicitors: Lord Mackay showed considerable strength of character in dismissing the arguments of his own advisory committee and pushing through the aims he had announced five years earlier. Bar Wars were not yet over: the barristers would still be trying to prevent Crown Prosecutors and employed lawyers from appearing in the Crown Court. But by the start of 1994 the score was clear enough – solicitors, one; barristers, nil.

Training for the law

Students are finding it harder than ever to train as barristers or solicitors. Unlike trainee teachers and doctors they are expected to pay their postgraduate fees themselves. Local authorities are now much less likely than they were a few years ago to give grants to law students: some have given up altogether. There are certainly not enough bursaries and scholarships to cover the needs of pupil barristers. And only the most prosperous commercial firms can afford to fund trainee solicitors through their finals courses. No legal aid practice has a spare £4,000 or more to pay a student's course fees.

Yet the sort of people who want to train in legal aid work are often precisely the people who most need financial help. While class barriers are breaking down in the legal profession there is a risk that financial barriers will deter all but the well off. Students will only take out huge loans if they can be sure of getting work when they qualify. In the early 1990s jobs were scarce to the point of non-existence.

Under the Law Society's training regulations, solicitors are obliged to pay any trainee solicitors they employ a minimum salary, which in 1993 was set at £12,150 in London and £10,850 in the rest of the country. It was a sign of the times that some solicitors felt they could not afford to pay their staff even these relatively modest sums.[94]

In November 1992 a consultation document was sent to 10,000 firms of solicitors. Of the 700 or so who replied, just over half wanted to abolish the compulsory minimum salary. Setting a minimum was thought to put some firms off taking trainees although it was not clear how many firms considered the salary levels critical: some paid much more anyway and others said that because of the time they would have to give a trainee they could not afford to take them on at any price.

In June 1993 the chairman of the Trainee Solicitors' Group, John Balsdon, told the Law Society's governing council there was no evidence that abolishing the minimum salary would increase the number of training places. It provided 'the only safeguard against the profession becoming an enclave of only the middle classes', he said. Although other council members said that it would be the trainees themselves who would suffer if firms could not afford to take them on, the council voted to keep minimum salaries at existing levels.

As well as advising on rights of audience the Lord Chancellor's Advisory Committee on Legal Education and Conduct – as its name would suggest – is responsible for keeping education and training under review. In 1993 it launched a full-scale study of legal education, the first for more than twenty years. This was to operate at a leisurely pace: the initial phase alone was expected to last three years. The advisory committee expected that it would be focusing particularly on funding problems. Lord Griffiths, the retiring chairman, said the legal profession had been making major efforts to ensure that the law was a career open to everybody. 'It would be a major backward step,' he said, 'if entry to the profession were in the future again to be largely restricted to those from wealthy backgrounds.'[95]

Discrimination against students on financial grounds was worrying, if not entirely surprising. Allegations of official discrimination on racial grounds were highly alarming. In the autumn of 1992 a group of black trainee barristers complained that their failure rate in the Bar's final assessments was nearly three times as high as the failure rate for white students. Official figures showed that 83 per cent of white students passed the Bar Vocational Course compared with 52 per cent of ethnic minority students. Their course included subjective tests of advocacy and conference skills which the black students claimed were inherently unfair, leading to racial discrimination.

Being law students, they applied for leave to bring judicial review proceedings against the Bar Council and the Council of Legal Education (which runs the course for trainee barristers). Mr Justice Potts said that if the students' grievances were well founded then each of them had cause for serious complaint against those responsible for running their courses. In his view, the best course of action would be for them to use the barristers' own appeal system, which would involve High Court judges being appointed 'Visitors' to the Inns of Court in order to hear the students' complaints.[96]

By the summer of 1993 the Council of Legal Education was so concerned by complaints of racial discrimination in the Bar Vocational Course that it appointed Dame Jocelyn Barrow, a leading campaigner against racial discrimination, to head an independent inquiry. In April 1994 her committee confirmed that there was a 'significant racial difference in failure rates' between white students and those from ethnic minorities although the inquiry found no evidence of discrimination within the meaning of the Race Relations Act. The Barrow Committee concluded that the Inns of Court School of Law had failed to meet the needs of black and ethnic minority students; it suggested a number of improvements in teaching and assessment methods.[97]

The Barrow inquiry was described by the Society of Black Lawyers as a 'whitewash': the society said it was 'extremely disappointed that the report did not find evidence of direct or indirect discrimination.'[98] The Council of Legal Education was relieved to find that it had not been accused of breaking the law by an inquiry it had paid for; it immediately started implementing the report's recommendations. These included an automatic right for students to re-sit the Bar School's vocational course.

But the Council of Legal Education was still not out of the hole it had dug for itself. Faced with three students fighting for every place on the course, it had called in occupational psychologists to find ways of selecting the best would-be barristers. The psychologists had said it was wrong to pick the people with the best university degrees; instead, places should be awarded on the basis of school 'A' level results and critical reasoning skills. As anybody but a psychologist might have foreseen, this led to disaster. Students with first-class law degrees, awarded scholarships by their Inns of Court, were refused places on the mandatory course because they had done relatively badly at school, in some cases many years earlier. Yet again, the Council of Legal Education had to back down. In June 1994 it announced that university results would be taken into account after all and it offered 250 more places to students with good degrees. The Bar Council then conceded that the Inns of Court School of Law should lose its monopoly; it decided that other approved colleges would be allowed to train students for the Bar.

Wigs and gowns

Interviewed by the BBC in October 1990 Lord Justice Taylor said he believed that 'at a stroke, we could disarm a good deal of public misunderstanding of the legal profession if we stopped wearing wigs and gowns in court'.[99] He repeated this view on many occasions after becoming Lord Chief Justice in 1992, but the matter proved controversial and it was agreed that nothing should be done until the issue had gone out to public consultation.

A discussion paper was issued in August 1992.[100] It revealed that High Court judges could claim the sum of £6,925 from public funds towards the cost of buying their robes. Any sum they had to spend above this figure could be set against their income tax bills (robes are considered 'plant' under the tax regulations).

Pity the poor High Court judge trying to work out what he should wear in the morning. He has five different costumes from which to choose. If he is sitting in the Court of Appeal or the Divisional Court he wears a plain black gown, but if there is a criminal trial going on it has to be the scarlet robe of the ceremonial dress faced with ermine but without the scarlet cloth and fur mantle. In the winter the judge also wears a black scarf and girdle and a scarlet casting-hood (incorrectly called a tippet). In the summer he has silk facing rather than fur on the same type of scarlet robe.

If the judge is hearing a civil case, that will not do at all. In winter-time there is a black robe faced with fur, a black scarf and girdle and a scarlet tippet. During the summer a violet robe faced with silk is worn instead. These are called *nisi prius* robes.

Just to keep the judges on their toes there is an exception for the Sovereign's birthday and certain saints' days. On those red-letter days all the judges wear whichever of their scarlet robes is appropriate for the season. The good news is that, since these robes run from neck to calf, they can wear what they like underneath.

There is even a problem over what barristers and judges should wear round their necks. Normally they wear white bands – small strips of cloth kept in place with elastic.[101] These can be worn with a normal turn-down collar but the effect is rather odd. For that reason, detachable wing collars are usually worn; but it is not easy to buy shirts without collars these days and it is even more difficult having wing collars properly laundered. That worries the Lord Chancellor who has to pay the bill for court staff obliged to dress in this way.

The ceremonial robes worn by High Court judges date from the time of Edward III (1327–77).[102] The usual colours worn in medieval times are believed to have been violet in winter and green in summer, with scarlet for best. But after 1534 it seems that only scarlet, violet and black were used – as they are today. Then, as on ceremonial occasions now, the judges wore a long robe, a full hood with a cowl worn around the shoulders and a mantle (or cloak) over the hood. During the summer these robes were faced with taffeta (a fine silk). In winter the facing was miniver (the white fur of ermine without the tails: ermine is the white coat of the winter stoat).[103] Since the fifteenth century the judges have always worn a black girdle or cincture.

By 1635, however, they had changed into something a little more comfortable for less formal occasions. Gone were the hood and mantle; instead the judge wore a black scarf around his neck and a scarlet casting-hood. This was the unlined hood of a serjeant-at-law, cast over the judge's right shoulder so that the cowl hung down the back.

By the middle of the eighteenth century even that was seen as a little excessive and the judges began to wear a plain black silk gown for some civil cases.

At the end of the last century things started getting out of hand again. High Court judges began to wear a casting-hood and scarf even when they were wearing the full hood and mantle. It was of course a dreadful solecism to wear two hoods at the same time.

It comes as no surprise to learn that different judges wore other sorts of robes. The county courts were created in 1846 and most of the judges there wore black gowns. But this did not satisfy them all, and from 1919 they were allowed to wear dark blue (or violet). To avoid any confusion with the violet robes of the High Court judge, their facings were to be of lilac or mauve taffeta. There was a black cincture but no scarf and a lilac tippet, worn this time over the left shoulder. (The tippet was really a kind of casting-hood whose origin had been forgotten by the robemakers; as a result they were making it in the wrong shape but remarkably nobody seemed to mind.)

All county court judges became Circuit judges when the courts were reorganised in 1971 and they were allowed to keep their existing robes, except that when sitting in the Crown Court they wear a red tippet instead of a lilac one. However, these robes are not compulsory and anyone who prefers to wear a black gown can do so – like the judges at the Old Bailey.

When the Court of Appeal was set up in 1875 the Lords Justices chose to wear the black silk gown previously worn by Chancery appeal judges. The Court of Criminal Appeal was created in 1908 and its judges continued to wear robes of scarlet, violet or black – according to season – as their predecessors had done in the Court for Crown Cases Reserved. Those robes were abolished with the Court of Criminal Appeal in 1966 and now all the appeal judges wear black in court.

On ceremonial occasions the Lords Justices of Appeal, as well as the Master of the Rolls, the Vice-Chancellor and the President of the Family Division, wear an elaborate gown of black flowered silk damask with gold lace and decorations. Beneath it they wear a court coat and waistcoat with a lace jabot, knee breeches, stockings or tights and buckled court shoes. According to the Lord Chancellor's discussion paper, these robes cost about £8,000 to buy new, perhaps more. Fortunately they come with the job and are passed down from Lord Justice to Lord Justice. It is not clear what happens when one judge is replaced by another of a different size.[104]

The law lords, sitting as they do at the pinnacle of the legal hierarchy, wear lounge suits and no wigs. On special occasions they throw caution to the winds and wear morning dress.

On the death of King Charles II in 1685 the Bar went into court mourning, for which junior barristers wore a black stuff gown with wide sleeves and a diminutive black mourning-hood cast over the left shoulder. They still do. By the early eighteenth century the normal court dress of King's Counsel had become a plain black silk gown with flat collar and long hanging sleeves. It still is.

Compared with some of the robes described above, wigs are

relatively modern; they were unheard of until the seventeenth century. But their introduction into polite society during the reign of Charles II was an innovation which could not be resisted: judges and lawyers started wearing them in the 1680s. At first they were of a natural colour, like the modern toupee, but they soon became larger and increasingly stylised. By the 1720s the legal wig was usually of powdered white or grey hair. Fashions changed, however, and by the end of the century wigs were generally worn only by lawyers, bishops and coachmen. Bishops were given permission by King William IV to abandon them in 1832.

By the beginning of the nineteenth century three different types of legal wig had emerged: all are still in use today. These are the long, full-bottomed, ear-flapping wig (which costs £1,590), beloved by cartoonists but only worn by judges and Queen's Counsel on ceremonial occasions; the bob-wig, now usually called the bench wig because it is only worn by judges, with frizzed sides rather than curls and a queue (or tail) at the back (costing £715); and the tie-wig worn daily by barristers, with a frizzed crown, rows of curls at the sides and back and a queue (a bargain at £345).[105]

The old legal wigs needed constant frizzing and curling. They also had to be perfumed and powdered every day. But in 1822 there was a breakthrough: Humphrey Ravenscroft invented a legal wig made of whitish-grey horsehair, which needed no servicing. His company still makes it today.

There was not a great deal of public comment in 1992 when the discussion paper on wigs and gowns finally appeared. Most lawyers and judges seemed happy enough with the way things were. Judges, in particular, valued the anonymity conferred by a wig. But Charter 88, a constitutional reform movement, called for judges and advocates to wear 'a simple black gown, without wig, bands or other paraphernalia'. They said:

A simple and dignified black gown would enhance the apparent as well as the actual objectivity of court proceedings; would adequately distinguish judges and advocates from members of the public; would provide a degree of uniformity that both masks inexperience and seniority and protects women from unnecessary comment on their appearance; would take from the impecunious the burden of buying several hundred pounds' worth of court dress at the start of their career; would prevent an irrelevant distinction being made between solicitor advocates and barristers and would thereby widen the pool of those effectively available as legal representatives; and would reduce the ordeal that an ordinary member of the public experiences in the unusual and stressful circumstances of appearing in court.[106]

This seems a persuasive argument although it has one or two flaws: prescribing a new uniform for solicitors would not of itself give them rights of audience, and dispensing with wigs and bands will not do a lot to reduce stress levels in the civil courts or the Crown Court (wigs and gowns are not worn by anyone in the magistrates' courts anyway).

Only just over 500 replies were received to the Lord Chancellor's consultation paper and two-thirds of the respondents favoured keeping court dress unchanged. Of the remainder, 14 per cent wanted to abolish wigs and 15 per cent thought court dress should be done away with altogether. The Lord Chancellor's figures did not reveal how much support there was from the judges for the status quo but it was again clear that they had no great wish to see any changes. The majority of those in favour of keeping court dress felt it had a significant role to play in maintaining respect for the authority and status of the court.[107]

This was in line with the findings of the Crown Court survey carried out in 1992 for the Royal Commission on Criminal Justice.[108] Some 9,000 jurors were asked if judges and barristers should continue to wear wigs and gowns.[109] There was a resounding verdict in favour of tradition: 78 per cent thought barristers should keep their wigs and gowns and 88 per cent wanted the judges' costume to remain unchanged.

In the light of this response the Lord Chancellor and the Lord Chief Justice decided that there should be no change in court dress. Lord Taylor said he accepted the strength of feeling among judges and the public even though he had personally been in favour of changes.

It was a disappointing outcome. Tradition is all very well but not when it makes it more difficult for people to do their jobs. Horsehair wigs have no place in the twenty-first century and elaborate gowns do nothing to enhance the dignity of their wearers. Magistrates and all those who appear before them have no need of any uniform. Lord Taylor was right to say that judges – and, indeed, barristers – need nothing more than a simple black gown to define their dignity and status.

4

Access to Justice

Making justice work

The key issue facing the legal system today is access to justice. Few of us give it a second thought. We assume justice will somehow be available, on tap, whenever we need it; but when the time comes to enforce our rights many of us will find it very difficult – if not downright impossible – to obtain true justice from the courts.

Why should this be, when for many years we have had a government wedded to law and order? It is a paradox we shall be exploring in the pages that follow. This chapter is mainly about access to civil justice. The remainder of the book deals with legal aid and the criminal justice system.

As we shall see in chapter 5, the cuts in legal aid eligibility introduced in 1993 meant that a lot of people who had been eligible for state assistance were eligible no more, while many others seeking legal aid were required to pay contributions which they could not afford. According to the Law Society, unless these cuts are reversed, 'for many people the legal aid scheme will be no more than a cruel deception – apparently available to help them when a problem arises, but in practice priced out of their reach.'[1]

What about those who *can* afford to go to court – those who still qualify for legal aid, the wealthy, large organisations and people supported by an employer or a trade union? What can they expect to find? According to the most recent independent review, it will be a civil justice system 'in urgent need of further fundamental reform and modernisation'.[2]

Of course there have been some welcome improvements in recent years. But Lord Woolf – one of the most thoughtful of our

171

recently appointed law lords – said in the spring of 1993 that the government should be looking for rather more fundamental reforms of the court system.[3] We should be much more imaginative, he believed, in trying to make justice available. Instead of cutting down on access to justice, which he thought was the most worrying feature of the whole legal scene at this time, Lord Woolf argued that the government should be looking at what resources it had and cutting its coat according to those resources:

> We must accept that our present way of dealing with cases is marvellous, but it is a Rolls-Royce type of litigation. I think we have got to have some rather more mundane forms of justice, if you are getting to a situation where you're having to cut down access. We had a Civil Justice Review, but quite frankly that was polishing the existing system. The government are playing with looking at Alternative Dispute Resolution. Moving a lot of work from the High Court to the county court was a substantial improvement, but I really feel we must be looking at the role of the judge. He has got to be prepared to perform functions which are different from those of merely being the referee and blowing the whistle when someone is offside.

Lord Woolf's remarks are worth closer study.

A Rolls-Royce system

Speaking later in 1993 Lord Woolf said a wealthy friend of his had recently bought a country house, only to find he had to spend £20,000 on a new roof. The man had 'always been partial to an entertaining fight in the courts' and he duly sued his surveyor for not spotting the problem. However, the case had already cost him more than £20,000 in legal fees and it looked as though he would have to drop the claim before trial. Lord Woolf reiterated that there was a danger of the system becoming so expensive that the public were being deprived of justice because of the costliness of going to law. 'Good as our system is,' he said, 'it is fatally flawed if the majority of the public, including the corporate sector, cannot afford to invoke it . . . If the alternative is between not going to court because you cannot afford a Rolls-Royce system and accepting a rough-and-ready model that does not produce such a refined product then I would prefer the second alternative.'[4]

Lord Woolf's 'fast track' approach would be inquisitorial in nature and based on the existing procedure for dealing with small claims in the county court. We shall be considering it later in this chapter.

The Civil Justice Review

In 1985 Lord Hailsham set up his Civil Justice Review. It had the appearance of an independent inquiry, with an advisory committee chaired by an industrialist: most of its members were non-lawyers. In fact, the review was strongly driven by Richard White, a senior official in the Lord Chancellor's Department. It commissioned numerous expensive reports from management consultants and published a number of provocative discussion papers, followed by a final report in June 1988.[5] The report correctly identified the main problems of civil justice as involving 'delay, cost, complexity and access to justice'.

Cost and delay have been causing problems for centuries. Over a hundred years ago the Judicature Commission suggested that the High Court and the county courts could be made more efficient if they were combined into a single system.[6] A combined court would certainly be more flexible: some cases would be reserved for High Court judges, others would always be handled by Circuit judges and there would be a broad middle band triable by either. It is an arrangement which seems to work for criminal cases in the Crown Court. But the idea was rejected by the Civil Justice Review, apparently because of opposition from the High Court judges. They were worried that a merger would damage the status of the High Court; cynics thought their real concern was that it would damage the status of the High Court judges.[7]

Instead the review proposed a more modest approach, giving unlimited jurisdiction to the county courts while reserving the High Court, in general, for cases involving more than £25,000.

These recommendations were broadly accepted. In July 1991 an order was made under the Courts and Legal Services Act[8] abolishing the existing limit on the county courts' jurisdiction and replacing it with more flexible criteria for allocating cases between the High Court and the county courts. The order also required all personal injury cases up to £50,000 to start in a county court.

At the same time the Lord Chancellor introduced a number of administrative improvements designed to discourage litigants from using delay as a form of 'gamesmanship'. Writs now had to be served within four months of issue instead of a year. Medical reports were to be provided at the start of proceedings. There was also a general devolution of work: cases up to £5,000 which previously had to be tried by a Circuit judge could now come before the District judge; some matters which were previously the responsibility of a District judge were transferred to court staff; other steps taken by court staff could now be dealt with by the parties themselves. These measures had the intended effect of reducing the number of cases being heard in the High Court.

The Lord Chancellor was proud of the 'dramatic increase in productivity' which had resulted, with completed trials rising from around 9,000 in 1989 to just under 25,000 in 1992.[9] But Lord Woolf was right to say that this amounted to no more than 'polishing' the existing system. The Lord Chancellor hardly needed to have spent half a million pounds on a two-and-a-half-year review simply in order to transfer a few cases from one court to another.

The Heilbron Report

It was against this background that the Bar and the Law Society set up an independent committee in July 1992 'to undertake a radical review of the business of the civil courts'. It was chaired by Hilary Heilbron QC, a prominent commercial barrister;[10] the vice-chairman was Henry Hodge, a leading legal aid solicitor.

In its report nearly a year later the Heilbron committee painted a gloomy picture of the civil justice system. 'An air of Dickensian antiquity pervades the civil process,' it reported. Virtually all court documents and records were compiled by hand and as a result information was often unavailable or difficult to obtain. The report also found:

- Procedures were unnecessarily technical, inflexible, rule-ridden, formalistic and often incomprehensible to the ordinary litigant.

- Some (but not all) lawyers and judges adhered steadfastly to traditional and time-consuming procedures and attitudes.

- The speed at which legal actions made progress depended on the parties and their lawyers rather than on the courts.

- Procedures and legal behaviour were geared to a trial rather than early resolution of a dispute.[11]

The Heilbron committee concluded – not unreasonably – that radical changes were needed.

Rebuilding the High Court

Although it is now some 120 years since the courts of Queen's Bench and Chancery were merged together with several others to form the High Court of Justice, there are still separate divisions in the High Court reflecting the two sources from which civil justice flows – the common law and equity. The Heilbron Report strongly recommended that the Queen's Bench Division and the Chancery Division should be merged into a single Civil Division of the High Court.[12] This would lead to much greater flexibility: at present, for example, Chancery Division judges cannot sit in the Commercial Court, even to help out. The change would not force specialist judges to try cases outside their particular areas of expertise: cases would be listed according to their subject matter and assigned to a judge who was experienced in that field. The Heilbron committee suggested there could be:

- A General List
- A General Business List
- A Commercial Court List
- An Admiralty List
- A Jury List
- A Company and Insolvency List
- An Intellectual Property List
- A Revenue List
- A Trust, Probate and Real Property List
- A Restrictive Practices Court List
- An Official Referees' Court List
- A Judicial Review List

This seems an excellent idea – although 'business' is an ambiguous term and the second list should be called the 'General Commercial List'. The scheme could be adjusted from time to time as particular areas became more or less busy and it would allow the Lord Chief Justice and the Vice-Chancellor[13] to move judges around in line with priorities. A new system of centralised listing would be needed, with full computer support.

Rebuilding the High Court should not stop there. Traditionally, cases are listed according to the principle that judges must never be kept waiting for a case. This means that lawyers and litigants are often kept hanging about in corridors for hours on end, just in case the previous case collapses. As a practice it may save judicial resources but it is expensive for the litigant who has to pay for his lawyer's time. It would be much more economical to keep the judge waiting a little while if necessary until the next case is ready: there are few judges who do not have a backlog of unwritten judgments and unread cases with which to occupy themselves.

There is also scope for simplifying court papers. Many people are familiar with the notion of a High Court writ – the formal document which begins an action in the Queen's Bench Division. The wording of the writ has become less intimidating and more accurate in recent years, making life easier for all concerned.[14] But most people would be mystified by an originating summons – the equivalent document in the Chancery Division – as indeed they would be by the sight of a petition or an originating application, which are other devices for starting legal actions. Although the Civil Justice Review said in 1988 that all cases should be started in the same way – by writ – this recommendation has unfortunately not been implemented. If the Lord Chancellor's Department cannot cope with changing the title of a common document, there is little hope that its officials will be able to combine the two huge rule books governing the High Court and the county courts (known, respectively, as the 'White Book' and the 'Green Book') to create the Heilbron committee's hoped-for single volume, available to all on computer disc (in, no doubt, a tasteful shade of eau de nil).

Although there are branches of the High Court throughout the jurisdiction, English justice is still highly centralised. Judicial review, remarkably enough, is available only in London. As we shall see, litigants are not allowed to challenge administrative decisions in the county courts,[15] presumably because ministers were worried that Circuit judges might run amok and find against the government at every opportunity. It may be desirable to keep a close eye on the sensitive and expanding areas of judicial review but there is no reason why cases should not be heard outside London, either by High Court judges on circuit or by approved Circuit judges sitting as Deputy High Court judges. It should also be possible for the Court of Appeal to sit in cities such as Birmingham, Manchester and Newcastle.

In March 1994, just before the first edition of this book was published, the government appointed Lord Woolf and a team of litigation experts to carry out a fundamental review of civil court procedures. The task of combining the two rule books was placed firmly on their agenda.

Lord Woolf decided to reveal his provisional conclusions two months later in an interview with *The Observer*.[16] This came as something as a surprise because it had been announced that his review would last for two years. He recommended that new *procedural judges* should be appointed to take control of cases at an early stage. They would fix timetables for hearings and set ceilings on costs. They would also appoint expert witnesses and reduce the number of documents before the court.

Lord Woolf's proposals received immediate and warm support from the Lord Chief Justice. Speaking at the Lord Mayor's dinner for the judges in July 1994, Lord Taylor described Lord Woolf's suggestions as 'bold and imaginative'.

But on the very next day, a deep rift opened between the Lord Chief Justice and the Master of the Rolls. While Lord Taylor wanted case management to be handled by lowly procedural judges, Sir Thomas Bingham said that control should be exercised by the trial judge himself. First, he said, it would be very hard for a more junior judge to be sufficiently bold and decisive without risking the wrath of the eventual trial judge. Secondly, the preliminary rulings would be of great importance: they needed the authority of a trial judge. Thirdly, Sir Thomas envisaged that the gradual narrowing down of the issues would lead to a process of 'creeping decision-making'. While he had no objection to this development – indeed, he seemed to welcome it – Sir Thomas said it would be much better to have the same judge in charge throughout the case. He realised this would mean more judges, but seemed less worried by this prospect than Lord Taylor had been.

The need for judicial intervention

The Heilbron Report recommended a new approach from the judges. 'They must exert their authority,' said the report, 'to ensure that the parties get on with the action and there is no unnecessary waste of court time.'[17]

This approach is new in the sense that it is only now being accepted by the judiciary; but it is what Lord Woolf was saying in the interview quoted at the beginning of this chapter[18] and it is consistent with the approach adopted by Lord Donaldson when he was Master of the Rolls.[19] At its most basic level it would operate before an action even came to trial.

At present, details of every writ are entered by hand in a cause book, 'as has been the practice for centuries'.[20] The Heilbron Report recommended that the process should be computerised, triggering 'prompts' whenever the time prescribed by procedural rules had expired. The computer would automatically warn the parties that their case would be struck out if no action was taken within a specified period.

The interventionist approach would not end there. Under the Heilbron proposals the judge would indicate to counsel at the start of the case how long he expected each part of the hearing to take. Barristers would be expected to keep to the time-limits. Since counsel would have lodged skeleton arguments, only brief opening statements would be needed in court. Cases cited in argument and written evidence would not be read aloud; if need be, the judge should adjourn the case in order to read the necessary documents. Closing submissions might also be in writing.[21] These are all admirable suggestions. The Heilbron Report also recommended that reserved judgments should be handed down in writing rather than read out in court – a suggestion already advocated in chapter 2 of this book.

The Heilbron proposals received a ringing endorsement from the Lord Chief Justice in October 1993. 'A trial is not a game,' he said. 'The role of the judge should not be restricted to that of an umpire sitting well above the play, intervening only to restrain intemperate language and racquet throwing.' The Lord Chief Justice advised his fellow judges that 'without being unpleasant or talking excessively, a judge can and should intervene to confine advocacy to the issues, to stop repetitious or oppressive cross-examination and to discourage long-windedness'.[22]

Lord Taylor's advice extended to barristers. He was not proposing rigid time-limits of the sort seen in the United States (where advocates are sometimes cut off in mid-sentence) but he agreed with the Heilbron committee that the judge should set a timetable for opening and closing speeches.

Judges and advocates would do well to heed this advice. If an advocate is given a fixed time-limit, he or she will generally manage to cover the required points in the time available. But there is only so much that can be done without government intervention. The Lord Chancellor was right to ask Lord Woolf to examine the civil justice system. But his report is not expected until 1996 and it will be 1997 at the earliest before any changes take effect.

Inquisitorial justice

Our system of justice is often described as *adversarial*. In the words of Lord Taylor, 'Judges in recent times have tended to leave it to the adversaries to determine the issues, how they should be contested, how long the contestants should take to gird themselves up for battle, and how long the contest itself should take.'[23] In general, this approach governs criminal cases as much as it does the civil courts; indeed the Royal Commission on Criminal Justice – like the Heilbron Report – said that 'judges must be prepared to intervene as and when necessary to expedite the proceedings . . .'[24]

There seems to be widespread support for a more hands-on *interventionist* approach from the judiciary. But some people want the judges to go further still.

The police believe that our criminal courts would be better able to convict the guilty if they took a more *inquisitorial* approach, with the judge playing a greater part in uncovering the facts by interrogating the defendant and witnesses.

That has been the way our coroners' courts have operated for centuries. Unlike other courts they are fact-finding bodies, designed to establish the cause of a sudden death. However, they are not a good advertisement for the inquisitorial system. Although there have been minor changes in recent years, the ancient origins of the coroner's inquest are demonstrated by an autocratic procedure which would have been abolished long ago if it had survived anywhere else in the legal system. The government should dust off the Broderick Report of 1971[25] and implement its proposals: that all coroners should be legally qualified, for example, and that they should be appointed by the Lord Chancellor rather than by the local authority. Better still, ministers should set up a new system of public inquiries into sudden deaths, with the power to conduct investigations, apportion blame and award compensation.

If inquests have nothing to teach us, can we learn anything from continental countries which have an inquisitorial system of criminal justice? The Royal Commission on Criminal Justice rejected suggestions that we should adopt an inquisitorial approach in England and Wales although the commissioners did make some recommendations aimed at moving the criminal justice system in this direction.[26] The Royal Commission doubted whether combining the functions of investigation and prosecution, and the direct involvement of judges in both, would serve the interests of justice better than a system in which the roles were kept separate. The commission believed that keeping the distinct roles of the investigator, the prosecutor and the judge offered better protection for the innocent defendant. In particular, there was less chance that he would be held in detention awaiting trial any longer than was necessary.

These are convincing arguments. An inquisitorial system of *criminal* prosecutions is not on the political agenda in England and Wales, and there is no sign that it ever will be.

Is there any scope for making the *civil* justice system more inquisitorial? This was the suggestion made by Lord Woolf as part of his search for a cheaper way of doing justice.[27] He gave as an example the way small claims are handled in the county courts.

The small claims court

Strictly speaking, there is no such thing as a 'small claims court' in England and Wales: small claims are heard in the county courts alongside what are now some very large claims. However, these courts have special arrangements for dealing with claims worth less than a specified amount. Instead of being tried in the normal way they are referred to an arbitrator, usually the District judge sitting informally and with no lawyers present. Arbitrators must apply the law of the land but they are free to ignore the finer points of evidence and procedure in reaching a decision. There is every reason to suppose that they adopt a more interventionist, inquisitorial role than they would if there were lawyers present.

When the arbitration system was introduced into the county courts in 1974 it was restricted to claims worth up to £75 and available only if one of the parties requested it. By 1991 all claims up to £500 were referred automatically for arbitration. In June of 1991 that figure was increased to £1,000. There were subsequent changes aimed at helping litigants in person: district judges were given greater responsibility to level out inequalities between the parties and claimants were given the right to lay representation.

Because these arbitrations are heard in private it is difficult to know how well they are being handled by the courts. Certainly those who use arbitration seem reasonably happy with the way it works. Indeed, the respected lawyers' organisation JUSTICE argued that the figure below which cases are automatically referred for arbitration should be increased from £1,000 to £5,000 (although JUSTICE would have allowed the parties to choose the traditional adversarial process if they preferred it).[28]

The Lord Chancellor said the major way in which he was aiming to reduce cost, delay and complexity in lower-value cases was by replacing courtroom procedures with arbitration procedures. But there are drawbacks. According to the pure theory of small claims arbitration, it should be possible to try cases without involving solicitors on either side. On that basis, runs the theory, there should be no need for the losing side to pay the winner's legal costs because there should be no legal costs. However, in practice it is not possible to conduct even the most straightforward personal injury case without professional help.

This means claimants have to think carefully before starting proceedings. Not only must a plaintiff be confident of success, he must also be sure that the amount he may win will be sufficient to cover his outlay and still leave him with enough to make the ordeal worthwhile. It follows from this that claimants were far from happy when the automatic arbitration level was raised to £1,000 in 1991; it meant there were more cases in which they were not entitled to claim their legal costs although in practice these costs were often paid by their opponent's insurance company when the case was settled.

There was therefore some comfort for claimants when, in October 1993, the Lord Chancellor published a consultation paper on small personal injury claims.[29] As we saw in chapter 3, he proposed that these claims should always go to arbitration unless the claimant said his case was worth more than £1,000. Lord Mackay recognised the need for claimants to take legal advice before starting legal action, if only because they needed to know how much their claim was worth. He proposed that successful claimants in personal injury cases should be able to recover a fixed sum for legal advice. But in August 1994 Lord Mackay announced that he would not be going ahead with these proposals after all.

Lord Woolf thought it might be possible to build on the small claims procedure and use it for much larger cases.[30] 'While obviously the larger the sum involved the more important the issue is to the parties,' he said, 'the issues for the judge can be equally difficult or easy whether the sum at stake is £50 or £50 million. It may be that if such a radical change is necessary it would have to be coupled with the establishment of a Director of Civil Proceedings with responsibility for overseeing the development of the civil law and access to the courts.'

Lord Woolf did not develop his ideas in detail; indeed, it would be hard to imagine that anyone with £50 million to lose would tolerate the rough-and-ready procedures he had in mind, with the judge having the power to exclude the normal exchange of documents or even legal representation in court. Our current procedures may be expensive but they do go some way towards safeguarding the parties' rights.

The less we spend on lawyers, the more we have to spend on inquisitors. The inquisitorial process only works if there is someone available to dig out all the facts. In small claims this can probably be achieved in the courtroom on the day of the hearing, provided the parties bring all their documents with them. For all but the simplest cases, however, an inquisition is not the answer.

Arbitration

Although we are not likely to see the abolition of an adversarial system in civil cases, we should certainly not write off arbitration as a means of providing access to justice. Lord Mackay said he was sometimes urged to make rules which provide for a judge in the county court to refer cases to an outside arbitrator with the consent of both parties. In fact, he explained, judges have had this power for nearly 150 years.[31] It is perhaps ironic that arbitrators are used to settle some of the largest disputes as well as the smallest. Arbitration is big business for lawyers and arbitrators (generally senior QCs and retired judges).[32] It may cost the parties more than conventional litigation because the arbitrator will command a hefty fee but the business community is often willing to pay what it takes to get a dispute settled quickly.

The crucial point about arbitration is that it is binding. Just like a judge, the arbitrator decides what the parties must do. But there is now another way of settling disputes. It is not binding but, strangely enough, it seems to work. It is called *alternative dispute resolution*.

Alternative dispute resolution

Alternative dispute resolution became popular in the United States during the 1970s. The business community found conventional litigation frustrating and expensive, whichever side won; unlike their English counterparts, courts in the United States do not make the losing side pay the winner's legal fees. Commercial organisations also realised that in many of their disputes it tended to be six of one and half a dozen of the other: both sides were often at fault and litigation was simply an expensive way of delaying the inevitable settlement at the door of the court.

But why wait until the judge is pacing up and down outside the courtroom? ('Just another half an hour, My Lord, and I am hopeful the parties can come to some arrangement . . .') With the aim of trying to get cases settled before the legal taxi-meter started ticking over at maximum rates, there was increasing support in England and Wales in the late 1980s for alternative ways of solving legal disputes.

One of these was *mediation*. This is a concept borrowed from the field of industrial relations.[33] It is quite different from arbitration. In mediation, after an initial joint session, the two sides gather in separate rooms. A neutral mediator moves between them, helping the parties to reach a settlement by pointing out to each side the strengths and weaknesses of their own case. The mediator will explore any options available to resolve the dispute and either party can insist that the mediator should recommend the terms of a settlement. In *evaluative mediation*, the mediator can say what he thinks of the positions taken by the two sides; in *facilitative mediation*, he must not.

In the hope that this technique could now be used to settle disputes between employers, in November 1990 the Confederation of British Industry launched a new organisation called the Centre for Dispute Resolution. It was an independent body with its own staff, supported by over 250 major companies and professional advisers.[34] In its first three years it trained more than 200 people as mediators.

The Centre for Dispute Resolution says that it is possible to achieve a result in almost any dispute if the parties genuinely wish to settle the problem. If no progress is made either side may withdraw. During the Centre's first eighteen months of operation 165 business disputes involving more than £550 million were referred to it. The success rate was put at 95 per cent. Its chairman reckoned that mediation would save the companies involved more than £30 million in potential costs and substantially more if management time was included.[35]

There are two variations on mediation, one more formal and the other less so. The *mini-trial* is a structured procedure in which executives from each party appear with their lawyers before a neutral adviser to present their arguments. After time for consideration the two sides begin negotiations with the adviser's help. If the negotiations fail the parties can ask the adviser how he or she thinks the case would be decided by a court. The parties can then settle on this basis if they wish. In a variation on this process, the parties appear instead before a panel of three people – one executive decision-maker from each party and a neutral chairman.

Conciliation is the name given to a much simpler form of alternative dispute resolution. The role of the conciliator is similar to that of a mediator although normally the conciliator will simply encourage the parties to reach a settlement without producing recommendations of his own. Confusingly, 'conciliation' and 'mediation' are often used as interchangeable terms.

There is another process known as *non-binding arbitration*. In this type of dispute resolution the arbitrator is simply expected to give his opinion of what would happen if the case went to trial. He may even be requested to select a 'jury' and ask them to reach a verdict. Faced with this information, the parties should be more likely to reach a settlement.

Alternative dispute resolution offers the advantages of speed, secrecy and convenience. It is flexible, allowing the parties to choose the level of formality they feel best suits their dispute. And that flexibility extends to the remedies available: for example, the loser may not be able to afford to pay compensation but both parties may be satisfied by a new contract on improved terms.

There are also disadvantages. In a dispute which has already attracted widespread publicity the parties may welcome a public hearing in court to restore their reputations. If the process fails the parties may have to resort to litigation or arbitration at additional expense. And because a settlement achieved through alternative dispute resolution is only binding if the parties agree, a defendant who has no wish to settle can drag the proceedings out and delay the inevitable writ.

The process suffers from obvious limitations. Alternative dispute resolution is only really appropriate where there is property or money at stake. It cannot be used, for example, to deal with applications for judicial review.

The one factor common to both arbitration and alternative dispute resolution is privacy. No doubt the opportunity to keep their disputes off the front pages and the television news is what makes the process so attractive to its users. They are hardly likely to be impressed by a journalist's assertion that the shareholders of public companies should be told what is being done with their money. Nor will they be too worried at the prospect of the courts losing touch with commercial realities if more and more disputes are settled behind closed doors. A public system of laws has the advantage of setting a benchmark against which disputes can be settled out of court. The common law is something of a vampire: without a steady stream of cases to feed on, it would atrophy and die.

Not that there was much likelihood of that in England and Wales in the early 1990s. Alternative dispute resolution has not been particularly successful in Britain. It has made a much greater impact in countries like Australia, Canada and Hong Kong – as well as the United States.

So what chance is there that alternative dispute resolution could supplant the courts? In November 1991 the Bar Council published the report of a committee chaired by Lord Justice Beldam. It called on the courts to adopt a voluntary system of mediation and recommended a series of pilot studies. The report said it was essential that parties should not lose their legal rights in attempting to solve their dispute by mediation. The 1993 Heilbron Report[36] endorsed Lord Justice Beldam's request for a pilot scheme, adding that it should cover legal aid cases as well.

Lord Mackay seemed far from enthusiastic about alternative dispute resolution. He said, not very helpfully, that he was 'very much in favour of alternatives to court procedures being provided in the private sector for those whose disputes can be resolved effectively without recourse to litigation'. However, he was anxious that people should not be encouraged to abrogate their legal rights.[37]

The real problem was, as always, resources: alternative dispute resolution would not be attractive to the Lord Chancellor's Department unless it was going to save money. In the short term it was going to cost the government more: someone has to pay the mediator. Resources apart, alternative dispute resolution has its virtues: they should not be overlooked by the government.

'No win, no fee'

In many parts of the United States, lawyers take cases on a 'no win, no fee' basis. If the claim fails the plaintiff generally pays nothing. If the plaintiff wins then the lawyer takes a share of the winnings – sometimes as much as half.

Plaintiffs are happy because this so-called *contingency fee* system gives them something at the end of the day, even if they have no money to fund a case: half a loaf is better than no bread. Lawyers are happy because they may end up with quite a large sum of money for relatively little work, provided they have chosen the right case to back. Insurance companies are happy because they can often negotiate an attractive settlement.

This is because there is frequently a stage in personal injury cases – generally a few days or hours before the hearing – when the defendant will offer a sum of money to settle the case. The plaintiff has to decide whether to accept the offer, which he will probably think is too small, or go ahead and fight the case in court. If he fights and loses he will end up with nothing.

Under the contingency fee system there is a strong incentive at this point for the lawyer to advise his client to accept. If the client fights and loses the lawyer will also get nothing; but if the lawyer is to be paid in any event he is more likely to offer impartial advice.

It is for this reason that contingency fees have been banned in England since the Statute of Westminster in the year 1275. Solicitors have not been allowed to charge a successful client more than they would charge someone who has lost his case. In fact many solicitors quietly did just that: they would charge a successful claimant as much as they thought he could now afford, while sharply reducing or even waiving their fees if the client lost.

In May 1993 the Lord Chancellor issued a consultation paper on what are called *conditional fees*. This scheme would allow solicitors and clients to agree a subtle variation on the American system. If the client lost the lawyer would still be paid nothing. If he won the lawyer would be able to charge 20 per cent more than normal. He would not have a direct interest in how much the client received but he would be paid more to compensate him for the cases where he received nothing.

Solicitors argued that a 20 per cent 'uplift' would be little incentive to take on the riskier cases. On the government's figures, a lawyer would clearly have to win five cases out of every six just to break even. The government soon recognised that this would make conditional fees quite unrealistic and dramatically increased the maximum uplift to 100 per cent.[38]

There were still obvious drawbacks. Naturally conditional fees apply only to cases where a successful plaintiff can expect compensation from the defendant: they are no use in criminal cases or most matrimonial disputes. Second, an unsuccessful plaintiff would still have to pay legal fees – not his own but his opponent's. In England and Wales, unlike the United States, the loser generally pays all the legal costs; and even if he does not have to pay his lawyer he will probably still have to pay the fees of his own expert witnesses. Not many claimants can afford to take the risk. Third, a successful claimant would have to pay his lawyer up to twice as much as he would have paid before: he should know exactly what he was letting himself in for.[39] Finally, the Lord Chancellor proposed that conditional fees should be restricted to cases involving personal injury, insolvency or applications to the European Court of Human Rights.

There is also a drawback from the defendant's point of view. As we have seen, an unsuccessful claimant has to pay the defendant's costs. In reality, however, the sort of person who resorts to 'no win, no fee' litigation is unlikely to have much money anyway so the chances are that the defendant would be out of pocket by a considerable sum even if he won the case. That means it will generally be cheaper for the defendant to pay the claimant a small sum of money to go away. But if claimants know this they are likely to 'try it on'. The system might therefore encourage speculative – or even fraudulent – claims by people who know they are not likely to succeed in court.

Shortly after the government had announced its support for conditional fees the Law Society unveiled a scheme which dealt with many of these problems. It would enable claimants in personal injury cases to insure against the risk of having to pay the other side's costs. The claimant would buy this insurance *after* the accident in which he was injured but *before* he started legal action. If he lost, the insurance company would pay the defendant's legal costs.

The beauty of the scheme was that there was not much chance that the claimant would lose. The solicitor would be backing the case with his own judgment. Since the solicitor knew he would not be paid anything unless his client won, he would not take the case to court unless he was reasonably confident of success. If he thought it would fail the solicitor would settle the case at an early stage: in that event, the claimant would hardly ever have to pay the defendant's costs. For these reasons the insurance would not cost much.

The Law Society announced that it had been working with an insurance company to offer so-called 'after the event' insurance for normally less than £100 per case, starting in late 1994.[40] In June 1994 it launched a scheme called Accident Line. This offers half an hour's free legal advice from an approved solicitor to any accident victim who telephones a free number (0500 19 29 39). One thousand solicitors' firms joined the scheme, confident that the fees they had paid the Law Society would be justified by the arrival of new clients.

This is clearly good news for solicitors: for the first time in recent years there were signs that a new area of work was opening up. It is also good news for clients: for the first time many of them can be reasonably confident of receiving at least some compensation for their claims. There might not be very much after the solicitor has taken his cut but as a result of competition some solicitors would no doubt charge less than a 100 per cent uplift. It might be bad news for hospitals, local authorities and other public bodies which receive a large number of personal injury claims but, in theory at least, they might take steps to reduce accidents and improve public safety. All in all, it seemed to be a rare shaft of sunlight in an otherwise gloomy picture.

Televising the courts

At present, cameras are banned from the English courts by law. Under the Criminal Justice Act 1925[41] it is an offence to take photographs or make sketches of judges, jurors, parties or witnesses in court. Nor may they be photographed 'in the building or in the precincts of the building in which the court is held', or if they are entering or leaving court buildings. This law is broken every minute of the day, and not just by journalists: some years ago those responsible for security at the High Court in London installed video cameras to monitor people entering and leaving the buildings and these cameras have now become universal.

In recent years the judges have taken an increasingly relaxed approach to the 1925 Act. No attempt is made to prevent filming immediately outside the High Court in London although photographers are kept to the public footpath where they cause more of an obstruction than they would if they were allowed to stand on the paved area leading to the main entrance. Film crews are kept a little way away from the main entrance of the Old Bailey but they are still allowed to film those coming and going. When Lord Denning was Master of the Rolls he allowed himself to be filmed by the BBC in his room at the law courts, but while Lord Lane was Lord Chief Justice he would not allow any of his fellow judges – not even Lord Denning's successor, Lord Donaldson – to be filmed inside the building. However, this rule was scrapped in 1992 by Lord Taylor who even gave press conferences there. Lord Taylor also allowed the BBC to film in the main hall of the Royal Courts of Justice after the public had gone home; but he drew the line at allowing cameras into an empty courtroom. Other courts are less sensitive and since 1990 Circuit Administrators have been responsible for deciding whether to grant requests of this type.[42]

Because of the ban on filming in courts, television news organisations rely heavily on artists' sketches of the defendants in court. These may be the only pictures available in criminal cases where the defendant is in custody; as a result they are frequently reprinted by the newspapers. BBC viewers are familiar with the careful pastel drawings of Julia Quenzler; ITN uses the rather more flamboyant crayon work of Priscilla Coleman. Those who complain that their likenesses are sometimes a little too impressionistic generally fail to realise that these pictures are drawn at some speed and entirely from memory. The artists are allowed to make written notes ('big nose, hooded eyes') but they must not make sketches of any kind in their notebooks.[43] There seems to be no reason for this restriction and the judges occasionally dispense with it although in fact they have no power under the Criminal Justice Act to do so.

In 1989 a committee of barristers chaired by Jonathan Caplan QC recommended that the government should allow the courts to be televised on an experimental basis. Mr Caplan argued that few people had the time or the inclination to sit through a court hearing but modern technology could bring the workings of a court to a much wider audience. He said BBC figures demonstrated that 70 per cent of adults in Britain learned most of what they knew about current events from television.[44]

As Jonathan Caplan acknowledged, the key issue in televising the courts is whether greater openness would put justice at risk. The Caplan Report answered that question with a resounding No. Would television trivialise the courts, destroy their dignity and turn them into mere entertainment? No, said the report: church services are not trivialised by television. Would television be intrusive or disruptive? No, thanks to miniature cameras and low lighting levels. Would television affect the parties and witnesses? No more than reporters do at present. Would television affect the jury in a criminal trial? No, because jurors would not be seen. Would television affect the judges or the lawyers? No, except that they might behave better. Would television be unfair to the defendant? No more than a public trial at the moment. Would an edited court report be prejudicial? No more than a report without television pictures.

These are convincing arguments. The Bar Council backed them in 1991 to the extent of supporting a Private Member's Bill which would have allowed a pilot study to take place,[45] but the bill was unsuccessful in parliament. In fact there was little pressure for televised trials from barristers as a profession and the judiciary was equally sceptical. Opponents of the cameras were alarmed at cases they had seen televised in the United States and they were reluctant to do anything that would discourage witnesses from giving evidence or make a criminal trial more difficult.

However, even those who were against televising criminal trials recognised that appeals were rather different. Without a jury, without perhaps any witnesses, there was less risk of prejudice to a trial.

With that in mind, the BBC approached the law lords in 1992 to see if they would agree to their hearings being televised. In 1989 the Lords of Appeal had allowed themselves to be seen giving judgment in the chamber of the House of Lords: the question now was whether they would allow legal argument, conducted in a committee room, to be recorded and broadcast. Everyone recognised that the vast majority of what was said would be meaningless to a lay audience but the BBC felt there would be cases from time to time which would be of great public interest and these could be edited in such a way as to make fascinating television.

The law lords were very encouraging: they were willing in principle to be the first British court to be shown on television. The ban on court photography seemed not to be a problem; the law lords proceeded on the basis that they were not a 'court' for the purposes of the Criminal Justice Act 1925. But some months earlier a programme shown on ITV had made the judges look rather silly.

Wise to the ways of the broadcasters, Lord Keith and his brethren insisted on a number of conditions before granting the BBC permission to film them. One caused the broadcasters particular difficulties: 'If any member of the committee which is filmed objects to any part of the programme depicting the committee, that part will be excised.' The BBC felt that it would be surrendering its editorial independence if it accepted this condition. The law lords were not prepared to change their minds and so there the matter was left. In the climate of the times the law lords were right to be wary; but it was a pity they were not prepared to trust the BBC.

As one door closed another opened. The most senior judge in Scotland, the Lord President of the Court of Session, revealed in August 1992 that he had been considering for some time whether the existing restrictions on televising the Scottish courts might be altered. It so happened that the 1925 legislation did not apply to Scotland and the Scottish judges had it within their power to let the cameras in if they wanted to.

The Lord President, Lord Hope, said he did not think it was in the long-term public interest to maintain a total ban on televising the Scottish courts.[46] Lord Hope said it was in the public interest that people in Scotland should become more aware of how justice was being administered in their own courts. 'There is a risk,' he explained, 'that the showing on television of proceedings in the courts of other countries will lead to misunderstandings about the way in which court proceedings are conducted in our own country.'[47]

Lord Hope issued practice directions making it clear that in future television cameras would be allowed in Scottish courts if their presence 'would be without risk to the administration of justice'. The directions drew a distinction between trials and appeals. There was still a ban on news broadcasts of current trials – either criminal or civil – because of the risks involved in televising the proceedings while witnesses were giving their evidence. But it would be possible for news programmes to show appeals – both civil and criminal – 'with the approval of the presiding judge and subject to such conditions as he may impose'.

The directions went further still. Requests to film actual trials for 'educational or documentary programmes' to be shown at a later date would be 'favourably considered' but, the directions continued, 'such filming may be done only with the consent of all parties involved in the proceedings and it will be subject to approval by the presiding judge of the final product before it is televised'.[48]

Clearly the BBC could not tolerate this last condition and, after lengthy and difficult negotiations, new guidelines were agreed. Broadly speaking, the judges kept control over what could be filmed in their courts and the BBC kept editorial control over its programmes. The BBC's television documentary department filmed five criminal trials in Scotland[49] and they were televised in November 1994.

However, the television companies had difficulties in making arrangements with the Scottish judiciary for news programmes to show appeals in progress. It was too expensive and by the summer of 1994 nothing had appeared on the screen.

The Lord Chancellor watched all this with interest. Lord Mackay made it clear that the government would want to see what happened in Scotland before deciding whether the law should be changed in England and Wales. There seemed little chance that the English judges would go any further than their Scottish counterparts in allowing cases to be seen on television.

Even so, the televising of hearings at the Court of Appeal is now on the long-term agenda in England. Sooner or later it will happen and the public will at last begin to see how justice is dispensed in its name.

The Law Commission

The Law Commission was set up by parliament in 1965. With a sympathetic Lord Chancellor (Lord Gardiner, a member of Harold Wilson's first Labour government) and an enthusiastic chairman (Mr Justice Scarman, later Lord Scarman) it made great strides. It has the job of keeping the law of England and Wales under review and recommending reform when it is needed. Its programmes of work must be approved by the Lord Chancellor and its recommendations have no effect unless or until they are implemented by parliament.

The chairman of the Law Commission is always a High Court judge. This is supposed to be a full-time appointment but Mr Justice Brooke, who became chairman in 1992, combined the job with his responsibilities at the Judicial Studies Board[50] and still manages to sit regularly as a judge. The other four commissioners are specialist barristers, solicitors or academics.

The Law Commission has evolved an efficient two-tier system of working. The commission will make an initial study of a legal topic, analysing the problems and looking for solutions. The options will then be set out in a consultation paper, together with arguments for and against each proposed change. The Law Commission may well give its provisional view, if it has one.

This 'green paper' is then published and comments are invited from lawyers, other professionals and those most affected by the proposed changes. It is only when all have had their say that the Law Commission publishes its recommendations, together with a parliament-ready draft bill. Further action is then up to the government.

The Law Commission was justifiably annoyed that none of its bills was included in the government's legislative programme in 1991 or 1992. Two of its reports were implemented in 1992 but these were Private Member's Bills, sponsored by individual peers. The commission told the Lord Chancellor in 1993 that there was 'a very serious backlog of Law Commission reports awaiting parliamentary consideration'.[51]

This was another serious failing to lay at the door of the government. Lord Mackay was spending more than £3 million each year on the Law Commission and he had virtually nothing to show for it. Worse still, the outdated laws which the Law Commission was seeking to replace were wasting incalculable amounts of time and money. Some of our most widely used criminal statutes were passed 130 years ago; as the Law Commission put it, 'Everyone who has anything to do with the operation of sections 18, 20 and 47 of the Offences Against the Persons Act 1861, which contain our criminal law's main armoury against violent crime, knows that they have long since earned their retirement from active service.'[52]

It seems remarkable that a body paid to review outdated laws should be ignored by the very institution which set it up. In what seemed a last desperate attempt to engage the government's attention, the Law Commission adopted the government's own political rhetoric:

We would hope that the new thinking which has ushered in the Citizen's Charter, the Courts' Charter and all the other charters which set out the quality of service which citizens are entitled to expect will embrace the right of citizens in a civilised country to expect that the laws which govern things which are very important in their lives – protection of home and family, protection from violence, or the buying and selling and renting of property for instance – should be as clear and straightforward to operate as human ingenuity and the work of this Commission can make them.[53]

But nobody took any notice.

Judicial review

One of the most important weapons in the citizen's armoury is the power to apply for judicial review of administrative action. Put simply, judicial review is a way of overturning a decision taken by a public body which has exceeded or abused its powers.

First, a word about terms. Lawyers generally speak about *applying for* judicial review, which means challenging a decision; or being *granted* judicial review, which means getting the decision overturned. It is only the newspapers who write of *a* judicial review – by which they mean a hearing in court, irrespective of its outcome. That usage is wrong.

The principles on which judicial review is granted or refused are part of what is called *administrative law*. One definition of administrative law is 'the law relating to the control of government power'. Another, more detailed definition would be 'the body of general principles which governs the exercise of powers and duties by public authorities'.[54] Both definitions are to be found in *Administrative Law*, the magisterial 1,000-page work by Professor Sir William Wade.[55]

These principles are, broadly speaking, part of the common law: in other words, they are derived from cases decided by judges[56] rather than from statutes passed by parliament. Even after Professor Wade's book was published in 1961 it was possible for Lord Reid, the distinguished law lord, to say 'We do not have a developed system of administrative law.'[57] But the case in which he made that observation, decided in 1963, itself marked a turning point for judicial review. Until the early sixties the judges were failing in their vital job of controlling the executive. As Professor Wade writes:

During and after the second world war a deep gloom settled on administrative law, which reduced it to the lowest ebb at which it had stood for centuries. The courts and the legal profession seemed to have forgotten the achievements of their predecessors and they showed little stomach for continuing their centuries-old work of imposing law upon government . . . [Administrative law] relapsed into an impotent condition, marked by neglect of principles and literal verbal interpretation of the blank-cheque powers which parliament showered on ministers.

In the 1960s, however, the judicial mood changed. New decisions re-established old principles and reactivated administrative law. The citizen had much to gain (and, Professor Wade maintains, the government had little to lose).

It could all so easily change back again. We must constantly be on the lookout for attempts to curtail judicial review, whether they come from an over-mighty government or an over-cautious judiciary. As Professor Wade writes: 'At the present time the courts are displaying enterprise and vigour, and there seems to be no danger of another period of relapse. But the recent past is a solemn warning.'

In late 1993 and early 1994 the judges were in a particularly strong position. Contrary to all the rules of practical politics, the government had appointed one of the most independent-minded and tenacious judges on the bench to inquire into its own alleged wrongdoing.[58] Lord Justice Scott was holding a public inquiry into the sales to Iraq of arms, and items that could be used for manufacturing arms, at a time when such sales were supposedly banned by the government. The judge, assisted by his chief interrogator Presiley Baxendale QC, was giving ministers and former ministers a thorough grilling, if not actually eating them for breakfast. It was felt that the government dared not take on the judiciary at such a sensitive time.

But rather as the BBC is said to practise self-censorship, the judges choose to exercise self-restraint from time to time. They feel, perhaps, that if they go 'too far' the government will step in and ask parliament to confiscate their powers. This is perhaps unlikely, although in 1984 the government did try to restrict the availability of judicial review.[59] On such occasions the judges tend to emphasise the constraints under which they operate.

Judicial review is all about the *way* in which public bodies take decisions. The courts are at pains to stress that they are not concerned with the decision itself, merely the decision-making process. That is an important distinction but it may not cut much ice with the parties involved. The applicant will probably not be very interested in the procedures followed by the decision-maker: his aim is simply to get the decision overturned. And cynical decision-makers may sometimes suspect that a court will first decide whether it likes the decision under attack; if it does not it will look for a way of ruling that the wrong procedures have been followed by the decision-making body.

What are those procedures? At the most basic level, public bodies which make decisions have a duty to act reasonably and fairly.

The principle of unreasonableness seems to be one of the most commonly used in applications for judicial review. Judges and lawyers often refer to it, without further explanation, as 'the *Wednesbury* principle' or '*Wednesbury* unreasonableness'. One might wonder why a perfectly harmless West Midlands town between Birmingham and Wolverhampton should be stigmatised in countless law reports as the epitome of unreasonableness, perhaps for one dreadful lapse many years ago. Anyone who troubles to look up the leading case of *Associated Provincial Picture Houses Ltd v. Wednesbury Corporation*[60] will find that in fact the Wednesbury council behaved perfectly reasonably; judicial review was therefore refused.

The case was decided in 1948. To operate their cinema, Associated Provincial Picture Houses needed a licence from the council. The law said this licence could be granted 'subject to such conditions as the authority think fit to impose'. In those more innocent days Wednesbury council imposed a condition that no children under 15 would be allowed in to the cinema on a Sunday. The cinema claimed this was unreasonable. The Court of Appeal said it was not: the council were entitled to have in mind 'the physical and moral health of children'. Giving judgment, the Master of the Rolls, Lord Greene, said that 'discretion must be exercised reasonably'. As he explained:

> A person entrusted with a discretion must, so to speak, direct himself properly in law. He must call his own attention to the matters which he is bound to consider. He must exclude from his consideration matters which are irrelevant to what he has to consider . . . Similarly, there may be something so absurd that no sensible person could ever dream that it lay within the power of the authority.

Lord Greene gave the example of a red-haired teacher, dismissed only because of the colour of her hair. Such a condition would clearly be struck down by the courts.

The *Wednesbury* test of reasonableness has formed the basis of judicial review for many years. In 1984 it was reformulated by Lord Diplock in his ruling on what became known as the GCHQ case,[61] brought to challenge the ban on trade unions at Government

Communications Headquarters (the base from which the Security Service monitors people's telephone calls and other international communications). Instead of unreasonableness Lord Diplock used the term 'irrationality' as a test of whether a decision should be overturned. By that he meant the sort of decision that was 'so outrageous in its defiance of logic or of accepted moral standards that no sensible person who had applied his mind to the question to be decided could have arrived at it'.

This seems a large hurdle to jump but the courts do not have much difficulty in finding examples of irrationality. As Professor Wade says, 'This is not because public authorities take leave of their senses, but because the courts in deciding cases tend to lower the threshold of unreasonableness to fit their more exacting ideas of administrative good behaviour.'[62]

Fairness is also an essential part of administrative law. As a concept it is similar to what was previously called 'natural justice'. This was a phrase much used by people who did not know what it meant: after all, what is 'natural' about justice? Used by lawyers, the concept comprised two rules: nobody can be a judge in his own cause, and a court must always 'hear the other side' – in other words, it must hear a person's defence. This failure to act fairly was recategorised by Lord Diplock in the GCHQ case as 'procedural impropriety'.[63] The concept may be extended in future to include a requirement that reasons should be given for decisions.

Fundamental to the whole subject of judicial review is the rule that a public body may not exceed its powers, that it must not act *ultra vires*. Lord Diplock recategorised this as a duty not to act 'illegally'. By that he meant that the decision-maker must understand correctly the law that regulates his power to make decisions and give effect to it. But to most people, acting illegally means committing a crime – breaking the criminal law. It is therefore better to speak of a duty not to act 'unlawfully'.

Summing up Lord Diplock's formulation, administrative law requires a decision-maker not to act irrationally, not to act with procedural impropriety and not to act unlawfully. Putting it more simply still, in cases where judicial review is available a public body must act reasonably, fairly and within its powers.

The modern law of judicial review dates from 1977 when Order 53 of the Rules of the Supreme Court was redrafted to incorporate reforms put forward by the Law Commission.[64] This provided a new and simplified procedure for seeking any of the old and quaintly named remedies of administrative law.[65] All the benefits of the law may now be obtained by making 'an application for judicial review'.

It has proved extremely popular; but there have been problems. In 1983 the law lords refused to allow claimants to use any other legal procedures if the case was one involving administrative law.[66] If it is a public law case the applicant must apply for judicial review; if private law, the claimant has to issue a writ in the normal way. If he picks the wrong form of action his case will be thrown out. This caused difficulties because it is not always clear whether a case is one of public law or private law. More recently the courts have softened their approach in borderline cases.

Judicial review has now become a victim of its own success. It is a bit like the M25 motorway: if you create a structure which people find useful, more and more people will use it until it becomes too overcrowded to get them to their chosen destination within a reasonable period of time.[67] It is necessary to seek 'leave', or permission, to apply for judicial review: in 1984 there were fewer than 1,000 applications for leave while in 1992 there were nearly 2,500.[68] In the first nine months of 1993 there was an increase of 25 per cent in applications for leave compared with the corresponding period in 1992. There was a similar increase in the number of applications for leave which were waiting to be heard in the summer of 1993. The current average waiting times are now ten months for cases heard in the Divisional Court and eighteen months for cases heard by a single judge.[69]

Writing in 1992 Lord Woolf said that the courts faced a 'crisis' over judicial review.[70] Cases were now taking up to two years from decision to judgment and matters were likely to get worse. Professor Wade had written of the judges vigorously scaling the high ground of judicial review and showing no signs of retreating. But, said Lord Woolf, unless changes were made quickly the judges would be swept back off the high ground they occupied in dismal retreat. If they allowed this to happen it would be the public who would suffer.

Lord Woolf added that public confidence in the legal system had been badly dented by the recent miscarriages of justice.[71] He thought matters would be made worse if judicial review ceased to provide the public with the protection it now offered them.

Finally, Lord Woolf anticipated the inevitable government response. Far from being too expensive, he said, the changes he was proposing would actually be cost-effective. They would reduce the hold-ups from which the government itself was suffering.

Lord Woolf said he was 'deeply concerned' by what was happening and that it was necessary, 'as a matter of considerable urgency', to divert some of the cases currently being heard by judges on the Crown Office List to other courts and tribunals. Some cases, he thought, could be heard by QCs sitting as Deputy High Court judges. And in cases where there was no great point of principle to be decided and the decision would affect only the individual bringing the challenge, applications should be heard by Circuit judges in the county court.[72] That would mean they could be heard locally, which was particularly valuable in homelessness cases.

This last suggestion was not implemented by the Lord Chancellor, although he did agree to appoint a number of leading silks as Deputy judges so that they could hear judicial review applications.[73] A senior judge responsible for judicial deployment insisted that these deputies should hear only homelessness cases under the Housing Act, on the spurious grounds that it would be wrong to ask a part-time judge to make a finding against the Crown but acceptable for a Deputy judge to find against a local authority.

The recently retired Master of the Rolls, Lord Donaldson, believed that homelessness cases should be taken out of the scope of judicial review altogether. This was part of his answer to the growing problem of delay. It was 'absurd', he said, that applicants were having to wait so long for their cases to be heard. 'If power is being abused, the abuse must stop at once.' If an abuse was alleged, the question should be resolved quickly so that decision-makers could know whether their planned course of action was lawful or not.

Lord Donaldson was well aware that reducing waiting times would probably lead to an increased case-load. His remedy was to create alternative structures for hearing certain types of case: appeals by homeless persons could be heard by specialist tribunals instead of scarce judges, leaving judicial review as a remedy of last resort if they were to go off the rails.[74]

Reviewing judicial review
In January 1993 the Law Commission issued a consultation paper outlining ways of improving the effectiveness of judicial review.[75] Its 'provisional' views, if accepted, would certainly make it easier for

applicants to challenge administrative decisions in the courts. The Law Commission suggested:

- Cases could be heard more quickly if High Court judges sat outside London, judges nominated to the Crown Office List spent more time hearing judicial review cases, or selected Circuit judges and Queen's Counsel sat as Deputy High Court judges.

- In cases where there were overlapping issues of public law and private law, applicants should not be restricted to the limited remedies available under judicial review.

- The present time-limit for making an application – three months from the disputed decision – should be extended, perhaps by another three months, provided the applicant was not guilty of delaying the proceedings.

- It should still be necessary for an applicant to seek leave before applying for judicial review but the respondent should be asked to give his views in writing rather than orally as is now increasingly the case.

- The courts should have the power to grant interim injunctions (temporary orders) against the Crown. (The House of Lords subsequently decided that the courts already had that power: see the case of *M. v. Home Office*[76] discussed in chapter 1.)

- In deciding whether an applicant has sufficient 'standing' to bring an application for judicial review the courts should continue their present broad approach. It should be easier for those less directly involved in a decision affecting the public in general to bring a 'citizen action' challenge.

The Law Commission's provisional report was well received although there was little confidence that the government would offer its support for the commission's considered views when these were published in 1994.

A report of a very different kind was released in June 1993. The Public Law Project, a charitable body established to undertake research into public law and to improve citizens' access to justice, published a major research study into the use of judicial review.[77] It looked in detail at all the applications for judicial review during the years 1987, 1988 and 1989, together with the first three months of 1991. The years 1987–9 may seem rather a long time ago for a fast-moving subject like judicial review but the analysis was based on information collected by one of the authors for a previous study, updated by further research on cases started early in 1991.

The authors discovered that while the overall number of judicial review applications in 1992 was more than four times the figure for 1981 much of that increase was covered by applications in a small number of subject areas. Immigration cases accounted for nearly 45 per cent of applications at their peak in 1987 but they subsequently declined to less than 23 per cent in 1991. Applications in housing cases rose steadily from less than 10 per cent in 1987 to nearly 24 per cent in 1991.

Since judicial review can be used to challenge such a wide range of government activities the authors were surprised to find few applications in certain key areas of government action. There were relatively few applications relating to the millions of decisions taken every year on social welfare benefits. Other areas which the authors said were largely untouched by judicial review included health, environmental protection, children's rights, social care and housing (other than homelessness). They suggested that however accessible judicial review may seem from a legal point of view other factors – such as the availability of funding or of legal advice – provided a major barrier to its use. [78]

The Public Law Project found that judicial review was not being used primarily as a challenge to central government despite its popular image as a restraint on the executive. In the first three months of 1991 there were more applications against local authorities than there were against government departments. [79] Looking in more detail at the central government cases the researchers found that a large (but diminishing) number involved the Home Office, which is the department responsible for immigration and asylum cases. There were only five other government departments that received ten or more challenges in any of the years covered by the research – Environment, Social Security, Transport, Inland Revenue and the Welsh Office. Applications against the Department of the Environment were rising steadily.

The report listed judges according to the percentage of cases in which they granted leave and found some very much less willing to grant leave than others. One judge had a strike rate, in successive years, of 21 per cent, 25 per cent and 37 per cent. This compared with other judges who granted leave in 82 per cent, 68 per cent and 78 per cent of cases during the same three years. There is no obvious reason for this remarkable difference of approach but the researchers noted that individual judges displayed a high level of consistency and they concluded that the judge's attitude had a good deal to do with the decision to grant or refuse an application for leave.

This conclusion is more than a little disappointing. The whole point of nominating a small number of judges to the Crown Office List (currently 18) was to encourage consistency. The answer must be to reduce the number of judges further and have them sit for longer periods. Specialisation would improve the quality and speed of their work, while a smaller group should produce greater consistency.

Judicial review has done much to improve standards of public administration. Officials are now well aware that they must act reasonably, that they must consult those affected by their decisions, that they must give reasons where appropriate and satisfy people's legitimate expectations. We have a lot to thank the judges for. They have forged for themselves a sword powerful enough to cut through great thickets of administrative action. Perhaps it is not so surprising that – in some areas of work at least – the government has let that sword become blunted by constant use.

The European Court of Justice

The European Court of Justice at Luxembourg is the common market court: its correct title is the Court of Justice of the European Communities.[80] As such, it is the court to which the twelve member countries and the community institutions bring their disputes. But it has another role of more direct relevance to citizens of the European Union (as the European Community has become since the Treaty of Maastricht came into force in November 1993).

European Community law (as we may perhaps still call it) is part of our own law.[81] European treaties are directly enforceable in the United Kingdom without the need for further legislation.[82] They amount to primary legislation. Secondary legislation includes *regulations* and *directives* made in Brussels by the Council of Ministers of the European Union and the European Commission.[83] Regulations are directly applicable in the United Kingdom; once made, they normally have immediate effect. Directives do not usually have any effect on the laws of the United Kingdom until they have been implemented by domestic legislation. However, member states which have not implemented directives within the time specified are not allowed to escape from their obligations: if a claimant takes action against the state he or she can generally rely on the directive as if it had been implemented. In this context the 'state' is given a broad interpretation, wide enough to include a local authority, a health authority or a nationalised industry.[84]

It should be a fairly straightforward task for a court in the United Kingdom to enforce Community law. If there is any doubt on how European law applies to a particular problem a court can ask the European Court for an authoritative 'preliminary ruling' under Article 177 of the Treaty of Rome.[85] Even a lowly tribunal or magistrates' court may do this. If the final court of appeal – which generally means the House of Lords – has doubts about Community law then it *must* refer the question to the European Court unless certain exceptions apply.

While all this is happening proceedings in the national court have to be suspended; interim relief may be granted to protect the parties' rights while they wait for a decision.

Needless to say, the European Court at Luxembourg works on the continental pattern. There is considerable reliance on written documents; the oral hearing is brief by English standards.[86] This is followed some weeks later by an *opinion* from an Advocate General at the court.

The Advocate General's opinion is not very easy to explain to people in Britain. Staff at the European Court insist that it is not a 'preliminary ruling' although this is the phrase most often used to describe it. The Advocate General is not in fact an advocate, still less a general.[87] He is, in reality, a judge: he listens to the case along with the other judges and gives his views on it before they do. His opinion is not the last word, however: that will emerge from the court some months later, after the other judges have had time to consider the Advocate General's views.

Perhaps the best known Advocate General is to be found in *The Merchant of Venice*. Portia offers the Duke of Venice her opinion that Shylock is entitled to his pound of flesh but 'no jot of blood'. The Duke is a layman, not a judge; he has sent for a 'learned doctor of laws' to 'determine' the case. Portia pretends to be that doctor of laws; her opinion is in fact a judgment which the Duke is more than happy to adopt as his own.

The judges of the European Court often adopt the Advocate

General's opinion, so it provides a good pointer towards the eventual outcome.[88] But as there is no guarantee that they will do so, celebrations by a successful litigant may be premature.

The European Court of Human Rights

While the United Kingdom hesitates about giving full rein to the European Convention on Human Rights, countries like Russia, Croatia and even Albania are showing no such doubts. They have all applied for full membership of the Council of Europe, the international organisation through which the Convention is enforced.

The Council of Europe was set up in 1949. By the end of 1993 it had 32 member states, including eight from the former Soviet bloc. Among countries which have joined since 1990 are Hungary, Poland, the Czech Republic and Slovakia.[89] Seven more countries were waiting to join. The Council of Europe is entirely separate from the European Union – although, confusingly, the parliament of the European Union generally meets at the Council of Europe's headquarters in the French city of Strasbourg.

The Council of Europe has reached agreement on some 150 conventions and treaties, on topics ranging from data protection to football hooliganism. They are binding on those countries that have accepted them: the United Kingdom has accepted more than 90. Of these, the European Convention on Human Rights is by far the most important. It is enforced through the European Court of Human Rights at Strasbourg – the Human Rights Court.

The Convention was drawn up in 1950 and signed by 15 countries. It took effect in 1953 although at first proceedings could only be brought in the Human Rights Court by one state against another.

In 1966 the British government agreed to allow individuals to go direct to the Human Rights Court and argue that their rights had been violated by decisions for which the government was responsible: *the right of individual petition*, as it is called. This momentous decision was taken by a Labour government with little public discussion: there was not even a debate in parliament on what amounted to a transfer of sovereignty from Westminster to the court at Strasbourg. Between 1966 and 1994 67 cases involving the United Kingdom were referred to the European Court of Human Rights. Of the 49 cases decided by September 1994 the United Kingdom had lost 31 and won 18.

This has been seen by many as a sad indictment of Britain's attitude towards human rights. Only Italy has a worse record: the Italians allowed the right of individual petition in 1973 and over the next twenty years Italy lost 81 of the 114 cases which were referred to the Human Rights Court. In mitigation of Britain's record it is fair to add that the United Kingdom has allowed individuals to take cases to the court for longer than some other major European countries: France did not introduce the right of individual petition until 1981 and in thirteen years the French government managed to lose 26 cases of the 56 sent to the court.[90] Britain also suffers from its refusal to incorporate the European Convention into domestic law: the fact that litigants cannot take proceedings under the Convention in the United Kingdom courts makes it inevitable that proportionately more cases will be taken to Strasbourg. The question of incorporating the Convention will be considered in the next section.

The procedure for taking a case to the Human Rights Court is daunting and cumbersome. An applicant begins by writing to the European Commission on Human Rights at Strasbourg. The Commission filters out cases which are inadmissible under the Human Rights Convention, as the vast majority turn out to be. Commission staff have been receiving about 5,500 cases a year, of which only about 200 are declared admissible. In 1992 just 12 British applications were found admissible out of 222 submitted.

This may well be because many people have only the haziest notion of what the European Convention actually says. 'I'm going to take my case to Europe' has become the refrain of defeated litigants and indeed almost anyone dissatisfied with some aspect of the legal system in Britain: most are rapidly disillusioned.

The Commission is made up of independent jurists put forward by the member states: in 1985 Britain nominated Sir Basil Hall whose former job as Treasury Solicitor – the civil servant who heads the government's legal service – gave him little opportunity to develop the jurisprudence of human rights. However, he was succeeded in August 1993 by Nicolas Bratza QC. Although Mr Bratza spent a great deal of time before his appointment defending the British government at the Human Rights Court he remained an independent barrister of liberal instincts. He would be well placed to become the British judge on the European Court.

If the Commission finds the case is admissible it then investigates the facts (in private) to see if a 'friendly settlement' is possible. If that fails, the Commission will announce its opinion of the case. It can then refer it to the Human Rights Court for a ruling but this is not inevitable. Some cases, generally those where there is thought to be a clear precedent, stay with the Committee of Ministers whose members are the foreign ministers of the member states. But these politicians are not expected to decide cases: in practice, decisions are taken by officials – the 'permanent representatives' of the member governments at Strasbourg. This has led to some questionable rulings in the past: it is clearly wrong that civil servants should have the power to dismiss allegations that governments have violated human rights.

There have been more than 20,000 applications to the European Commission but by April 1994 only 461 cases had been referred to the Human Rights Court. The court has one judge for each of the member states although judges do not have to be nationals of the countries which nominated them. When Liechtenstein could not find a judge of its own it nominated a Canadian called Ronald Macdonald.[91] States put up three names for consideration by the Parliamentary Assembly of the Council of Europe, but this is less democratic than it appears because the Assembly invariably votes for the candidate whose name has been placed at the top of the list by the government concerned.

Britain's judge is Sir John Freeland, a former legal adviser to the Foreign Office. So was his predecessor at the court, Sir Vincent Evans.[92] It is remarkable that the British government should appoint people with no judicial experience to a position of such sensitivity and influence. However distinguished they may be as lawyers, retired civil servants are not likely to have the independence of mind required of a judge. Sir John is a man of the highest integrity and was well used to giving the government of the day independent legal advice. One Foreign Office source said he was clearly the best person for the job, adding that other countries happily made political appointments to the European Court of Human Rights. But according to another Foreign Office source ministers had belatedly realised that it was wrong to nominate lawyers who would not qualify for appointment to the English courts as members of the European Human Rights Court and Commission. The source said the recent appointment of Nicolas

Bratza QC to the Commission demonstrated that the policy had now changed. This is all very well, but as Sir John Freeland's appointment is due to run until the year 2000[93] his tenure may not be entirely comfortable. It is an acknowledged part of the national judge's role to explain the idiosyncrasies of his own legal system to other judges on the court; but it takes a brave judge to stick up for what he believes to be right when he knows he will be accused of supporting the government which previously employed him and which nominated him to the Human Rights Court.

This was indeed the accusation levelled against Sir John in the case of *Campbell v. United Kingdom*.[94] The court held, by eight votes to one, that the government was in breach of a prisoner's human rights by opening letters from his solicitor. Sir John was the only judge persuaded by the British government's arguments. In the *Costello-Roberts* case[95] the court decided by five votes to four that the 'slippering' inflicted on a seven-year-old boy by his headmaster did not amount to degrading treatment or punishment. Sir John was one of the five judges who accepted Britain's defence of corporal punishment although he conceded that the case was 'at or near the borderline'. If he had come down on the other side of that line Jeremy Costello-Roberts would have been awarded compensation and corporal punishment would have been ended in British schools.

If a case is referred to the Human Rights Court there will be a brief oral hearing. The judges will then take several months to prepare their written judgments. The court often agrees with the European Commission's view but in recent British cases the court has seemed more reluctant than the Commission to rule against the British government.

If the government loses the case there is no immediate effect on the laws of the member state. The court's rulings do not have the same status as decisions of the European Court of Justice at Luxembourg which at once become part of the laws of the United Kingdom. Decisions from the Human Rights Court in Strasbourg are binding in the sense that failure to comply with the court's ruling would be a breach of the United Kingdom's treaty obligations under the Convention. The government is therefore required to amend the law accordingly.

This has had a significant effect on human rights in Britain. As a result of decisions by the Human Rights Court:

- The rules were changed so it was no longer necessary for prisoners to petition the Secretary of State for permission to consult a solicitor.

- A number of interrogation techniques in Northern Ireland were discontinued.

- The law on contempt of court was modified by the Contempt of Court Act 1981.

- It was made easier for workers to opt out of joining a trade union.

- Changes were made to the prison regulations to end automatic censorship of correspondence.

- Telephone tapping was brought under legislative control.

- The Immigration Rules were changed in 1985 so that men and women should be treated equally.[96]

- The Access to Personal Files Act 1987 enabled individuals to see personal information held on them by local authority departments.

- The Criminal Justice Act 1991 allowed the parole board to decide on the release of discretionary life sentence prisoners.

In observing the letter of a ruling from the European Court of Human Rights successive governments have generally changed the law as little as possible; but they have never simply ignored a decision of the court.

There is, however, a get-out clause. Article 15(1) of the Human Rights Convention says:

> In time of war or other public emergency threatening the life of the nation any High Contracting Party may take measures derogating from its obligations under this Convention to the extent strictly required by the exigencies of the situation, provided that such measures are not inconsistent with its other obligations under international law.

The power to 'derogate' from the Convention – in effect, to ignore its provisions – was tested in a series of cases relating to terrorism in Northern Ireland. They date from the autumn of 1984 when four men were arrested and detained under the Prevention of Terrorism Act for periods ranging from four days and six hours to nearly seven days. Article 5(3) of the Convention says that:

> Everyone arrested . . . shall be brought promptly before a judge . . . and shall be entitled to trial within a reasonable time or to release pending trial.

In November 1988 the European Court of Human Rights decided that the Convention did not allow detention even for as short a time as four days and six hours without a court appearance.[97]

A month later the United Kingdom Permanent Representative to the Council of Europe presented his compliments to the Secretary General of the Council and with them a *note verbale* announcing that the United Kingdom had 'availed itself of the right of derogation conferred by Article 15(1) of the Convention and will continue to do so until further notice'.[98] So much for the court's ruling.

Sure enough, within a couple of weeks two more men were detained under the Act for periods which turned out to be longer than four days and six hours. They too complained that there had been a breach of Article 5(3) – the right to be brought promptly before a judge. Crucially, they claimed that the derogation lodged in December 1988 did not comply with Article 15 because measures taken by the British government were not 'strictly required by the exigencies of the situation'. The case came before a court of 26 judges and in May 1993 the judges rejected the men's claim by a majority of 22 votes to 4.[99]

The Human Rights Court ruled that states should be allowed a wide 'margin of appreciation', or discretion, in deciding whether there was a 'public emergency threatening the life of the nation'. In any event, the judges had no doubt that there was just such an emergency at the present time. The court concluded that the British government 'had not exceeded their margin of appreciation in considering that the derogation was strictly required by the exigencies of the situation'. It followed that the derogation was valid.

This was a disappointing decision. No doubt the other countries of Europe did not wish to be seen telling the British government how best to fight terrorism. Also it is arguable that the emergency in Northern Ireland does threaten the life of the province. However, despite all the killings and the bombings in Great Britain it is hard to maintain that the life of the United Kingdom as a whole is threatened by the terrorists. If that were really so, the IRA would have won.

The European Convention on Human Rights has now become too successful for its own good.[100] It currently takes five or six years, on average, to get a decision from the European Court, not counting the time taken to hear the case in its country of origin. This comes as less of a surprise when one realises that the European Court of Human Rights and the European Commission on Human Rights are still part-time bodies, meeting only for some sixteen weeks a year (although there is a huge full-time administrative staff). In 1993 the Council of Europe agreed to simplify and streamline the two-tier system of handling cases. The growing number of member states made this a particular priority.

A single Human Rights Court

At a summit meeting in Vienna in October 1993 the 32 members of the Council of Europe agreed to replace the existing Commission and court with a new single European Court of Human Rights. The United Kingdom was originally holding out for some sort of two-tier process but Britain came round to the idea of a single court in May 1993 when it became clear that the vast majority of member states supported it. Officials had hoped to finalise the structure of the new court in time for the Vienna summit but there was still disagreement on some important details. The political leaders extended the deadline for finalising the new structure to May 1994.[101] However, the reforms will have to be ratified by all the member states and so the new court may not hear its first case much before the end of the century.

The planned single court will sit full-time. It will consist of one judge for each of the countries which are members of the Council of Europe at the time when the court is set up. Judges will now have to retire at the age of 70. And there will be an end to the questionable practice of allowing ministers, or effectively officials, to decide individual applications.

Hopeless cases will be thrown out at an early stage by a *committee* of three judges. The remaining cases will normally be heard by a *chamber* of seven judges, one of whom will be from the country in the dock. But if a case 'raises a serious question affecting the interpretation of the [Human Rights] Convention' or if the court is considering overturning one of its earlier decisions the chamber 'may, at any time before it has rendered its judgment, relinquish jurisdiction in favour of the *Grand Chamber*, unless one of the parties to the case objects'.[102] The Grand Chamber will consist of 17 judges.

The British government was keen that the new court should have 'a proper appeal system'.[103] It seemed the United Kingdom wanted two bites at the cherry: if there was no longer to be a two-stage process Britain wanted a second chance to argue its case before the court. This seems undesirable: one of the great merits of a decision from the existing European Court of Human Rights is its finality. However, Council of Europe officials were persuaded that there should be a rehearing in 'exceptional cases'. This is meant to 'ensure the quality and consistency of the case-law'.[104]

There is to be no appeal from a decision of the Grand Chamber: its decisions will be final. But if the case has been decided by a chamber of seven judges then any party will have three months to ask for the case to be referred to the Grand Chamber. A panel of five judges from the Grand Chamber is bound to accept that request if the case raises a 'serious issue affecting the interpretation or application of the Convention' or 'a serious issue of general importance'.[105] That means the judgment of an ordinary chamber will only become final if the parties announce that they will not be asking for it to be referred to the Grand Chamber, or if the panel of judges refuse leave to appeal, or if nothing has happened within three months.

This is most unsatisfactory. The court's reasoned judgment will be published, but not until it has become final. In the meantime, the judgment of a chamber will, of course, be given to the parties so that they can decide whether to seek a rehearing. As a result the parties will be able to sit on a judgment for up to three months. It is much more likely that the winning side will leak it selectively to the media. Individual chambers should publish their decisions immediately they are delivered, even if there is the possibility of a further hearing.

Although the broad structure of the new court had been agreed by the time of the Vienna summit in October 1993 a crucial issue remained outstanding: the right of individual petition. As we have seen, individuals may only challenge a decision in the European Court of Human Rights if the government responsible has granted them this right. It is the practice of the United Kingdom to renew the right of individual petition for fixed periods of around five years at a time.

Under this arrangement the British government can decide from time to time whether its citizens should retain the right to challenge its decisions in the Human Rights Court. So long as the right of individual petition is optional, it can be withdrawn if ministers find they are losing too many cases. At the least, disgruntled ministers could fire a shot across the court's bows by renewing the right of individual petition for a shorter period than normal – three years perhaps, or even one year.

Most countries in the Council of Europe believed that individuals should be guaranteed the right to take cases to the new European

Court of Human Rights. They rejected the idea that states should be able to withdraw this fundamental right if they pleased.

Council of Europe officials put the issue before a 'committee of experts'. Confidential minutes of a meeting held by the Steering Committee for Human Rights in September 1993 show that 'twenty-three experts thought the right of individual petition should be mandatory'. Just three experts said it should be optional. One of them was a senior Foreign Office lawyer.

If Britain's view had prevailed individuals would not have been able to take a case to the Human Rights Court unless there was a current declaration from the state involved that it recognised the competence of the court to receive such applications. Under the majority proposal there would be an automatic right for an individual to bring a case against a government.

It was disappointing to see the British government holding out, in the face of overwhelming opposition, for the power to withdraw human rights from its citizens. Lord Mackay, representing the British government at the Vienna summit in the absence of the prime minister, seemed reluctant even to admit that this was the government's position. Asked whether individuals would be guaranteed the right to take cases to the court in Strasbourg, the Lord Chancellor said that was 'a separate question' from reorganisation of the court. Pressed on whether the right of individual petition would be renewed under the new arrangements Lord Mackay replied: 'That question doesn't arise for some time and I would think the government will decide it in the light of circumstances at the time but, as far as I personally am concerned, I would expect the right of individual petition to be renewed when the time comes for that.' Pressed further he said that 'in the new circumstances we shall have to reconsider' the right of individual petition, while stressing that it had worked perfectly well in the past as far as the United Kingdom was concerned.[106]

This public ambivalence reflected a private disagreement between government departments. The Home Office was tired of losing cases at the Human Rights Court and it wanted the theoretical option of picking up the stumps and walking off the pitch. This was a miserable and narrow-minded approach which simply confirmed the popular image of the British as 'bad Europeans'.[107] Other countries will not have been too impressed when Lord Mackay reminded them that much of the European Convention on Human Rights had been drafted by his predecessor (and fellow Scot) Lord Kilmuir.[108]

However, the Foreign Office realised that this was not the way any future British government would want to play the game. It was inconceivable that the right of individual petition would ever be withdrawn. Why, then, give people the impression that it might be?

Eventually, the Home Office caved in and the Foreign Office view prevailed.[109] Britain dropped its opposition to a mandatory right of individual petition at the last moment and duly signed the new Protocol to the European Convention on Human Rights at a meeting in Strasbourg in May 1994. Article 34 says the Court may receive an application from any person claiming to be the victim of a violation by a member state.

A Bill of Rights?

The fact that the European Convention on Human Rights has not been incorporated into the domestic legal systems of the United Kingdom means, broadly speaking, that the English courts are under no obligation to enforce its provisions. Although some other European countries have also not incorporated the European Convention they all have written constitutions establishing fundamental human rights. In having neither, Britain stands alone.

Many people feel the time has come to incorporate the European Convention. That would require legislation: parliament would be asked to approve a new Bill of Rights.

In his Dimbleby Lecture towards the end of 1992 the Lord Chief Justice, Lord Taylor, said, 'We should have the courage of our treaty obligations and incorporate the convention.' At present, we fell between two stools:

> The United Kingdom was a signatory to the European Convention and ratified it in 1950. We are bound by it as a treaty and we have accepted the compulsory jurisdiction of the Court of Human Rights at Strasbourg. But we have still, 40 years on, not made the convention part of our domestic law . . . Our judges are not bound by the convention. Where there is a conflict, English law prevails. The aggrieved party then takes his case to Strasbourg. If the court there finds in his favour, four results follow. First, the government is bound under the treaty to amend our law to accord with the Strasbourg judgment. Secondly, the final result of the instant case is delayed, usually by several years. Thirdly, other cases may have been similarly and, as it turns out, wrongly decided by our domestic court meanwhile. Fourthly, the standing and reputation of our justice system becomes badly bruised . . . It is as if we said, in 1950, the well-known prayer: 'God make us good – but not yet.'[110]

The Lord Chancellor disagreed. Lord Mackay argued that the present arrangements gave the government more flexibility in changing the laws after an adverse judgment. And he pointed out that incorporating the Convention would not stop people taking their cases to Strasbourg, although he conceded that it was likely that fewer people would need to do so. Lord Mackay made it clear that the government had no plans to incorporate the Convention.[111] He also argued that the Convention was not suitable for direct incorporation because of the broad language in which it was drafted.[112]

However, there was support for incorporation from other judges such as the Master of the Rolls, and from opposition politicians such as the leader of the Labour Party. In March 1993 the Law Society's council unanimously supported incorporation of the Convention.

Giving the Denning Lecture in 1993 Sir Thomas Bingham conceded that incorporating the European Convention would not usher in the New Jerusalem:

> But the change would over time stifle the insidious and damaging belief that it is necessary to go abroad to obtain justice. It would restore this country to its former place as an international standard-bearer of liberty and justice. It would help to reinvigorate the faith, which our eighteenth and nineteenth century forbears would not for an instant have doubted, that these were fields in which Britain was the world's teacher, not its pupil. And it would enable the judges more effectively to honour their ancient and sacred undertaking to do right to all manner of people after the laws and usages of this realm, without fear or favour, affection or ill will.[113]

In calling for incorporation of the European Convention the Lord Chief Justice and the Master of the Rolls were echoing the pioneering campaign of Leslie Scarman. Lord Scarman retired in 1986 after all too short a period as the senior law lord. He became known to the public as the author of the report into the Brixton riots of 1981 but among lawyers he is respected for his tireless campaign in favour of a Bill of Rights. That campaign began with Lord Scarman's Hamlyn Lectures in December 1974;[114] nearly two decades later he was still arguing in favour of incorporating the European Convention.[115] It is time his words were heeded.

That will not happen, however, until there is a change of government. What can be done in the meantime? In a lecture delivered in 1991 Lord Browne-Wilkinson explained that there was already a good deal the judges could do by themselves.[116]

First, there is the chance of using European Community law. As we have seen, European law is part of our own law; in any conflict European law will prevail. And, argued Lord Browne-Wilkinson, the European Court of Justice generally complies with the European Convention on Human Rights when reaching decisions on European Community law. 'It seems,' he said, 'that in those areas affected by the European Community Treaties the European Convention on Human Rights is already incorporated into English domestic law.' This ingenious theory has yet to be tested; our courts have been reluctant to bring in the Convention by the back door while parliament has left the front door firmly bolted.[117]

Lord Browne-Wilkinson therefore turned instead to the common law and pointed to examples where the courts had applied strict rules of statutory construction. 'In each case, the statutory provision, although wide enough on its literal meaning to authorise the act complained of, was strictly construed so as to exclude the doing of acts which curtailed individual freedom.' Within the common law itself, he argued, there were to be found tools which, if it was thought fit, could protect our freedoms from anything short of a deliberate wish by parliament to invade them.

Lord Browne-Wilkinson managed to unearth those tools while hearing the case of *Derbyshire County Council v. Times Newspapers Ltd.*[118] As we saw in chapter 1, the law lords concluded that the common law was consistent with the Human Rights Convention. This is perhaps not so much of a surprise as all that: the British lawyers who drafted the European Convention drew heavily on the common law for their inspiration.

The Labour leader, John Smith, argued in March 1993 that 'Parliament should pass a Human Rights Act that incorporates the rules of the Human Rights Convention directly into British law and gives citizens the right to enforce those rules in the courts.'[119] To help people assert their rights John Smith called for an independent Human Rights Commission in Britain along the lines of the Equal Opportunities Commission and the Commission for Racial Equality. Under Labour's plan, the protection offered by the Human Rights Act would only be available to individuals, not companies: Labour was worried by the sight of large corporations in other countries trying to resist social legislation by claiming that it infringed their 'human' rights.

Speaking to the constitutional reform group Charter 88 in March 1993 John Smith acknowledged that there would be nothing to stop parliament overruling that Act in subsequent legislation. However, Mr Smith planned to erect political obstacles which he thought would protect his Human Rights Act from being undermined by the courts: these would include a section saying that any further legislation intended to introduce laws inconsistent with the Convention would have to do so in express terms.

Here we are in murky waters. Some supporters of a Bill of Rights believe it should be 'entrenched', in other words protected from amendment or repeal unless there was support from a special majority of MPs – say two-thirds or three-quarters. But most commentators believe that would be impossible because no parliament may bind its successors. And if that is the law, no parliament can insist that its successors must use express terms if they wish to amend earlier legislation.[120]

In any event, what seemed to worry Mr Smith was the risk of being 'undermined by the courts' rather than by parliament. John Smith QC MP seemed more concerned by his colleagues in the law than by his fellow MPs. This was even more apparent in an earlier part of his speech. The justification for Britain's refusal to incorporate the European Convention was said to be that British citizens had the protection of the common law. But, Mr Smith argued,

> the extent and limits of those rights are controlled by the judges and not by parliament. This is a significant weakness. The task of the judges is to interpret and apply the law, not to make it. Democracy demands that fundamental rules governing citizens' behaviour, and fundamental rights protecting citizens' freedoms, should be decided by parliament and not by the judges.

So spoke a Member of Parliament, calmly asserting that MPs can provide for every eventuality and the judges will not need to make new law. But that is a counsel of perfection. Incorporating the European Convention will not relieve our judges of having to make new law – in fact, the opposite is true. The European Convention on Human Rights is indeed couched in much broader terms than the statutes we are familiar with in Britain. That is hardly surprising: it was intended to lay down fundamental laws in a rapidly changing world.

Here, then, was the basic inconsistency in Mr Smith's speech. By giving our own courts the power to interpret its provisions we are giving the judges a huge measure of discretion to fashion human rights law in the way they see fit. They would indeed be 'making' law and, because of the political obstacles erected by Mr Smith, parliament would be almost powerless to stop them.

This is something that would worry any politician: it must be the main reason why successive governments have not let British judges loose on the European Convention. But it may be no bad thing. It all comes down to who we believe will be better at protecting human rights. We may not think much of our judges in that role but successive British governments do not have a particularly impressive record either. And we have already noted (in chapter 2) how the judges have supplanted the parliamentary opposition in recent years. To paraphrase Lord Denning: we have got to trust someone – let it be the judges.

5.

Legal Aid

The rise and fall of civil legal aid

The introduction of a system of legal aid funded by the state was rightly described by a senior judge as one of the major legal reforms of the twentieth century.[1] But many fear the life will have gone out of the legal aid system long before the twentieth century itself draws peacefully to a close. Legal aid is costing more and doing less. During its brief existence the system has gone through four distinct phases: foundation, expansion, looming crisis and – most recently – sharp decline.[2]

The foundation period started in 1945 – when a committee chaired by Lord Rushcliffe first proposed that civil legal aid should be available for people of 'small or moderate means'[3] – and continued until 1970, when the first law centre was opened in North Kensington. A period of rapid expansion followed from 1970 to 1986, when the last major improvement was introduced – the police station duty solicitor scheme. By 1986, however, there were signs of a growing crisis as the cost of legal aid began to spiral out of control. That crisis suddenly arrived in 1992, bringing with it a new period of sharp decline. The examples quoted below are taken from this period. Its start can be dated, quite precisely, to 24 October 1992 when the Lord Chancellor made a keynote speech on legal aid to the Law Society's annual conference in Birmingham – what we shall call his 'Birmingham Manifesto'.[4] We shall begin this chapter by considering each of these periods in turn.

> • *A 75-year-old widow from Birmingham approached a solicitor on 23 April 1993 in connection with a personal injuries claim. The client has no savings and her only source of income is her old age pension of £61.52 per week. If she had applied two weeks earlier she would have been eligible for legal advice and assistance without having to pay a contribution. She now falls outside the scope of legal advice by just 52 pence.*
>
> • *A Rochdale man sought legal advice on hearing from his former cohabitant that she intended to move to the Shetland Islands with their 10-year-old daughter. The daughter has indicated that she wishes to stay with her father. The client therefore wanted assistance in making applications for parental responsibility, prohibited steps and residence orders. The client's disposable income has been assessed at £138.86. Before 12 April 1993 he would have been eligible for legal advice and assistance, provided he paid a contribution of £70. He is now ineligible.[5]*

Foundation

Most of the Rushcliffe committee's recommendations were implemented in 1950 when the Legal Aid Act 1949 took effect. Parliament created a system of civil legal aid which pays for solicitors (and, where appropriate, barristers) to help people bring or defend cases[6] before the civil courts (but not tribunals). The broad shape of the scheme has remained unchanged. Applicants have to pass a means test although those with disposable income or capital above certain limits must pay a contribution:[7] astonishing though it may seem now, when the scheme was established 80 per cent of the population were eligible for legal aid on income grounds. In addition to the means test there is a merits test, designed to ensure that every case has a reasonable prospect of success before public money is spent on it. There is also the notorious *statutory charge* under which a person who gets legal aid may find to his surprise that some of the money he has recovered or preserved is taken to pay for any costs of the action which have not been met by the other party: in that sense, legal aid is a loan rather than a grant.

Crucially, it was decided that legal aid would be 'demand led' rather than 'cash limited' so that everyone who qualified would get legal aid – whatever the government had to pay for it at the end of the year. At least in theory, this is still the case.

The Rushcliffe committee had accepted the Law Society's view that legal aid should be provided by solicitors in private practice. That meant they would continue to do the sort of work they had always been doing: crime, matrimonial work and personal injury. The only real change was that they would be paid by the state (and at slightly lower rates) rather than by the client. It also meant that access to justice depended on whether a suitable solicitor had chosen to set up shop in the area where a potential client happened to be. The Legal Aid Act 1949 even allowed the Law Society – the solicitors' representative body – to run the legal aid scheme (a state of affairs which continued until the Legal Aid Board took over in 1989).

Although the Rushcliffe committee had rejected more adventurous proposals for a publicly run system based on the wartime network of Citizens' Advice Bureaux[8] the seeds of just such a movement germinated in the heady days of the late 1960s, blossoming in 1970 into the country's first law centre.[9] The law centres movement was born of a growing feeling that, despite legal aid, most people would not willingly climb the dusty stairs to a solicitor's office – and even if they did, the solicitor would have little interest in (and even less idea about) areas of social welfare law such as landlord and tenant, housing benefits, employment law, debt, immigration and welfare rights. So by the start of the seventies legal aid had come of age.

Expansion
Between 1970 and 1986 there was a steady expansion in the scope of legal aid. New services were made available: the *Green Form scheme* in 1973 which allowed solicitors to conduct a quick means test and provide immediate 'legal advice and assistance' on any matter of English law;[10] *assistance by way of representation* in 1979 which extended the Green Form scheme to cover certain proceedings in the magistrates' courts;[11] and the *duty solicitor scheme* introduced in 1983 to help unrepresented defendants appearing before magistrates' courts and extended in 1986 to provide instant advice for people arrested by the police (or 'helping with inquiries').[12] Perhaps not surprisingly there was a huge increase in expenditure on legal aid

during this period: from £8 million in 1969–70 to £265 million in 1986–7.[13]

New types of legal aid did not by themselves account for this massive increase in spending. Against the background of a growing crime rate[14] there was a sharp rise in the number of people getting criminal legal aid in the magistrates' courts in 1967 when parliament implemented the Widgery Report[15] (discussed later in this chapter). The Divorce Reform Act of 1969 led to a soaring divorce rate which meant more work for the lawyers and more money being spent on legal aid. It was also a time of social change: the more people who own cars, the more litigation there is against those who sell unroadworthy vehicles; the more people who own houses, the more there is to fight over in the event of a divorce.[16] Bigger workloads for courts and solicitors lead to greater delays which in turn push up costs.

Of course the cost of legal aid depends on how many people are eligible for it. As we have seen, 80 per cent of the population qualified on income grounds in 1950. By 1973 that figure had slumped to 40 per cent. Some six years later the last Labour government announced a dramatic increase in eligibility just before it left office. This was implemented by the incoming Conservative administration and, by 1979, the level was back up to almost 80 per cent again.[17] But in 1993, on the Lord Chancellor's own estimate, just 48 per cent of the country's households were eligible.

Looming crisis

Until 1986 the government had played very little part in the legal aid scheme. The first signs of a legal aid crisis came in the spring of that year when allowances for dependants were suddenly cut – making it more difficult for people with children to meet the financial conditions for help. In 1986 the government also set up a four-month 'scrutiny' of the scheme, organised by the Cabinet Office Efficiency Unit and conducted by three junior officials. Its most controversial recommendation[18] was that large areas of the Green Form legal advice scheme should be taken away from solicitors and transferred to the Citizens' Advice Bureaux (who would then pass on to solicitors cases they could not handle). The Bureaux were initially tempted by this additional role but they later changed their mind and refused to co-operate. The scrutiny report also called for the establishment of a Legal Services Board with overall responsibility for legal aid and advice. There was cautious support among lawyers for an independent body to run the legal aid scheme.

In March 1987 the government responded to the Efficiency Unit scrutiny with a White Paper on legal aid.[19] Like so many other superficially attractive government theories to founder on the harsh rock of practicality, the Citizens' Advice Bureaux proposal was to be shelved – at least in that form.[20] However, the White Paper revealed that a Legal Aid Board would indeed be created, under the guidance of the Lord Chancellor. The government's own Legal Aid Advisory Committee was disappointed that this was not to be the broader Legal Services Board which the scrutiny report had recommended.[21]

Under the Legal Aid Act 1988 the Legal Aid Board was given wide powers to provide legal services. The Board took over the Law Society's job of administering civil legal aid in 1989 although more radical changes were postponed while members and staff built up the necessary expertise. By 1993 the Board was saying it would be willing to take on responsibility for criminal legal aid in 1995, provided fundamental changes were introduced in the meantime.[22]

In November 1989 the Lord Chancellor announced a general review of eligibility for civil legal aid. This was designed to operate at a more leisurely pace than the Efficiency Unit scrutiny. It was to start at the beginning of 1990 and parliament was told it was 'likely to complete its work in two or three years'. In June 1991 it came up with the idea of a 'safety net' to replace the current arrangements for civil legal aid: would-be litigants would have to spend all it was calculated they could afford before being considered for legal aid to continue with the case. If legal aid was refused and the litigation had to be abandoned they would probably end up having to pay the other side's costs as well as their own. Critics of the proposal dismissed it as absurdly misconceived, designed to deter all but the most foolhardy from bringing or defending legal action. At first Lord Mackay seemed unimpressed by the criticism but the government had to back down when the Legal Aid Board itself said that the safety-net proposal was 'too complicated and too burdensome'.[23] The 1989 review was never heard of again; but the Lord Chancellor made it clear that although he had lost this particular battle he was determined to win the legal aid war.

Sharp decline

In October 1992 Lord Mackay launched his Birmingham Manifesto.[24] Legal aid, he said, could not continue to take an ever-increasing share of public expenditure. The net cost of legal aid in 1991–2 was more than £900 million. The figure would rise above £1 billion during 1992–3, more than double what it had been four years earlier. If the current trend were to continue the cost of legal aid would be approaching £2 billion by the middle of the decade.

Noting, with dry understatement, that the safety-net proposals 'were not universally welcomed' Lord Mackay said he was disappointed that many of those who found fault with his ideas could see the way forward only in terms of pouring more public money into the scheme: 'In the present financial climate, that is not realistic. What is certain is that the overall cost of legal aid must be made more affordable. It must also be better targeted – towards those people whose need is greatest and towards those areas of work where it provides the most cost-effective service.'

In other words – cuts. Solicitors had less than a month to wait before discovering where the knife was to fall.

Eligibility cuts

In November 1992, on the same day as the Chancellor of the Exchequer published his Autumn Statement, Lord Mackay announced what he described with deceptive simplicity as measures 'to control the growth of legal aid expenditure'. The importance of a government announcement is often in inverse proportion to the degree of government effort put into publicising it and this announcement was slipped out as a written answer to a parliamentary question. Its significance was immense: the cuts were to be even more dramatic than expected.

These mainly affected civil legal aid, together with advice and assistance under the Green Form scheme: it turned out that the changes – which came into operation in April 1993 – would have hardly any effect on those applying for criminal legal aid.[25]

The first cut reduced the number of people eligible for free civil legal aid. In order to get legal aid without paying a contribution an applicant must show that his 'disposable income' – what he has left after deducting essential living expenses[26] – is below a certain level. In 1992–3 that level was £3,060 a year. From 1993, instead of being increased in line with inflation, it was reduced to £2,294 – the level at which an applicant would be entitled to income support.

Dependants' allowances were also cut to income support levels. This was another way of reducing the number of people eligible for legal aid. In calculating his or her 'disposable income' a claimant can deduct a fixed allowance for a dependant partner or children. Instead of being increased in line with inflation in 1993 the deduction allowed for a partner was reduced from £2,122 to £1,304; for a child under 11 it was down from £948 to £785; and for a child aged 11 to 15 there was a reduction from £1,395 to £1,155.

Certain people are only entitled to legal aid if they are willing to pay part of the cost. But in order to qualify for this 'contributory' legal aid their income must also be below a certain level. In 1993 that 'ceiling' – the maximum disposable income a successful applicant can have – was frozen at £6,800 (or £7,500 in personal injury cases). This was yet another way of reducing the number of people who qualified for legal aid: as people's wages increase in line with inflation they cease to be eligible for assistance unless the eligibility ceiling goes up by the same figure. The government estimated that 8 per cent of households would lose the right to legal aid under these changes.[27]

Higher contributions were introduced and for a longer period: all those granted civil legal aid now have to pay one-third of their disposable income above the lower limit instead of a quarter under the previous arrangements. And – perhaps the last straw for some – those contributions now continue for the lifetime of the case instead of for just one year as before.

People paying small contributions faced enormous increases. Those who had previously paid a contribution of £30 found themselves asked to pay £332 each year in the case of a single person; £463 a year in the case of a couple with no children; and £619 each year for a couple with two children. Lawyers said it was almost inconceivable that their clients could afford these contributions, particularly as they would last as long as the case.[28]

Perhaps the most dramatic change applied to those seeking legal advice and assistance under the Green Form scheme.[29] As with civil legal aid the number of people eligible for free assistance was reduced by restricting it to people whose disposable income was at income support levels. Before the changes anyone with a disposable weekly income below £75 could get assistance free of charge. From April 1993 only those with disposable incomes of less than £61 a week qualified. (The figure went up to £70 in 1994).[30]

That was bad enough. In addition the Lord Chancellor had decided that anyone above this new, low, 'free' level would no longer get legal advice under the Green Form scheme at all. Under the previous arrangements people with disposable weekly incomes above £75 could still get legal advice and assistance so long as they were left with no more than £145 a week after deduction of allowances for their dependants; they then had to pay a contribution ranging between £5 and £75. In 1993 those people who would previously have qualified by paying a contribution were taken out of the scheme altogether. Those with disposable incomes of between £61 and £75 were the worst affected: overnight they were transformed from being so poor that they needed free help into being so rich that they were supposed not to need any help at all.

Solicitors were apoplectic when they grasped what the Lord Chancellor was planning to do – and with every justification. The president of the Law Society, Mark Sheldon, said it was 'the most devastating attack on the legal aid system since it was introduced 40 years ago'.[31] The Legal Action Group, well-respected for its work in the field of welfare law, was right to say that it amounted to an 'unspoken assault on one of the fundamental principles that has underlain legal aid since 1945 – the idea that legal aid should be available to all those who could not otherwise afford lawyers and not just to those "normally classed as poor".'[32] Lawyers subsequently estimated that around 14 million adults would be affected by the proposals, either by having to pay a contribution for the first time or by having to pay a higher contribution than before or by losing eligibility for legal aid altogether.[33]

The poverty trap had widened to a chasm. For years those on middle incomes had known they went to law at their peril. They were unable to afford lawyers' fees except for the most straightforward of personal transactions but had too much money to qualify for legal aid. Now it was only the poorest of the poor who could defend their rights with impunity. A cynic could still claim that the doors of the courts were open to all – not so much like the Ritz Hotel of legal legend[34] but more like the shop doorways opposite where the homeless slept rough every night.[35]

Family lawyers were particularly alarmed by the Lord Chancellor's announcement. The Solicitors Family Law Association predicted that people would not be able to afford to get divorced. Legal

- *A Dorset woman sought urgent legal advice in May 1993 having suffered violence at the hands of her husband over a number of years. The husband had taken steps to prevent his wife gaining access to the matrimonial home and stated that he intended to keep the couple's two children with him. The client alleges she has been repeatedly threatened by her husband. She works seven days a week as a cook and earns £103.15 net. She has no savings, receives no financial support from her husband and has to pay rent. Before 12 April 1993 she would have been eligible for legal advice and assistance if she paid a contribution of £32. She is now ineligible.*

- *A London couple with four children sought legal advice after their youngest child developed severe disabilities following an accident. The family urgently needed advice on whether they could take action under the Children Act to oblige the local authority to rehouse them in suitable accommodation (so that their disabled child would not have to be taken into care). The client is a student with an income of £119 a week. He and his wife are entitled to child benefit so their total income is £154 per week. After making deductions for his wife (of £25) and for the children (of £60.20) he is left with a disposable income of £67.70. Before 12 April 1993 the family would have been eligible for legal advice and assistance with no contribution. Now they are ineligible. They cannot afford to pay privately for advice.[36]*

aid is not available for divorce as such (it was abolished when divorce law was simplified in 1976) but advice about financial matters and children can be obtained under the Green Form scheme. By restricting that advice to people who qualified for income support the Lord Chancellor was severely restricting access to matrimonial help for some of the neediest members of society. The National Consumer Council said it was wrong to abolish contributory Green Form legal advice and assistance. The Council objected to the idea of a single cut-off point: 'instead', it said, 'graduated help should be available for those who are not poor but who cannot afford the full cost of a complex case'.

Even the Lord Chief Justice weighed in on behalf of those who would lose the right to legal aid. In his Dimbleby Lecture Lord Taylor said there were two 'blots' on the justice system – its cost and its delays. 'The shrinkage of those eligible for legal aid,' he said, 'means large numbers of our citizens are denied access to justice.' If citizens' rights were not safeguarded 'the result may not only be injustice but even unrest, especially during high unemployment'.[37]

But it was all to no avail. Pressed to justify these apparently devastating cuts the Lord Chancellor said his aim was to protect the poorest members of society. Lord Mackay maintained that he was not reducing the scope of legal aid: it would still cover the same areas as before. Reducing scope would have been a way forward, he acknowledged, but he thought the solution he had adopted was a more 'imaginative way' of dealing with the problem. 'It protects the people who need the service most,' he said, 'and it continues to give the protection of legal aid to people who are prepared to make a contribution out of their disposable income.'[38]

According to Lord Mackay the cost of legal aid would continue to rise, apparently by a staggering £400 million.[39] However, this unprecedented largesse was more apparent than real. It was true that previous estimates had shown the cost of legal aid for 1993–4 as £885 million; and the Treasury was indeed offering an increase of 45 per cent for that year. For a long time it had been traditional for the Lord Chancellor to get his figures past the Treasury by wildly underestimating the true cost of legal aid. When the bills came in his officials professed surprise that the estimate had turned out to have been too low and asked for a few more millions to make up the difference: it was always granted.[40] Now the Treasury's patience was running out. Reports[41] said it rejected the proffered figures as fiction and the Lord Chancellor conceded that he could no longer defend them as realistic. So, for the first time, the Lord Chancellor was being forced to use real figures and this time he would have to stick to them.

These figures, revised in November 1993, showed that the Treasury was allowing £1,284 million for 1993–4; £1,406 million for 1994–5; and £1,539 million for 1995–6. That meant increases of about 9.5 per cent each year – which the Chancellor of the Exchequer no doubt thought was a reasonably gentle attempt to rein in and control the rising cost of legal aid.[42] The number of people getting legal aid would continue to rise.[43]

The Lord Chancellor's eligibility cuts were meant to save £43 million during 1993–4, the first year of operation. In 1994–5 the estimated saving was to be £110 million, and in 1995–6 it was estimated at £173 million. What nobody could predict was whether the true savings would turn out to be much less – or indeed much more. In fact, the savings turned out to be very much greater than the government had expected: the legal aid bill turned out to be £73 million less than the government had budgeted for in 1993–4, even when the planned savings of £43 million had been taken into account. With hindsight, the cuts turned out to have been much deeper than they needed to be.

Lord Mackay's proposals came under savage attack from the legal profession in the months before they were implemented. In February 1993, for the second year running, solicitors queued up outside the House of Commons to lobby their MPs. At the same time representatives of more than forty consumer groups were meeting in a Commons committee room to explain how clients would suffer from the planned changes. That evening the Lord Chancellor was roundly condemned in the House of Lords.

Speaking from the Labour front bench Lord Irvine of Lairg QC accused Lord Mackay of 'reducing our legal aid system to a rickety ambulance to pick up only the poorest of the poor'. His plans were 'the worst conceivable way of making cuts in the legal aid budget'.[44]

Lord Donaldson, a former Master of the Rolls who might well have become a Conservative Lord Chancellor, added his support: 'I never for one moment thought that it would be necessary to say in your Lordships' House that justice is not an optional extra in a society which is based on the rule of law.' Lord Alexander QC, a former chairman of the Bar who might well become a Conservative Lord Chancellor in the future, expressed 'the gravest qualms' about the government's decision: 'In civil cases,' he said, 'it will inevitably mean that many people will just not be able to pursue their legal rights.'[45]

In a powerful speech, the Lord Chief Justice said that cutting eligibility involved 'an abdication of responsibility to a large section of those for whom the legal aid system was devised'. They were 'draconian cuts'. A 'large band in our community' who 'will become ineligible for legal aid' would have no access to the courts unless they were willing to appear without a lawyer. He continued: 'There is concern not only for those who will become totally disentitled but for those whose required and increased contribution will effectively put them out of court even though they are technically eligible for assistance. I consider that not only deplorable but a surprising proposal from my noble and learned friend on the Woolsack [Lord Mackay].'

Lord Taylor went on to say that the Lord Chancellor's proposals, coupled with plans to 'franchise' legal aid firms (which will be considered later in this chapter), would lead to fewer firms of solicitors doing legal aid work. The government had introduced the Courts and Legal Services Act in 1990 to increase competition and here was the Lord Chancellor introducing measures which would actually cut competition. Lord Taylor urged the Lord Chancellor to consider the plans proposed by the lawyers for saving money. He disclosed that he and the Master of the Rolls, Sir Thomas Bingham, had written to Lord Mackay asking him to look for other ways of controlling expenditure.[46] The Lord Chancellor did not budge an inch.

Parliamentary approval

At the end of March 1993 the House of Commons debated and approved the regulations which implemented Lord Mackay's eligibility cuts. Labour's spokesman, the barrister Paul Boateng, said the Lord Chancellor's proposed changes represented a betrayal of the bipartisan approach which had governed the legal aid scheme since it was introduced in 1949. He blamed the Treasury for its desire to save money at the expense of justice. And he gave poignant examples of the people who would be affected by the changes.

In response to Labour's comments John Taylor, the Lord Chancellor's junior minister, stressed that legal aid would continue to grow at about 10 per cent a year. Almost half of all households would still be eligible for civil legal aid. More than a fifth would be eligible for advice and aid free of charge. And Mr Taylor quoted with satisfaction a comment made by the Labour peer Lord Williams of Mostyn QC: 'Ours is probably the most generous system of legal aid in the world.'

Both men were right. But the government should never have let the legal aid scheme run out of financial control.

Judicial review

Early in April 1993, a few days before the eligibility cuts were due to take effect, the Law Society was granted leave to seek judicial review

- *A Filipino woman living in London with an extremely limited command of English wished to appeal against a decision to refuse her disability benefit. Currently the lady is employed as a waitress and earns £100 a week gross. She has reasonable medical evidence to show that the Department of Social Security may have assessed her case unduly harshly. The client has no capital or savings and is not able to afford to pay privately for the help she needs. Before 12 April 1993 she would have been eligible for legal advice and assistance provided she paid a contribution of £32. She is now ineligible.*

- *Two London women needed advice and assistance in relation to divorcing their abusive husbands. Both women have children and disposable incomes of £65.92 per week and £64.86 per week respectively. Before 12 April 1993 they would each have been eligible for legal advice and assistance free of charge. They are now ineligible.*[47]

of the Lord Chancellor's proposals. The solicitors argued that Lord Mackay had exceeded his powers under the Legal Aid Act and had failed to consult properly before introducing such major changes.

In June 1993 the High Court dismissed the Law Society's application. The eligibility cuts were regrettable but not irrational, it concluded: 'hard . . . choices have to be made by those whose responsibilities include the apportionment of finite resources between competing public services.' Lord Justice Neill and Mr Justice Mantell accepted that a failure to consult those affected may in some circumstances have amounted to a procedural impropriety – which is a ground for judicial review. They acknowledged that the Law Society had a legitimate expectation that it would be consulted in this case. However, Lord Justice Neill said the eligibility cuts had been 'put forward in order to meet a situation which had become much more urgent and critical than had been envisaged only a short time before'. That meant there was no need for the Lord Chancellor to consult the Law Society. And even if he had, it would not have made any difference in the end. Lord Justice Neill concluded: 'It is plain that urgent decisions had to be taken, but reading the papers in this matter I can see no clear recognition on the government side of the fact that the Law Society are capable of looking beyond their own sectional interests and of offering advice and guidance as to what the *public interest* requires.'

This was some consolation to the Law Society for being ordered to pay 75 per cent of the government's costs. The bill was estimated at between £35,000 and £40,000;[48] the Law Society was not entitled to legal aid.

The eligibility cuts are now firmly in place. As we shall see later in this chapter, the cuts, and the hardship they represent, could certainly have been avoided.

Civil legal aid: the future
Quite apart from having to cope with the cuts in eligibility, those solicitors who were still willing to do civil legal aid work had to face more bad news in 1993. The Lord Chancellor was planning to introduce a form of payment for civil cases which solicitors doing criminal work had been fighting to resist.

Standard rates
In his Birmingham Manifesto[49] the Lord Chancellor complained that rates paid for legally aided civil work were 'leaping way ahead of inflation'. Civil work was also paid at a much higher rate than criminal work. Lord Mackay said the rates had to be 'properly controlled' and he made it clear that he planned to introduce a prescribed hourly rate for civil legal aid work (except in matrimonial cases). He added ominously: 'In setting these rates for the future, it is my intention to place emphasis on what is affordable and what is the market rate for legal aid work: that is, the rate which will attract sufficient firms to do the work.'

The rate he proposed was £65 an hour, starting in February 1994. Solicitors said this was a cut of almost 25 per cent compared with current levels of pay: far from attracting sufficient firms it would encourage experienced practitioners to give the work up. Even though it was proposed that rates would be increased in exceptional circumstances (or where there had been 'exceptional competence and dispatch') the Law Society tried to persuade the Lord Chancellor that there should be higher standard rates if the work had been done by a partner or by London-based firms with higher overheads.

Henry Hodge, a legal aid lawyer on the Law Society's Council, recalled that conveyancing solicitors had 'cut each other's throats bidding down rates to keep the dullest of residential conveyancing work'. He suggested that the Lord Chancellor might want legal aid litigators to do the same.[50]

Standard rates ran into difficulties. By July 1994 the Lord Chancellor was saying he hoped to introduce them 'early in 1995'. The hourly rates were still to be fixed.

Franchising

The legal aid solicitor is often to be found in the bleakest of urban landscapes. From his shabby office on the edge of a run-down council estate, or looking out from his upstairs window on a once prosperous high street, he wonders how much longer his bank manager and his family commitments will let him work to help ordinary people with real problems. The desolation he sees all around him is symbolic of the legal aid scheme he seeks to administer. In a dark corner of this grim townscape a small tree is putting down its roots. That young sapling, recently planted by no less a person than the Lord Chancellor, may grow into the great oak which will shelter and nourish the entire legal aid scheme. Or it may be snapped in half by neighbouring solicitors who see it as yet another threat to their precarious livelihood. The new seedling was apparently named after the branches of the fast-food shops that surround it. It is called 'franchising'.

The idea of giving solicitors 'franchises' to do certain types of work can be traced back to a notion first proposed by the Efficiency Unit scrutiny in 1986 – that Green Form advice work should be transferred from solicitors to advice agencies. It soon became clear that this idea would be impracticable in its original form because Citizens' Advice Bureaux were not in a position to take on all the work available. But the Lord Chancellor was keen to find alternative ways of doing legal work. If that meant giving it to people who were not solicitors, there had to be some way of checking that the work was being done to the right standards.

At the same time the government was starting to lay down standards for public services in general. In May 1988 Lord Mackay told the new Legal Aid Board that he expected it to make sure civil legal aid work was done to proper levels of quality. This led the Board to think of ways of ensuring that Green Form work would meet specified requirements.

What should those be? It is not always easy to tell when legal work has been done well; the client's expectations might have been unreasonably high or low. But if it became possible to identify practitioners who were meeting defined standards then the whole idea of legal aid work would change. Instead of allowing *all* solicitors to do legal aid work it would be possible to restrict legal aid to those practitioners who were giving value for money. Indeed, some legal aid work could be done by people who were not lawyers at all. There would be a stick-and-carrot approach: those who applied for a 'franchise' to do legal aid would receive greater rewards than other solicitors and eventually the non-franchised solicitors might lose the right to do legal aid work altogether.

One of the rewards of a franchise would be financial: franchised firms were promised they would receive payments on account instead of having to wait until each case was over. In the long run they might be able to negotiate their own fees for large areas of work. The other reward was administrative. Instead of having to ask the Legal Aid Board for permission to begin work on a case the solicitors would be given delegated authority to grant certain types of legal aid applications themselves – or refuse them where their clients did not qualify. That in itself would save the Board a significant amount of time and therefore money.

This, then, is the essence of franchising: legal aid practitioners are given financial incentives and delegated powers in exchange for meeting specified quality standards. Or, as the Legal Aid Board put it: 'The Board's objectives in promoting franchising are to work in partnership with the profession to provide an accessible and quality assured legal aid service to clients giving improved value for money to the taxpayer.'[51] It is not a game for the small player. Lord Mackay envisaged that 'in some areas and for some types of work, only accredited firms which give an assured standard of service might be eligible to do legal aid cases'.[52] The writing was on the wall for the one-person all-purpose general legal aid practice.

At first the Law Society's support for franchising was less than wholehearted. In 1989 its governing council said that 'franchising as a concept was welcome but its terms needed careful scrutiny'. When the Law Society was asked to endorse the first experimental use of franchising among solicitors in the West Midlands its initial view was that franchising 'offers too little to solicitors'.[53] It was only when the Legal Aid Board offered new forms of payment on account that the solicitors allowed the experiment to begin in the summer of 1990. The Law Society found that negotiating with the Legal Aid Board was 'a much more life-enhancing experience than negotiating with the Lord Chancellor's Department'.[54]

The franchising experiment turned out to be something of a success. One leading Birmingham solicitor who took part said it meant he could help his clients more quickly and more effectively. Graham McGrath wanted to see the scheme extended: he was perfectly happy about the involvement of the Legal Aid Board and the system of quality controls they had imposed on his practice. Indeed, quality monitoring had alerted him to shortcomings among his own staff which of course he had dealt with immediately. But Mr McGrath was concerned about solicitors' pay: he said there was a risk that the Legal Aid Board would 'claw back' the financial advantage that franchised firms had been given.[55]

In the summer of 1993 the Legal Aid Board published the terms on which it was prepared to do business with solicitors. Applications for franchises could be made from October 1993 and it was planned that the first contracts would take effect from 'mid-1994'. They would last for five years.[56] At least 2,600 applications were expected[57] and as the Board was clearly worried about being swamped it encouraged solicitors not to apply until they were ready. Franchises would be offered to independent advice agencies and law centres employing a practising solicitor as well as to firms of solicitors. They would be available in nine types of work and solicitors could apply for franchises in one, some, or all of them. The Board's initial categories were:

- Matrimonial/family
- Crime
- Housing
- Debt
- Employment
- Personal injury
- Welfare benefits

- Consumer/general contract
- Immigration/nationality[58]

Those granted franchises would be permitted to issue emergency legal aid certificates without prior authority from the Legal Aid Board.[59] They would also be allowed certain additional powers connected with the Green Form scheme; in particular they would not need authority to exceed the normal financial limit. And they would be allowed to represent people in court under the assistance by way of representation scheme.

All this was something of a disappointment: the powers were no greater than those given to solicitors involved in the West Midlands experiment. Solicitors had been pressing for the right to authorise full civil legal aid certificates. These would have been almost as good as blank cheques, allowing practitioners to spend substantial sums of money without further authority. But that was for the future. 'In the light of experience,' suggested the Board cautiously, 'it may be possible to extend powers to suppliers whose standards of management control are high, possibly including the grant of civil legal aid under strict conditions.'

The Board recognised the importance of keeping small rural firms in business by its decision to allow all legal aid practitioners to apply for franchises. However, those who were not doing the required number of cases, or who were not doing them to the required standard, would not immediately be given the delegated powers available to other franchise holders. And these powers might be granted only for certain types of work. For example, a firm which did a lot of matrimonial work but little housing might get a franchise for both areas although to begin with it would only be given devolved powers for matrimonial work.

Even if the powers delegated to solicitors were somewhat disappointing the financial incentives for franchised firms were well worth having. Every time solicitors properly granted themselves emergency civil legal aid they would receive £250 on account. 'Assistance by way of representation' would lead to a payment of £150 on account. Green Form cases would be rewarded with payment for the equivalent of two or three hours' work. All these payments would be made within 28 days. However, solicitors would not receive any money if the Board thought they had acted outside the guidelines and misused their delegated powers.

There were other incentives for solicitors franchised to do criminal work. Solicitors would receive the standard fee for this type of work as soon as a legal aid order was granted (rather than at the end of the case). And nine months after the issue of a civil legal aid certificate they would receive 75 per cent of their costs.

It soon became clear that every serious legal aid practitioner would need to apply for a franchise. There were roadshows and seminars to help firms anxious not to be left behind. Solicitors who could not face the paperwork merged with other firms or closed their practices.

The requirements for getting a franchise are demanding. First the Legal Aid Board makes checks on an applicant with the Solicitors Complaints Bureau and the Board's own fraud investigation section. Then a detailed audit is carried out: one of the Board's Liaison Managers monitors the firm's files for up to six months to check how well it is being managed. Before a franchise is granted the Liaison Manager will also check up on the firm's applications for emergency legal aid certificates and extended powers under the Green Form scheme: if too many of these were being refused by the Legal Aid Board, the Board would have reason to doubt whether the firm would authorise its own applications correctly. Bills submitted during this evaluation period will be checked to make sure the applicants are not charging too much.[60] Finally the firm must be willing to go along with certain bureaucratic-sounding standards of organisation and quality – the 'management standards' and the 'transaction criteria'.

Management standards
The Legal Aid Board made its first attempt at setting management standards for solicitors in October 1992.[61] In the language of the times they were to include:

- a strategic management plan covering the medium-term strategy;

- a performance management system based on a staff appraisal process; and

- a financial management system with time recording, cost control, budget forecasts, cash flow statements and a profit and loss account.

Some solicitors saw these requirements as an unwarranted inter-ference with their right to decide how to run their own practices.

The Legal Aid Board disagreed. 'It is not our intention to dictate business decisions,' insisted the chief executive, Steve Orchard, 'it is our intention to see that arrangements are in place that will give the Board certain assurances about the level of service the client will receive.'[62]

Traditionally solicitors' firms, and especially the smaller ones, have been badly managed. Many of them relied on a humble bookkeeper – often a low-paid, long-serving, elderly member of staff – to keep track of hundreds of thousands of pounds. Because the partners were always too busy looking after their clients these highly respected bookkeepers occasionally got away with little-publicised but spectacular frauds, siphoning off huge sums of money which the partners did not know they even had.

For many years the Law Society had had little success in persuading solicitors to improve the way they ran their businesses. It therefore seized the opportunity presented by the Legal Aid Board and set to work on its own draft Practice Management Standards. By April 1993 the solicitors had come up with a document which the Legal Aid Board was willing to incorporate into its own management criteria.[63] All firms were encouraged to adopt these standards, even those which did not do legal aid work.

They amounted to a highly detailed set of requirements for running a modern solicitors' office. Practices had to have a 'written management structure' with an 'outline strategy for the future'. There was emphasis on keeping the client informed and ensuring that any complaints were dealt with. Some of the requirements should hardly have been necessary: solicitors were told that documents must be 'arranged in the file in an orderly way' and staff must have 'ready access to up-to-date legal reference material'.

Behind the jargon was a serious attempt to make the legal profession more professional. Firms were encouraged to adopt a systematic approach to staff recruitment, to provide initial training for new members, to evaluate and appraise employees and to provide continuing training where necessary. It was not the sort of thing that small or medium-sized firms were used to. One said it was a waste of time to give staff regular training and appraisals because none of them stayed very long anyway. Another said that if an employee did not fit in, it was 'cheerio' and time to get someone else.[64]

Transaction criteria

The Legal Aid Board's next task was to discover whether franchising work was being done competently. The Board believed it could get objective evidence of how well a client was being advised and represented by applying what were called 'transaction criteria' to a random selection of files. Transaction criteria were defined as a series of points and questions that a trained observer checking the file after the event would use to evaluate what was done and the standard to which it was done. The Board's first transaction criteria – covering Green Form and emergency civil work – were published in a 100-page booklet in December 1992.[65]

It was a remarkable document outlining, for the first time, what a legal aid lawyer was meant to do at every stage of a case. Areas covered included matrimonial work, crime, housing, debt, personal injury, welfare benefits, employment, immigration and consumer law. The work under each topic was divided into three phases:

- Getting information from the client.

- Advising on this information.

- Further investigation, research and action.

Under each topic the lawyer was given a check list of the things to be done, invariably beginning with an instruction to write down the client's full name, address and telephone number. Although some legal aid practitioners were clearly offended at seeing their work being 'set out as a plumbing manual' (as the booklet's introduction candidly put it) others were no doubt grateful for detailed advice on such puzzles as what is meant by 'severe behavioural problems' in an application for the mobility component of disability living allowance.

The Legal Aid Board said that in order for the transaction criteria to work, firms had to record the necessary steps in each case on their files. Quality Auditors would go through a random sample of files looking for systematic omissions (where the same information was omitted from a number of files) or frequent random omissions (where several files each had something different missing). Total compliance with every point on the check list was not expected but a benchmark level of compliance would be set and practitioners would have to meet it in order to keep their franchises.

Even so the approach was to be 'co-operative rather than confrontational'. Firms which failed to comply with the criteria would be encouraged to take remedial action once the difficulties had been pointed out. According to the university researchers who worked on the transaction criteria, Professor Avrom Sherr of Liverpool and Professor Alan Paterson of Strathclyde, co-operation between lawyers and the Legal Aid Board had been 'a feature of the franchising experiment over the past two years and appears to have fostered a level of trust and understanding which might have been thought of as unlikely given the political climate within which legal aid reform currently takes place'.

The Birmingham solicitor Graham McGrath argued that the Legal Aid Board could tick boxes on a check list without knowing whether the work done had met the required standards: 'the question is how good was the bail application, not whether the client got a letter.'[66] Other solicitors thought the criteria were useful for staff training and supervision but could lead to problems if employees relied on them to indicate the next steps that should be taken in dealing with a particular problem.

The researchers themselves said that transaction criteria would not force firms to 'paint by numbers' but they would ensure that practitioners were using the right paints and painting the right type of picture: 'Transaction criteria would never seek to replace the ability of a lawyer but they do seek to provide a meaningful basis for ensuring a basic level of service is provided to clients.'[67]

Some solicitors feared that transaction criteria would increase the cost of legal aid as lawyers would be required to demonstrate that they had followed the necessary steps. Others were more sanguine, however. Tony Edwards, who runs a leading legal aid practice in the East End of London, believed it might push up costs to follow the criteria but did not consider that was a reason for not doing a job properly.

The Law Society was much more worried about transaction criteria than it had been about management standards. It said that systems to test the quality of solicitors' competence were largely 'unknown territory' and it persuaded the Legal Aid Board to agree that the granting of a franchise would not depend on whether the applicant complied with these criteria, at least to begin with.[68]

The Board conceded that:

Organisations will not be expected to demonstrate 100 per cent compliance with the transaction criteria . . . If an organisation shows lower than average levels of compliance . . . within the category of work or less than 65 per cent compliance, whichever is the lower, that will not result in the refusal of a franchise. Instead, the Board will seek explanations and may also re-examine other information gathered from both the [transaction criteria] audit and its own monitoring.

In other words, if the solicitor did not measure up to the criteria there was probably something wrong with the criteria. This seemed a remarkable concession to solicitors, all the more so because the quality required of them by the criteria was never going to be of a very high level anyway. This diagram shows how the researchers attempted to define and measure the quality of legal work:

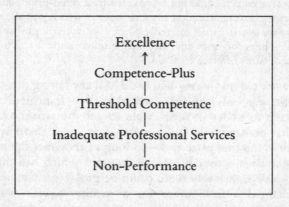

Excellence
↑
Competence-Plus
|
Threshold Competence
|
Inadequate Professional Services
|
Non-Performance

They explained that standards should not be set at the level of excellence to be found in a top commercial firm. That would be too expensive. Instead the aim was 'threshold competence' – defined as 'a basic level of competence to be achieved by a lawyer specialising in the area concerned'.[69]

This must be a cause for concern. Some government officials took the view that it was better to start at a level which firms could meet rather than set standards at a level which would force existing firms out of business. They thought that the level of competence was a floor which would slowly move upwards. But it could just as easily turn out to be a ceiling which will move downwards. There is a real risk that 'threshold competence' will drift into 'inadequate professional services' owing to the demands of the marketplace.

Because solicitors will be under pressure to get through the work as cheaply as possible it will be very tempting for them to cut corners. In his Birmingham Manifesto speech[70] Lord Mackay said: 'I would like to see firms entering into long-term contracts with the Legal Aid Board to undertake blocks of cases, both civil and criminal. This could be done following competitive tendering and would of course be against defined quality standards.'

The Lord Chancellor returned to the theme of competitive tendering in January 1993. He said he expected to see

> the Legal Aid Board offering contracts to accredited firms of solicitors for undertaking blocks of cases following competitive tendering. In the largest cases, which could not be covered by a fixed-price contract, fees and rates will be negotiated in advance in ways which will allow firms to compete for work. Firms offered a block contract will probably seek an assured volume of cases and this may require some restriction on the number of firms offering legal aid.[71]

Now what did that mean? Was Lord Mackay saying that obtaining a franchise was only the first step, that even franchised solicitors would have to undercut their rivals to get the work? Or was he saying that perhaps only half a dozen firms in a town would get franchises in the first place and – so long as they met the minimum quality standards – they would be the ones which had offered the cheapest deal? Either way there could be problems. Certainly firms which charged a little more for a quality service would find themselves losing their franchises, just as some television companies did at the end of 1992. Meanwhile the big cases, like murders and serious frauds, would presumably be hawked around town and sold to the lowest bidder.

Needless to say Lord Mackay maintained that this was not what he had in mind. 'What I am proposing,' he said, 'is that this system may be developed to allow the taxpayer to get the best value . . . I am assuming there are people who are able to provide the service to a competent standard who are willing to compete with one another to provide it.'[72]

Eventually the Law Society realised what the Lord Chancellor was getting at. At the end of March 1993 it asked Lord Mackay for an assurance that competitive price tendering would not be introduced without the authority of parliament. The solicitors were worried about a 'hidden agenda', which – since the Lord Chancellor had announced his plans at the Law Society Conference some five months earlier – was perhaps a little uncharitable. Their main concern was that competitive tendering 'would destroy the principle that legal aid clients – like all others – are free to choose their own solicitor'.[73] The Law Society threatened to withdraw its support from franchising if the matter was not resolved.[74] However, in April 1993 the Legal Aid Board chairman, John Pitts, told the solicitors: 'There can be no question of franchise holders being compelled to participate in any competitive tendering exercise and no question of franchise holders being excluded from legal aid work because they choose not to participate in any tendering exercise or do tender and fail.'[75]

In the spring of 1994 franchising ran into serious difficulties. Solicitors threatened to boycott the scheme in protest over the way it was to be run. But improvements were made and in July 1993 the Law Society withdrew its objections, allowing franchising to start a month later.

The future of franchising

Officials in the Lord Chancellor's Department privately acknowledged that legal aid solicitors might not warm to the concept of competitive tendering but they pointed out that it was the way many professionals were moving. Large commercial clients seeking solicitors for a particular project were now holding what were called 'beauty parades' in which different firms line up against each other and compete for the job.

The Lord Chancellor was clearly contemplating the possibility that firms which did not get franchises would lose the right to do legal aid work. Is this a protection for the client, who will know that his solicitor has met the prescribed standards? Or is it a restriction on his right to be represented by a firm of his choice?

The client will have to rely on the Legal Aid Board to ensure that the solicitors available locally have achieved 'threshold competence' although he may not have quite as much confidence as Lord Mackay in the Board's ability to weed out incompetent lawyers. On the other hand he is likely to be better off with some sort of quality control than he was when there was none at all.

Franchising will not by itself produce firms which can do particular types of work to an agreed level of competence. However, it will allow solicitors to demonstrate that they have achieved that level, in the reasonably objective view of the Legal Aid Board. Franchising should therefore be given a cautious welcome by consumers.

Criminal legal aid

The present criminal legal aid arrangements date from 1967 when parliament enacted the main recommendations of the Widgery Report.[76] Under the current system people facing criminal charges must make their application for legal aid to the courts rather than to the Legal Aid Board. This means legal aid can be granted much more quickly. Like applicants for civil legal aid they must jump two hurdles. First, they must satisfy the magistrates (or in practice their clerk) that it is desirable 'in the interests of justice' for criminal legal aid to be granted.[77] Second, they must show that their means are modest enough to qualify for legal aid on financial grounds.

The interests of justice

Under the Legal Aid Act 1988 it is 'in the interests of justice' to grant criminal legal aid when the defendant, if found guilty, is at risk of losing his liberty, his livelihood or his reputation. These criteria – the *Widgery criteria* as they are called[78] – also say that legal aid should be granted if there are substantial questions of law to be argued or if the defendant needs help to follow the proceedings.[79]

The chances of getting legal aid in the magistrates' courts vary widely from one part of England and Wales to another. In September 1992 the Legal Aid Board published research highlighting the inconsistencies.[80] There was an astonishing variation in the rate at which criminal legal aid was granted: in 1990 it had ranged from 35 per cent to 100 per cent. The researchers found that this variation was attributable to the approach taken by individual court clerks: in deciding whether a case merited legal aid they looked mainly at the seriousness of the charges rather than at the Widgery criteria.

This was perhaps unsurprising in view of the inadequate way in which some applications were completed. One applicant stated that he was in real danger of losing his job (and would therefore qualify for legal aid) 'because I am already unemployed'. Another claimed that his case was complex because 'the offence was committed on the spur of the moment'. The researchers said that the reasons given in an attempt to satisfy the Widgery criteria were occasionally nonsensical. 'Much more frequently, they are vague, absent, or irrelevant.'

Why should this be? They found that many application forms were completed by unqualified assistants, trainee solicitors, and other junior staff. This again is unsurprising: many solicitors say it is the only way of making legal aid pay.

The researchers rightly called for a greater consistency in approach. 'It cannot be right,' they said, 'that virtually identical applications can be determined in such radically different ways.' They doubted whether consistency was possible unless responsibility for making decisions was taken away from 'a large number of separate authorities exercising a wide discretion'. The report concluded:

> Whether an applicant receives legal aid can depend as much upon the personal views and idiosyncrasies of the court clerks as it can on the strength and nature of the defence or mitigation to be put forward at court. In the final analysis, it may be questioned whether a decision-making process as open-ended and opaque as that now operated by magistrates' courts is in the best interests of justice.

It may indeed.

In July 1993 the National Audit Office published a report criticising the way criminal legal aid was granted. Responding to the report, the Lord Chancellor issued new guidance in May 1994 on how courts should interpret the 'interests of justice' test. Lord Mackay said he was confident the new guidance would promote greater consistency. He also promised that courts would have to give reasons for rejecting applications.

The means test

The vast majority of people facing criminal charges are sufficiently poor to qualify for criminal legal aid. However, some defendants have to pay a contribution towards the costs of representation. From April 1994 any applicant earning more than £47 a week after deductions has to pay a third of the excess towards the costs of his case.[81] Anyone with capital of more than £3,000 must put the excess towards his legal fees.

Applicants have to fill in a statement of their means, but in the experience of Judge Jeremy Fordham, 'any serious check on the truth or accuracy of this information is very rare.'[82] Judge Fordham said in 1992 that 'dishonest people nearly always get legal aid with a "nil" contribution'. Even those who were meant to pay towards the cost of their legal aid were unlikely to end up much out of pocket.

Experienced defendants generally did not pay many of their contributions before the case came to trial. They knew it was unlikely that the court would use its power to withdraw their legal aid order: the last thing the judge wanted was an unrepresented defendant appearing before him to slow down the proceedings. And once the trial was over it was too late. If the defendant ended up in prison he could hardly be expected to pay his legal aid contributions with no money coming in. If he was acquitted the state would pay the full cost of his defence.

In 1991–2 less than 6 per cent of those granted criminal legal aid were ordered to pay a contribution. Critics like Judge Fordham argued that anyone meeting the 'interests of justice' criteria should have an automatic right to free legal aid. But this proposal – previously endorsed by the Royal Commission on Legal Services in 1979[83] – was rejected by the Lord Chancellor in his Birmingham Manifesto: 'where an individual facing a criminal charge has the means to pay a contribution towards the cost of his defence, I believe it is both fair and right that he should continue to do so,' he said.[84] Surely it must be more trouble than it is worth to collect contributions which could be as low as £2 a week? No, said Lord Mackay in the same speech: 'Evidence we have recently collected shows that contributions received[85] more than pay for the whole cost of administering the grant of criminal legal aid.'

The Royal Commission on Criminal Justice found that the initial means test for criminal legal aid was causing 'administrative difficulties'. The commission suggested that it would be better to postpone the means test until the outcome of the trial was known. Implicit in the suggestion was that those found not guilty should not have to pay a contribution at all. This seems fair. The Royal Commission also said that it would be very concerned if the government's proposals had the effect of increasing the number of defendants who had no legal representation, particularly in the Crown Court.[86]

Keeping an eye on the pennies

By the late 1980s government spending on criminal legal aid had become a national scandal – not because it was too low but because it was too high. The Lord Chancellor's Department was happily spending large sums of public money without any idea whether it was going to people who were entitled to it. It was an alarming demonstration of how government departments can behave when there is insufficient parliamentary scrutiny.

In 1986 the influential House of Commons Public Accounts Committee first expressed 'serious concern' about the escalating cost of legal aid and the fact that the Lord Chancellor's Department had no way of knowing why the cost was rising so steeply.[87] Responding to the criticism the government 'acknowledged that there had been gaps in the availability of management information on legal aid and said that measures were in hand to fill them'.[88] But in November 1991 the National Audit Office, which monitors government spending, found things were as bad as ever. In a devastating indictment it said there was '. . . significant and material uncertainty as to the propriety and regularity of substantial sums of expenditure on criminal legal aid'.

As a result the Comptroller and Auditor General, who heads the National Audit Office, refused to give his unqualified approval for the Lord Chancellor's 1990–91 Appropriation Account,[89] a serious matter in Whitehall. In particular he was concerned that applications for criminal legal aid were granted without enough information and corroboration, that there were inconsistencies and delays in the enforcement of contribution orders and that there was a lack of guidance to the courts.

This was bad. Spending on criminal legal aid in the year 1990–91 was £333 million. While not actually accusing anybody of dishonesty the public auditor was saying he could not be sure that nobody had put his hand in the till.

There is no particular reason to suppose that magistrates' clerks were handing out questionable legal aid certificates to local solicitors in exchange for a few drinks in the pub afterwards. But there is every reason to think that many courts were giving applicants the benefit of the doubt. For one thing, the law said they should.[90] For another, it meant that the courts would not have too many unrepresented defendants to deal with. The real problem was that the government had no way of checking whether those granted legal aid were in fact eligible for it. The forms completed by applicants did not give enough information to make this possible.

The person ultimately responsible for money spent by the Lord Chancellor's Department is its most senior civil servant, the Permanent Secretary. Tom Legg[91] took up that post in September 1989 and early in 1992 Mr Legg was called in by the Commons Public Accounts Committee to face accusations that his department had taken a 'very relaxed approach' to 'potential abuse' of the criminal legal aid regulations.

Relaxed? Surely not. Indeed Mr Legg told the committee that as long ago as 1990 he had commissioned an internal audit report on criminal legal aid. By June 1991 that report had already been completed. And a mere five months later, in November 1991, the Lord Chancellor's Department and the Home Office (which at that time was still responsible for magistrates' courts) had 'set to work on implementing it'. This they had done by setting up a working party which Mr Legg said was expected to finish its work in March or April 1992. No doubt the intention would then have been to put options to ministers which could have been studied in detail and put out to consultation with interested parties before being acted on when the time was right.

Some MPs were clearly exasperated at what they saw as a grindingly slow rate of progress, as this extract from Mr Legg's cross-examination demonstrates:[92]

> *Sir Ian Stewart MP* (Con): For 18 months or more you were content to let the thing ride without trying to tighten up in any way?
> *Mr Legg*: Those words imply a state of mind which was not quite the one we had. We were concerned about the problem and had set in hand this major review of it.[93]

It is easy to make fun of this apparently dilatory approach but behind it lies a real policy dilemma. As Mr Legg was well aware, most justices' clerks simply did not have the resources to check whether applicants came within the financial limits. But that cut no ice with the Public Accounts Committee whose report stated: 'We regard it as unsatisfactory, and contrary to the reassurances given to us in the Treasury Minute of 22 October 1986, that management information systems and monitoring within the Lord Chancellor's Department were inadequate to alert the department to the scale or significance of the problems on criminal legal aid.' The committee said the government had 'shown a failure to deal with the growing problems of criminal legal aid, with little apparently done since the matter was addressed and guidance issued in 1984'. The MPs expected the Lord Chancellor's Department 'to introduce without further delay strengthened administrative procedures and controls for the handling of criminal legal aid awards within magistrates' courts'.[94]

By then the government had pressed the panic button. Tom Legg had promised the Public Accounts Committee that he would remind magistrates' clerks of their responsibilities and in April 1992 the Lord Chancellor's Department sent them a circular.[95] It informed them that the auditors had discovered legal aid was often being granted without proof that the applicant met the financial conditions and it reminded them that employed defendants were meant to send in wage slips covering the past 13 weeks when they applied for legal aid. The circular said that without this evidence the application must be refused. It added, in bold type: **There is no discretion to waive this requirement.**

But there was. The law[96] did not require any specific documents to be produced before legal aid was granted. As a matter of law, a circular could not impose such a requirement.

The Law Society and the Justices' Clerks' Society patiently explained this to the Lord Chancellor's Department. Meanwhile many courts were simply ignoring the circular. In Liverpool, however, the Lord Chancellor's words were taken very seriously indeed. This caused 'chaos' according to one Liverpool solicitor: Robert Broudie said[97] that case after case was being adjourned – at substantial expense – because the legal aid applications had not gone through. He applied for judicial review of the circular. Another solicitor pointed out that his clients could not even manage to keep their charge sheets while they were in the cells overnight; they were hardly the sort of people who would file away thirteen consecutive wage slips. In some courts at least the circular was clearly causing injustice to people who were wrongly denied immediate legal aid. But the Liverpool justices' clerk, Malcolm Marsh, replied that defendants could normally provide the information required, given time. He pointed out that his court was referring, on average, one application a month to the police because fraud was suspected.[98]

Was the circular lawful? After all it would hardly inspire confidence if the Lord Chancellor, who presides over the highest court in the land, was advising courts throughout England and Wales to apply a requirement which had no foundation in law.

In May 1992 the junior minister at the Lord Chancellor's Department, John Taylor MP, told Labour's front-bench spokesman that 'he had been advised that the circular was correct in law'. Mr Taylor announced bluntly that the circular would not be withdrawn.[99]

Less than a month later Mr Taylor informed MPs that paragraph

10 of the circular – the clause dealing with wage slips – would be withdrawn after all.[100] Shortly afterwards Mr Taylor, a solicitor by training, was interviewed by the BBC. Did he now think that the circular was lawful or not?

> I don't consider myself in a position to make judgments about whether it is lawful or not. I'm a politician. I think the Lord Chancellor's Department was quite right to respond quickly. When there were problems perceived with clause 10 about 13 weeks' payslips, I think it was also prudent to suspend that element of the circular and to continue to examine the regulations.[101]

It was alarming to hear the minister for justice say that he did not know whether his own department's advice to the courts was lawful. Afterwards officials said the circular had set out what everyone in the Lord Chancellor's Department believed was the law even though they knew it was a law that was widely ignored. As things turned out, the department was in the process of examining the regulations when the Liverpool solicitor, Mr Broudie, applied for judicial review.

This whole episode, though trivial in itself, provokes a number of thoughts about the working of the Lord Chancellor's Department. First it suggests that the quality of legal advice on middle-ranking issues is poor. But this is hardly surprising: until the recession of the early 1990s most lawyers would not dream of joining the government legal service when they knew they could make more money in industry or in private practice. The fact that the Lord Chancellor's Department has a judge for a Secretary of State, a solicitor for a minister and a QC for a Permanent Secretary does not in itself mean that its officials will get the law right every time.

It might have been the case that sound legal advice was overruled for reasons of political expediency. This would not have been surprising either; the government knew it was going to come under fire from the Public Accounts Committee and may have wanted to get its retaliation in first. But on the facts this seems unlikely.

Above all the episode demonstrates the perils of acting in isolation. Before taking action governments frequently sound out those most affected by their proposals. That allows time for those involved to warn ministers about the errors of their ways. One organisation, the Justices' Clerks' Society, was represented on the working party which helped draw up the circular but there should have been greater consultation with the courts and the legal profession.

In December 1992 the government tried again. Miraculously a consultation paper appeared.[102] This time it proposed that an applicant's statement of means should be accompanied by whatever supporting documents were needed to enable the court to assess his income, capital and maximum contribution. No documents would mean no legal aid.

The Law Society found this flexible approach perfectly unobjectionable. However, the Legal Aid Board believed that an applicant should be granted criminal legal aid on the basis of what he said in his application form, provided he could satisfy the court or its clerk that he was unable to produce any supporting evidence. The Board offered the government two reasons for this. 'One was that criminal defendants tend to be socially inadequate, mentally disordered and self-destructive more often than the general population. Another was that it is often in the interests of other agencies and individuals that a defendant should be represented.'

From this it was clear that those who understood the system could have warned the government about the folly of its plans. Ministers might have avoided the elephant trap they found themselves in if only they had issued their original circular for advance consultation.

Keeping control of the pounds

While the storm clouds were gathering over civil legal aid, criminal practitioners were not exactly basking in the sun. Take, for example, solicitors' rates of pay. When fixing rates the Lord Chancellor was previously obliged to 'have regard to the principle of allowing fair remuneration according to the work actually and reasonably done'.[103] Those words were removed by the Legal Aid Act 1988 and instead the Lord Chancellor takes into account a number of other factors including the cost to public funds.[104]

For some years the Legal Aid Board had been worried by the rapidly rising cost of criminal legal aid: in 1992 the cost per case had been increasing at roughly twice the rate of inflation. Solicitors felt they were being blamed for the failings of the criminal justice system. Go to any magistrates' court, they said, and you will see solicitors spending much of their time waiting for their cases to be heard, time which the Legal Aid Fund had to pay for at nearly £25 an hour.[105] If courts had more efficient scheduling arrangements instead of listing all cases for the same time, and if prisoners, prosecutors, police and probation officers were always in the right court at the right time, then the cost of criminal legal aid would not be increasing so fast.

By the summer of 1993, however, there were signs of progress. The Legal Aid Board's figures for 1992–3 showed that criminal legal aid was taking a smaller slice of the cake than before: net spending on criminal legal aid in the magistrates' courts was virtually unchanged at £287 million (compared with £286 million the year before) while net expenditure on civil legal aid had increased from £434 million to £586 million over the same period. John Pitts, chairman of the Legal Aid Board, said this was 'due in large part to a reduction in the number of people being prosecuted'. Also the average cost of each case had increased by less than 3 per cent, which Mr Pitts said was 'a welcome reduction from the high levels of increase in each of the last six years'.[106]

It was not clear why this should have happened; but it was clear that the frustration solicitors felt with the legal aid system was leading to a steady drift away from magistrates' court work. In 1992–3 the Legal Aid Board made payments for this type of work to 7,011 solicitors' offices.[107] The figure was down 5 per cent on the year before.

Standard fees
Standard fees were the government's answer to the rising cost of criminal legal aid. Under the original payment arrangements a solicitor's fee was based on the amount of work done for a defendant: the bigger the case, the higher the fee. That meant every case had to be assessed by officials to see how much the solicitor should receive. In 1986 the government's Efficiency Unit scrutiny recommended replacing these detailed and time-consuming arrangements with standard fees for most cases.[108] And at the beginning of 1987 the Lord Chancellor, Lord Hailsham, told the Law Society that he was 'committed to the introduction of a standard fee system for solicitors in the course of the next few months'.[109] It was to take rather longer than the government had planned.

In the summer of 1991 Lord Hailsham's successor started discussions with the Bar and the Law Society. Lord Mackay's target date for introducing standard fees was then April 1992. However, the Lord Chancellor soon found that solicitors were determined to oppose them.

The essence of standard fees is swings and roundabouts: in some cases solicitors would be paid more than was justified by the work done and in others the solicitor would receive less. The Law Society feared more people would lose on the swings than would gain on the roundabouts. That was because there were not many cases which could be concluded without much work. The Lord Chancellor countered this by saying that solicitors could expect to be paid more quickly than they had been before. That was because standard fees were easier to administer.

The key question was whether standard fees would lead to a poorer service. The Lord Chancellor's Department said: 'There is no evidence that this has happened in the Crown Court since standard fees were introduced there in 1988. Standard fees encourage efficiency and that is not incompatible with quality of service.'[110] The Law Society, on the other hand, said standard fees would 'penalise solicitors who prepare cases thoroughly, and will reward only those who skimp on preparation'.[111] This seemed much more plausible.[112]

In November 1991 solicitors in Devon actually voted to support industrial action in protest against the proposals: they announced that they would be withdrawing from the 24-hour police station duty solicitor scheme. At first the Law Society was embarrassed – the solicitors' president, Philip Ely, said that such action would be 'inappropriate and premature'.[113] But within a few weeks Mr Ely had become much more sympathetic to the cause of legal aid solicitors.[114] After pressure from the Legal Aid Practitioners Group, a ginger group of legal aid lawyers, the Law Society agreed to hold an unprecedented mass meeting at Westminster in February 1992. As many as 2,000 solicitors attended and during the afternoon a few of them even queued outside the House of Commons and lobbied their MPs.

The Lord Chancellor displayed a strong sense of duty by attending the conference and speaking to an audience which was unsympathetic if not outwardly hostile. He conceded that it would not be possible to introduce standard fees in April 1992, as planned, but said he intended to have the new system in place by the summer of that year. Meanwhile management consultants would be brought in to work out the detailed figures.

In the event, the consultants' report was not published until the end of September. It agreed that government plans amounted to 'a mechanism for gaining speedy control of the rate of increase in expenditure on criminal legal aid in the magistrates' courts, and thus achieving a key policy objective set by the Lord Chancellor'. Lord Mackay provisionally accepted the consultants' detailed recommendations and said he intended to introduce standard fees by the end of 1992.[115]

Yet again the timetable slipped. It was announced that standard fees would be introduced for magistrates' court work during April 1993. With only a month to go the Law Society made known its intention to seek judicial review of the Lord Chancellor's proposals. To allow time for the law to take its course the Lord Chancellor responded by agreeing to postpone his plans yet again.

In court the Law Society argued that Lord Mackay had acted unlawfully and irrationally. The solicitors claimed that they were entitled to proper payment for each case even though their total income might not change because of the 'swings and roundabouts' principle. But the High Court rejected the Law Society's arguments. The judges decided there was nothing in the Legal Aid Act to indicate that parliament had intended to outlaw standard fees. Lord Justice Leggatt said the Lord Chancellor had been given a broad measure of discretion by the legislation.[116] Standard fees for magistrates' court work were finally introduced in June 1993.

Why all the fuss? Was it simply that the solicitors were after as much as they could get? Or was there an issue of principle at stake over standard fees?

From a financial point of view the Lord Chancellor was able to say that standard fees would be introduced on a 'cost-neutral' basis. What this meant was that 'at the time of introduction, the income to the profession from criminal legal aid in the magistrates' courts will not be reduced as a result'. But the Lord Chancellor had an important caveat: 'It is expected, however, that standard fees will help to control costs in the years to come.'[117] That meant fee increases could be kept down each year to below the rate of inflation if the Lord Chancellor so wished – even though the amount of work on each case was likely to increase (because cases tend to get more complicated year by year). In response to solicitors' fears that they would be paid less and less for more and more work the Lord Chancellor's officials pointed out that he would not be able to make cuts on a purely arbitrary basis: he would have to act reasonably or face judicial review.

The Lord Chancellor's junior minister, John Taylor MP, believed that standard fees were 'a genuine incentive to the person who can dispose of cases well and competently'. If anything, he said, they would lead to a better quality of service for the client. Pressed to explain what incentive there was for a solicitor to do the job well rather than just quickly he said any suggestion that solicitors would cut corners was an insult to a learned profession: solicitors could be relied on to do all that was required.[118] Mr Taylor was himself in practice as a solicitor: it was heartening to see that he had such confidence in the selflessness and devotion to duty of his professional colleagues, men and women who he apparently believed were willing to carry on working without pay rather than see their clients suffer.

Other solicitors were much less sanguine. They pointed out that some of the recent miscarriages of justice were the result of failure by solicitors to do their job properly when preparing cases for trial. This was backed up by academic research by Mike McConville and Jacqueline Hodgson of the University of Warwick Legal Research Institute.[119]

Professor McConville and Dr Hodgson examined 1,000 criminal cases handled by 50 firms of solicitors over a three-year period. They found that much of the work in solicitors' offices was not done by solicitors at all: it was delegated to other staff on a routine basis. Those people ranged from trainee solicitors to former police officers.

In most cases suspects who asked to see a solicitor at the police station were visited by an unqualified representative. Many of these people seemed to lack confidence in dealing with the police. They were either unclear about their role in the process or tended to over-identify with the police. Mike McConville believed that clients were at 'great risk' when an unqualified or inexperienced person was called on to advise them at the police station. He said that if the person there to 'defend' the client did not have the necessary skills, the whole system would fail.

That view was starkly demonstrated by the case of the Cardiff Three in 1992.[120] The Court of Appeal said the solicitor who sat in on police interviews in 1988 'seems to have done that and little else . . . It is of the first importance that a solicitor fulfilling the exacting duty of assisting a suspect during interviews should follow the guidelines and discharge his function responsibly and courageously. Otherwise, his presence may actually render disservice.'

Mike McConville's research clearly points to the alarming conclusion that people are wrongly convicted because solicitors' firms *are* cutting corners. In his view, standard fees would simply pay the solicitors for what they were already doing, which was standard work. Standard fees might save money but they would also confirm bad practice:

> Solicitors for their part also are in some cases guilty of not looking actively for defences which might be available, or indeed discovering what precisely is the defendant's story, because they see the case as simply one more of a given class of case to which routinised treatment can be applied . . . It is indeed a 'boilerplate' defence and that's very clearly seen when we move to the courtroom where solicitors mostly operate. We see very often recycled material being applied to whoever is the defendant before the court and the client's story never emerges in many of these cases . . . The very strong tendency in these firms is to 'routinise' cases in particular ways and the particular way which is most favoured is a guilty plea.[121]

Responding to Professor McConville's findings the Law Society announced in April 1993 that solicitors' representatives would have to meet specified standards before they could advise clients at the police station. The Law Society and the Legal Aid Board agreed that, from October 1994, solicitors' representatives would not be paid under legal aid unless they had been trained and had passed a written test.[122]

Under the system introduced in 1993 there are two different standard fees for magistrates' court work – a lower level covering the least expensive 70 per cent of cases and an upper level covering the next 20 per cent. The remaining 10 per cent of cases are assessed on a case-by-case basis by the Legal Aid Board. At the end of each case the solicitor looks at the work done and decides whether it fits into the lower category. If so, he or she claims the lower fee which is set at a little more than halfway between zero and the maximum figure of the lower category. If the cost of the case takes it into the higher band the solicitor produces the necessary evidence and claims the higher standard fee. Travel and waiting times are extra and solicitors in London get paid higher rates.

Under the initial rates set by the Lord Chancellor the crucial figure for guilty pleas was £261. If a case was worth anything up to that figure (calculated on the old hourly rate) then the solicitor would receive the lower standard fee of £140. If the case was worth between

£261 and £451 he would be paid the higher standard fee of £336. For summary trials the lower standard fee was £247 (for cases worth up to £447) and the higher standard fee was £556 (for cases worth between £447 and £745).

There can be little doubt that standard fees are an unsatisfactory way of paying solicitors to do work which is far from standard in nature. Either solicitors will cut corners or they will turn away the more difficult types of work. From the Lord Chancellor's point of view, however, it is silly to spend scarce resources on administering a complicated scheme when the money can be better used paying for solicitors to do the work itself. In principle it cannot be unreasonable for the Lord Chancellor to take steps to control rising costs.

Like so many aspects of legal aid the introduction of standard fees in the magistrates' courts was not the best way of coping with a growing problem. But it was not as bad as the solicitors had claimed. By crying wolf they devalued their own currency in the public mind when the time came to complain about the eligibility cuts introduced in 1993.[123]

The future: Early Cover?

In January 1992 Charles Everett of the Lord Chancellor's Department asked John Pitts of the Legal Aid Board to consider how the Board could take on responsibility for the grant of criminal legal aid in the magistrates' courts. It had always been envisaged that the Legal Aid Board would eventually control all aspects of legal aid administration. The Comptroller and Auditor General's finding of 'significant and material uncertainty as to the propriety and regularity' of criminal legal aid spending in 1990–91[124] had made matters more urgent.

The Board said it would be willing to take responsibility for criminal legal aid from the start of 1995 provided major changes were made. Its advice to the Lord Chancellor[125] correctly identified the fundamental flaw in the existing arrangements. Legal aid, to be effective, must be granted immediately a defendant is brought before a court. At that stage, however, it is often difficult to decide whether the applicant is entitled to legal aid, either on the merits of the case or on his means. Until the prosecution discloses its case it is not always clear whether the 'interests of justice' criteria will be satisfied. And until the applicant can provide proof of his means it is not possible to decide whether he qualifies on financial grounds.

The Board's answer was a new type of criminal legal aid, to be called 'Early Cover'. It would be similar to legal advice and assistance under the Green Form scheme: solicitors would decide whether their clients met the financial criteria and would collect any contributions their clients had to pay for as long as the case continued. People in custody would get Early Cover without having to pass a means test.

Early Cover would only apply to the first stages of a case. After that, defendants would apply for legal aid in the normal way except that applications would be handled by the Legal Aid Board instead of the magistrates' courts.

Certain types of work would be excluded from the new scheme. The Board proposed that Early Cover should be available to everyone facing a charge which could be tried before a jury. Those facing summary charges would only get Early Cover if they were in custody and wanted to apply for bail.[126]

The proposed new scheme was immediately denounced by the *New Law Journal* as a waste of time and money.[127] The magazine's main concern was that Early Cover would not allow a solicitor to do urgent preliminary work: this would have to wait until a full legal aid certificate was granted some weeks later. It also rejected the suggestion that defendants charged with summary offences should not get Early Cover if they were on bail. The magazine rightly said that a defendant needs advice before deciding whether to plead guilty.

That concern was shared by other solicitors. What of a defendant facing the summary charge of assaulting a police officer? During the initial stages of the case he would not be entitled to be represented in court by a solicitor. He might get legal advice under the Green Form scheme but even that was unlikely after the eligibility cuts of 1993. Lawyers wondered how the Legal Aid Board was proposing to ensure that vulnerable and inadequate defendants were legally represented in the early stages of summary cases. As solicitors pointed out, they would no longer be able to negotiate with prosecutors at court, make applications to vary bail conditions and apply for cases to be discontinued if there were special circumstances or dismissed if the prosecution was guilty of undue delay.

There was also concern about the proposal that solicitors should collect contributions for the duration of the case. What if the contributions dried up during a lengthy Crown Court trial? Law Society officials thought solicitors would be reluctant to chase up contributions from clients who could not afford to pay them: that would mean some clients going unrepresented and others being subsidised by their solicitors. The Legal Aid Board had the grace to acknowledge that its approach 'may not be popular with the profession' but said this was 'in line with the Lord Chancellor's stated preferences for the payment of contributions generally'.[128]

In December 1993 the Lord Chancellor announced that he would not after all be transferring responsibility for criminal legal aid to the Legal Aid Board 'for the time being'. He was worried that this might put at risk 'the speed and efficiency of criminal procedures'. The Law Society welcomed this development.

Collective government amnesia

The story of legal aid is the tragedy at the heart of this book. It is a sombre catalogue of the misfortunes which befall our fellow citizens. One of those citizens found the problems of legal aid particularly painful. His name is Tom Legg.

We last met the Lord Chancellor's Permanent Secretary early in 1992 when he was called in by the Commons Public Accounts Committee to face accusations that his department had taken a 'relaxed' approach to potential abuse of the legal aid regulations. A year later the newly knighted Sir Thomas Legg was asked back by the committee to explain what had been done 'to tighten things up'. Sir Thomas explained that in April, when his department had become responsible for the magistrates' courts, he issued the controversial 'wages slip' circular discussed earlier. By the autumn it had become clear that the circular by itself would not solve the problem and so shortly before Christmas 1992 he had issued a consultation paper proposing changes in the legal aid regulations. The Permanent Secretary seemed to be implying that this was pretty swift action and MPs seemed happy enough.

As Sir Thomas took his leave of the Public Accounts Committee he might well have thought he had come through the interrogation with his dignity still reasonably intact. As it turned out, the questions were only just beginning. For this distinguished but hapless civil servant the episode was to end some months later in high farce and bitter public humiliation.

Towards the end of his questioning by the Labour MP Alan Williams, Sir Thomas Legg said he would be concerned if people who could no longer afford to see a solicitor tried to represent themselves in court. There were two reasons for his concern. The first and more important one was that 'in an adversarial system like ours people who represent themselves obviously are not as well equipped to secure full justice to their cause'; the second was that 'it tends to take up the time of the court more than is otherwise necessary when litigants represent themselves.'[129]

So far so good. But then, in an inspired piece of questioning, Mr Williams asked Sir Thomas: 'Have judges actually warned you that a result of what is happening is that more people might represent themselves and that this might lengthen court processes? Have they actually given you and the Lord Chancellor warning that this is a risk you are running?'

Sir Thomas replied: 'No, I have not had that said to me. I am not aware that has been said. I cannot say that it has not, but it has not to me.'[130]

The fates were unkind to the Lord Chancellor's Permanent Secretary. In another part of the Palace of Westminster, a matter of minutes after Sir Thomas Legg had finished giving his evidence, the Lord Chief Justice rose to speak in a debate on legal aid. Lord Taylor told peers that a litigant in person might indeed cost the system more than someone who was legal aided. 'He is likely to take more of the court's time,' said Lord Taylor, 'partly because he may have difficulty in presenting his case intelligibly and partly because the court needs to be more indulgent to him in case there is some point he has not been able to articulate.'

Lord Taylor went on to say that he believed there were 'other cost-cutting measures which could be considered short of slashing eligibility'. And then he added: 'It was with those considerations in mind that the Master of the Rolls and I wrote jointly to the Lord Chancellor last week asking him to explore all other methods of controlling the escalation of legal aid expenditure rather than proceeding with his present proposals.'[131]

Wait a moment. Hadn't Sir Thomas Legg said the judges had *not* written to the Lord Chancellor about the problems of unrepresented defendants? Surely Lord Taylor and Sir Thomas Bingham couldn't have written to the Lord Chancellor about that very issue? In fact they had. Surely the Permanent Secretary had not misled the Public Accounts Committee of the House of Commons? Inadvertently he had. Surely Sir Thomas Legg could not have forgotten about a letter from the Lord Chief Justice? Indeed he had. As Sir Thomas explained, he had realised his mistake a day after giving his original evidence.

> What happened was that quite late on in the evening, about halfway through the evening of the following day, I happened to be dining at my Inn of Court and my private secretary came and told me there had been a press inquiry[132] about how it came about that I had answered Mr Williams as I had when the Lord Chief Justice had written in the way that he had. At once, but for the first time I am afraid, the penny dropped and I realised that I should have answered Mr Williams' question in the affirmative.[133]

Sir Thomas wrote to the committee explaining that he had 'forgotten' about the letter from the Lord Chief Justice and the Master of the Rolls and saying he was sorry he had unintentionally misled MPs. The committee called him back in March 1993 for a rare second interrogation. Was he aware of the letter? Yes, he was. Did his junior officials know about it? Yes, those dealing with legal aid did so. How, then, could it have slipped his memory? Probably because the letter was about proposed changes in eligibility. But were those changes not germane to the subject the Public Accounts Committee was looking at? He and his colleagues did not think so. Did other officials accompanying Sir Thomas know about the letter? Certainly, two or three did. Why had they not told him he had made a mistake at the time? Probably because, like him, they had not thought it was relevant to the matters he was being asked about. Did Sir Thomas mean that it was 'collective amnesia'? Sir Thomas preferred to call it 'collective categorisation'. Rightly or wrongly they had put these matters into two different categories.

Finally it was the turn of Alan Williams, the MP whose perceptive questioning had wrongfooted the Permanent Secretary some weeks earlier. When the letter from Lord Taylor and Sir Thomas Bingham had arrived, he asked, did Sir Thomas 'just read it, put it aside and say "Oh, it's just them again" or did it merit a bit of discussion?'

Sir Thomas gave a revealing reply:

> We get many letters from the Lord Chief Justice of course, a steady stream of letters from the Lord Chief Justice and a steady stream of telephone calls to and fro. Obviously all of them are important. I did not myself deal with the top copy of the letter. It was sent straight to the division which deals with legal aid in order to assist the Lord Chancellor

with an early advice and answer, in part in preparation for the debate which took place on the same day as the hearing before this committee and in part to prepare a draft answer which was sent shortly after that debate.

Mr Williams had the last word: 'If this is the attention a Lord Chief Justice's letter receives from your department, I now begin to understand some of the replies we get as members of parliament when we write to the department with complaints on behalf of our constituents.'[134]

It would be wrong to make too much of this incident. But it does cast some light on management standards within the Lord Chancellor's Department. When things go wrong one's suspicions are naturally aroused: the committee noted that the original answer it received from Sir Thomas had 'blocked off a line of questioning'.[135] However, on this occasion, as with so many other incidents related in this book, the cock-up theory is more plausible than the conspiracy theory.

An opportunity lost?

Could the Law Society have avoided the legal aid crisis of 1992–3? Perhaps not: like any representative body it had to support the interests of its members. Those doing legal aid work were mostly solicitors in private practice, determined to carry on working in the way they always had before. There was little enthusiasm for 'new ways of delivering publicly funded legal services'.

Even so, the Law Society had tried to help. In December 1990 its president, Tony Holland, had offered the Lord Chancellor a 'partnership' to tackle the rising cost of legal aid. In a letter to Lord Mackay Mr Holland said: 'We are prepared to help to identify and tackle areas of inefficiency – including any which may be our profession's responsibility – and to commit the necessary resources on our side. Together we should aim to establish an efficient, properly resourced court system whilst ensuring that legal aid is made available to those who cannot afford the full cost of solicitors' services . . .'

But nothing came of it. Law Society officials said afterwards that they thought Lord Mackay wanted to make changes on his own terms; they believed the Lord Chancellor's Department did not like solicitors trying to set the government's agenda. The Lord Chancellor's officials rejected this analysis: they said that in the past they had been too close to the Law Society and the Bar but they were now developing a healthier relationship.[136] Even though there were constant meetings at all levels government officials thought the Law Society was finding it hard to adapt to this new 'arm's length' approach.

These officials stressed that they would have welcomed specific proposals from the solicitors. There must be some doubt as to whether the Law Society was talking about new ways of delivering legal services or about ways of making the courts more efficient so that solicitors could get through more cases in a day. Certainly the Lord Chancellor's Department thought the Law Society had nothing specific to offer at that time.

The Bar had also tried to do its bit. In November 1991 the Bar Council said the time had come for a 'complete review of the whole legal aid system'. It said that 'to deal piecemeal with legal aid can lead to disparity and injustice'. The Bar commissioned a series of internal reports on ways to handle cases more efficiently in the courts.

Nevertheless opportunities had been missed. In June 1991 the Lord Chancellor published a consultation paper on eligibility for civil legal aid.[137] It said this could not be extended without greater efficiency. But, as Lord Justice Neill has remarked,[138] 'It does not appear that either then or during the course of the following year the Law Society appreciated that there was any risk that the conditions for eligibility were likely to be made *more* restrictive.'

November 1992 was probably the last opportunity the Law Society had to stop the axe falling. For the first time the Lord Chancellor indicated how much the Treasury was prepared to spend on legal aid in the years ahead, and the lawyers should have been looking for a better way of using that money. It was then that the Law Society should have been sowing the seeds of change.

They would not have fallen on stony ground. Early in December 1992 Lord Mackay had written to Mark Sheldon, president of the Law Society, saying he would welcome 'suggestions on how the legal aid budget might be contained otherwise than I have proposed'.[139] However, the thrust of the Law Society's policy at that time was still to try 'to persuade the Lord Chancellor to think again'.[140] So Mr Sheldon's reply was short on ideas and long on rhetoric.

His letter reminded Lord Mackay that the Law Society had offered two years earlier to 'join with the government in working together to control the rising cost of legal aid'. It added that for some years the Society had been suggesting ways of reducing waste in the magistrates' courts and that 'a strategic approach to the setting of priorities' was essential for the medium and longer term. As far as the short term was concerned, the best the Law Society could come up with was: 'We invite you to discuss with us urgently an alternative set of money-saving measures so that the proposed eligibility changes may be withdrawn.' And 'for the longer term', the Society suggested, there should be a new body 'to plan the priorities for legal aid to avoid similar crises in the future'.[141]

The Lord Chancellor's answer was scathing. 'I am not persuaded that any new body is necessary to provide me with advice in this area,' he said. He went on to snub the Law Society's feeble attempts to appear magnanimous. In their letter the solicitors had said they would have been willing to accept a pay freeze in April 1993 if the Lord Chancellor agreed to drop his original plans. Although described by the Law Society as a 'dramatic, even drastic step to take'[142] this was not in fact a very generous offer: legal aid rates had only gone up by a grudging 3 per cent the previous year and with a public-sector pay ceiling set at 1.5 per cent the Law Society could not have been expecting much. Not surprisingly Lord Mackay's response was, in essence: What makes you think you are going to get any more next year anyway? He said he 'had already arrived at the view that no increase would be appropriate' in April 1993.[143]

But the door was still open. Lord Mackay told Mr Sheldon: 'I am not clear from your letter whether you have any further specific measures to suggest. If you have, I should be pleased to consider them.' He explained that he was already taking measures to make the courts more efficient but these would not be enough to control the overall cost of legal aid. He repeated: 'If you have further specific proposals for achieving such control, I would welcome them.'

The lawyers tried again. After consultations with the Bar they announced an alternative package which they reckoned would save £43 million, exactly the sum which the Lord Chancellor was hoping to find through eligibility cuts.[144] But around one-third of the solicitors' figure was based on the savings to be made from their offer to forego their expected pay rise. Since they knew by then that they were not going to get one, this was hardly magnanimous.

However, another £14 million could be saved if it was agreed that a solicitor's representative[145] need no longer attend court if a barrister was instructed.[146] The solicitors offered to make further savings by agreeing that lawyers would not need to attend magistrates' courts for unopposed adjournment applications.

These were sensible measures – although there were many in the profession who asked why their leaders were doing the Lord Chancellor's dirty work for him. The Law Society was willing to consider even more radical moves in future years to meet the Lord Chancellor's target. It was said these might include:

- Allowing conditional or contingency fees in personal injury cases.

- Abolishing legal aid for defendants pleading guilty in the magistrates' courts, provided they had already received legal advice and there was no risk of prison.[147]

- Looking for cheaper ways of providing advice to clients under the police station duty solicitor scheme.[148]

The Law Society said in January 1993 that the eligibility cuts 'would do untold damage to the fabric of the legal aid scheme for comparatively modest savings'. It maintained that its own proposals – while in many respects representing a reduction in service to those on legal aid – would be less damaging and it called for a 'broadly based group' to advise on priorities for the future.[149] But critics took the view that solicitors had been pricing themselves out of the market. Their proposals were too little, too late.

Within days those critics were proved right. Lord Mackay told the president of the Law Society that there was not enough in the solicitors' proposals to make him change his mind. There was no money to be saved from a pay rise because there was not going to be a pay rise. Lord Mackay told the Law Society: 'It is clear, even on your own figures, that your remaining measures would not save anything like the required £43 million.'[150]

Writing in *The Times*[151] Lord Mackay set out his Conservative, indeed Thatcherite, thinking more starkly than ever before.[152] If people could not afford to go to court, he implied, then they would have to do without the law's protection: 'People must consider their priorities and in particular whether proceeding with litigation, with its inevitably uncertain outcome, takes precedence over other financial demands and other ways of dealing with the problem they face.'

What the Law Society had failed to grasp was that Lord Mackay was deliberately altering the entire philosophical basis of legal aid:

> Much of the present legal aid system would be entirely familiar to Lord Rushcliffe, whose report led to the 1949 Act which set legal aid on a statutory basis . . . Its objective was to place those who could not afford to pursue cases in the courts in as near as possible the same position as private clients and for the lawyers to be paid as if they were being funded by the clients themselves . . . In too many areas of legal aid work lawyers are still paid by the hour, a system which dates back even to before 1949. It is an arrangement which positively encourages the inefficient. The normal basis for paying lawyers for legal aid work must become a standardised fee, set at a level which will attract enough lawyers of the appropriate quality to do legal aid work.[153]

By the time the eligibility cuts took effect in April 1993 Lord Mackay was making no secret of the fact that he was doing what the Treasury wanted. But far from being pushed around by the other Chancellor in the cabinet Lord Mackay himself clearly espoused the undiluted doctrines of the 1980s Conservative Party. Asked to respond to the charge that a quarter of a million people were being denied access to justice the Lord Chancellor explained that naturally he was anxious to secure as much money for legal aid as possible:

> But I have a responsibility for public expenditure and for the need of this country – if it is to be competitive in an increasingly competitive world – to make sure that the burden on the wealth-producing sector is kept within reasonable limits. And therefore I have to co-operate with the rest of my colleagues in seeking to restrain expenditure. The people you are referring to, so far as civil legal aid is concerned, are people who will be asked to pay a contribution now which hitherto they might not have been asked to pay. But I can't see any good reason why the taxpayer should be obliged compulsorily to fund a person's case, if that person is not prepared to put at least something towards the cost of the case himself or herself.[154]

In January 1993, with the wolf no longer simply at the door but starting to bite through it, the Law Society had little difficulty in finding ways of saving money. Staff in the Lord Chancellor's Department thought that these savings – though welcome – did not go far enough. 'The solicitors' expressions of hurt are somewhat misplaced,' said one official.[155] Their proposals would certainly have led to an inferior service for the client but the Law Society was right to think that they would have been less harmful than those announced by the government.

When Lord Mackay showed no signs of accepting the Law Society's proposed cuts the solicitors came up with another bright idea. During late 1992 and early 1993 there had been a mysterious shortage of customers for the criminal courts. It appeared that the police were becoming reluctant to bring charges as frequently as before; instead they were making more use of formal cautions.[156]

A number of reasons were offered for this unexpected drop in prosecutions.[157] Police forces were concentrating scarce resources on complaints which were more likely to lead to a successful conviction. There was a greater understanding of how much evidence would be needed in court and a reluctance to investigate cases which it was thought would be thrown out by the Crown Prosecution Service. The police also saw little point in prosecuting if the offender was likely to receive a non-custodial sentence because of new legislation.[158] The same legislation allowed 17-year-olds to be dealt with by Youth Courts instead of the magistrates' courts. It was believed that the Crown Prosecution Service were also discontinuing weak cases more frequently and bringing less serious charges to secure convictions.

Research commissioned by the Law Society suggested there had been an 8 per cent reduction in the number of legal aid orders granted, which the solicitors thought would be enough to save the government £25 million in the coming year. Figures provided by the government suggested that the amount might be even higher: the number of legal aid orders had dropped by 13 per cent between the last quarter of 1991 and the last quarter of 1992, which the Law Society reckoned would produce a saving of approximately £37 million out of the £43 million the Lord Chancellor was seeking to save in 1993–4.

Lord Mackay was unimpressed. Giving evidence to the House of Commons Select Committee on Home Affairs in February 1993 he said that on the figures available it was too early to say whether these savings would continue: he would be keeping an eye on the trend but he thought it unwise to base his budget plans on it.[159] He was 'disappointed' with the Law Society's proposals, estimating that they would save £8 million at most – a figure hotly disputed by the solicitors. And he condemned as 'absurd' suggestions that 14 million people would be at a disadvantage due to the cuts in eligibility: his own estimate was that some 120,000 fewer civil legal aid certificates would be issued as a result. This meant a reduction of more than 30 per cent on his department's original estimate that 410,000 legal aid certificates would be issued in 1993–4.[160] Lord Mackay conceded that the number of people turning down contributory legal aid – around 20 per cent – could double.[161] But he insisted that, even with his cuts, the poorest 21 per cent of households would get free legal aid and another 27 per cent would be eligible if they paid a contribution. This meant that 48 per cent of households in all would still be eligible for legal aid compared with an estimated 50 to 55 per cent before the changes.[162]

The Home Affairs Committee concluded[163] that 'clearly the eligibility cuts will deprive some ordinary people of the protection they now enjoy from the law'. They calculated that in practice 'fewer than 250,000 people' would be adversely affected by the changes – 120,000 who would not get civil legal aid plus some 100,000 who would lose the right to Green Form legal advice.[164] In the committee's view, the cuts in eligibility were 'unfortunate. They do not sit easily with the government's strategy to make the consumer and the citizen more aware of his or her rights and more tenacious of them.'[165]

The overall conclusion of the Home Affairs Committee was that both sides needed to find a better way of spending the existing legal aid budget:

> If we achieve one thing by this report, it will be to knock the heads of the legal professions [sic] and the Lord Chancellor's Department together. Both have as their aim the delivery of justice. Both have told us that they see the need for change in the way public funds are used to provide legal assistance. Our inquiry has demonstrated that unless the whole legal aid system is fully reviewed and all the relevant parties act together and constructively in undertaking that review, cuts will continue to be forced on governments. The principal sufferer will then inevitably be the one person everyone seeks to help – the person of modest means with a legitimate case who seeks the protection of the law.[166]

The committee believed that the government should restore the cuts in real terms when compensatory savings could be found and this somewhat pious hope was subsequently endorsed by the Lord Chancellor's Advisory Committee on Legal Aid.[167] That committee had been set up in 1949 although in recent years its views on the key issue of eligibility had been largely ignored by the government. This policy seems likely to continue. In its first report since it was unexpectedly revived in 1991 the advisory committee expressed its 'deep concern' at the Lord Chancellor's eligibility cuts. There was no suggestion that Lord Mackay was unduly disturbed by this conclusion.

Perhaps there was little the Law Society could have done to stave off the plans outlined in Lord Mackay's Birmingham Manifesto. Its members would have revolted if the Law Society had supported the government's planned cuts any earlier than the eleventh hour. Indeed, it is fair to say that the Law Society was working to its members' advantage by putting off the cuts for as long as possible. As for the government, it could undoubtedly have stepped in earlier. Instead of asking the Law Society for support, instead of prophesying the forthcoming apocalypse, the Lord Chancellor should have taken action while there was still time to do so. A minister more attuned to the demands of the Treasury, an elected politician who did not also have to preside over the judiciary and the House of Lords, might have avoided the crisis merely by thinking ahead.

Even at the fifty-ninth minute of the eleventh hour there was one proposal Lord Mackay might have leapt at: capping the amount of money available for legal aid each year, which would have involved the legal profession agreeing to cash limits. That would have meant an even more fundamental change than the Lord Chancellor was proposing: legal aid has always been demand-led, which means the Treasury has paid for every case that meets the eligibility criteria. Solicitors would not have welcomed any change in that policy but it had already been slipped in through the back door. The realistic figures published in November 1992 were more than just targets. They were cash limits in all but name. That would have been the time to take the money on offer and show the government how best to spend it.

Indeed, what the Law Society really needed at this time was a strategy for justice. Strangely enough one had just dropped through its letterbox.

A strategy for justice

A Strategy for Justice was published in November 1992 by the Legal Action Group, a well-respected organisation which campaigns for reform of legal services. It took the form of a 150-page booklet in which the Legal Action Group said that 'legal aid has suffered from a lack of planning and overall strategy since its inception in 1949'. The booklet argued that the current division of responsibility between the Lord Chancellor's Department and the Legal Aid Board was not working. The way forward, it suggested, was to expand the role of the Legal Aid Board so that it became more autonomous and independent – in short, to create a Legal Services Commission.

Towards a Legal Services Commission
An independent, publicly funded Legal Services Commission would have four objectives:

- to ensure the provision of advice, assistance and representation so that every member of society has equal access to justice;

- to initiate and carry out educational programmes designed to promote people's understanding of their rights and duties;

- to monitor the legal system and propose reform of the law; and

- to undertake research into all aspects of legal aid, including different methods of providing publicly funded legal services.[168]

Such a commission would have a much broader role than anything we have yet seen in England and Wales. It would take responsibility for the full range of publicly funded legal services, from initial help by Citizens' Advice Bureaux to the advocacy services of Queen's Counsel. But its main task would be to provide legal aid.

The Legal Services Commission would be responsible for planning, funding and delivering legal services to all who needed them. It would have to make hard choices: the commission would receive an annual grant from the government and although it would have total control over its own spending it would be expected to keep within its budget. There is certainly no suggestion that legal services should be available to all without charge: means testing would remain for those seeking legal aid. However, initial diagnostic advice should be free, as it already is for those detained by the police.

The Legal Action Group believed there were other areas of 'essential' legal need which merited free advice: these would include housing, custody, children, personal injury, employment protection, all but the most minor criminal cases, wrongful imprisonment and immigration cases. There is not a lot left: nobody would suppose that eligibility for free legal aid could be extended to cover all these services in the foreseeable future. The Legal Action Group's wish for a relatively high proportion of the population to be financially eligible is also a counsel of perfection. One should always aim high but there is no point in asking for pie in the sky.

At present legal aid policy is broadly a matter for the Lord Chancellor while implementation is the responsibility of the Legal Aid Board. Officials in the Lord Chancellor's Department sometimes appear to be living in an ivory tower rather than an anonymous office block behind the Department of the Environment: the Citizens' Advice Bureaux Green Form plans, the 'safety-net' scheme and the 13 weeks' wage-slips proposal (all described earlier in this chapter) demonstrate the dangers of splitting policy and administration. Bringing the two together in a Legal Services Commission would mean a more practical approach towards policy-making. The new commission would also be looking for better ways of providing publicly funded legal services.

A Legal Services Commission should be responsible for education and law reform as well as research into legal aid. Education is more than just telling people where to find a solicitor. It means teaching citizens about their rights and duties, it means teaching schoolchildren how the law works in practice.[169] It also means teaching people how they might be able to resolve some of their legal problems without a solicitor, perhaps through local self-help groups or community action projects.[170]

Law reform can also have a major part to play in ensuring that money is spent wisely. For example, the law was changed in England and Wales during the 1970s so that couples could be divorced without attendance at court. As a result legal aid was no longer needed for undefended divorces (although it remained available for applications involving financial arrangements or children) and the money saved was put to better use.

There are publicly funded Legal Services Commissions in several other common law jurisdictions. In Australia there is a Legal Aid Commission for each state in the Commonwealth. Commissions receive a fixed amount each year from state and federal funds. Their budgets are not open-ended; they are increased each year in line with average earnings or the consumer price index and there is some provision for extra cash to meet unexpected demands. These bodies have a considerable degree of autonomy. Within a fixed budget they can choose how services should be delivered and money spent. That means they decide the scope of legal aid and who is to be eligible on financial grounds. It also means they can provide legal services through their own network of salaried lawyers if they think this would be more efficient. The Director of the South Australia Legal Aid Commission said that in many states the commission was working within the justice system to make the courts more efficient. This has two benefits. It helps the clients by making the system easier to understand. And 'as a result of greater efficiencies, legal representation for clients becomes less expensive for commissions, thereby releasing funds for "preventative" advice and education programmes'.[171]

The Lord Chancellor's officials thought it was unrealistic to suppose that such a system would work in England and Wales without a much higher level of government intervention. In their view, legal aid could no longer be separated from politics, however much the profession – as they saw it – might hark back to a golden age when legal aid policy was decided away from the public gaze by the Law Society, the Legal Aid Advisory Committee and the Lord Chancellor's Permanent Secretary. Lord Mackay's officials thought it would be impossible for any government to hand over issues of eligibility and scope to an independent body and leave them to get on with spending up to £2 billion a year, knowing that they would always be asking for more.

Indeed, any system of fixed funding has one obvious drawback: there may not be enough money to go round. In fact one might as well accept that there *will* not be enough money; however much is available, more can always be spent in increasing eligibility, improving scope or reducing contributions. Some Australian commissions do not even have the funds to pay for certain essential services which are provided in England and Wales: neither New South Wales nor Victoria has a police station duty solicitor scheme and New South Wales does not normally provide assistance in family law cases where only property is involved. The Victorian Legal Aid Commission was forced to make heavy cuts in services after funds ran out in the summer of 1993.

Even with the huge sums spent on legal aid in England and Wales it would be naïve to imagine that a legal aid commission here would get all the money it needed. When the Crown Prosecution Service was set up in 1986 it was badly under-funded by the government – as ministers subsequently admitted. There is little likelihood that legal aid would do any better: indeed, the chances are that it would do worse.

But that seems no reason to dismiss the idea out of hand. The government was wrong to let the Law Society run the legal aid system for so many years. The Lord Chancellor was also wrong to set rigid eligibility limits for legal aid. It seems absurd to risk serious damage to the legal aid system simply in order to save £43 million. The government may be right to say that it cannot give total autonomy to a legal services commission. But, at the very least, it should allow the Legal Aid Board much greater discretion in the way it spends taxpayers' money.

Law centres

In 1970 a group of lawyers and community workers in North Kensington set up the country's first neighbourhood law centre with donations of £4,000 from two charities. Until then there had been only one solicitor doing legal aid work in what was a deprived area of West London. Against all the odds law centres have survived for more than twenty years. They were feared by solicitors who saw them as a threat to their practices, disliked by local authorities who found themselves paying for agencies which would then turn round and sue them, [172] and apparently despised by Conservative governments which rejected their requests for more funding.

Meanwhile those law centres which managed to survive in difficult financial times have developed expertise in unmet areas of social welfare law, using the Green Form legal advice scheme for its original purpose and representing clients before tribunals where legal aid is not available.

From the government's point of view law centres should have considerable advantages. The Legal Action Group sees them as something of a springboard for its integrated approach to the provision of legal services: 'Harnessing the ideals of their workers and volunteers, they have the capacity to provide services much less expensively than private practices, whose work methods and expectations, in terms of remuneration and otherwise, are those of a small business.' [173]

The Law Centres Federation has argued that private practice by solicitors should be replaced, in the long term, by a salaried legal service. That proposal is unrealistic and undesirable: people should always be able to pay a lawyer privately just as they can still see a doctor privately despite the existence of a National Health Service. There is no doubt that greater support for law centres would pay dividends. They could indeed play a major role in providing legal services more efficiently and effectively. But that by itself would not be enough.

A fundamental review

As both the Legal Action Group[174] and the Commons Home Affairs Committee[175] have recognised there must be a fundamental review of publicly funded legal services as a whole. The review should investigate the scope for using salaried lawyers for certain types of work instead of solicitors in private practice. It should re-examine the potential of using organisations like the Citizens' Advice Bureaux to provide initial legal advice. And it should consider how to build on the precarious network of law centres with their valuable expertise in social welfare law.

The Home Affairs Committee called for 'an inquiry into the scope for savings and efficiency gains in the way legal services are delivered and the courts run'. It said: 'This inquiry must be approached with an open commitment to radical change from the government, from the legal professions, the judiciary. There should be full involvement of consumer groups in the work.'[176]

A review of legal services should not confine itself to the problems of legal aid, fundamental though those are. Legal aid must not be looked at in isolation. What is needed is a much wider review of the restrictions on access to justice. And reviews are no use at all if governments are not prepared to act on their recommendations.

6

Planning Criminal Justice

A criminal justice policy?

In a mature democracy, with one party holding the reins of political power for the best part of a decade and a half, it should not be too difficult for the government to formulate and execute a coherent criminal justice policy. There ought to be no need for violent shifts between legislation aimed at clearing the prisons of all but the most hardened criminals and policies designed to satisfy the public's wish for punishment and retribution. It should be possible for the government to formulate a general approach, experiment if necessary to find the best way of implementing it and then stick to its policies. Sadly, life in Britain is not like that. In this chapter we shall look at how the government has coped with the problems of criminal justice in recent years. We shall see that money has had a major influence on policy-making. Above all we shall examine the remarkable series of U-turns executed by government ministers. Our first stop will be at the magistrates' court.

Local justice

As the government itself has acknowledged, magistrates' courts have a long and proud history.[1] If we were starting again from scratch there is little chance that anybody would design a system in which nine out of ten cases were tried by unpaid, unqualified lay people. But it would be hugely expensive to replace lay magistrates with full-time professionals even if there were enough lawyers to do the work. So it is hardly surprising that, in its most recent policy statement, the government said it was 'wholeheartedly committed to

275

the concept of summary justice provided by lay people drawn from their local communities'.[2]

Despite this commitment the government introduced a bill at the end of 1993 which those who worked in the courts saw as a threat to the independence of the magistracy. The story begins in 1989 when the Home Secretary ordered a review of magistrates' funding. It was known, in the fashionable phrase of the time, as a 'scrutiny'.

The Home Office scrutiny

The magistrates' scrutiny was carried out by a small team of officials headed by Julian Le Vay, an Assistant Secretary at the Home Office.[3] Mr Le Vay and his team remarked that although the arrangements for running and funding magistrates' courts had been reformed in 1949[4] they still had 'the local, part-time, almost amateur flavour of an earlier age'. The Le Vay Report described the service as 'highly fragmented', the highest organisational unit being the magistrates' courts committees of which there were 105. The reported noted that:

> There is no coherent management structure for the service. At the national level, the role of the Home Office is so uncertain,[5] and its powers so limited, that it might be truer to say that there are 105 local services, each run by a committee of magistrates. But the local structure is just as confused, with 285 justices' clerks enjoying a semi-autonomous status, under committees which are fundamentally ill-suited to the task of management.[6]

The Le Vay scrutiny was primarily concerned with controlling resources. Imagine, then, how Mrs Thatcher and her ministers must have reacted to the report's conclusion:

> It would be difficult to think of any arrangements less likely to deliver value for money than the present ones. The [government] provides most of the funds but has no say in how these resources are allocated or used, or even the total level of spending, other than by operating detailed approvals which are themselves an obstacle to optimum value for money. The immediate funding body, the local authority, has too little at stake in the service to provide an effective budgeting discipline, whilst magistrates' courts' committees are too dependent on local authorities, and their management capacity is too underdeveloped, to plan or manage resources effectively.

Clearly Something Had To Be Done and the Le Vay scrutiny's preferred solution was to set up an executive agency, which happened to be another politically fashionable notion of the time.[7]

Under the Le Vay plan justices' clerks would no longer have managed their own courts. Instead there would have been 'court managers' – legally qualified but trained in management.

But all this was not to be. Critics thought the government had baulked at the prospect of naked state control in the field of criminal justice.[8] Ministers put it rather differently: they said magistrates and staff had been opposed to the 'dilution of local justice which they feared a national service would entail' and moreover the cost would have been 'substantial'.[9] In any event the government decided to think again.

The White Paper

In February 1992 the government published its revised proposals in a White Paper.[10] A more modern management structure was still needed 'to improve performance and accountability', it said, but ministers had decided that 'management of the courts should continue to be locally based'.

On closer inspection the management turned out to be not quite so local. Around half the magistrates' courts committees – which run the local courts – were to be abolished. Those left – between 50 and 60 – would be restricted in size. Their chairmen would not be able to take office unless they had been approved by the Lord Chancellor. Justices' clerks would have to work within a policy framework laid down by the new magistrates' committees. There would be an extra tier of chief justices' clerks. There would also be a new magistrates' courts inspectorate: in the last resort the Lord Chancellor would be able to step in and take action.

Before examining these far-reaching proposals in more detail it is worth mentioning that initial reaction to them was surprisingly muted. Magistrates themselves appeared not to be too worried about the plans and the justices' clerks, whose jobs were on the line, kept their heads down and said nothing for a year and a half.

This was not as strange as it might now seem. Justices' clerks are not the most militant of public servants and their professional body, the Justices' Clerks' Society, has more apostrophes than press officers. They were no doubt preoccupied for much of 1992 and 1993 with the vexed issue of unit fines (which we shall explore later in this chapter) but the clerks were more than a little naïve in thinking that quiet discussions with government officials might persuade Lord Mackay to change his mind.

Justices' clerks must be solicitors or barristers. Under the existing arrangements they are appointed by the magistrates' courts committees to provide legal advice to lay magistrates, manage the courts and take certain judicial decisions on their own initiative (such as extending bail and granting adjournments). They are accountable to the benches themselves and can be dismissed by the magistrates' courts committees. The justices' clerks are responsible for managing the other court staff who include court clerks and administrative staff. Court clerks, like justices' clerks, sit in court to advise the magistrates: they normally have some form of legal qualification.

There are currently some 250 justices' clerks serving 105 magistrates' courts committees: it follows that each committee is responsible for an average of between two and three clerks. However, the government decided that in future there should be a single employee responsible for all the paid staff in each committee's area. They were originally to be called chief justices' clerks;[11] this was changed to justices' chief executive, a title designed to emphasise their management functions rather than their quasi-judicial status. Justices' clerks would remain responsible for their local benches, but the chief executives were a new tier of management between them and their committees.

Justices' clerks have always held office 'at the pleasure' of magistrates' courts committees. The government decided that in future they should be employed under contracts of employment incorporating performance standards. These contracts would be for unspecified fixed terms although the Lord Chancellor 'expected' that a justices' clerk who was performing satisfactorily would have his or her contract renewed. The contracts would also provide for pay to be linked to performance. The new tier of chief justices' clerks was to be appointed on the same basis.

Both justices' clerks and chief clerks would be subject to supervision by a proposed new Magistrates' Courts Inspectorate, responsible to the Lord Chancellor. Its job would be to make sure the government, which provides 80 per cent of the expenditure on magistrates' courts, got good value for money.

It was this line of command to the Lord Chancellor which alarmed the Justices' Clerks' Society in September 1993. They saw the introduction of fixed-term contracts as the first sign of direct influence by the executive. John Friel, the society's president, gave two examples of how the government had tried to put pressure on the courts. A year earlier the Lord Chancellor's Department had told applicants for criminal legal aid that they would have to produce 13 weeks' payslips as proof of their means. As we saw in chapter 5, the courts had no power to insist on this requirement and it was eventually withdrawn. Mr Friel said his members had no hesitation in ignoring this unjustified instruction. And during the miners' strike of 1984–5 he himself, as clerk to the magistrates in north Nottinghamshire, had also happily ignored a government request to speed up hearings of cases against striking miners. However, in Mr Friel's view, justices' clerks would think twice about ignoring government circulars if their contracts were coming up for renewal.[12]

The Lord Chancellor dismissed this approach as 'completely wrong'. Justices' clerks would be employed by the local magistrates' court committee, he said, not by the government; they would have nothing to fear from the executive. Moreover they would get more protection under contracts of employment than they had when they were subject to dismissal at any time. Lord Mackay said he was at least as concerned as the justices' clerks to ensure the independence of the magistrates. On the other hand he was also concerned that the magistrates' courts should have a 'proper management structure', to make sure public money was properly spent. That was why he would be appointing a Magistrates' Courts Inspectorate. Lord Mackay emphasised that the inspectors would be independent and not connected with those members of his department who were responsible for the policy and finance of the magistrates' courts.[13]

The Lord Chief Justice was less sanguine about the planned Police and Magistrates' Courts Bill. 'I'm worried about it,' he said in July 1993. 'I've seen the Lord Chancellor about it and I'm still worried . . . The danger of a fixed-term contract is that the clerk is going to worry that someone above him will think he's too lax or too severe and he will exercise his functions accordingly.'[14]

Lord Taylor repeated his concerns in November 1993. In his view, the contractual terms on which justices' clerks were engaged should be a matter for their employing committee and not laid down in a central blueprint. He did not agree that the area chief executive should himself be a justices' clerk who was empowered to act as such, nor that he should be involved in giving advice to the magistrates since that too would undermine the judicial independence of justices' clerks. As Lord Taylor said: 'In order for a person properly to exercise judicial functions, he or she must not only *be* independent, but *feel* independent, and *appear* independent.'[15] The government subsequently insisted that chief executives would not be able to tell justices' clerks what legal advice they should give to magistrates.

The Justices' Clerks' Society held a special meeting in September 1993 to express their 'grave concern' at the government's proposals. They called on Lord Mackay to withdraw. To nobody's surprise the Lord Chancellor stood firm. He thought it strange that the justices' clerks should hold an emergency meeting in protest against proposals which had been announced some eighteen months earlier.

Meanwhile magistrates in the outer London boroughs were particularly worried by plans to reduce the number of magistrates' courts committees in the capital. Under the existing arrangements there was a committee for each of the twenty London boroughs. The Lord Chancellor proposed to reduce this number to just three covering North-East, South and North-West London (or Middlesex as it was to be called, after a county abolished some thirty years earlier). The Outer London Magistrates' Courts Action Group said this would create regional bureaucracies unable to respond to local needs.[16]

In February 1994 the Lord Chancellor backed down. He no longer insisted that justices' clerks should have fixed contracts or performance-related pay. Magistrates' courts committees would still be able to appoint their own chairmen without the Lord Chancellor's approval. The Lord Chancellor would not be able to block a justices' clerk's reappointment. These U-turns were announced in response to parliamentary criticism from the Lord Chief Justice. Lord Taylor welcomed the government's announcement while calling for further changes to ensure that chief executives would not exercise judicial functions.

What are we to make of the government's attempts to reform the magistrates' courts? As taxpayers no doubt we should be pleased if there is greater control over how our money is spent. It must be right for those who receive public money to be properly accountable. But whenever the government mentions money, justice and reform in the same breath, it is time to start looking for where the cuts are going to fall. The government claims that justice and efficiency go hand in hand. Sadly it is not so simple. Spending a lot of money on the system may not be very efficient but it can often be the best way of securing justice. When the money begins to dry up, injustices become more likely.

Sentencing policy: Lord Taylor steps in

In the spring of 1993, for reasons never fully explained, the Lord Chief Justice of England chose to launch a lethal attack on English sentencing policy while addressing a gathering of Scottish solicitors at Gleneagles in Tayside.[17]

In his speech Lord Taylor criticised two provisions of the Criminal Justice Act 1991 which, he said, many people felt 'run counter to all the principles of good sentencing policy . . . and in fact defy common sense'. One of those sections provided 'restrictions on imposing custodial sentences'. The other dealt with the 'effect of previous convictions'.[18]

Restrictions on custody

Section 1 of the Criminal Justice Act 1991 read in part:

> (2) The court shall not pass a custodial sentence on the offender unless it is of the opinion –
>
> (a) that the offence, or the combination of the offence and one other offence associated with it, was so serious that only such a sentence can be justified for the offence; or
>
> (b) where the offence is a violent or sexual offence, that only such a sentence would be adequate to protect the public from serious harm from him.

Previous convictions

Section 29 of the Criminal Justice Act 1991 read in part:

> (1) An offence shall not be regarded as more serious . . . by reason of any previous convictions of the offender or any failure of his to respond to previous sentences.
>
> (2) Where any aggravating factors of an offence are disclosed by the circumstances of other offences committed by the offender, nothing . . . shall prevent the court from taking those factors into account for the purpose of forming an opinion as to the seriousness of the offence.

Later in this chapter we shall consider what, if anything, these sections may have meant. But first we should look at the long period of discussion and consultation which led up to them. Only then might we be able to see where the government went so badly wrong and how it might be possible to avoid such mistakes in the future.

281

Punishment, Custody and the Community

To understand the Criminal Justice Act 1991 we must return to its origins some four years earlier. As Lord Windlesham put it: 'The man and the moment came together in the aftermath of the General Election in June 1987.'[19] Douglas Hurd, back in the Secretary of State's room at the Home Office, 'sensed that the time was right to draw together several strands of policy, weaving them into a coherent pattern and projecting them as a whole'.

The most important of those strands was sentencing. There had always been a twin-track approach to sentencing: the policy was to punish violent and serious crimes severely while trying where possible to keep less serious offenders out of prison. Mr Hurd's challenge was to make the non-custodial option seem credible to his supporters in parliament.

The entire Home Office ministerial team and their most senior officials met at Leeds Castle in Kent on 28 September 1987. It proved a key moment in the reappraisal of non-custodial penalties. 'Given the popular identification of punishment with imprisonment,' the meeting asked, 'was it possible to stiffen non-custodial options so that the aims of punishment, deterrence and rehabilitation . . . were pursued not in prison but in the environment in which the offender would normally have to come to terms with everyday life?'[20] The answer – yes – came the following summer.

In July 1988 the government published a Green Paper – a discussion document – called *Punishment, Custody and the Community*.[21] It recognised that imprisonment was not the most effective punishment for most criminals. Instead the government proposed a new plan to supervise and punish offenders 'in the community'. Where possible it believed the penalty should involve three principles:

- restrictions on the offender's freedom of action, as a punishment;

- action to reduce the risk of further offending; and

- reparation to the community and, where possible, compensation to the victim.[22]

The Green Paper held out the prospect of allowing courts to pick and mix from an assortment of penalties. These might include:

- community service;

- residence at a hostel;
- prescribed activities at a day centre;
- compensation to the victim;
- staying away from football matches, specified pubs or streets.

The Green Paper said that imprisonment was likely to add to the difficulty which offenders found in living a normal and law-abiding life. It pointed out that sending people to prison 'reduced offending only by restricting the opportunities for a limited period' and it insisted that 'custody should be reserved as punishment for very serious offences, especially where the offender is violent and a continuing risk to the public'.

It was this last point which the government wanted to stress – especially to its supporters in the Conservative Party. The Home Office press release[23] began – rather oddly for an announcement which was apparently about punishment in the community – by saying: 'The government is committed to providing the prison places needed, particularly for serious violent offenders, and is spending £1 billion on prison building.' This was naturally ignored by the following day's newspapers. Many of them chose instead to concentrate on one of the silliest ideas ever put forward by the Home Office: electronic monitoring of offenders, or 'tagging'.[24] The Green Paper suggested that a criminal could be ordered to wear 'a miniature transmitter which emits a continuous signal. This is retransmitted from his home, e.g. by telephone, to a central monitoring point and the offender cannot move very far away from the telephone without alerting the central monitoring system.' The Home Office explained that tagging could be used to make sure an offender stayed at home for a limited period – in other words, to enforce a curfew.[25]

Making prisoners wear an electronic ball and chain may have looked like a tough non-custodial punishment but the drawbacks were obvious. Not all offenders have telephones in their homes. Some, indeed, do not even have homes. And who would pay for the calls? Was the telephone line to be kept busy twenty-four hours a day by conversations between the tag and the central computer? Or would the offender ring in occasionally to reassure the computer that all was well? What would happen if someone else was on the phone? Or would a special telephone and line be installed? Would the police be sent round if there was no reply from the tag? If the offender was taken into custody for non-compliance surely that would defeat the object of the exercise? To these questions there were no answers in the Green Paper. One problem had been anticipated by Home Office officials, however. They had been wearing prototype tags in the bath to see if they would still work.[26]

The Green Paper of July 1988 had been heavily trailed by the Home Office junior minister, John Patten. It had been planned at a time when the number of people in prison was 50,000 – nearly 6,000 above capacity, with many of the surplus prisoners overflowing into police cells and army camps. The government was worried that the prison population would rise to well over 60,000 and possibly to 70,000 by the year 2000.[27] Mr Patten's aim was to stop that happening. To achieve this he had to persuade judges and magistrates that 'community sentences' were a tough and demanding form of punishment, that prison was not the only way of dealing with young thugs. And that meant he had to change the image of the probation service: he needed to persuade the public that probation officers who had been trained to befriend and support offenders could also be involved in punishing them. In all this he had some success. The prison population began to decline steadily. But it was to be more than four years before the government's planned legislation came into force.[28]

John Patten had been lunching hard in order to drum up support for the government's proposals. For a period of just over a year his Parliamentary Private Secretary invited groups of between six and ten Conservative backbenchers to working lunches with Mr Patten in his room at the Home Office: the minister saw some 150 MPs in this way. At these meetings Mr Patten appeared tentative and open-minded, indicating that he was trying out ideas while they were still in the formative stages. Lord Windlesham, the source of this insight, said that when the government's proposals were finally made public 'there was widespread support on the Conservative benches, primarily because so many people felt that they had been part of the sequence which had led to their formulation'.[29]

Meanwhile others in the Home Office were working on the judges. The Home Secretary, Douglas Hurd, had won the respect of the Lord Chief Justice: Lord Lane and his deputy, Lord Justice Watkins, had regular meetings with Mr Hurd at the Home Office after 1986.[30] Even more remarkably, Lord Lane agreed to attend the first of a series of national conferences on criminal justice held at

Ditchley Park in Oxfordshire during September 1989. This was to be followed by a series of residential seminars for key figures in the middle ranks of the criminal justice system which brought together, for the first time, judges, ministers, officials, magistrates, lawyers, police officers, prosecutors, probation officers, prison governors and even journalists; the aim was to give participants a picture of the system as a whole, to make them understand how decisions taken by one group might affect the others. These pioneering seminars were devised and run by David Faulkner, the Deputy Secretary at the Home Office responsible for criminal justice policy.

With the backing of Douglas Hurd, Mr Faulkner had been working behind the scenes at the Home Office to steer criminal justice policy in a more liberal, humane direction. His great success was in persuading sceptics that the moral duty of keeping people out of jail whenever possible coincided with the political imperative of clearing overcrowded prisons. This approach was embodied in the government's subsequent declaration of intent.

Crime, Justice and Protecting the Public

In February 1990 the Home Office published a White Paper – a policy document – called *Crime, Justice and Protecting the Public*.[31] It was said to 'carry forward the ideas in the earlier Green Paper'.[32] John Patten, still Minister of State at the Home Office, was reputed to have written it all himself. This seems unlikely since a former Oxford don and future Education Secretary would hardly have stated that the government's aim was to make sure that criminals got their 'just desserts'.[33] He would surely have known that desserts are puddings.[34]

The new Home Secretary, David Waddington QC, described the government's proposals as a 'balanced package of measures'. By this he meant that 'the most serious offenders should receive long prison sentences . . . but non-violent offenders should, as far as possible, be punished in the community'.[35] It sounded like a compromise between opposing forces: critics said the government was putting out a contradictory and confusing message and doubted whether the proposals would have any effect on the judges unless sentencing rules were enshrined in statute.

Some jurisdictions in the United States do just that. A sentencing commission prescribes the normal sanction to be imposed for each combination of offence and offender; the court can read off the appropriate sentence from a grid. Put like this the system appears unacceptably rigid but of course there is some discretion within the specified range and, if the sentencer can justify his decision, even outside it.[36]

Nevertheless a more realistic way of gaining some control over the sentencing process in England and Wales would be for the government to set up a Sentencing Council. This idea was first proposed by Professor Andrew Ashworth in 1983.[37] A Sentencing Council would be chaired by the Lord Chief Justice and would build on the existing series of guideline judgments issued by the Court of Appeal. Instead of having to wait for a suitable case to come up, it was suggested that the Sentencing Council could discuss problems on a hypothetical basis and issue Practice Directions which would then influence future sentencing decisions. Professor Ashworth recommended that the Sentencing Council should include magistrates, a senior Circuit judge, a probation officer, a prison governor, a prosecutor, a Home Office official and an academic. In his view:

> What the Sentencing Council should aim to produce is sets of detailed sentencing ceilings for different grades and types of offence, which have their basis in certain relativities between offences, together with declared principles for use in calculating the precise sentence beneath that ceiling – principles to deal with persistent offenders, multiple offenders, breaches of suspended sentences and so forth.

However, this idea was firmly rejected by the White Paper. 'It is not the government's intention that parliament should bind the courts with strict legislative guidelines,' it promised.[38] 'The courts will properly continue to have the wide discretion they need if they are to deal justly with the great variety of crimes which come before them.'[39]

This seemed to give the courts a free hand. But the Home Office then went on to cut down that wide discretion. It began by reminding judges of the existing law:

> An offender can receive repeated financial or community penalties, if his offences merit that level of penalty. As the Court of Appeal has said, an offender should not be 'sentenced for the offences which he has committed in the past and for which he has already been punished. The proper way to look at the matter is to decide a sentence which is appropriate for the offence . . . before the court' (R. v. Queen, 1981).[40]

The White Paper argued that 'injustice is more likely if the courts do not focus on the seriousness of the offence before them when they sentence'.[41] Later on the policy was spelled out much more clearly:

> The government intends to introduce legislation which would require a court, before it gives a custodial sentence, to be satisfied that the offence for which the offender has been convicted by the court is so serious that only a custodial sentence is justified or that a custodial sentence is necessary to protect the public from serious harm. The length of a custodial sentence should be justified by the seriousness of the offences for which the offender has been convicted or which have been taken into consideration by the court.[42]

The White Paper made it clear that these restrictions would not apply to the most serious crimes which are tried only in the Crown Court. Indeed, the courts would be able to give persistent violent and sexual offenders longer sentences than would be justified by the seriousness of the offence.[43]

This was part of the sterner touch demanded by David Waddington when he became Home Secretary. Lord Windlesham records that Mr Waddington was apprehensive about how his Bill would be received:

> So a subtle process of toughening up the Bill began: here the addition of some new wording; there an increase in emphasis on the punitive aspects at the expense of the aim of diverting offenders from custody. Taken on their own, few of the retreats seemed to be of major significance, but cumulatively they amounted to a drawing back from the coherence of the strategy drawn up after the Leeds Castle meeting. That some advance took place cannot be denied, but the objectives were diffused and a rare opportunity to change the direction of public opinion, as [Douglas] Hurd had begun to do, was allowed to pass by.[44]

The White Paper was generally well received. However, Lord Justice Glidewell, the then chairman of the Judicial Studies Board, immediately spotted the fatal weakness which was to cause the government so much trouble three years later:

> Anybody whose home has been burgled normally feels pretty bitter. But time and again, judges get somebody in front of them of, say, 20 – with 14 previous convictions, having been burgling steadily since 15, none of them perhaps enormous crimes. Is the public really going to accept that even on the third or fourth offence the burglar should be left out in the community? I do think there is a real problem in seeking to give

non-custodial sentences to the recidivist house-burglar after a time, but that is left grey in the paper.[45]

It appears that Lord Justice Glidewell communicated his concerns to the Home Office while there was still time to take account of them. Lord Windlesham reveals that David Faulkner 'obtained ministerial sanction to take the previously unheard of step of showing a draft of the Criminal Justice Bill to two or three judges in order to obtain their reactions'.[46] Lord Justice Glidewell was one of them. Although they supported the main thrust of the bill, 'the judges were critical of certain provisions when they saw them in cold print'.

Some years later the then Home Secretary Kenneth Clarke said that the Lord Chief Justice had been consulted about the Criminal Justice Bill and, so far as Mr Clarke was aware, he was satisfied with the outcome.[47] In fact this was not the case, as the Home Office minister David Maclean later acknowledged.[48] It turned out that Mr Clarke was recalling what he had been told about a discussion between Lord Lane and Douglas Hurd at the Ditchley Park conference in 1989. Mr Maclean accepted that this discussion could not be interpreted as approval for a bill which was not published until much later.[49]

The Criminal Justice Bill

The government's Criminal Justice Bill was published in November 1990. David Thomas, Fellow of Trinity Hall, Cambridge, and the country's leading authority on sentencing, said it was 'the biggest load of codswallop' he had ever seen. According to Dr Thomas its only saving grace was that it was so incomprehensible it was possible nobody would take any notice of it. 'If this bill is enacted in this form,' he said, 'it will cause endless chaos. Everyone who knows anything about the subject is too busy to be bothered about the bill. They will only start to read it when it is too late.'[50] Unfortunately, despite later amendments to the bill, it all turned out just as Dr Thomas had predicted. His remarkable prescience was simply ignored at the time.

The bill as drafted was a watered-down version of the earlier White Paper, *Crime, Justice and Protecting the Public*. Originally, as we have seen, the government wanted to restrict custody to offences which were 'so serious that only a custodial sentence is justified'.[51] Now the courts would look at two offences together: an offender who did not quite deserve custody for one crime would still get a custodial sentence if he was convicted of another almost-serious offence. Or so it appeared.

What of the offender's criminal record? In the White Paper the emphasis was on 'the seriousness of the offence before the court'.[52] The bill did indeed have a clause saying that an offence should not be regarded as more serious 'by reason of any previous convictions'. But it then went on to say that 'in so far as the circumstances of any offences of which an offender has been previously convicted are relevant for the purpose of forming an opinion as to the seriousness of the offence, nothing . . . shall prevent the court from taking those circumstances into account for that purpose'.[53] Now what did that mean? Should previous convictions affect the sentence or not? The contradiction was immediately obvious.[54]

The Criminal Justice Bill appeared to represent a compromise between the reforming instincts of Douglas Hurd and the cautious conservatism of David Waddington. Like most compromises it ended up pleasing nobody. The bill was further amended while it was passing quietly through the parliamentary process but that served only to make the provision dealing with previous convictions even more incomprehensible.

The Criminal Justice Act 1991

The Criminal Justice Act was passed by parliament in July 1991. The Home Office minister, John Patten, boldly asserted that the new Act would be seen as 'a benchmark which sets out to increase the confidence of the community in the criminal justice and penal systems'. Nothing could have been further from the truth.[55] For good measure he added that it would 'affect the way in which the courts operate and the way in which offenders are dealt with for many decades into the future'.[56] As we shall see, part of the Act lasted for less than twelve months.

Although the Criminal Justice Act received the Royal Assent in 1991 another year was to pass before it came into effect. The government decided not to implement the legislation until October 1992 to allow time for training those who would have to use the new provisions. The Act had only been operating for a few months when doubts began to surface.

The Criminal Justice Act 1991 turned out to be just the sort of measure people did not want to see. Prisons were no longer bursting at the seams: from a peak of more than 50,000 in 1987 the numbers had dropped to 45,600 by September 1992. If public opinion had ever supported a policy of trying to divert offenders away from custody it had long ago succumbed to more basic instincts; there was increasing enthusiasm for giving young thugs lengthy sentences. But if the custody provisions were seen as too soft, the new financial penalties were apparently too harsh: people were getting huge fines for comparatively minor crimes. To make matters more complicated still, some fines were thought to be far too low. Well might Home Office officials bemoan the fickleness of public opinion.

Now that there was no longer a crisis in the prisons the Home Secretary, Kenneth Clarke QC, seemed happy to look again at measures rejected by his supposedly more right-wing predecessors.

The use of custody

It is now possible to understand the sentencing provisions set out earlier in this chapter – or at least the thinking behind them. They can be seen in the context of a long-standing government policy aimed at reducing the prison population, a muted judicial and academic response which was largely ignored, a Home Office whose public face had been trying to look in two different directions at the same time and a parliamentary draftsman who was apparently required to produce self-contradictory clauses.

Along came a new Lord Chief Justice, one who was not involved in the original consultation process and who was not as liberal as some people had supposed. Lord Taylor supported what he saw as the philosophy behind the 1991 Act, that an offender should only be sent to prison when it was necessary to do so.[57] On sentencing policy, however, Lord Taylor reckoned there were two schools of thought: one believed in the need for punishment and the other did not. He himself clearly fell into the first category:

> There are powerful arguments for custody, not as a sentence of first resort, but certainly as one weapon in the court's armoury. If an offender, even a very young offender, has been given the benefit and assistance of probation, has been conditionally discharged and has been given a

community service order, what is the court to do when he comes back again and again and again? Short of repeating the same threats and wagging the same finger once more (which the offender soon learns to treat with contempt) there must surely be a custodial sanction available. True, it may not necessarily reform the offender; but at least it punishes him in a way society would regard as just.[58]

Faced as he was with legislation which stopped judges sending persistent offenders to prison it was not surprising to find Lord Taylor critical. Faced with legislation which had been so badly drafted his scorn was equally unsurprising.

Take Section 1(2) which said, in effect, that prison must be reserved for people who commit a serious offence, or two quite serious offences together. Well, of course, said Lord Taylor, it was reasonable not to impose a custodial sentence unless the seriousness of the *offending* requires it. 'But, for goodness sake, why,' he asked, 'has consideration to be limited to one offence or – even more strangely – the combination of that offence and only one other?'[59]

Then take Section 29(1) which said, in effect, that an offence was not to be regarded as more serious because the offender had previous convictions. Well, again, said Lord Taylor, there was a sensible idea behind the provision – that you sentence a man for an offence rather than on his record. He agreed that it had never been the practice of the courts to punish twice for the same offence: an offender with a long record is given the punishment he deserves and no more although someone of good character who commits the same offence will receive a much reduced punishment.[60] But take the example of two offenders jointly charged with burglary. 'For one of them, it is his first offence; the other has been convicted of burglary five times before and has breached probation orders and failed to comply with community service orders. How,' asked Lord Taylor, 'can it be just to treat them both the same?'

The answer was that they did not have to be treated the same if 'any aggravating factors of an offence were disclosed by the circumstances of other offences committed by the offender'. What was that supposed to mean? How can the circumstances of one offence disclose 'aggravating factors' of another?

For a while the judges were left to sort out the whole sorry mess. But perhaps that was only their 'just deserts'. If Lord Lane had chosen to say publicly in 1990 what Lord Taylor in fact said in 1993 parliament would have found it much more difficult to enact these provisions. At the very least MPs would have understood rather better the legislation before them.

Unit fines

Critics of the Criminal Justice Act 1991 did not confine their ire to the restrictions on sentencing. There was a great deal of public concern early in 1993 about the system of 'unit fines' introduced in October 1992. Although some individual magistrates had expressed misgivings at the time, the furore that broke out during the following months was rather more unexpected.

For many years the law had allowed courts to reduce a fine if the offender could not afford to pay it but there had been doubts as to whether a fine could properly be increased to punish a wealthy offender more severely. In 1990 the White Paper *Crime, Justice and Protecting the Public*[61] proposed a system of linking fines more closely to the means of offenders. It said 'this would include a requirement for defendants to provide information about their means and for the courts to reduce or increase fine levels according to the means of convicted offenders'.

Broadly speaking, under section 18 of the Criminal Justice Act 1991 if magistrates wanted to fine an offender they had to order him to pay a certain amount of units instead – the more serious the offence the more units he had to pay up to a maximum of 50. How much was a unit? That depended on how much 'spare income' the individual offender had after proper household expenses had been deducted. A unit was deemed to be one-third of whatever was left. However, maximum and minimum 'disposable weekly income' figures were set by law. The minimum value of a unit, however little income the offender had, was £4. The maximum level of a unit, however well-off the offender might have been, was £100.

This was a serious mistake. The range was far too wide. It meant one offender would be fined 25 times as much as another for exactly the same offence. It was also a mistake to remove the magistrates' discretion to increase or reduce fines according to the offender's personal circumstances.

Offences which can be tried in the magistrates' courts are graded according to their seriousness: there are five different levels. Under the old system maximum fines were set for each level; the highest fine the magistrates could impose for the most serious offence was £2,000. It would have been possible to keep these maximum levels when unit fines were introduced. Alternatively, the government could have used its existing powers[62] to increase the levels slightly in line with inflation. Instead the maximum levels were increased by 250 per cent, 400 per cent, or even 500 per cent.[63]

Offence	Old Maximum	New Maximum
Level 1	£50	£200
Level 2	£100	£500
Level 3	£400	£1,000
Level 4	£1,000	£2,500
Level 5	£2,000	£5,000

It was another grave mistake to have increased maximum levels at the same time as unit fines were introduced: unit fines became linked in the public mind with a succession of very high fines for apparently trivial offences.

Why should this have been? The answer lay in the strange behaviour of many offenders. Before they came before the court, defendants were asked to fill in what the Home Office described as 'a simple means inquiry form'. It was in fact quite a complicated document and convicted defendants who refused to fill it in faced prosecution.[64] But there was a much simpler sanction for offenders who refused to disclose their means: the court could assume they had the maximum disposable income of £100 a week.

It turned out that a number of defendants were unwilling to tell the court how much money they had coming in each week. Perhaps this reticence arose from a reluctance to admit they had some undeclared income; perhaps it stemmed from the antipathy some people have to the very concept of a means test; or perhaps it was merely due to the fact that people who receive complicated forms through the post from a magistrates' court tend to stuff them behind the clock and forget about them. Whatever the reason, the result of this reticence was that huge fines were imposed. Indeed a number of defendants said on the form that they were willing to let the court fine them on the basis that their spare income was £100 a week – even if it was not. Possibly they had assumed that £100 would be the amount they were fined. In fact, the amount they were ordered to pay was £100 multiplied by the number of units set by the court.

One widely reported example was the case of an unemployed man from South Wales who was fined £1,200 for dropping litter. There had been a number of aggravating factors and so the magistrates at Cwmbran in Gwent fined Vaughan Watkins, aged 20, a total of 12 units. Mr Watkins, from Pontnewydd, had failed to complete the means-test form which should have been posted to him before the hearing and so the magistrates had assessed each unit at the maximum level of £100. He told reporters it was 'absolutely ridiculous'. Mr Watkins said: 'I am unemployed and I have no savings, so I don't know how I could be expected to pay a fine like this.'[65] The answer, of course, is that he was not: once he had disclosed his means to the court as well as to the press, his units were reassessed at the minimum level of £4, making a fine of £48.

As was always intended, the people worst affected by unit fines were the middle classes – the comfortably off for whom fines had been no more than a minor inconvenience in the past.[66] What the government had failed to anticipate, however, was the anger of magistrates, most of whom came from the same middle classes. Several of them resigned over the Criminal Justice Act.

A magistrate in Bradford was quoted as describing the Act as 'a criminal's charter' which was making JPs look foolish. 'Hardened young criminals are leaving the court laughing,' he said. Another West Yorkshire magistrate resorted to magnificent hyperbole: 'The little thugs who wreck three cars a week are having their nappies changed by the probation service while honest motorists who have driven at 38 mph in a 30 mph zone are being hit for hundreds of pounds. It offends the British sense of justice.'[67]

The idea of means-based fines in England and Wales came from David Chandler, clerk to the Bradford justices, whose paper on the subject was published in 1984. But much of the impetus for unit fines came from Bryan Gibson, the magistrates' clerk at Basingstoke in Hampshire. His court was one of four where pilot schemes were carried out with some success. Mr Gibson said that the problems over unit fines were caused mainly by the changes made when the system was introduced on a national basis. In the pilot schemes the maximum weekly disposable limit was set at £25, which Mr Gibson said 'commanded a reasonable degree of support'. Setting the figure at £100 meant that people with relatively modest incomes had to pay much higher fines.[68]

The arrangements for assessing an offender's means were fairly crude. Capital was not taken into account so someone with a huge house but no income might be fined a pittance. And not enough was done to check the information supplied by offenders. Lying about one's means was itself an offence but there can be little doubt that it was going on.

The government acts

By the summer of 1993 the Home Secretary, Kenneth Clarke QC, had recognised the political damage that the new legislation was causing. At the beginning of May Mr Clarke said he agreed with the principle of unit fines but he went on to say that the system 'plainly needs to be amended to avoid some of the absurd decisions we have seen recently'.[69] After a meeting with leaders of the Magistrates' Association he announced plans to change both the unit fines provisions and the restrictions on taking previous convictions into account.[70]

At that stage Mr Clarke was suggesting that improvements to unit fines could have been made within two or three months by changing the regulations. However, changes to the rules on previous convictions needed new primary legislation which he thought would take somewhat longer.

Asked[71] whether the government had been wrong to increase the maximum level of a unit from £25 during the experiment to £100 when the legislation came into force Mr Clarke explained that magistrates had wanted the fine levels generally to be increased. But nobody had 'read across from what was seen to be the desirable introduction of unit fines combined with the desirable increase in the maximum fines to catch up with inflation'.

Magistrates and their clerks disagreed. They said they had warned the Home Office about the risks of changing the figures. Would the government accept the blame for what had gone wrong?

'I think the government has been involved in all this,' the Home Secretary cautiously conceded. But it was not as if the Criminal Justice Act had been controversial:

It went gently through the House of Commons. It was not opposed by the Labour Party. It was not opposed by the Liberal Party. I don't criticise them, because it was supported, so far as anyone was aware, by the Magistrates' Association, by the judiciary, and by most other people who had been consulted on it. It shows that even the fullest process of consultation can make its mistakes.

Mr Clarke was right about the lack of opposition but this was surely taking the principle of government by consent too far. Governments are responsible for what they do and when things go wrong they should not blame others for not protesting loudly enough. Certainly Mr Clarke did not give Labour and the Liberal Democrats any credit for the many parts of the Act he thought were working well.

The following week Mr Clarke discovered a way of implementing his recommendations much more quickly. Originally, he had thought he would have to wait until the 1993–4 session of parliament to introduce amending legislation. He had now been advised that he could use the Criminal Justice Bill, at that time passing quietly through parliament, as an engine of change.

Mr Clarke announced plans to:

- amend section 1 of the 1991 Act to allow courts to take account of all the offences for which the offender was being punished;

- repeal section 29 so courts could take account of an offender's criminal record; and

- abolish the unit fine system and replace it by provisions which required magistrates to consider an offender's means but not to fine by application of a mathematical formula.

'Never have we seen so quick a collapse of government policy,' said Labour's shadow Home Secretary, Tony Blair. No longer was the unit fine scheme to be modified: it was now to be scrapped.

Before the Home Secretary's announcement David Faulkner, the Home Office Deputy Secretary most closely involved with the Criminal Justice Act 1991, had believed that fine tuning was all that was required. 'With hindsight, one could wish these things had been ironed out beforehand,' he said. 'One of the difficulties is the rush and pressure of parliamentary business. It is very difficult to ge the detail right.'[72]

These remarks had a hollow ring to them. Mr Faulkner was a fine civil servant and many thousands of offenders have benefited over the years from his enlightened approach to criminal justice. But he had the best part of four years to get the detail right – virtually the whole of one parliament.

Mr Faulkner conceded that 'there may now be a case for expressing the provisions on previous and related offences more flexibly and for modifying the rules for assessing disposable income for the purpose of unit fines'. But, he insisted, 'the principles remain sound and should be preserved in whatever changes are made'.[73] Later Mr Faulkner was to maintain that the principles behind the Criminal Justice Act 1991 were taken from current legislation and existing rulings from the Court of Appeal. Those who had criticised the Act's treatment of previous offences and means-related fines had not acknowledged the extent to which the Act reflected what had gone before, he said, or indeed 'the courts' considerable flexibility and discretion'.

Supporters of the 1991 Act said its failings were mostly the result of sloppiness and were trivial when set against the enlightened principles on which the legislation was founded.[74] But they were soon to discover that battles which they thought they had won were now being fought afresh. Vivien Stern, director of the National Association for the Care and Resettlement of Offenders (NACRO), recalled that Britain had been imprisoning more people per hundred thousand than anyone else in Western Europe even though imprisonment was widely acknowledged to be an expensive way of making bad people worse:

> There is a suggestion that the Act has been dreamed up by left wing lunatics, when in fact it was devised by a Conservative government after wide consultation . . . The idea that you should not impose a more severe sentence simply because an offender has previous convictions is not a burst of revolutionary madness. It is in fact what the Court of Appeal expected courts to do before the Criminal Justice Act.[75]

The National Association of Probation Officers urged the Home Office 'not to tamper with the basic aim of the Criminal Justice Act'. The probation officers called for 'more training and clarification rather than wholesale and premature reform of the legislation'.[76]

Kenneth Clarke went ahead with his U-turn all the same. David Faulkner said he was surprised that the Home Secretary had decided to act so quickly; he had hoped – in vain – that there would have been an opportunity for consultation and discussion.[77] In Mr Faulkner's view, the areas of concern amounted to 'relatively straightforward points which can be corrected'. They did not undermine the 'fabric' of the Act.

Bryan Gibson, the man behind unit fines, was shocked and disappointed at the government's decision. He thought the scheme could have been made to work. 'Given a fairly short phasing-in period,' he said, 'people would have become accustomed to what in fact is a very progressive and positive way of looking at the punishment of offenders.'[78] Mr Gibson took some comfort from the fact that magistrates would still be able to operate an informal system of unit fines, as his court had done before the Criminal Justice Act took effect.

As for the Lord Chief Justice, he was naturally pleased that his complaints had been heeded so speedily. Lord Taylor acknowledged that unit fines were a 'very good idea' but he said that to fix an arithmetical formula had produced some 'bizarre' results.[79] The Lord Chief Justice stressed the need to give judges full discretion to do what was appropriate in the individual case.

At the end of July 1993 the Criminal Justice Act 1993 became law. Michael Howard QC, who by then had replaced Kenneth Clarke as Home Secretary, was able to depict the collapse of his government's sentencing policy as some sort of triumph. 'We have acted decisively and quickly to amend the 1991 Criminal Justice Act,' he said, perhaps forgetting who had introduced it in the first place. From August 1993, he announced, the courts would be able to take account of an offender's previous convictions in deciding what sentence to impose. And from September 1993 the unit fines system would be abolished. 'Magistrates will still be expected to take an offender's income into account,' said Mr Howard, 'but they will not be hampered by a mechanistic formula.'[80] Meanwhile, the prison service gloomily prepared itself for the inevitable rush of new customers.

David Faulkner had been right to say that the principles behind the Criminal Justice Act remained sound but this did not make it any easier to put them into practice. It was not surprising that judges and magistrates resented the loss of their discretion. They would hardly welcome artificial restrictions on their ability to send offenders to prison, just as magistrates did not want to lose the power to decide how much an offender should be fined.

In an ideal world the government would have gained the support of the judges before taking action. That might have avoided some of the problems which the judges had clearly expected. Indeed, if the judiciary had backed Mr Hurd's aim of reducing the overall prison population there might not have been any need for the restrictions on custody contained in the Criminal Justice Act. While Lord Lane was Lord Chief Justice, that level of co-operation was out of the question but his successor took a very different approach. The government will not be able to plead ignorance if it chooses to disregard the judges' views in future.

In an ideal world the government would also have stuck to its guns. As originally conceived, the policy behind the Criminal Justice Act was wise and humane. But in the real world policies are modified to fit in with political realities. And that is where the problems arise.

The restrictions in sections 1 and 29 of the Criminal Justice Act had emerged so badly mangled from the legislative sausage machine that the government was probably right to get rid of them. However, unit fines were a different matter: they work effectively in other countries. If operated properly they must be fairer than a system where each offender is fined the same amount – in other words, a poll tax. If only the opposition had opposed – and if only the government had listened – a successful system of unit fines would have been perfectly possible.

Meanwhile, as we have seen, Mr Howard was busy telling his supporters that 'prison works'. Lord Taylor, who more than anyone else was responsible for persuading parliament to amend the Criminal Justice Act, was beginning to worry that things had gone too far. His approach was rather more subtle than that of his long-standing friend Lord Woolf. The Lord Chief Justice stressed that the principles underlying the 1991 Act remained valid: custodial sentences, he said, would be imposed only where the seriousness of the offending behaviour made prison the only justifiable option or where the public needed to be protected from a dangerous offender. The Criminal Justice Act had extended the range of community penalties available to the courts, a measure intended to prevent offenders from committing further crimes. 'Retribution and deterrence,' said the Lord Chief Justice, 'must be balanced against the need to rehabilitate offenders back into society.'[81]

Mr Howard changes tracks

The Home Secretary was singing a rather different tune. Michael Howard told his party conference in October 1993 that it was time to frighten the criminals rather than law-abiding members of the public: 'In the last 30 years the balance in the criminal justice system has been tilted too far in favour of the criminal and against the protection of the public. The time has come to put that right.'

Mr Howard announced a 27-point plan. Its objectives were: 'action to prevent crime; action to help the police to catch criminals; action to make it easier to convict the guilty; action to punish them once they are found guilty.' The most controversial of the 27 points was his plan to abolish the right of a defendant to remain silent without adverse comment. That and the other points derived from the report of the Royal Commission on Criminal Justice will be considered in chapter 8. The remaining proposals in Mr Howard's speech had been on the Home Office agenda for some time: they were included in what was to become the Criminal Justice and Public Order Act 1994.

The general tone of Mr Howard's speech was perhaps more important than its content. He accepted that the new reforms might well see more people going to prison but he did not flinch from that: 'We shall no longer judge the success of our system of justice by a fall in the prison population.' Four new private prisons would be built in addition to two already announced: they would be 'decent but austere'. Mr Howard's message was clear and simple: 'Prison works. It ensures we are protected from murderers, muggers and rapists, and it makes many who are tempted to commit crime think twice.'

Judges and magistrates had no difficulty in understanding what Mr Howard was telling them. If the courts wanted to send people to prison he would find the places. If necessary, it emerged a few weeks later, he would keep prisoners in police cells, in army camps, and even in converted ships: the modern equivalent of the notorious 'hulks'. The wheel had truly come full circle and the prison population was rising at an alarming rate.

Within a week of Mr Howard's conference speech Lord Woolf had given his own views on prisons: it was 'short-sighted and irresponsible' to talk of getting tough on crime.[82] The columnist Hugo Young immediately remarked on this startling reversal of roles:[83]

While the politician spouts the monosyllables that were once the prerogative of the bench, the mantle of social concern has fallen on the judge. It is now the judge, in the person of Lord Woolf, who feels obliged to reach for the most comprehensive understanding that might once have been called, with proper dignity, political. He is the one who has studied the causes of crime and the consequences of prison.

Hugo Young concluded: 'Woolf shows Howard up as a lightweight opportunist, far happier pandering to discredited public prejudice than reading the voters a lesson in reality.' Deep down, he said, Mr Howard knew Lord Woolf was right. It seemed a long way from the sunlit uplands of Leeds Castle.

7

When Justice Miscarries

An appalling vista

Until the late 1980s it was still possible to believe that Britain's criminal justice system was the best in the world. But in 1989 that myth was shattered for ever. An 'appalling vista' opened up – to use Lord Denning's notorious phrase[1] – as it gradually became clear that a number of people had been wrongly convicted of the most serious offences in the criminal calendar. So many miscarriages of justice came to light between 1989 and 1992 that it is sometimes difficult to remember each individual case. But it is only by looking in detail at what went wrong that we will have any chance of putting it right.[2]

The Guildford Four

In October 1975 Patrick Armstrong, Gerard Conlon, Paul Hill and Carole Richardson were convicted of the five murders arising from the bombing in October 1974 of the Horse and Groom pub in Guildford. In addition Mr Armstrong and Mr Hill were convicted of two murders arising from an explosion in November 1974 at the King's Arms pub in Woolwich. The prosecution case had been based almost entirely on confessions they had allegedly made to the police. All were sentenced to life imprisonment.

In January 1989 the Home Secretary, Douglas Hurd, referred their case back to the Court of Appeal after a long campaign by church leaders and others. He had done so because of doubts about the state of Carole Richardson's health while she was being questioned and in the light of new alibi witnesses.

Whether this new evidence would have been enough to secure the acquittals of the Guildford Four is something we shall never know. While lawyers were preparing their cases for the Court of Appeal, the Avon and Somerset police were checking through original interview notes made by detectives from the Surrey police force. Early in May 1989 Detective Inspector Doreen Bryant compared handwritten notes of interviews with Patrick Armstrong against rough typed notes of the same interviews. Her suspicions were aroused. The typed notes contained deletions and additions, both typed and handwritten, as well as some rearrangement of material. And yet the handwritten notes corresponded with the typed notes *in their corrected form*. It therefore looked to the Avon and Somerset police as if the rough typed notes had been made before the handwritten notes. At the original trial, however, Surrey police officers had claimed they had made handwritten notes during their interviews.

Patrick Armstrong's confession was central to the prosecution case. Anything which cast doubt on it would undermine all four convictions. By early October, a full five months after Inspector Bryant's discovery, the Director of Public Prosecutions, Allan Green, had decided he should not oppose the forthcoming appeal.

The appeal was rapidly brought forward. As had by then become customary in such cases the Court of Appeal sat at the Old Bailey – which has more secure facilities for handling prisoners. But there was no need for security. The four people who were brought to court in an armoured convoy left the same day as innocent citizens.[3]

It was another nine months before the Avon and Somerset police had completed their investigations into the case. In November 1990, more than a year after the Guildford Four were cleared, the Director of Public Prosecutions announced criminal proceedings: retired Detective Chief Inspector (later Superintendent) Thomas Style, Detective Sergeant John Sutherland Donaldson and Detective Constable Vernon Attwell would be prosecuted for conspiracy to pervert the course of justice. (Mr Donaldson and Mr Attwell had been suspended from police duties since October 1989 and later retired.)

Committal proceedings began in February 1991. They were to end, suddenly and dramatically, four months later. The Bow Street magistrate, Ronald Bartle, discharged the three men after ruling that the process of the court had been abused. His reasons included the seventeen years' delay in bringing the case; the adverse media comment since the Guildford Four appeal; and the fact that the Surrey officers had not been cautioned by the Avon and Somerset police before being interviewed a month before the Court of Appeal hearing.

At the beginning of 1992 the High Court granted judicial review of that decision. Lord Justice Neill, Lord Justice Taylor (shortly to become Lord Chief Justice) and Mr Justice Rose decided it was unreasonable. The delay would not prejudice a fair trial in a case based mainly on documentary evidence. The adverse media comment in 1989 would not prevent a jury deciding the case on the evidence in late 1992 (or, as it turned out, the spring of 1993). And the aim of the investigating officers in 1989 had been to obtain relevant information for the Court of Appeal.

The three former police officers stood trial at the Old Bailey in April 1993. A month later they were acquitted of all charges. They had chosen not to give evidence but the jury were shown written statements they had made to investigating officers from Avon and Somerset in October 1990. In their statements all three said that the handwritten notes had been made at the time of their interviews with Patrick Armstrong and not later, as the Crown alleged. Mr Attwell could not recall why he had made rough typed notes of the handwritten interview notes but he thought it looked as if he had made a rough copy for internal police purposes. It might not have been fully accurate because the emphasis would have been on speed. Mr Style and Mr Donaldson accepted that some of the manuscript additions and alterations appeared to have been written by them. They believed this would have been to help police typists prepare a typed copy of the original handwritten document for use later in court: instead of having to decipher the handwriting they could refer instead to the amended typed copy. These explanations clearly made an impact on the jury. But there was more to come.

During the course of the trial Edmund Lawson QC, for the defence, said that Patrick Armstrong 'sang like a canary' about his IRA contacts and activities. The jury was told that Mr Armstrong had freely confessed to the Guildford pub bombings in subsequent interviews with other police officers, including Peter Imbert who was later to become Commissioner of the Metropolitan Police.

Giving evidence Sir Peter Imbert told the court he had recorded his interview with Patrick Armstrong in shorthand. He said two other members of the Guildford Four, Paul Hill and Carole Richardson, had repeated their confessions to involvement in the bombings. And the fourth member, Gerard Conlon, had given the police a 'catalogue' of names and information about the IRA.

None of this evidence had been before the Court of Appeal in 1989. One can only speculate on whether it would have made any difference to the appeal of the Guildford Four. As we shall see in chapter 8, there are known to be many reasons why people confess to crimes they have not committed. At the trial of the Surrey police officers in 1993 defence counsel had asked rhetorically why the three detectives should want to fabricate what he said was the truth. But the evidence against the Guildford Four, whatever impact it may have had on the jury in 1993, could not have thrown much light on whether the former detectives had actually manufactured a confession.

Needless to say the jury's verdict on the Surrey officers left the public bemused. How could it be that both the Guildford Four and the Surrey officers were not guilty? The answer of course is that a 'not guilty' verdict means the prosecuting lawyers have failed to prove their case beyond reasonable doubt – no more and no less. Unless they do so a defendant must be acquitted. The courts do not claim to be able to find out whether something actually happened: all they do is decide whether or not there is enough evidence to prove that it almost certainly did happen.

There needs to be only a reasonable degree of doubt about a conviction for someone to be acquitted. A much higher standard of proof is required before a defendant can be convicted. The evidence uncovered by the Avon and Somerset police was quite enough to cast doubt on the convictions of the Guildford Four but it was not enough to prove that the Surrey detectives had conspired to pervert the course of justice.

Should it be easier to acquit than convict? The answer must be Yes. The consequences of a miscarriage of justice are so serious that we must tilt the scales heavily in favour of the accused. It may be galling to see the guilty walk free but it is infinitely worse to see innocent people convicted.

In October 1989, on the day the Guildford Four were freed, the Home Secretary announced a public inquiry into their case. It was to be chaired by Sir John May, a retired Lord Justice of Appeal. However, Sir John said his inquiry could not start taking evidence in public while there was still a possibility of charges against the Surrey police officers. He felt it was essential to avoid prejudicing any future trial. Sir John grossly underestimated the time it would take to dispose of those charges. The estimate he gave in November 1989[4] was 'two or three months'. In fact, it was three and a half years.

By July 1992 it had become clear that there would be little or no time between the end of the Surrey detectives' trial and completion of the report by the Royal Commission on Criminal Justice, which had been appointed following the release of the Birmingham Six in 1991, of which Sir John May was also a member. The Royal Commission had wanted to take account of whatever lessons could be learned from the case. To save time Sir John therefore announced that there would be no public hearings into the Guildford Four case after all. It would all be done in writing or in private.

The result was to satisfy nobody. The hearing before the Court of Appeal in 1989 had been cursory in the extreme: it lasted just half a day. The Crown Prosecution Service was so anxious to see the Guildford Four let out of prison that it made the mistake of conceding the appeal immediately. That meant the lawyers for the Guildford Four had no chance of putting their evidence forward in court. Neither, for that matter, did the Surrey police officers who had been accused of lying. So there never was a full hearing into the case.

The trial in 1993 was also unsatisfactory from the point of view of those who wanted to know what had been going on. The three officers did not give evidence. Neither did Patrick Armstrong. Speaking afterwards to the media Mr Armstrong said he had not been asked to appear as a witness; the jury had been told he had refused. In fact, Mr Armstrong's medical advisers had laid down certain conditions for a proposed police interview some four months after his sudden release, which his solicitor said the police were not willing to accept. The psychiatrist who was treating him for what was diagnosed as post-traumatic stress disorder had insisted that any police interview should be video-recorded, that it should be held in familiar surroundings, that his solicitor and his psychiatrist should be present and that he should be allowed to end the interview at any time.

The acquittal of the Surrey officers should have cleared the way for publication of the report of the May Inquiry. But there was still one matter outstanding. Paul Hill had been cleared of the Guildford offences but he had also been convicted of murdering a former soldier in Northern Ireland. He had lodged an appeal against that conviction and was freed on bail shortly after he was acquitted of the Guildford bombings. In April 1994 Mr Hill was cleared by the Court of Appeal in Northern Ireland. He had claimed he was induced to confess to the soldier's murder by an incident in which an unloaded revolver had been 'fired' at him through a flap in the door of his cell at Guildford police station. Since the Crown was unable to disprove that claim the Court of Appeal considered that his confession would have been ruled inadmissible. On that basis Mr Hill would have never have been convicted of murdering the former soldier.

Sir John May's 300-page report was finally published at the end of June 1994.[5] He concluded that the case of the Guildford Four was a miscarriage of justice. Sir John said that if the trial judge Mr Justice Donaldson (later Lord Donaldson MR) had known about the handgun incident there could be little doubt he would have declared Mr Hill's statements inadmissible and directed the jury to acquit the Guildford Four.

After they were cleared in 1989 a number of prominent people suggested that the Guildford Four – or some of them at least – were guilty all along. Sir John May deprecated this 'whispering campaign': in the eyes of the law, the Guildford Four were not guilty. However, Sir John was not prepared to say whether *he* thought the Guildford Four were guilty or innocent. That, he felt, was not something a public inquiry could or should decide. It was impossible to discover the full truth twenty years on.

Sir John May's report did little to reassure the public. Individuals were to blame, he said; the police may have behaved improperly, prosecuting lawyers should have disclosed vital alibi evidence; the courts should have approached confession evidence with a more open mind. But Sir John believed the miscarriages of justice 'were not due to any specific weakness or inherent fault in the criminal justice system itself.' That seemed hard to reconcile with a Royal Commission which recommended 352 specific improvements to the criminal justice system. Sir John was one of its members.

The Maguire family

In March 1976 Anne Maguire, her husband Patrick (known as 'Paddy'), her sons Patrick and Vincent, her brother Sean Smyth, her husband's brother-in-law Patrick Conlon (known as 'Giuseppe') and a family friend called Patrick O'Neill were convicted of unlawfully possessing the explosive nitroglycerine in December 1974 (though not of 'running a bomb factory' as the press often claimed). Mrs Maguire and her husband were each sentenced to fourteen years in prison. The other adults were sentenced to twelve years (Patrick O'Neill's sentence was reduced to eight years on appeal). Vincent Maguire, then aged 17, was sentenced to five years and Patrick Maguire, who was 14, got four years' detention. In 1980 Giuseppe Conlon died in custody. All the others served their sentences and were released.

Giuseppe Conlon was the father of Gerard Conlon, one of the Guildford Four. Under questioning Gerry Conlon was alleged to have told the police that Anne Maguire, his aunt, was the person who had shown him how to make bombs at her home in London. That was why the police went to her house in the first place, two months after the Guildford bombings. Though no explosives were ever found, and there was no evidence of what the family were supposed to have done with them, the Crown alleged that the people arrested in the house had been moving or disposing of nitroglycerine. Tests were said to have detected minute traces of explosives on their hands (or, in the case of Mrs Maguire, on her gloves). The Maguire family always maintained their innocence.

The freeing of the Guildford Four led directly to the clearing of the Maguire family. Though in fact there was no overlap between the two cases, it was taken for granted in the public mind that the bombs which exploded in Guildford were somehow linked to Mrs Maguire and her family. They were not.

That link was preserved when the time came to investigate the case of the Guildford Four. In October 1989 the Home Secretary also asked Sir John May to inquire into the circumstances surrounding the trial of the Maguire family.

As we have seen, the inquiry into the Guildford Four case was thwarted by the impending prosecution of the police officers who investigated that case. No such problem arose over the Maguire family: their convictions rested on scientific evidence[6] rather than disputed confessions. Sir John May therefore started on the Maguires' case.

One of the grounds on which their conviction had been challenged was the possibility that the Maguires had become 'innocently contaminated' with nitroglycerine – in other words it was suggested that the Maguires could have had traces of explosives on their hands without having deliberately or knowingly handled a prohibited substance.

In April 1990 Sir John May commissioned the distinguished analytical chemist Professor Duncan Thorburn Burns to test this theory. He carried out experiments, using a towel as the possible source of contamination because (not surprisingly) members of the Maguire family had said in evidence that they had washed and dried their hands on a towel in their bathroom. First Professor Thorburn Burns handled a stick of explosives containing nitroglycerine. He then washed his hands and dried them on a clean towel which was subsequently used by others in the laboratory. The tests proved that significant amounts of nitroglycerine could be picked up from a contaminated towel and smaller traces could be obtained by handling other contaminated household objects. This contradicted the evidence of scientists at the Maguires' trial.

Faced with this evidence, the Director of Public Prosecutions conceded in June 1990 that the convictions were unsafe and unsatisfactory on the ground of innocent contamination (but on no other ground). The case was referred to the Court of Appeal and in June 1991 the Maguire family was cleared – but again 'on the ground that the possibility of innocent contamination cannot be excluded and on this ground alone'.[7]

This ruling was hardly the vindication the Maguires had hoped for. It implied that at least one of them had either been handling nitroglycerine or had let somebody into their house who had been in contact with explosives. 'There never were any explosives in my house,' said Mrs Maguire after the judgment.

The Birmingham Six

In August 1975 Hugh Callaghan, Patrick Hill, Gerry Hunter, Richard McIlkenny, Billy Power and Johnny Walker were convicted of the 21 murders arising from the bombing of two Birmingham pubs in 1974. All were sentenced to life imprisonment. The prosecution case rested mainly on confessions they had allegedly made to the police, together with scientific evidence which was said to prove that two of the men had handled nitroglycerine.

In January 1987 the Home Secretary, Douglas Hurd, referred the case back to the Court of Appeal. He gave two reasons: there was fresh scientific evidence casting doubt on the tests for nitroglycerine and there had been allegations from a former policeman, Tom Clarke, that some of the men had been ill-treated while in police custody. But a year later all their appeals were dismissed.

Giving judgment in January 1988 the Lord Chief Justice, Lord Lane, sitting with Sir Stephen Brown and Lord Justice O'Connor, said that Mr Clarke was 'a most unconvincing witness'. The judges had no doubt that evidence 'suggesting his erstwhile colleagues in the West Midlands police force treated these applicants with brutality was false'. Other witnesses were also dismissed as lying or mistaken.

The court then dismissed claims that there had been a police conspiracy to fabricate evidence. Investigating officers from the Devon and Cornwall police had found a document in the handwriting of former Detective Superintendent George Reade who had been in charge of the West Midlands inquiry. The court said this document – which became known as the 'Reade Schedule' – could not have amounted to 'a blueprint for perjury', as counsel for the men had claimed. It followed that their confessions, which the court had said were the true foundation of the prosecution's case, had not been undermined.

The judges went on to say that nothing had emerged which had caused them to doubt that the scientific evidence proved one or more of the six to have been in recent contact with explosives. And quite apart from the alleged confessions and the scientific evidence there was 'a wealth of evidence as to the surrounding circumstances . . . which by undesigned coincidence greatly strengthened the case' against the six men.

Lord Lane ended the court's judgment with remarks which were to become notorious. 'As has happened before in references by the Home Secretary to this court under section 17 of the Criminal Appeal Act 1968,' said the Lord Chief Justice, 'the longer this hearing has gone on the more convinced this court has become that the verdict of the jury was correct. We have no doubt the convictions were both safe and satisfactory.' Not only was Lord Lane saying that Douglas Hurd had been wrong to refer this case to the Court of Appeal, he was suggesting that the Home Office was too ready to refer other hopeless cases to the court as well.

In 1990 a different Home Secretary, David Waddington, sent the case of the Birmingham Six back to the Court of Appeal once more. He announced that he was acting on the strength of new information discovered by the Devon and Cornwall police. Electrostatic document analysis had suggested that notes of a police interview with Richard McIlkenny had not been recorded contemporaneously, as West Midlands detectives had claimed at the original trial.

A month before the appeal hearing started the Crown announced that it would no longer be relying on the scientific tests which were said to have detected traces of explosives. Three weeks later the Crown went further and conceded that the police evidence was no longer reliable either. Since the remaining circumstantial evidence was not by itself enough to keep the men in prison, counsel for the Director of Public Prosecutions, Sir Allan Green, took the bold step of telling the Court of Appeal that he was no longer seeking to sustain their convictions.

Although the outcome was by then in no doubt the Court of Appeal decided it should hear the evidence in public and decide the appeals in the normal way. At the end of March 1991 Lords Justices Lloyd, Mustill and Farquharson gave their reasons for allowing the appeals.

First, it was no longer safe to rely on the evidence given by the former Home Office scientist, Dr Frank Skuse, at the original trial. Prompted by what Sir John May's team had discovered about the Maguires' case forensic scientists had reviewed Dr Skuse's tests for explosives. Their findings were quite remarkable. It appeared that soap or detergent used to wash laboratory dishes could produce the same test results as nitroglycerine. They had also looked at evidence given by another scientist at the previous appeal. Experiments by Dr Janet Drayton had made Lord Lane's court 'sure that Hill's left hand is proven to have had nitroglycerine on it for which there is and can be no innocent explanation'. However, the review team had found evidence, which Dr Drayton now accepted, that other substances might have produced the same readings: it appeared – almost unbelievably – that she might have got a positive test result from anyone who smoked cigarettes. That effectively disposed of the scientific evidence.

The Court of Appeal then turned to the alleged confessions. Detective Sergeant Colin Morris and Detective Constable Terence Woodwiss of the West Midlands police had testified at the original trial that they interviewed Mr McIlkenny on Friday 22 November, 1974, the day after the bombings. Superintendent Reade said he was present. All three swore that a contemporaneous note was taken. Mr McIlkenny always denied that the interview had ever taken place.

In 1988 the Court of Appeal had declared: 'McIlkenny's assertion that he was not interviewed by the West Midlands officers on the Friday is plainly unacceptable.' By the time of the second appeal, however, the court had the benefit of electrostatic document analysis – the ESDA test, which is used to detect missing pages from the indentations made on subsequent sheets. That test, said the court in 1991, appeared to show that the note of the interview with Mr McIlkenny 'could not have been contemporaneous'.

Sergeant Morris and Constable Woodwiss had also signed notes of an interview which they said Mr McIlkenny gave the following day, 23 November, in Birmingham. The Court of Appeal said: 'On any view, the second interview could not have been noted contemporaneously, as the officers insisted.'

The court then turned to a discrepancy in the so-called Reade Schedule. 'In the absence of any explanation from Superintendent Reade,' said the judges, 'it must cast additional doubt on the honesty and reliability of his evidence.'

In 1988 the Court of Appeal had stated: 'We are certain that Mr Reade did not seek to deceive the court.' In 1991 the Court of Appeal announced: 'On the evidence now before us, Superintendent Reade deceived the court.'

The Court of Appeal judges concluded their 1991 judgment by saying:

In the light of the fresh scientific evidence, which at least throws grave doubt on Dr Skuse's evidence if it does not destroy it altogether, these convictions are both unsafe and unsatisfactory. If we put the scientific evidence on one side, the fresh investigation carried out by the Devon and Cornwall Constabulary renders the police evidence at the trial so unreliable that again we would say the convictions are both unsafe and unsatisfactory. Adding the two together, our conclusion was inevitable. It was for those reasons that we allowed the appeals.

In May 1992 George Reade, Colin Morris and Terence Woodwiss were committed for trial on charges of perjury and conspiracy to pervert the course of justice. Another retired detective, Rex Langford, was cleared of all charges by the Bow Street magistrate.

More than a year later Mr Reade, Mr Morris and Mr Woodwiss stood in the dock at the Old Bailey and answered 'not guilty' to the charges against them. But before the jury could hear any evidence, counsel for the three men spent three days arguing that the proceedings were an abuse of the process of the court. After considering the matter overnight Mr Justice Garland agreed that the case should go no further. He discharged the jury from giving verdicts and the case was suddenly over.

A week later[8] the judge explained why he had decided that the defendants could not possibly receive a fair trial. His written judgment was not particularly impressive and it did little to allay the public's unease at what had happened. Mr Justice Garland gave three main reasons for his decision to grant a stay of any further proceedings: delay, adverse publicity and the difficulty of isolating the narrow issues which the jury were being asked to decide from 'the whole matrix of events from 1975 to 1991, about which there are strong public perceptions'.

The issue of delay was simple enough: in Mr Justice Garland's view, the defence were put 'at a substantial disadvantage' in having to deal with events which had taken place nearly nineteen years earlier. It is worth recalling that a similar argument was rejected by the High Court in the case of the Guildford Four police officers.

The issue of adverse publicity was, needless to say, the one that interested the media most of all. Mr Justice Garland said the volume, intensity and continuing nature of the publicity had made the case of the Birmingham Six 'synonymous' with false confessions. In the judge's view, that publicity started in 1985 and had continued right up until the day before the trial was stopped. There was 'a snowball effect each time a new case was added to the list of miscarriages of justice'. The judge said it was inevitable that the reasons given by the Court of Appeal in 1991 for finding the convictions of the Birmingham Six unsafe and unsatisfactory would appear to have been findings of perjury and conspiracy against the defendants in this case. However, he was not suggesting that the press should have restricted or moderated their coverage of the 1991 appeal in order to avoid prejudicing the present trial. He also drew a distinction between the publicity in the case of the Birmingham Six officers and the publicity in the case of the Guildford Four officers: in this case, he said, it was much more damaging.

The third reason put forward by Mr Justice Garland was perhaps the most important. This prosecution had a very narrow focus: all that the Crown had sought to do was to prove that notes of an interview with Richard McIlkenny had not been recorded at the time alleged by the officers in the dock. Like the officers in the Guildford Four case the three retired Birmingham detectives were planning to argue that the man they interviewed had indeed confessed to the pub bombings and that indeed his confession was true. If that was the case, defence counsel would have asked the jury, why should the detectives have invented notes of their interviews?

What would the jury have made of all this? The judge said that some jurors, at least, would have been left in a state of confusion. Why, they might have asked, was the prosecution complaining about the contemporaneity of the interview notes when the jury were only too well aware that for years it had been accepted that the men's confessions were obtained by force? And why, they might also have asked, were the defence contending that the Birmingham Six were guilty all along when the jury knew perfectly well they had been cleared by the Court of Appeal? The Crown, moreover, was not willing to say whether it thought the alleged confessions of the Birmingham Six were genuine or not. It was the difficulty of isolating the narrow issue before the jury from the other issues which were bound to be in the jurors' minds which weighed heavily with the judge.

Ultimately, the question for Mr Justice Garland was whether, on the balance of probabilities, the men could get a fair trial. He concluded that they could not. Each case turned on its own facts and circumstances. In this case, he implied, it offended the court's sense of justice and propriety to be asked to try the accused.

Critics had pointed out that the Guildford Four officers had received a fair trial in similar circumstances: they must have done, the argument went, because they were acquitted. But the judge said this did not follow: juries had been known to react to perceived unfairness by acquitting, sometimes in the teeth of the evidence.[9]

The most intriguing issue of all was only hinted at in the judge's ruling. When the Birmingham Six were cleared in 1991 the West Midlands police immediately reopened their investigations into the original pub bombings. By the autumn of 1993 the police had completed their report. Mr Justice Garland said: 'I have had the advantage of seeing the material gathered during this further inquiry.' Later he added: 'I re-emphasise that I have had the advantage of reading . . . the enormous amount of new material arising from the Devon and Cornwall and West Midlands [police] inquiries all of which has been disclosed by the Crown.' What could this new inquiry have concluded? And why was it an advantage for the judge to have seen it? Leaks suggested that the report was not entirely favourable to the Birmingham Six. That could hardly have influenced Mr Justice Garland's decision, which could only have been based on the arguments put to him in court. Why, then, did he mention it – twice?

The three retired officers made no comment as they left court after their acquittal. But they did give an interview to the *Sunday Telegraph*[10] in which they all maintained they were innocent of the charges they faced. Colin Morris said the evidence against them was so trivial it would never have stood up in court. Both Mr Reade and Mr Morris felt a 'lingering regret' that they had not been cleared by a jury. This was, of course, their choice: they could have let the trial proceed if they had wanted to. But, as Mr Reade explained, 'if you are offered a lifeline you would be foolish to reject it'.

George Reade also repeated the allegations he had been planning to make in the privileged surroundings of the courtroom. Those comments cannot be justified, and indeed four weeks later the *Sunday Telegraph* published a front-page apology to the Birmingham Six. 'We unreservedly accept that the Birmingham Six are, and were, innocent of the charges preferred against them,' said the newspaper, 'and we deeply regret any impression to the contrary which may have been given by the article.' In the course of its lengthy apology the *Sunday Telegraph* said it fully accepted that the convictions of the Birmingham Six were quashed 'for good reason' and not 'as the result of any factor other than the most careful review of the evidence by the Court of Appeal'.[11]

George Reade had told the *Sunday Telegraph*: 'As God is my judge, we never did anything wrong.' Again, that remark cannot be justified. Perhaps God will be the judge of George Reade. It was not a role Mr Justice Garland was prepared to play. And that is perhaps the final tragedy of the Birmingham pub bombings. As far as the courts are concerned it seems we shall never know what happened.

Judith Ward

In September 1991, when Kenneth Baker was Home Secretary, he referred the case of Judith Ward to the Court of Appeal. Miss Ward had been given a life sentence in 1974 for the murder of twelve people who died when a bomb exploded in a coach on the M62 motorway. She never appealed against her conviction. During her trial she made admissions and confessions, some of which it could be shown were clearly not true.

Part of the scientific evidence against Judith Ward was given by Dr

Frank Skuse, the Home Office forensic scientist who also gave evidence against the Birmingham Six. After his evidence in that case was declared unreliable the Home Office started reviewing other cases in which Dr Skuse had been involved. Judith Ward's newly appointed solicitor, the tenacious Mrs Gareth Peirce, had already started making representations to the Home Office but the Home Secretary proudly announced that this was the first time the Home Office had reviewed a case on its own initiative. Officials claimed that this showed a new approach to alleged miscarriages of justice, and indeed taking the initiative was an approach which the Home Office itself had effectively ruled out less than five years earlier.

Judith Ward's appeal opened in May 1992. On the fifth day of the hearing, when it became inevitable that she would be cleared, Miss Ward was freed on bail. She had spent eighteen years in prison for crimes she did not commit. Giving judgment in June 1992 Lords Justices Glidewell, Nolan and Steyn said they greatly regretted that a 'grave miscarriage of justice' had occurred. It had happened because:

> in failing to disclose evidence [to the defence] . . . one or more members of the West Yorkshire police, the scientists who gave evidence at the trial and some of those members of the staff of the Director of Public Prosecutions and counsel who advised them . . . failed to carry out . . . their basic duty to seek to ensure a trial which is fair to both the prosecution . . . and the accused.

The judges said three senior scientists from the Royal Armament Research and Development Establishment – Douglas Higgs, George Berryman and Walter Elliott – 'took the law into their own hands and concealed from the prosecution, the defence and the court, matters which might have changed the course of the trial'.

Three weeks later the Director of Public Prosecutions, Barbara Mills QC, asked the West Yorkshire police to investigate the roles of Mr Higgs and Mr Berryman (Mr Elliott had since died). She said at that time there were no grounds for action against anyone else involved in the case, including one of the case lawyers who was still on her staff and a prominent QC who was still in practice at the Bar. After receiving the police report Mrs Mills announced in April 1993 that there was 'insufficient evidence to justify criminal proceedings'.

Lessons for the future

In the wrongful conviction of the Birmingham Six there was a part to be played by almost every actor in the criminal justice system. The police of course were first on the scene, with officers from the West Midlands force interviewing suspects in the way they no doubt thought was expected of them. The second act unfolded when the forensic science service carried out tests on the men in custody. That convinced the police that they had caught the bombers. Most disturbing of all, the third vehicle of the criminal justice system to fail the Birmingham Six was the appeal system itself – the three judges who dismissed their appeal in 1988. Why did the Court of Appeal remain convinced in 1988 that the jury's verdict was correct?

The judges genuinely believed in the confession evidence, the scientific evidence and important circumstantial evidence. And that apparently made them reluctant to accept the alleged police conspiracy put forward by the six men. In 1988 the judges did not have the latest evidence from explosives experts or new scientific tests suggesting that police notes had been altered. Their devotion to the jury system made them rely too heavily on the original verdict, and a jury is only as good as the evidence it is given.

Ironically, the three parts of the system that failed the Birmingham Six in 1988 were to come to their rescue in 1991. The men owed their freedom to new police inquiries, new scientific tests and, above all, to a more open-minded approach by the Court of Appeal. But none of that would have happened without a sustained campaign by journalists, lawyers and the men's supporters. Victory, though sweet, had come more than sixteen years too late.

The government's response to the freeing of the Guildford Four in 1989 had been to set up the inquiry chaired by Sir John May. Cynics thought this was a way of buying time; if so, the price was rather higher by the time the Birmingham Six were cleared. This time it was to be a full-scale Royal Commission, the first to be appointed since 1977. However, it would be wrong to be too cynical about the government's reasons for setting up the Royal Commission on Criminal Justice: by 1991 there was a clear feeling in government circles that fundamental reforms could no longer be avoided. And the woman who was thought to be most against the idea of a Royal Commission was no longer living in Downing Street.

The Royal Commission on Criminal Justice was ordered to examine the effectiveness of the criminal justice system of England and Wales in securing the conviction of the guilty and the acquittal of the innocent. Minutes after the Birmingham Six had walked out of the Old Bailey it was announced that the commission would be chaired by Viscount Runciman of Doxford, an academic and a businessman. From then on it was something of a public relations disaster. 'Gary' Runciman, though otherwise the ideal person to chair a major inquiry of this type, appeared painfully shy in public and did nothing to reassure people that matters were now under control. Surrounding himself with officials who were equally frightened of the media, he got off to a bad start by delegating press inquiries to a junior Home Office press officer who was generally 'too busy' to return telephone calls.

Public relations improved slightly with a change of staff in the Home Office press office although there was little sign that the commission was taking the press office into its confidence. Commission officials remained largely unapproachable and no effort was made to publicise the substantial volume of research material which they had set in train, some of which was still trickling out after the commission had published its report. And the few 'photo-opportunities' which did occur were thrown away by a commission which clearly did not think it was under any obligation to restore public confidence during the two years in which it was sitting.

On a personal level many of the commission's members were charming and co-operative. But they decided at an early stage that all their work should be done in private. There were a number of weekend seminars at which the commissioners discussed their provisional views with interested parties. These too were held in secret: there was no attempt to stimulate a wider public discussion as Lord Justice Woolf had done in preparing his report on the Strangeways prison riots a couple of years earlier.

All this would not have mattered if the commission had taken seriously the advice it was given by the media on how to publicise its final report. As their deliberations drew to a close, the commissioners became frightened that their conclusions might leak out before their report was published. As a result, despite pleas from the media there was no advance briefing of journalists. That simply encouraged the press to use its own initiative, which it did to devastating effect. The commission's main recommendations were widely reported in the days leading up to the release of the final report,[12] mystifying commissioners who had sworn one another to secrecy. They seemed not to have realised that the people who had been consulted about proposals had not taken the same vow of silence as themselves.

Paradoxically the one way that the commissioners could have avoided leaks would have been to have taken the media into their confidence. Most people now know that documents are often released to the media under embargo: reporters are given documents in advance of publication on the understanding that nothing will be published before a specified time. If that procedure had been followed there would have been no need for reporters to compete with one another for leaks.

So nervous were Lord Runciman and his fellow commissioners about advance publication that they allowed the media just two hours in which to read, digest, analyse – and, in the case of the electronic media, summarise and report – the commission's findings before they held their only press conference.[13] These tactics are often adopted by government departments so that journalists cannot read enough of the report in time to work out any difficult questions. In the case of the Royal Commission it meant that the vital initial impression conveyed by the media was based on a quick skim through the report's recommendations, mixed in with occasional leaks and seasoned with suppositions. It was scandalous that journalists were not given a chance to read the report properly, even if only overnight. Asked to explain his apparent contempt for the media Lord Runciman answered lamely that the commission had been advised to withhold the report until the morning of publication – presumably by the Home Office.

Consequently reporters could do little to assess whether the commission's proposals would meet their objectives. Instead the media concentrated on the proposed restrictions on trial by jury (discussed in the next chapter). Lord Runciman had failed to realise the impact these proposals would have. 'What has surprised me to some extent,' he said, 'is the importance which some people have attached to some of our recommendations and in particular the interpretation which has been put on our recommendation that the mode of trial should be decided . . . by the magistrates.'[14] A few days earlier Lord Runciman had been even more candid: 'I was very surprised,' he said, 'at the furore which appeared to be generated by what I thought was an uncontroversial, indeed commonsense, recommendation.'[15]

As far as immediate media coverage was concerned it was therefore the worst of all possible worlds. Reports were dominated by a topic which seemed at best tangential to the commission's main conclusions, while those conclusions themselves were not given the careful assessment they deserved. And it was all the fault of the Royal Commission.

8

The Royal Commission

A disappointing report

The report of the Royal Commission on Criminal Justice[1] turned out to be something of a disappointment. Its members seemed well satisfied with their work but practitioners thought it was impractical, academics considered it unacademic and reformers regarded it as unreformed.

There was widespread criticism of the commission for not putting more emphasis on measures designed to reduce the risk of miscarriages of justice. Surely, people said, that was what it was set up to do? In fact, it was not: the commission's terms of reference required it to 'examine the effectiveness of the criminal justice system in England and Wales in securing the conviction of those guilty of criminal offences and the acquittal of those who are innocent, having regard to the efficient use of resources'.

Michael Zander, who was a member of the Royal Commission, acknowledged that he and his fellow commissioners might have been at fault in not sufficiently stressing in their report and at their press conference that those were the terms of reference within which they were working.[2] He candidly admitted that on some issues (such as supporting the right to silence in the police station) the commissioners put the emphasis on avoiding conviction of the innocent while on others the emphasis was on convicting the guilty (for example, in allowing the police to take mouth swabs by force).[3]

Professor Zander pointed out that the Royal Commission had made about ninety proposals designed to assist the defence as against some thirty that were designed to assist the prosecution.[4] He rejected suggestions that the commission should have 'given primary weight in every instance to the issue of avoiding the conviction of the innocent'. This was obviously of great importance, 'but so too is conviction of the guilty – and so, for that matter, is achieving efficiency and due economy in the system'.[5]

Which is the more important? It used to be argued that it was better for ten guilty men to go free than for one innocent man to be wrongly convicted. Is this the basis on which the commission worked? Was it in fact fewer than ten men: five, perhaps, or even two? Or is it more complicated now: better for ten guilty men to be freed cheaply by the magistrates than for one innocent man to be convicted after an expensive trial in the Crown Court? We simply do not know.[6]

According to the Legal Action Group, the commission's report would do little to alleviate the problem it was set up to address: far from reducing miscarriages of justice the recommendations would simply make them harder to reverse.[7] This view was shared by Michael Mansfield QC who said the commission's proposals would increase pressure on defendants to plead guilty: he attacked the Royal Commission for 'turning its back' on the victims of the system whose wrongful convictions had led to its establishment in the first place.[8]

In its initial response the Legal Action Group immediately grasped the fundamental flaw at the heart of the Royal Commission's report. Despite being chaired by a distinguished academic[9] it was without intellectual substance. It had no sense of the moral foundations on which our criminal justice system should rest. The report read more like the submissions of an interdepartmental working party than the conclusions of a Royal Commission. Its pages lacked any feeling that the report was dealing with matters which were vital to a free society. It was only in Michael Zander's 'Note of Dissent' that there was any hint of the ethical standpoint which should have infused the whole report. Professor Zander ended his note by saying: 'The integrity of the criminal justice system is a higher objective than the conviction of any individual.' Far from appearing as the last sentence of a brief dissent this should have been the first sentence of the entire report.

So much for the theoretical basis of the Royal Commission; what about the practical effects of its 352 detailed proposals? An experienced Circuit judge who had looked at some of the commission's key recommendations concluded that they would not work in practice. The recommendations on defence disclosure would be 'pointless'. The plea-bargaining proposals would be 'cumbersome, they would be time-wasting and they would put too much pressure on defendants'.[10]

Professor Mike McConville, one of the academics who was invited to do research for the Royal Commission, thought the report was not 'empirically grounded'. In his view, it deployed defective reasoning in support of its recommendations, it was based on a flawed understanding of the organising principles of criminal justice and it amounted to little more than 'opinion and assertion'. The commission had done no research on crucial issues such as the quality of justice in the magistrates' courts, the reliability of guilty pleas, the quality of legal advice or even on miscarriages of justice. He considered that the report was a 'miscarriage of judgment'.[11]

Responding to these points Michael Zander said:

- The commission thought the proposition that the quality of justice generally in magistrates' courts was lower than in Crown Courts too obvious to require research.

- It was not clear how any research could be done on the reliability of guilty pleas.

- The commission had the benefit of Professor McConville's own research on the quality of legal advice and made a number of recommendations designed to improve matters.

- The research programme touched on miscarriages of justice in a variety of ways.

The Royal Commission examined the criminal justice system progressively from the initial investigation by the police, through questioning of suspects and the role of the prosecution, to pre-trial procedures, the trial, the appeal and the mechanisms for correcting miscarriages of justice. There was, however, no discussion of the desirability or effectiveness of jury trial; and there was no mention of the twin roles of the media in uncovering past miscarriages of justice while at the same time contributing to future miscarriages by sensationalist reporting.

Michael Zander revealed that the Royal Commission was aware throughout its work that 'many people had built up wholly unreal expectations' of its report. He noted that these people were bound to be disappointed although he failed to explain why the commission had done nothing to dampen their unreal expectations during the two years it was sitting. He concluded that the public's disappointment might in part have been caused by the commission's decision to reject proposals designed to prevent the innocent being convicted (such as a rule requiring confessions to be corroborated).[12] Professor Zander said that such proposals were dismissed only because it was thought they would not work or because 'there were other likely negative consequences that outweighed the potential advantages'.[13] He believed that critics who did not object to – or even welcomed – most of the recommendations had expressed their disappointment with the report as a whole because they strongly disagreed with a few of its proposals.

The government's response

Home Office officials had assumed they would have a year to consider the Royal Commission's recommendations before any decisions were taken. In the normal course of events, one would have expected the government to publish a White Paper in the summer of 1994 outlining its considered proposals; this would have been followed by a bill in November or December of 1994 which would have become law during the following year.

However, political realities intruded into this cosy scenario. Michael Howard had become Home Secretary in May 1993 and by the late summer he had decided to seize the initiative. Law and order had become the key political issue and Mr Howard seemed determined to stop his Labour shadow, Tony Blair MP, from making the running. Perhaps Mr Howard had also remembered that many of his recent predecessors had not spent long in office; he must have reasoned that he too might not have a second chance to make his mark on criminal justice policy.

Besides, Mr Howard was not a man racked by self-doubt. Labour had moved to the right in recent years, particularly on law and order, and the only vacant ground for the Conservatives was to be found even further in the same direction. That did not seem to worry the government which knew its most vocal supporters were inclined so far to the right that they were off the political map. These were people who fondly believed that hanging and flogging never did anyone any harm and that the only way to deal with offenders was to lock them up and throw away the key.

There was already a Criminal Justice Bill planned for the 1993–4 parliamentary session. It was intended to deal with squatters, trespassers and young offenders. Mr Howard decided that this would be the perfect vehicle for implementing some of the Royal Commission's proposals and the cabinet gave him its full support-.The Criminal Justice and Public Order Bill, as it was called, was slipped out in the traditional way on the last working Friday before Christmas 1993, on the same day as another major government bill.

The Criminal Justice and Public Order Bill only contained those of the Royal Commission's recommendations which appealed to the government and which ministers felt they could implement easily. Even so, the bill had a stormy passage through the House of Lords. The government had hoped it would become law by the time parliament rose for the summer recess in July 1994. However, peers unexpectedly inflicted a series of defeats on the government. Although Michael Howard undertook to reverse these amendments[14] he had to wait until the so-called 'spill-over period': a couple of weeks around the end of October before parliament is prorogued for a few days and a new session begins with the Queen's Speech. This must have irritated Mr Howard: having announced the government's plans in his famous 27-point speech at the Conservatives' conference in October 1993, Mr Howard would have wanted to tell his party the following year that they were already on the statute book.

Before the trial begins
A number of the Royal Commission's recommendations were perfectly sound, even desirable. In this chapter we shall concentrate on those which caused the most concern. Many of these related to the period before the trial begins.

The right to silence
In general, a citizen has no legal duty to answer questions from the police.[15] And nobody has suggested it should become a crime to remain silent in the face of police questioning. The crucial question for the Royal Commission was whether a person's silence should count against him in court. It was a question on which informed opinion was sharply divided.

That division was reflected in the recommendations of the Royal Commission. Nine commissioners wanted to keep the right to silence. Two did not. The government chose to accept the views of this tiny minority.

Under the old law the police must 'caution' a person they are questioning as soon as they have grounds to suspect him or her of an offence. That means the suspect will be told he need not say anything unless he wishes to do so but what he does say may be used as evidence. The caution must normally be given before the suspect answers any questions (or before he answers any further questions if it was his previous answers which gave rise to the suspicion). It is this right to remain silent *without penalty* which is usually referred to as the right to silence.[16]

The police, the Crown Prosecution Service and a majority of the judges told the Royal Commission that they favoured amending this right to silence.[17] They thought it should be possible for the prosecution or the judge to invite a jury to draw adverse inferences if people reasonably suspected of a criminal offence failed to give the police an explanation of the evidence against them. Of course there would have to be a new caution, something like: 'You do not have to say anything. But if you do not mention now something which you later use in your defence, the court may decide that your failure to mention it now strengthens the case against you.'

Supporters of this argument do not say that adverse comment should automatically follow an accused person's refusal to answer questions: they accept that the judge would use his discretion in deciding whether to mention the defendant's silence. But they believe that abolishing the right of silence would reduce the chances of an 'ambush' in the courtroom. Their concern is that a defendant may fabricate a defence and then spring it on the police at his trial, by which time it is too late for investigation. The police also believe that innocent suspects should respond to the allegations against them as soon as possible, both to exonerate themselves and help the police catch those who are guilty.

The Home Secretary said he found these arguments totally convincing.[18] This was fortunate for Mr Howard, since the change in the law had been on the Home Office agenda for some years.[19] Others disagreed with the government, however, notably the Law Society and the Bar Council. They said:

Not only are the circumstances of police interrogation disorientating and intimidating in themselves, but there can be no justification for requiring a suspect to answer questions when he or she may be unclear both about the nature of the offence which he or she is alleged to have committed and about the legal definitions of intent, dishonesty and so forth . . . Innocent suspects' reasons for remaining silent may include, for example, the protection of family or friends, a sense of bewilderment, embarrassment or outrage, or a reasoned decision to wait until the allegation against them has been set out in detail and they have had the benefit of considered legal advice.[20]

And as the Royal Commission itself pointed out, some people – even those who are not mentally ill or handicapped – will confess to offences they did not commit. The threat of adverse comment at the trial may increase the risk that confused or vulnerable suspects will make false confessions.

The Royal Commission reviewed the research evidence on the right to silence. This suggested:

- The right to silence is exercised in only a minority of cases.

- It may tend to be exercised more often in the more serious cases and where legal advice is given.

- There is no evidence which proves that silence is used disproportionately by professional criminals.

- There is no evidence to support the belief that silence in the police station improves the defendant's chances of an acquittal.

- Most of those who are silent in the police station either plead guilty later or are subsequently found guilty.

- Nevertheless if the prosecution and the judge were allowed to suggest to the jury that silence can amount to supporting evidence of guilt, it is possible that some defendants who are silent and who are now acquitted might be convicted – *rightly or wrongly*.[21]

It was this last point which weighed heavily with most members of the Royal Commission. They believed that although more guilty people might be convicted if the right to silence were abolished, the possibility of that happening was outweighed by the risk that more innocent people might be found guilty because of the extra pressure on suspects in the police station. While acknowledging the frustration of the police most commissioners doubted whether the possibility of adverse comment would make as much difference as the police supposed. The experienced criminals who had previously remained silent would continue to do so even if the law was changed: at their trial they would justify their silence by saying that they had been advised by their solicitors to say nothing until the allegations against them had been fully disclosed.[22]

All but two (unnamed) members of the Royal Commission agreed that defendants should not have to answer the charges against them while they were being questioned by the police. They were fortified in that conclusion by the fact that the Royal Commission on Criminal Procedure had reached a similar (majority) view in 1981.[23] They did however conclude (by a different majority) that defendants should have to disclose their defence at a later stage in the proceedings. We shall deal with this under the heading of *defence disclosure*.

Lawyers and commentators breathed a sigh of relief when a majority of the Royal Commission agreed that the right to silence at the police station should remain. Their relief turned to despair three months later when the Home Secretary told the Conservative Party Conference that he would abolish it after all.[24]

The government intended that the law would operate as it had done in Northern Ireland since 1988.[25] Ministers suggested that a defendant's silence might tip the balance against him. But the chances are that he would not be a hardened criminal. According to the Royal Commission: 'It is the less experienced and more vulnerable suspects against whom the threat of adverse comment would be likely to be more damaging.'[26]

In vain do we search the Royal Commission's report for research on the effect of abolishing the right to silence in Northern Ireland. Those commissioners who urged a change in the law can hardly have been surprised that the government had chosen to model its new arrangements on the provisions already introduced into another part of the United Kingdom. Professor Simon Lee, of Queen's University Belfast, thought it 'astonishing' that the commission should ignore the experience in Northern Ireland and the 'burgeoning case-law, much of it Strasbourg-bound'.[27]

There was strong criticism of the government's plan to abolish the right to silence when the Criminal Justice and Public Order Bill was announced in the Queen's Speech in November 1993. The Law Society said it was basic to the English system of criminal investigation that people should not be required to prove their innocence by having to explain their actions.[28] Liberty (the National Council for Civil Liberties) said the government's proposal would undermine the presumption of innocence and erode the right to a fair trial.[29] The lawyers' organisation JUSTICE said there should be no attempt to increase pressure on defendants in police stations by introducing the possibility of a penalty for silence or incomplete answers.[30]

Nothing could have been more insulting to the Royal Commission than to have a key recommendation overturned in such a short space of time. There was not even any pretence of consultation: the government decided to make the changes at the first legislative opportunity. Speaking as a former member of the commission Michael Zander seemed to be suggesting it might even be unconstitutional to appoint a Royal Commission and then reject its recommendations in this way.[31] This was clearly going too far, and indeed Professor Zander said later that he had been misunderstood. Governments are certainly under no duty to implement the recommendations of a Royal Commission or anyone else. But if ministers are going to follow their own political judgments, why bother to ask a Royal Commission for its views in the first place? The commission was set up to ensure that the guilty would be convicted and the innocent would be acquitted. Removing the right to silence may help convict the guilty, but it will also make it easier to convict the innocent.

The Criminal Justice and Public Order Bill was published in December 1993. As expected, the clauses dealing with the right to silence were designed to allow courts to draw adverse inferences if a suspect failed to mention material facts to the police or account for suspicious circumstances. But that was not all. Whenever a defendant was denying the charges, clause 28 would have obliged the magistrates or judge to call the defendant into the witness box and order him to give evidence in his own defence. The magistrates or jury could then have drawn adverse inferences if the accused person failed to answer questions.

The Lord Chief Justice announced shortly after the bill was published that the judges were seriously troubled by this proposal. 'It may produce undesirable and unfair results,' he said. 'It might lead the jury to consider that the defendant was defying the judge if he exercised his right not to give evidence.' Giving the Tom Sargant Memorial Lecture in January 1994, Lord Taylor said the clause 'would tend to introduce an element of inquisitorial procedure into

the judge's role. It would be an unnecessary piece of ritual procedure.'

This came as something of a surprise to the Home Secretary. He
had simply imported the measures from Northern Ireland and he
understood that the Lord Chief Justice supported the package as a
whole. Lord Taylor, it may be surmised, had not realised the full
extent of what was proposed for England and Wales; as soon as he
found out, he objected.

The Lord Chief Justice had no trouble persuading the Home
Secretary to revise his proposals. Under the amended clause, the
court will still be able to draw 'such inferences as appear proper'
from the defendant's refusal to give evidence or answer specific
questions. But the judge no longer has to order the defendant into
the witness box: he simply has to make sure the defendant knows he
can give evidence in his own defence and that his refusal to do so may
count against him.

This was a good example of the power wielded by the Lord Chief
Justice. His support was clearly very important to the government.
In the Tom Sargant lecture, Lord Taylor brushed aside the majority
recommendations of the Royal Commission. In his view, the
government's proposals had a 'respectable genesis': they were
derived from a report of the Criminal Law Revision Committee and
had been 'successfully operated in Northern Ireland since 1988.' Lord
Taylor saw nothing unfair in what was proposed. 'The burden of
proof remains on the prosecution,' he said. 'But it is sensible that the
jury may take account of the fact that no answer has been given.'

As well as having to answer questions in court, a defendant is
obliged by Part III of the Criminal Justice and Public Order Act to
supply the police with certain specific types of information; again,
his refusal to do so may count against him. These measures will
come into effect on a date to be fixed by the Home Secretary: the rest
of this chapter is written on the assumption that the relevant sections
are enacted as they stood in July 1994.

The main provision in this part of the Act is designed to persuade
an accused person to disclose the facts he may relay on in his defence.
Again, courts will be able to draw such inferences 'as appear proper'
from a defendant's failure to mention these facts while being
questioned or when he is charged. As originally drafted, the clause
would have put a defendant at risk in a police car or on his own
doorstep: if he did not disclose his defence as soon as he was stopped

by the police, his silence could have counted against him. The provision would have allowed inferences to be drawn from the silence of someone who was regarded only as a potential witness – a person questioned during house-to-house inquiries, for example. And worse still, it would have widened the scope for what may be called 'non-verballing'. To 'verbal' a defendant is to put words into his mouth (such as 'it's a fair cop; you've got me bang to rights'). To 'non-verbal' a suspect is to put silence into his mouth (in other words to disregard the answers he gives and maintain, at the trial, that he said nothing).

In the light of these concerns, Lord Taylor persuaded the government to provide that a defendant would have to be cautioned before his silence could count against him. As the Lord Chief Justice told parliament: 'The new caution will make clear to the suspect that the law has changed and that he may no longer be safe in refusing to give any account of himself.' Secondly, the caution would ensure that the provision would apply only to someone under active suspicion of criminal activity. And as far as the non-verballing was concerned, Lord Taylor thought that could be dealt with if the police were required to repeat the questions at a formal interview in the police station.

This particular provision applies to questions asked by anyone 'charged with the duty of investigating offences or charging offenders'. This definition is clearly broad enough to cover investigators employed by Customs and Excise, the Inland Revenue, the Department of Social Security, and other public bodies. But what about a store detective employed by Marks and Spencer? What indeed about a private security firm? Is a defendant effectively obliged to provide these people with information? The courts will have to decide.

It is not just the defendant's refusal to answer questions that may count against him. A person arrested by the police or by Customs investigators must also account for 'any object, substance or mark' if the investigators tell him they reasonably believe its presence may be 'attributable to the participation of the person arrested in the commission of an offence . . .' The object, substance or mark may be on the defendant's person, his clothing, his footwear, or otherwise in his possession or in any place in which he is at the time of his arrest. When asking for an explanation, the investigating officer must warn the defendant that his refusal to answer could be held against him.

The new powers go further still. They apply where someone is arrested 'at or about the time' when the alleged offence was committed. It does not matter how far the defendant is from the scene of the crime. If the police or Customs reasonably believe that his presence at the place where he was arrested 'may be attributable to his participation in the commission of the offence' then his failure to account for his presence may count against him. Again, the investigating officer must tell the suspect what may happen if he refuses to provide an explanation.

In summary, then, an accused person is at risk if he disobeys a request from anyone 'charged with the duty of investigating offences' to provide facts he will rely on in his defence. He need only account for objects, substances, or marks – or his presence at a particular place – if asked by a police or Customs officer (the reference to Customs was added while the bill was passing through parliament). His silence may not just count against him at his trial. Adverse inferences can also be drawn by judges and magistrates who have to decide whether a trial should go ahead.

Confessions and corroboration

False confessions have led to serious miscarriages of justice, as the Royal Commission of course acknowledged.[32] Why should people confess to crimes they have not committed? The commission offered four explanations:

- People may make voluntary confessions as the result of a morbid desire for publicity or notoriety; or to relieve feelings of guilt about a real or imagined previous transgression; or because they cannot distinguish reality from fantasy.

- A suspect may confess from a desire to protect someone else from interrogation and prosecution.

- People may see an immediate advantage from a confession (such as an end to questioning or release from the police station) even though the long-term consequences will be far worse. (Confessions obtained by improper police pressure come into this category although they are not mentioned by the Royal Commission at this point.)

- People may be persuaded temporarily by their interrogators that they really have committed the act alleged.

Because of these risks many who gave evidence to the Royal

Commission argued that confessions should not be admissible unless made or confirmed in the presence of a solicitor. These witnesses maintained that this would reduce the pressure on the defendant to make a false confession at the police station. In addition, the solicitor would ensure that interviews were carried out fairly and confirm that the confession had not been fabricated.

However, the commission raised a number of objections to the idea.[33] First, a suspect might not wish to have a solicitor present. It turned out that this was the case with almost 70 per cent of those questioned in the police station. No doubt some suspects would have been put off the idea of having a lawyer by the police but there must be at least a few who want to talk to detectives privately. Second, a confession may be made somewhere other than in a police station and the suspect might subsequently refuse to confirm it in the presence of a solicitor. This scenario should have sounded an alarm bell to the commissioners, if only because it could mean that the original confession was improperly obtained. But the Royal Commission seems to have regarded such a case as one of cold feet, implying that the defendant's refusal to co-operate should not stand between him and his conviction. The third argument is that the presence of a solicitor at the interview would not prevent improper pressure being put on the suspect before the interview began. This is true, but the police might be less likely to mistreat a suspect if they knew he would be seeing his solicitor shortly afterwards. Finally, the quality of work done by solicitors in the police station was far from satisfactory. This too was true – in one notorious case[34] the solicitor sat silently through what was clearly an oppressive interview – but the answer should have been to improve the quality of work by solicitors, not to take away existing safeguards.

After considering these objections the Royal Commission concluded that it would be wrong to exclude a confession because it was made before the solicitor's arrival or after the suspect had declined legal advice. The Legal Action Group did not agree with this approach. 'The presence of a competent solicitor is a major safeguard against oppression,' it argued. 'Enforcement would result in police officers encouraging suspects to seek legal advice and help prevent the widespread abuse that is current police practice.'

The argument is finely balanced but it becomes less important if confessions have to be corroborated by other evidence.

In Scotland there is a general rule that the accused's guilt cannot be established by the evidence of only one witness. But if there is a clear confession, the Scots require very little more evidence by way of corroboration. The Scottish courts have also developed what is known as the *special knowledge principle*. This says that confession evidence may be corroborated by facts mentioned in the confession which only the guilty person could have known about (such as exactly where the body was buried). However, this principle opens the door to abuse: 'special knowledge' can easily be passed to the accused by the police. So the Scots' much praised insistence on corroboration seems pretty thin.

In England and Wales the evidence of a single witness is generally enough to prove any issue. The Royal Commission considered whether that rule should be changed.

The recent miscarriages of justice have demonstrated, above all, the dangers of relying on unsupported confessions. The Royal Commission frankly conceded that people do confess to crimes they have not committed (for the reasons mentioned above). In a striking paragraph[35] the commission said:

> The legal system has always allowed in evidence statements that are made against the interests of the maker in the belief that individuals will not make false statements against themselves. This belief can no longer be sustained. Research has conclusively demonstrated that under certain circumstances individuals may confess to crimes they have not committed and that it is more likely that they will do so in interviews conducted in police custody even when proper safeguards apply.

The main argument against insisting on corroboration is, of course, that it would allow a number of guilty people to walk free. In the convoluted prose of the Royal Commission: 'a significant number of people plead guilty after a confession who might be strongly advised by their lawyers not to do so if the confession were the only evidence against them. There is no reason to believe that *most of them* are not in fact guilty.'[36] Passing rapidly over the wrongful convictions implicit in that last sentence the commissioners hinted at the principles underlying their recommendations. Far from believing that it was better for ten guilty men to go free than it was for one innocent man to be wrongly convicted, the commission said that if some defendants did walk free when 'most of them' were guilty 'not only will justice not have been done in the individual case but there would be a cumulative effect on the public's perception of the effectiveness of the criminal justice system'. In other words, a few innocent people have to be locked up so that the public does not think the judiciary has gone soft on crime.

The Royal Commission went on to consider whether uncorroborated confessions could be admitted if the judge gave the jury a warning about the risks involved. The commissioners all agreed that a strong warning should be given if the prosecution was relying on uncorroborated evidence: they considered that a judge should tell the jury, where appropriate, that other defendants had made false confessions in similar circumstances. That seemed an admirable recommendation.

However, the Royal Commission could not agree whether confessions should in fact be acceptable in the absence of corroboration. Three (unnamed) commissioners concluded that a conviction should never be based on a confession alone. They believed that there should always be evidence supporting the identification of the defendant: 'special knowledge' in the Scottish sense would not be sufficient. The remaining eight members of the Royal Commission took the view that if a confession was credible and had not been obtained by oppression or inducements the jury should be able to consider it even in the absence of other evidence, provided the judge had warned them of the risks. Commenting on this recommendation Lord Scarman said he was 'not persuaded by the commission on confession evidence; that in a murder case, for instance, you can get a conviction on the strength of a confession alone. That,' he said, 'was partly the mistake in the Guildford Four case.'[37]

There can be little doubt that the Royal Commission's majority recommendation would lead to some wrongful convictions. Equally, the minority view would produce some wrongful acquittals. How many there would be in each category is impossible to say: it would depend on how rigorously the rules and safeguards were enforced. Clearly, the phrase 'miscarriages of justice' includes wrongful acquittals as well as wrongful convictions. And implicitly, as we have seen, the Royal Commission seems to accept that some wrongful convictions are the price we must pay for an effective criminal justice system. Nowhere did the commission spell out its priorities. The nearest it came was in its opening chapter where the commissioners said:

It is widely assumed – and we are in no position to contradict it – that the guilty are more often acquitted than the innocent convicted. To some

335

extent, an inevitable and appropriate consequence of the prosecution being required to prove its case beyond reasonable doubt must be that not every guilty person is convicted. But there is only a handful of cases in which it is possible to be certain, with hindsight, that the jury's verdict was mistaken. We have simply to acknowledge that mistaken verdicts can and do sometimes occur and that our task is to recommend changes to our system of criminal justice which will make them less likely in the future.

But this was not an answer to the fundamental question.

Corroboration in rape cases

At the time of the Royal Commission's report a judge hearing a case of rape or sexual assault was obliged to warn the jury that it could be dangerous to convict the defendant solely on the complainant's uncorroborated evidence. Many women found this deeply offensive and the Law Commission had already recommended that the rule should be abolished.[38] Although the Royal Commission made no specific recommendation on this point its members would presumably have wanted the judge to decide what warning was appropriate in each individual case.

However, this was one matter on which the government had already made up its mind. The Criminal Justice and Public Order Act 1994 abolishes the need for the judge to warn a jury about convicting a defendant on the uncorroborated evidence of the alleged victim (or an accomplice of the accused). It also abolishes the corroboration requirements for certain other sexual offences.[39]

Mode of trial

The most serious offences must be tried *on indictment* by a judge and jury in the Crown Court. These include murder, manslaughter, rape, robbery, wounding with intent, conspiracy, blackmail and spying.

The least serious offences can only be tried *summarily* by a magistrates' court. Some of these are quite trivial but others are not: they include assaulting the police, driving while drunk, threatening behaviour and causing up to £2,000 worth of criminal damage.

All other offences can be tried *either way* – in other words, either by the magistrates or in the Crown Court. From time to time offences are 'downgraded' so that they may no longer be tried by a judge and jury. In 1975 a committee chaired by Lord Justice James[40] recommended that small thefts – of no more than £20 – should be tried by the magistrates alone. The Labour government of the day put the proposal to parliament in 1976 but after passionate opposition in the House of Lords the issue was shelved by the Home Office.

Theft is therefore still an 'either-way' crime. Others include fraud, burglary, arson and certain sexual offences. In these cases the defendant has the important right to insist on trial by jury if he wishes – although he cannot insist on summary trial. In practice, the magistrates hear argument from the prosecution and the defence on where the case should be heard. They then decide which court would be more suitable. If they send the case to the Crown Court that is the end of the matter. But even if they would prefer to hear it themselves the defendant may still insist on being tried by a judge and jury, as defendants do in over 35,000 cases a year.

Some defendants prefer the quicker, simpler procedures in the magistrates' courts. But those who are pleading not guilty realise that they are more likely to be acquitted by a judge and jury. Research cited by the Royal Commission, and carried out by the commission's own director of research, found that the chances of acquittal in comparable cases were significantly higher in the Crown Court (57 per cent) than in the magistrates' courts (30 per cent).[41]

The Royal Commission found that the mode of trial arrangements were not working as intended. 'The magistrates send for trial a large number of cases that they could try themselves,' it said, 'while defendants opt for trial on the basis that they are going to plead not guilty but then usually plead guilty.'[42] The commission suggested a new procedure 'to secure a more rational division of either way cases'[43] (not, it should be noted, to improve the quality of justice). Unless the prosecution and defence could agree in advance where the case should be heard it would be up to the magistrates to decide the mode of trial.

The Royal Commission specified a number of factors which the magistrates would consider in deciding whether they should send a case to be heard by a judge and jury. One of these would be the defendant's potential loss of reputation. Others would include the defendant's past record and the likely effect on him of the sentence he might receive.[44] The implications of these proposals are clear enough. A middle-class person in responsible employment charged with an offence of dishonesty would be tried by a jury. A young unemployed lad with a string of convictions would have his case heard by the magistrates.

This proposal was widely condemned. The Lord Chief Justice was right to reject it in his initial comment on the Royal Commission's report. 'I do not accept that a defendant with a criminal record has, by that token, a weaker claim to jury trial,' said Lord Taylor. On the contrary, 'he or she may feel specially vulnerable. "Round up the usual suspects" may not be just an old joke.'[45] The Lord Chief Justice thought the proposal might well lead to a 'socially divisive regime'. That criticism had already been put to the chairman of the Royal Commission, Lord Runciman; he had rejected it out of hand.[46]

Although Lord Runciman repeatedly denied accusations that the proposal to curb the defendant's right to choose jury trial was simply a cost-cutting measure, his own report suggested it would lead to 'savings' which could be used to ensure that 'more serious cases going to the Crown Court are not only better prepared but more quickly heard'.[47] The Law Society was among those critics who said that the proposals 'could only have been based on the interests of cost-cutting, not of justice'.[48] It pointed out that there were safe-guards in a jury trial which were more likely to produce a just result.

As we have seen, the Royal Commission maintained that its proposals would lead to a more 'rational' allocation of cases. But it is hardly irrational for defendants pleading not guilty to choose the mode of trial which is more likely to lead to their acquittal. It is implicit in the Royal Commission's recommendations that jury trial is less likely to lead to wrongful convictions. Otherwise what justification would there be for making it more readily available for those with more of a reputation to lose?

The commission said that 'defendants should not be able to choose their court of trial solely on the basis that they think they will get a fairer hearing at one level than the other'.[49] But are defendants right to think that a trial by jury will be more fair? This question is neatly side-stepped by the report. It simply asserts that 'magistrates' courts conduct over 93 per cent of all criminal cases and should be trusted to try cases fairly'. Where is the evidence for this? We have just seen that magistrates convict almost twice as often as juries. If trial by jury really is fairer, the government should not take it away from cases where it is currently available.

Significantly there was support for Lord Runciman's proposals from the Director of Public Prosecutions, Barbara Mills QC. She pointed out that eight out of ten people who choose jury trial then plead guilty when they get to the Crown Court, causing great inconvenience to witnesses who had come to give evidence. 'I certainly would not be supporting anything which I thought was socially divisive,' she said, 'or anything which would tend to suggest that the criminal justice system favours the rich and powerful against the poor and not so well known.' Mrs Mills said it was 'a much more sensible way of using resources in the widest sense' but she stressed that the proposals were not a cost-cutting exercise.[50]

Is it important to discourage people from electing trial by jury if they are going to admit the charges anyway? Mr Justice Judge agreed that it could be frustrating when someone changed his plea to guilty 'at the doors of the court'. Even so he insisted that a defendant had the right to plead guilty at a time of his own choosing, not when it happened to suit the administration of justice. 'Even a very late plea is better than a trial,' he said. 'For example, even if a woman has come to court to give evidence about rape, and the defendant pleads guilty at the last moment, at least she won't have to go into court and tell what happened to her: that represents a considerable saving.'[51]

Michael Zander, who frequently sprang to the defence of the Royal Commission in the months following its report, insisted that the debate over mode of trial was not just an argument about saving public money. 'Sending cases to the Crown Court that could appropriately have been dealt with by the magistrates involves not only higher costs but also longer delays for all Crown Court defendants and, even more important, longer sentences.'[52]

However, Professor Zander accepted that the quality of justice was 'probably lower' in magistrates' courts. This, he said, was implicit in a two-tier system. But since magistrates already tried most 'either-way' cases, 'the commission's view was that there is no valid reason why the quality of justice in magistrates' courts is not adequate for some either-way cases that are presently heard by juries'. Professor Zander stressed that the main purpose of the commission's proposal was not to deprive defendants of the chance of jury trial: it was to deal with the fact that the great majority of defendants who opt for Crown Court trial end by pleading guilty.[53]

In February 1994, the government promised in its interim response to the Royal Commission that its decisions on this issue and any proposals for change would be announced 'as soon as possible'. By August 1994, nothing more had been heard from the Home Office. However, ministers were right to tread warily.

Michael Howard might have been able to persuade the voters that the right to silence protected only the guilty but few people took that view about the right to trial by jury.

Committal proceedings

As we have seen, committal proceedings are designed to filter out weak cases before they reach the Crown Court. The vast majority – an estimated 120,000 a year – are what are known as *paper committals*. In such cases defendants are sent for trial on the basis of written statements and the magistrates are not required to decide whether these statements disclose a case to answer. In addition it is estimated that there are nearly 9,000 *old-style committals* a year, where the magistrates take oral evidence and decide whether the prosecution has made out an arguable case.

Committal proceedings can be bypassed in an increasing number of cases: in serious frauds,[54] for example, and in certain cases where there are child witnesses.[55] If the prosecution believes there is enough evidence to justify a trial the prosecutor can issue a *notice of transfer* and the case will move automatically to the Crown Court. The defendant is given details of the evidence against him: if he thinks it is insufficient to justify the prosecution he can ask the Crown Court to have the charges dismissed.

The Royal Commission found that 'the present system of paper committals has no useful purpose, apart from any associated time limit' for serving the papers – and that can be provided by other means.[56] The commission was therefore right to recommend that full committal hearings should be abolished. Under its proposals the defendant would still have an opportunity before the start of the trial to submit that there was no case to answer although witnesses would not be called in support. But it would not be left to the magistrates to decide. In a case which *must* be tried by a jury the Crown Court judge would decide. In a case which *may* be tried by a jury – the middle-ranking, 'either-way' cases – a full-time, legally qualified, stipendiary magistrate would make the decision. That was because 'the main purpose of the new procedure would be to hear legal argument on the sufficiency of the evidence'.

This, however, was a very curious suggestion. Outside London there are only about 35 stipendiaries to cover the whole of England and Wales and they are based mainly in the larger provincial towns and cities. If the Royal Commission's proposals were accepted they would presumably have to spend all of their time travelling around the country, briskly dismissing cases as they went. There is also an objection of principle. Lay magistrates are expected to understand the law well enough to decide when someone should be sent to prison. Indeed, the Royal Commission wanted to give lay justices the right to try cases which had previously been reserved for trial by jury. Those decisions involve a much greater responsibility than deciding whether to dismiss a case before it gets to the jury: if the magistrates refuse to stop the case the defendant can try again when the case reaches the Crown Court. Why then should lay magistrates lose the right to decide if there is no case to answer?

From private conversations with members of the Royal Commission it appears that they envisaged the creation of more stipendiary magistrates. More full-time magistrates would be needed anyway if they were to try even a small proportion of the 35,000 cases a year which could be moved down from the Crown Court. But stipendiary magistrates are something of an anomaly: there should be no more of them than is absolutely necessary. They are not 'magistrates' at all, of course, but very junior judges. Yet, unlike the more senior judges in the Crown Court and even the High Court, stipendiaries decide whether the defendant is guilty. Everywhere else in our criminal justice system the initial finding of guilt or innocence is made by ordinary people – juries or magistrates. But a stipendiary decides the facts as well as the law: he or she is given less pay than a Circuit judge for more responsibility. Any move towards the greater use of stipendiaries should be resisted.

Sensibly enough, the government heeded these suggestions. The Criminal Justice and Public Order Act 1994 abolishes committal proceedings while leaving it to lay magistrates to decide if there is no case to answer. Under the new procedure, which comes into force on a day fixed by the Home Secretary, the prosecutor sends the magistrates and the defendant a list of the charges together with all the documentary evidence in support. If he wishes, the defendant may then make a written application to the magistrates for the charges to be dismissed. The prosecutor has an opportunity to oppose this application. This too must be in writing. However, in complex or difficult cases the court may allow oral representations on both sides. A defendant who does not have a lawyer is always allowed to make an oral application for the case to be dismissed. A single magistrate can then rule on the application for dismissal. The magistrate considers the written evidence and any oral representations which have been allowed. If the magistrate concludes that there is 'not sufficient evidence against the accused to put him on trial by jury for the offence charged,' then the charge must be dismissed. However, the magistrates can substitute a different charge if they think it is supported by the evidence. Even if the magistrates throw out the charge, the prosecutor may have a second bite at the cherry; he can still apply to a judge for a voluntary bill of indictment (under the procedure described on page 131).

If there has been no successful application for dismissal within a prescribed period, the magistrates must transfer the proceedings to the Crown Court for trial. Magistrates' courts must display a list of the cases they have sent for trial but the new transfer proceedings are subject to the same sort of reporting restrictions as there were for the old committal proceedings.

Prosecution disclosure

We saw in chapter 7 how important it is for the prosecution to disclose all the available evidence to the defence, whether they intend to use it in court or not. Judith Ward was wrongly imprisoned for eighteen years because the prosecution had failed to do just that. But the ruling in her case was thought to have put an impossible burden on police officers. Until then, under guidelines issued by the Attorney General in 1981, the police had been allowed to hold back a wide variety of 'sensitive' documents. Now, it seemed, they had to hand over every scrap of paper even if they had only scribbled a telephone number on it. As a result, the Court of Appeal laid down new guidelines in the case of the so-called M25 Three.[57] Broadly speaking, these allowed the prosecution to withhold certain material but only if it asked the court's permission first.

The police maintained that even this ruling made things too difficult for them. The Metropolitan Police Commissioner, Paul Condon, admitted in July 1993 that police forces throughout England and Wales had dropped at least 60 major cases – such as drug trafficking and armed robbery – because of the disclosure rules. Mr Condon said that disclosure would have put at risk the lives of informants and undercover officers; the police would also have had to make public a number of secret technical devices. In its report the Royal Commission took heed of the police arguments and proposed that the existing rules should be replaced by something less onerous for the prosecution. Under its proposals disclosure would come in two stages. To begin with the prosecution would automatically disclose material which it thought was relevant to the offence or the offender. If the defence wanted to see any further material it would have to show – in court if necessary – that the material it sought was relevant.

These recommendations were largely accepted by the government[58] although they were not included in the 1994 legislation. However, the Legal Action Group expressed concern about any further restrictions on prosecution disclosure. It said that 'with so many miscarriages of justice arising from partial disclosure, it is necessary to have strong, even draconian, rules'. This perhaps goes too far. It is possible to argue that fair rules are better than extreme provisions: unfair rules will simply be ignored by the police. It is true that some prosecutions would become impossible if the police had to disclose the names of informants or undercover officers. On the other hand, the less disclosure there is, the more likely it becomes that defendants will be wrongly convicted. Yet again the Royal Commission's priority seems to have been to convict the guilty even if a few innocent people were swept up in the net.

Defence disclosure

The issue of defence disclosure was another that divided the Royal Commission. Even the majority view bears all the signs of a hasty compromise: like most compromises it pleased nobody. On this issue there were no instant decisions from the Home Office: the government acknowledged that defence disclosure could not be separated from the difficult issue of prosecution disclosure.

At present there are not many things a defendant is required to do, so long as he turns up in court. If he intends to rely on an alibi he must give the prosecution advance details and the names and addresses of any witnesses he plans to call in support of it. He must also give advance notice of any expert evidence he wishes to call. These provisions are supposed to make it more difficult for defendants to fabricate alibi or expert evidence; they are also aimed at preventing juries being misled by last-minute evidence which the prosecution have had no opportunity of checking.[59] In practice defendants hardly ever meet the prescribed time-limits; judges generally let them call their evidence anyway and allow the prosecution an adjournment if it needs to do any checking up.

The Royal Commission proposed a major extension of the defendant's duty of disclosure. It thought this would have practical advantages as well as discouraging 'ambush' defences – something which, as we have seen, the police were very worried about. The commission said that defendants who intended to contest the charges against them should be obliged to disclose their defence in advance of their trial, or to indicate that they would simply be arguing that the prosecution had not produced enough evidence to justify its allegations. In most cases defence solicitors would simply have to tick boxes on a standard form, selecting from a list of possibilities such as 'accident', 'self-defence', 'consent', 'no dishonest intent', 'no appropriation', 'abandoned goods', 'claim of right', and, no doubt, 'it weren't me, it was me mate like, honest guv, straight up'.

It seems clear from the commission's report[60] that the police wanted still more information; Lord Runciman's team considered whether the defence should have to reveal the names and addresses of all its witnesses. That would enable the police to interview them before the trial (with a defence solicitor in the room, of course). The commission decided this would be too helpful to the prosecution because prosecuting counsel could then call any of the witnesses which the defence might subsequently decide not to use. The possibility that some defence witnesses might be a little less keen to give evidence after a quiet word with a couple of burly detectives apparently never entered the commission's collective mind.

What sanction would there be if the defendant suddenly sprang an unexpected defence? In that case the prosecution, with permission from the judge, 'should be able to invite the jury to draw adverse inferences'.[61] The same would apply if the defendant had ticked two mutually inconsistent boxes (for example: 'she agreed to let me do it' and 'it was actually my twin brother'). But the judge would not have to allow adverse comment if he or she thought there was a good reason for the change of defence. As well as a stick there would be a carrot: the more information the defendant handed over, the more of its case the prosecution would have to disclose under the provisions just mentioned.

Behind this proposal is perhaps the feeling that lawyers have tended to treat criminal trials as a game which the prosecution team must win with most of the cards stacked against them. Give the Crown a better hand, runs the argument, and they will succeed more often. This is a dangerous notion: a trial is not a game. Just as we should not be putting unnecessary obstacles in the way of the prosecution, we should not be looking for ways of making things harder for the defence. We should turn instead to the basic principle underlying criminal trials in English law.

Every jury is told that it is for the prosecution lawyers to prove their case: it is not the job of the defendant to help them. To these principles Michael Zander added another: that a defendant need only respond to the case the prosecution makes in court, not to the case it says in advance that it will make. He rightly concluded that defence disclosure is wrong in principle.

In his 'Note of Dissent' Professor Zander pointed out that it is also unnecessary in practice. According to his survey[62] of prosecuting counsel, 'ambush' defences only occurred in 7 per cent of contested cases; while the Crown Prosecution Service thought they caused 'serious problems' in just 3 per cent of not guilty pleas. That is because a competent prosecutor can anticipate the defence in the vast majority of cases. Ticking a few boxes will not tell him or her who the witnesses are going to be and what they will say. But defence disclosure would be the thin end of a much larger wedge – the full disclosure which the police are seeking.

The Royal Commission believed greater defence disclosure would lead to increased efficiency. Professor Zander rightly said this assertion was unconvincing; indeed, the contrary is likely to be true. He pointed out that the proposed rules would never be enforced in practice; no judge wants to stop a defendant putting forward his defence.

The government would do well to heed Michael Zander's advice on this point. But all the signs were that it would not.

Plea-bargaining

The term 'plea-bargaining' is something of a misnomer in England and Wales. In the United States judges will openly reduce the charges if the defendant agrees to plead guilty. In England plea-bargaining usually refers to a plea of guilty in return for a shorter sentence, a process more accurately described as 'sentence-bargaining'.[63]

Until the Court of Appeal stopped the process about twenty-five years ago, barristers representing defendants on trial at the Crown Court would often arrange to see the judge in his private room before the hearing started. However discreetly it was phrased, there was only one question the barrister wanted to ask: if the client pleads guilty, will he go to prison? Once the judge promised a suspended sentence or probation, the defendant would be advised to change his plea to guilty; there would then be a short speech in mitigation and everyone could go off to lunch.

That was broadly what happened in the case of *Turner* in 1970.[64] The accused changed his plea to guilty during an adjournment after he had been led to believe that, as a result, he would avoid the prison sentence which he was told would inevitably follow a finding of guilt by the jury. His appeal was allowed on the basis that he might have been deprived of the right to make his plea freely and voluntarily. The Lord Chief Justice, Lord Parker, ruled that judges should never say they would impose a particular sentence on a plea of guilty and a more severe sentence on conviction following a plea of not guilty.

This is somewhat mysterious because it is well known that a defendant who pleads guilty can expect his sentence to be reduced by at least a quarter and possibly as much as a third. The reduction is supposed to be a reward for penitence and remorse but in fact it is an inducement designed to save the time of the court, spare the witnesses from giving what may be distressing evidence and avoid the risk of an acquittal by the jury.

This arrangement can be justified on pragmatic grounds if there is a clear-cut case against the defendant. But what if there is not? What, indeed, if the defendant is truly innocent but is afraid he will be wrongly convicted? Will he plead guilty to something he did not do in an attempt to get a lighter sentence?

In 1977 the answer was 'Yes' according to research conducted by John Baldwin and Mike McConville.[65] But were they right? And was that still the case? To find out the answer to this and many other questions the Royal Commission funded a major survey of the Crown Court. Questionnaires were issued to judges, jurors, lawyers, police, court clerks and defendants in every contested case in the Crown Court during the last two weeks of February 1992. In all, there were some 22,000 questionnaires relating to more than 3,000 cases. The survey was masterminded by Michael Zander. Not surprisingly, he wanted to know if innocent people were still pleading guilty. In cases where the defendant had pleaded guilty to all charges, defence barristers were asked for their response to the following paragraph:

An innocent defendant sometimes decides to plead guilty to achieve a sentence discount or reduction in the indictment. Were you concerned that this was such a case?

This is possibly the worst example of drafting ever seen in a publicly funded questionnaire. It begins by asserting what it seeks to discover. It offers no explanation of what is meant by 'innocent'.[66] It puts forward two alternative explanations without giving respondents an opportunity to indicate which is true – one, the other, or both. It uses the word 'concerned' in such a way as to allow several shades of ambiguity.[67] And finally, it gives no hint that it was intended to cover only those cases where the barrister thought the defendant was innocent of *all* charges.

In 53 out of the 846 replies – 6 per cent – the barristers answered 'Yes' to the question as asked. This seemed a matter for concern: it implied that there were 1,400 cases a year where innocent defendants were pleading guilty. But in reality it meant nothing of the sort. Some barristers had said 'Yes' because the defendant was said to be not guilty only to one of several charges. In other cases the defendant had claimed to be innocent although the barrister was highly sceptical. No doubt there were also cases where the barrister said 'Yes' because he or she was 'concerned' to ensure that the defendant did not plead guilty if he was really innocent. Professor Zander had the grace to admit that his drafting was 'imperfect'.[68]

However, this part of the survey was not entirely valueless. Defendants pleading guilty were also asked whether they had committed the offence which they had admitted (or a similar offence). In 31 out of 269 cases – 11 per cent – the defendants said they had not. These explanations were typical of those they gave:

- If I had pleaded not guilty, I would have received a bigger sentence, I think. (The defendant received a conditional discharge.)

- I was out to steal that day but I never actually attempted to steal what the store detective claimed. I pleaded guilty because my barrister spoke to the judge and got assurance that if I pleaded guilty I would not be sent to prison. However this guarantee did not extend if I pleaded not guilty and was found guilty. (Again, this defendant received a conditional discharge.)

- It seemed easier at the time to get it over with. (A suspended sentence was passed.)

- Because my solicitor told me to. (The defendant was put on probation.)

The Royal Commission recognised the risks of offering inducements: 'it would be naïve,' the commission said, 'to suppose that innocent persons never plead guilty because of the prospect of the sentence discount.'[69] Against this it weighed the benefits, to the system and to defendants, of those who really were guilty admitting their guilt. In the event, the resource arguments appear to have triumphed: the commission argued that the system of sentence discounts should remain.

Professor Mike McConville thought the Royal Commission was turning its own terms of reference on their head: it had been asked to examine the effectiveness of the criminal justice system . . . in convicting the guilty and acquitting the innocent, having regard to the efficient use of resources, and not to save resources at the cost of convicting innocent people.[70] Indeed, the commission went on to recommend that some defendants should get larger discounts for a guilty plea than others, perhaps even bigger than they were receiving under the existing arrangements (the report was not specific).

This proposal was aimed at making the system more 'effective': the earlier a defendant pleaded guilty, the higher his discount would be. Commissioners thought it would help to reduce 'cracked' trials, where the defendant changed his plea to guilty at the doors of the court.

They also thought it should be made easier for defendants to find out what the judge had in mind. This would be achieved through what the Royal Commission called a sentence 'canvass'. If the defendant wanted to know what punishment he could expect his counsel would go and ask the judge. To avoid misunderstandings, prosecuting counsel and a shorthand writer would also be present. The judge would hear 'brief statements from the prosecution and defence of all the relevant circumstances, which should include details of the defendant's previous convictions if any and, if available, any pre-sentence report required by the Criminal Justice Act 1991'.[71] The only question the judge could answer would be: 'What is the maximum sentence if my client were to plead guilty at this stage?'[72]

It is clear that the commission did not want the judge to go further and say what the defendant would get if he was found guilty by a jury; the report acknowledges that giving a defendant the choice between a lower sentence on an immediate plea and a higher sentence on conviction by the jury 'does amount to unacceptable pressure'.[73] The commissioners thought this pressure could be avoided if the defendant was not told what he could expect after being found guilty.

This was absurd. If the defendant is told that he will get no more than three years for a plea of guilty, and he knows that the discount at this stage is 25 per cent, he will not have to be much of a mathematician to work out that he can expect four years if the jury find him guilty. It follows that all defendants would face 'unacceptable' pressure' if these proposals were implemented, precisely the situation which the Royal Commission wanted to avoid.

Lord Runciman and his colleagues seemed to have forgotten which Queen had granted their Royal Commission. It was the Queen of Hearts[74] who said 'Sentence first – verdict afterwards'. Yet that was precisely what their report was proposing. The judge would decide the sentence before hearing the full facts of the case or any of the witnesses. If the defendant did not like the sentence he could wait for the jury's verdict. In the meantime the judge would be locked into the sentence indication he had given. 'Stuff and nonsense!' as Alice said. 'The idea of having the sentence first!'

Needless to say, the commission did not devote a moment's thought to whether sentence-canvassing was right in principle. In the typical case a defendant asks what he would get for a plea of guilty. Unless this is purely a matter of idle curiosity it must mean one of two things. Either he is innocent of the charge but prepared to plead guilty. Or he is guilty as charged and willing to admit it. If he is innocent it cannot be right to let him plead guilty, still less to encourage him. If he is guilty he should be given a full opportunity to have his case put – in his presence and in public – before his fate is decided.

What if the defendant rejects the judge's offer and tries his chances before the jury? The judge is unlikely to believe he was innocent of the charge if he was apparently contemplating a guilty plea. How can that judge preside over a contested trial and direct the jury to give him the benefit of the doubt? How can the judge increase the sentence if he changes his mind during the trial? How indeed can a defendant solemnly plead not guilty when he has effectively told the judge he committed the crime?

Michael Zander dismissed the argument that the commission's

ecommendations would increase the risk of innocent people pleading guilty. He suggested that the risk was created by the existing sentence discount rather than the proposed sentence canvass: he believed that risk would not be increased by giving defendants more information about their options. Professor Zander also justified the proposal on pragmatic grounds: if it resulted in more defendants pleading guilty more quickly, then they would get shorter sentences and the system as a whole would benefit.[75]

Mr Justice Sedley said that the old form of plea-bargaining was 'pretty unseemly. One particularly undesirable outcome was that people who were charged with quite serious crimes could sometimes, where the evidence was weak, induce the court to let them off very lightly indeed in return for an admission of guilt.' He went on: 'Part of the logic of plea-bargaining and sentence-canvassing is that punishment becomes proportionate not to the gravity of the crime but to the strength of the case, a principle which, if it is to be defended, needs first to be articulated.'[76]

The government settled for a reasonably inoffensive compromise. The Criminal Justice and Public Order Act 1994 says that in deciding what sentence to pass on an offender who has pleaded guilty, the court must take account of the stage in the proceedings at which the offender indicated his intention to do so and the circumstances in which this indication was given. If the court decides to pass a less severe punishment as a result, it has to say so publicly.[77]

DNA testing

DNA profiling is one of the most exciting developments in forensic science for many years.[78] It was first used in 1986 and in principle it is remarkably simple. Each individual is supposed to have a unique 'genetic fingerprint'. Criminals fleeing the scene of the crime often leave parts of themselves behind: body fluids such as blood and semen, or tissues such as skin and hair. These biological samples can be analysed in the laboratory to produce a pattern of lines faintly resembling a supermarket bar code.[79] Scientists then perform the same tests on a sample taken from the suspect. DNA profiling allows the scientists to compare the two samples and decide how likely it is that they came from the same individual.

The success of this technique clearly depends whether the police can obtain a sample from the defendant. Criminals may be understandably reluctant to provide the evidence which they suspect will secure their conviction. What happens if they refuse to co-operate?

Under the Police and Criminal Evidence Act 1984 the police were allowed to take *non-intimate samples* from a defendant without his consent, provided a senior officer reasonably suspected the defendant of involvement in a 'serious arrestable offence'. Non-intimate samples included hair (although not pubic hair); nails and nail scrapings; and swabs taken from anywhere other than a body orifice. The police could not take *intimate samples* unless the suspect agreed. These included body fluids and swabs taken from a body orifice.

The Royal Commission recommended that saliva – at that time classed as an intimate sample – should be reclassified as non-intimate. This would allow mouth swabs to be taken from a suspect without his consent. The commission also recommended that the definition of 'serious arrestable offence' should be widened for this purpose to include assault and burglary. This would allow the police to take samples by force from people suspected of these crimes.

The government accepted these proposals and decided to go further still. It announced that the police would be able to take non-intimate samples by force in all 'recordable' criminal offences – effectively, all crimes. This would produce about 500,000 samples a year which would go into a national database of convicted criminals' DNA profiles.

There was some concern about this latest step from civil liberties organisations. They were not convinced that those responsible for the database would destroy samples from suspects who turned out to be innocent, particularly as the police were keen to keep *all* samples for statistical purposes.[80] Critics were also worried about too much reliance being placed on a relatively new scientific method. And the Legal Action Group said police officers should not be allowed to take saliva samples without consent because 'considerable force' might be needed to open a suspect's mouth.

On this occasion the government was right to introduce legislation. DNA profiling, if performed competently and honestly, may turn out to be the most reliable way of linking a suspect to a crime. There is always scope for error and corruption. But it is easier to fabricate an entire confession than it is to manufacture a single drop of saliva.

The Criminal Cases Review Authority

Almost everyone who gave evidence to the Royal Commission on Criminal Justice supported what turned out to be its key innovation: that the Home Secretary should no longer decide whether suspected miscarriages of justice should be referred to the Court of Appeal and that the decision should be taken instead by a new independent tribunal. Even the Home Office was keen to give up its responsibilities.[81] The government had been against any such change some ten years earlier[82] but that was before the inadequacies of the existing arrangements were exposed by the miscarriages of justice discussed in the previous chapter.

As we saw in chapter 1, a defendant who has been convicted in the Crown Court has very restricted rights of appeal and once these have been exhausted he cannot ask the Court of Appeal to look at his case again – even if fresh evidence subsequently comes to light. Only the Home Secretary can do that. However, successive Home Secretaries have used their powers to refer cases to the Court of Appeal[83] very rarely indeed. The Home Office receives details of between 700 and 800 alleged wrongful convictions a year. From 1981 to 1988 an average of between four and five cases annually were referred to the Court of Appeal. In the years 1989 to 1992, after the floodgates had supposedly opened, the Home Office referred an average of just seven cases a year to the court.

Ministers and officials took a highly restricted view of their powers. Rather than initiating their own investigations, Home Office staff tried to pick holes in the sometimes feeble arguments put forward by convicted prisoners and their advisers to show what had gone wrong in a case. That at least is the inference to be drawn from a memorandum published by the Home Office in January 1987 in support of its decision not to refer the cases of the Guildford Four and the Maguire family to the Court of Appeal.[84] Its tortuous reasoning was clearly designed to persuade the then Home Secretary, Douglas Hurd, not to reopen those two cases. And it succeeded.

The Royal Commission rightly concluded that the Home Secretary's role was 'incompatible with the constitutional separation of powers as between the courts and the executive'. The commission thought it wrong for the Home Secretary to be responsible for investigating alleged miscarriages of justice while at the same time having responsibilities for law and order and for the police.

Instead it said there should be a new body to deal with alleged miscarriages of justice. The Royal Commission suggested this should be known, somewhat ponderously, as the Criminal Cases Review Authority. If the authority decided that a case needed further investigation it would be able to call in an outside police force and order detectives to follow specified lines of inquiry. The authority would also be able to commission expert advice, from forensic scientists, for example. Once the investigation was over the authority would either refer the case to the Court of Appeal or tell the applicant why his case was being turned down. The authority itself would have no powers to quash a conviction.

If the new authority thought the results of its investigations should be considered by the Court of Appeal it would provide the court with its reasons and 'such supporting material as it believes to be appropriate and desirable in the light of its investigations, and which in its view may be admissible, though without any recommendation or conclusion as to whether or not a miscarriage of justice has occurred'.[85] The Court of Appeal would then treat the case as a normal appeal from the Crown Court.

This recommendation is not as generous to appellants as it might first appear. Some of the material uncovered by the authority might well be favourable to the prosecution. Some of it might not even turn out to be admissible in court: the authority would only need to believe it 'may' be admissible. The Crown would still be able to resist the appeal and the judges would have the last word.

The Criminal Cases Review Authority would be independent of the Court of Appeal although the court would be able to refer cases to it for investigation. It would consist of both lawyers and lay people, supported by a specialist staff, and the chairman would be appointed by the Queen on the advice of the prime minister. That recommendation was apparently made so that the post appeared comparable to that of a Lord Justice of Appeal, although it was not suggested that the chairman should have similar security of tenure and the Royal Commission specifically ruled out the appointment of a serving judge to the post.

If the commission had really wanted to emphasise the authority's independence from the courts it should have ruled out the appointment of a retired judge as chairman. It is only fair to say, though, that there are some judges who would make an excellent job of running the new authority – Judge Stephen Tumim, for example, who has made a major contribution to prison reform as HM Chief Inspector of Prisons.

The Royal Commission recognised that some prisoners become obsessive about their cases. It therefore said there should be no right of appeal if the authority decided not to investigate a case or not to refer it to the Court of Appeal – although an applicant would be able to try again if he had fresh evidence or new arguments. If the authority goes about its work conscientiously this proposal may just be acceptable in the interests of finality. But the commission went on to recommend that the authority's decision should not be subject to judicial review. That notion was attractive to Home Office ministers who were worried that the judicial review procedure would give disgruntled appellants a second bite at the cherry. It is quite unacceptable. If the authority acts unreasonably or irrationally its decisions should be subject to review by the courts just like those of any other public body. It should not be allowed special treatment.

One aspect of the Royal Commission's blueprint was particularly welcome. It recommended that the new authority should be able to discuss a case with the applicant if it was thought this would help the authority to decide whether the case should be investigated further. The commission rightly perceived that people who believe they have suffered injustices feel they have a right to be heard and are frustrated that they are not able to put their case in person to the anonymous Home Office officials who are considering it. Members of the authority would certainly benefit from face-to-face meetings with the prisoners whose futures they effectively control.

It came as no surprise when the Home Secretary moved quickly to accept the idea of a Criminal Cases Review Authority.[86] This was a highly desirable reform: indeed, Professor Simon Lee said, 'Its need was so stunningly obvious that its advent was merely delayed by the commission's appointment'.[87] However, it soon emerged that getting the review authority off the ground would involve yet more delay: the Royal Commission had only sketched in the broad outline and the details would take time to work out.

This was a major disappointment. The Home Office could hardly have been taken by surprise when the Royal Commission recommended a new review authority to deal with suspected miscarriages of justice: it was an idea that the Home Office itself supported. Officials there must have worked up proposals for a new review body into a reasonably advanced form but clearly the Home

Secretary saw less urgency in this area than in, say, abolishing the right to silence. The irony was that there would almost certainly have been a review body in operation by 1993 if the Royal Commission had not been set up.

Although reformers had to accept that the government would not be ready to introduce legislation until the end of 1994, interested parties were led to believe that they would not have to wait any longer than that. But in March 1994 there was a faint tinkling of alarm bells. The Home Office issued a discussion paper which made it clear that the government did not know how to proceed on a number of key issues. Throughout the Home Office paper, there were phrases like 'the government will wish to give further thought to this question in the light of consultation' and 'the government intends to give further consideration to the need for statutory provision for this purpose.' So, for example, the government said it was 'minded' to introduce new arrangements dealing with summary cases but 'the details will need careful working out.' At one point the paper said: 'The government will wish to give further consideration to the arguments for and against empowering the Court of Appeal to appoint its own counsel in uncontested appeals.' At another point it said: 'The government's provisional conclusion is that the power [to commission investigations] could be valuable in certain exceptional circumstances, but that difficult constitutional and practical questions are raised which it will be essential to resolve before the scope and definition of any new power can be decided.'

The Home Office asked people to write in with comments by the end of May 1994. Responses were to be sent to Miss C.F. Byrne of C3 Division – the very department whose powers were under threat. The discussion paper helpfully said that further copies could be obtained from Miss A. Byrne, her sister perhaps. But although this deadline should in theory have allowed time for the Misses Byrne and their colleagues to prepare the necessary legislation, it became known by the summer of 1994 that the government would not be ready to introduce a bill in the forthcoming session of parliament. At a news conference in July 1994, the Lord Chief Justice said the Review Authority was extremely important and should be brought into being as soon as possible. He'd earlier expressed concern at the apparent delay in setting it up.

In 1993, the Legal Action Group had been worried that the planned new authority would be 'as marginal in its effect and as lacking in credibility as, for instance, the Police Complaints Authority'. If the Criminal Cases Review Authority was starved of resources it could be 'reduced to a role little better than the existing Home Office arrangements'. The Legal Action Group was right to be concerned. Governments are adept at neutralising sweeping reforms. The Crown Prosecution Service, set up in response to an earlier Royal Commission, was indeed starved of resources at its birth: it has still not fully recovered. It came in for much criticism during 1993 over the quality of its decisions and its apparent reluctance to bring prosecutions.[88]

A great deal will depend on the Criminal Cases Review Authority. Despite the tremendous public concern that lay behind the appointment of the Royal Commission on Criminal Justice there can be little confidence that its recommendations – even if fully implemented – will do much to prevent further wrongful convictions. The government's highly selective approach towards implementing the commission's proposals makes it all too likely that we shall see defendants wrongly convicted for many years into the future. Their only hope will be the Criminal Cases Review Authority. If the Home Office can complete work on the details of the new authority in time for a Bill in the autumn of 1995, the Criminal Cases Review Authority could be up and running some time in 1997[89] – the tenth anniversary of Douglas Hurd's decision to refer the Birmingham Six case to the Court of Appeal. For those innocent people languishing in our overcrowded prisons that day will not come a moment too soon. Not until then can they begin their final search for justice.

Notes and References

Chapter 1: Her Majesty's Judges

1 Speech at the Lord Mayor's Banquet, quoted in R. M. Jackson, *The Machinery of Justice in England* (Cambridge University Press, 7th edn, 1977). In his memoirs, *Not Without Prejudice* (Hutchinson, 1937), Lord Hewart explained that his 'natural caution' prompted him to insert the word 'almost'.

2 In the Richard Dimbleby Lecture, BBC1, 30 November 1992.

3 Asked if people were ever justified in taking the law into their own hands, a representative sample said:
   Sometimes justified: 76%
   Never justified: 21%
   Don't know: 3%
   (Gallup Poll, *Daily Telegraph*, 30 August 1993)

4 Lord Gifford QC calculated that 67 per cent of the judges were from public schools and 64 per cent had been to Oxford or Cambridge. His figures are drawn from a survey of 967 judges ranging from law lords to Assistant Recorders. His survey was done in 1985 but the figures are unlikely to have changed a great deal. See Tony Gifford, *Where's the Justice?* (Penguin, 1986). (He will have cringed at the cover picture, which wrongly shows an English judge holding a gavel. The solecism is frequently repeated on television, despite the author's best efforts.)

5 *London Borough of Wandsworth v. National Association of Schoolmasters and Union of Women Teachers* [1993] IRLR 334.

   This seems a good moment for a note on references. In the above citation the date 1993 is an essential part of the reference; the initials refer to the *Industrial Relations Law Reports* for that year, starting at page 334. If there is more than one volume in a single year, the volume number is given before the report's initials. Round brackets are used for dates which are informative rather than essential: the volume is identified by a separate volume number. This book uses the traditional way of citing case references but other sources of reference have been cited in a way which should be easier for non-lawyers to follow.

6 *R. v. British Coal Corporation and Secretary of State for Trade and Industry ex parte Vardy* [1993] IRLR 104.

7 *R. v. Foreign Secretary ex parte Rees-Mogg, The Times*, 31 July 1993. Although Lord Rees-Mogg was granted leave to seek judicial review, his action was dismissed by the High Court on its merits.

8 And Northern Ireland.

9 The Lord Chancellor's woolsack is a large square bag of wool (and a little horsehair) inside a wooden frame, covered with red cloth and placed in front of the throne. It has no formal back or sides, but a small temporary backrest provides some comfort during a long debate. See R. F. V. Heuston, *Lives of*

the Lord Chancellors 1940–1970 (Oxford University Press, 1987), p. 13.

10 As Lord Hailsham and Lord Havers were by Mrs Thatcher.

11 There are no restrictions on grounds of sex or religion: Heuston, *Lives of the Lord Chancellors 1940–1970*, pp. 3, 5.

12 These 'wax' seals are still affixed to certain formal documents such as letters patent: they are moulded on to a piece of string which is suspended from the parchment. Other state documents – such as the Royal Proclamation dissolving parliament – are sealed with a 'wafer' or paper seal, which is rather smaller. A new seal is made for each monarch. The present one shows the Queen on horseback.

13 There is now a junior minister in the Commons: see page 12. The Lord Chancellor still answers for the Attorney General in the House of Lords.

14 For a discussion of this paradoxical relationship, see Joshua Rozenberg, *The Case for the Crown* (Thorsons, 1987), chapter 10.

15 The Attorney General is known within Whitehall as 'the Attorney' and the Solicitor General is referred to as 'the Solicitor' – which is confusing because he is normally a barrister.

16 At the time of writing, the Attorney General was Sir Nicholas Lyell QC MP and the Solicitor General was Sir Derek Spencer QC MP.

17 The last Labour law officers, Sam Silkin and Peter Archer, refused knighthoods in 1974. However, both were given peerages on retirement from the Commons.

18 In his Mishcon Lecture, 'The Lord Chancellor in the 1990s', University College, London, 6 March 1991, para. 25. It might have been thought that Lord Mackay was referring to Lord Hailsham, who had said '. . . a Lord Chancellor is a useful working member of the cabinet . . . and capable of giving useful advice in cabinet in foreign and legal matters . . .' (*A Sparrow's Flight*, Collins, 1990, p. 423) In fact, Lord Mackay had in mind Lord Kilmuir who offered the cabinet advice on international law during the Suez crisis 'in conjunction with, or maybe in competition with, the law officers of the time' (Lord Mackay, interview with

the author, 18 June 1993, referring to published documents).

19 Planned spending for 1995–6: £2,445m (legal aid £1,528m). *The Government's Expenditure Plans 1993–94 to 1995–96*, Cm 2209 (February 1993).

Command Papers are official government documents published by Her Majesty's Stationery Office. Before 1870 they carried numbers without any prefix. In 1870, when the numbers got too big, the authorities began again from number 1, this time adding the prefix *C*. Whenever the numbers approach 10,000, they start again with a new prefix. So papers issued from 1900 had the prefix *Cd*; those published after 1919 were *Cmd*; papers issued from 1956 were *Cmnd*; and in December 1986 the prefix changed (rather cleverly this time) to *Cm*. These abbreviations may be confused, so J. R. Spencer wisely advises us to include the year as part of the reference.

20 Lord Hailsham, *A Sparrow's Flight*, p. 427.

21 By the author, interview, 18 June 1993.

22 See the comments on Lord Donaldson later in this chapter.

23 See Lord Mackay, 1991 Mishcon Lecture, para. 36.

24 Press conference, 28 May 1993. The shortage of judges will be discussed in chapter 2.

25 In a lecture to the Holdsworth Club.

26 There will be detailed discussion of these points later in the book.

27 Interview with the author, 18 June 1993.

28 A move that had been resisted by Lord Hailsham. We have now seen the Lord Chancellor cross-examined by the Committee on his cuts to legal aid eligibility (in February 1993).

29 And of course he has no involvement whatsoever in the Lord Chancellor's responsibilities in the House of Lords.

30 The Parliamentary Secretary is based in the Lord Chancellor's Department at Trevelyan House, Great Peter Street, Westminster.

31 The Lord Chancellor is also chairman of the Judicial Committee of the Privy Council (see p. 134) and President of the Court of Appeal, the High Court, and the Crown Court (s. 1(2) Supreme Court Act 1981). As if this was not

enough, he is also the controlling authority for the county courts.

32 *Pepper v. Hart* [1993] 1 All ER 42. He said afterwards that there were precedents for a Lord Chancellor sitting in tax cases.

33 He argued that the courts should not be able to consult Hansard in order to interpret an ambiguous statute. Unusually there were seven law lords sitting: six disagreed with him on this point. In his partly dissenting judgment Lord Mackay said that there could be an 'immense increase in the cost of litigation in which statutory construction is involved'. He went on: 'The costs of litigation are a subject of general public concern and I personally would not wish to be a party to changing a well established rule which could have a substantial effect in increasing these costs . . .' (*Pepper v. Hart*, see n. 32). His fears were perhaps justified when Westminster City Council's privatised library service offered to make searches of Hansard for £60 a clause (press release, 2 April 1993).

34 So does the senior law lord when he presides over a judicial sitting in the Chamber.

35 A wooden changing hut, panelled in the Palace of Westminster 'linenfold' style, sits just behind his desk: few visitors and even fewer television viewers realise what it is.

36 Sir Francis Purchas, Joseph Jackson Memorial Lecture, 3 November 1993, reprinted in *New Law Journal*, 12 November 1993.

37 Lord Mackay, 1991 Mishcon Lecture, paras 5, 65.

38 Interview with the author, 18 June 1993.

39 This is a figurative expression: in reality he only has one. It is of the long full-bottomed variety and lives on a wooden stand on the table just inside the door of his room.

40 Address to the Special General Meeting of the Law Society, 25 January 1918, *Law Society's Gazette*, February 1918.

41 *Report of the Machinery of Government Committee*, Cd 9230 (1919).

42 Haldane's proposals were never implemented. Professor Drewry concludes that this was because of opposition from Sir Claud Schuster who was Per-

manent Secretary of the Lord Chancellor's Department from 1915 to 1944. See Gavin Drewry, 'Lord Haldane's Ministry of Justice – Stillborn or strangled at birth?', *Public Administration*, vol. 61 (1983), p. 396.

43 Discussed on pp. 77–81.

44 Just as our Treasury minister is called the Chancellor of the Exchequer. Other 'Lords' who sit as ministers in the Commons from time to time are the Lord President of the Council and the Lord Privy Seal.

45 Gifford, *Where's the Justice?*

46 Discussed on pp. 192–4

47 Lord Hailsham, *A Sparrow's Flight*, p. 423.

48 It was handed over by the Home Office in April 1992.

49 Professor Heuston says: 'Claims have been made for an initial date of AD 615, but Edward the Confessor (1042–66) was the first English king to have a great seal and a Chancellor to keep it.' See Heuston, *Lives of the Lord Chancellors 1940–1970*, p. 1. However, Lord Mackay has said: 'Since AD 605, 210 people have held the office of Lord Chancellor of whom one was a woman, Queen Eleanor in 1253.' See 1991 Mishcon Lecture, para. 3.

50 Lord Mackay, speech to the Society of Scottish Lawyers in London, 16 March 1988.

51 Lord Hailsham once said: 'I am a lawyer and the son of a lawyer and the father of two lawyers, and the well-being and prosperity of the legal profession is one of the causes nearest to my heart.' (Speech to the City of London Solicitors' Company Ladies' Banquet, 15 April 1987) Lord Havers was the son of a judge, the brother of a judge and the father of a prominent barrister.

52 Cmnd 7648 (1979).

53 Interview with the author, 19 June 1993.

54 See pp. 229–20.

55 See pp. 91–2, 94–5.

56 Hansard, House of Lords, 7 April 1989, col. 1307.

57 Asked by the author at one press conference whether his proposals would meet their stated objective, he replied: 'I'm not a prophet, Joshua.' This did not strike anyone as particularly funny

at the time but others (including Lord Taylor) have cited it publicly as an example of the Mackay wit.

58 Although his insistence on giving a detailed answer to the precise question asked makes him the despair of those who have to mine 'soundbites' from his interviews.

59 Lord Mackay regarded it as important for the Lord Chancellor to sit judicially on a regular basis. Between October 1987 and March 1991 he sat twice as a member of the Privy Council and eleven times in the House of Lords.

60 Subject to the Parliament Acts 1911 and 1949 which allow Acts to be passed in certain limited circumstances without the assent of the House of Lords. The War Crimes Act 1991 was passed under this legislation, after it was rejected by the House of Lords in 1990 and 1991.

61 This means they can – and do – take part in parliamentary debates: see p. 63.

62 Scottish judges are even more confusing. The Scottish equivalent of an English High Court judge is called 'the Hon. Lord Smith' in court but that does not entitle him to a seat in the House of Lords.

63 No offence is meant to all those people called Smith who object to their name being used as a generic: the author has simply followed the precedent set by Anthony Sampson in his seminal work, *The Anatomy of Britain* (Hodder & Stoughton, 1962, p. 155, and *The Essential Anatomy of Britain* (Hodder & Stoughton, 1992), p. 48.

64 Hence the Lord Chancellor had to be Lord Mackay of Clashfern. The names taken by Scottish peers vary from the obscure to the whimsical. On Lord Mackay's appointment it was said he was not so widely known – even in Clashfern. The chief of the clan Mackay is – confusingly – Lord Reay. Those with un-Scottish names have less to worry about. A Scottish peer could be known simply as Lord Rozenberg – unless he was considered to be a rather distant member of the clan Montrose. There has been an Earl of Montrose since the year 1505.

65 Or the equivalent appeal courts in Scotland and Northern Ireland. Lord Slynn served as a judge at the European Court of Justice instead.

66 Interview with the author, 30 March 1993.

67 Judgments are generally delivered on Thursdays at 2 p.m.

68 The law lords asked for what the BBC saw as an effective veto over how the BBC might use recordings of their proceedings: see p. 191.

69 Criminal Justice Act 1925, s. 41.

70 Interview with the author, 18 June 1993.

71 European Communities Act 1972.

72 If they can understand it. Decisions are sometimes so opaque or incomplete that they have to go back to the European Court once more: in *Stoke-on-Trent City Council v. B & Q Plc* (Case 169/91; [1993] 2 All ER 297) the House of Lords asked the European Court to interpret its decision in the earlier case of *Torfaen Borough Council v. B & Q* (Case 145/88; [1990] 2 QB 19).

73 In very limited circumstances it is possible to 'leapfrog' the Court of Appeal.

74 Practice Statement [1966] 1 WLR 1234.

75 Lord Templeman interviewed by Hugo Young, *The Judges*, BBC Radio 4, 13 April 1988.

76 These are called 'speeches' or 'opinions' in the House of Lords.

77 There are now five lawyers working in the Court of Appeal Civil Division, but they tend to be fully occupied with helping litigants in person. They are not attached to individual judges as they would be in other common law countries.

78 Interview with the author, 18 June 1993.

79 He added that Lord Slynn had been quite happy to join the House of Lords before his term of office at Luxembourg had expired.

80 It was thought the Act would come into effect on 1 June 1994.

81 [1993] AC 70.

82 And may therefore be classed with the younger law lords for the purposes of this slightly contrived comparison.

83 [1993] AC 534.

84 See p. 215.

85 [1992] QB 770.

86 There are three distinct jurisdictions in the United Kingdom: England and Wales, Scotland, and Northern Ireland.

Laws passed by parliament may apply to one jurisdiction, two, or all three: the last section of an Act usually makes this clear. The Channel Islands and the Isle of Man are not part of the United Kingdom (although they are usually included in the phrase 'British Isles') and they have separate legal systems. In July 1992 the author watched the last man sentenced to death for murder in the Isle of Man before the law was changed: he was later retried. Disappointingly, the judge did not wear the traditional black cap over his wig. 'We're more civilised than that over here,' he explained when asked.

87 [1993] 2 All ER 75.

88 Colin Laskey, interview with the author, *Nine O'Clock News*, BBC1, 11 March 1993.

89 The Law Commission – which advises the government on reform of the law – announced shortly after the decision in *Brown* that it would be looking at the question of consent to physical injury across a whole spectrum of activity that includes sports, games and 'what is sometimes called rough horseplay'.

90 *Airedale NHS Trust v. Bland* [1993] 1 All ER 821.

91 [1993] 3 WLR 433.

92 [1932] AC 562. A woman bought a bottle of ginger beer. She claimed it contained a decomposed snail (although this was never proved) and sought to sue the manufacturers for negligence. There was no contract between the purchaser and the manufacturer. Until that case it had only been possible to sue the supplier under the law of contract.

93 Junior Counsel to the Crown at Common Law, the 'Treasury Devil'.

94 This was the term used although Secretary of State for the Home Department is more commonly used as the Home Secretary's formal title. Statutes simply refer to 'the Secretary of State'.

95 Criminal Justice Act 1988, s. 36.

96 Although he is a member of the House of Lords he does not sit as a law lord; otherwise he could hear appeals from his own decisions.

97 See p. 120.

98 [1991] 4 All ER 481.

99 6 December 1993.

100 (1980) 71 Cr. App. R. 102 at 104.

101 [1980] 1 WLR 1193.

102 Lord Windlesham, *Responses to Crime*, vol. 2 (Clarendon Press, 1993), pp. 181–4.

103 *Sunday Times*, 22 November 1981.

104 Speech to mark Lord Lane's retirement, Court of Appeal, 15 April 1992.

105 Interview with the author, *Nine O'Clock News*, BBC1, 25 February 1992.

106 For example, by Melanie Phillips, *The Guardian*, 26 February 1992.

107 Court of Appeal, 15 April 1992.

108 *The Guardian*, 20 July 1992.

109 Lord Taylor, speech to the Law Society of Scotland, 21 March 1993.

110 A minor scholarship.

111 Interview with the author, 25 February 1992.

112 *R. v. Bibi* [1980] 1 WLR 1193.

113 Speech to the Law Society of Scotland, 21 March 1993. Lord Taylor's views on the Criminal Justice Act are discussed more fully on pp. 281–92.

114 Press conference, 28 May 1993.

115 He had been appointed before the compulsory retirement age for senior judges (then 75) was introduced in 1959. He regularly said he had all the Christian virtues except resignation.

116 He was an Independent although his ratepayers' group generally voted with the Conservatives.

117 Informality was to be the keynote. Those appearing before the court were told that the judges were not bothered with formal modes of address. Donaldson was normally addressed as 'Sir John' but occasionally he was called 'brother' by trade union representatives appearing before him, which he took as a compliment: Hansard, House of Lords, 22 June 1992, col. 354.

118 In the Court of Appeal, 31 July 1992.

119 Profile, *The Observer*, 25 October 1992.

120 Interview with the author, 12 August 1992.

121 12 August 1992, *Nine O'Clock News*, BBC1.

122 Reports in *The Times* and *The Guardian*, 28 September 1992. Sir Thomas Bingham was referring to the case of *Costello-Roberts v. the United Kingdom* which was first lodged before the European Commission on Human Rights in January 1986. The applicant,

then aged 7, had been hit by his headmaster three times with a gym shoe in October 1985 for misbehaviour. The hearing at the European Court took place in September 1992. In March 1993 the court ruled by a majority of five judges to four that the slippering in this case had not been severe enough to amount to degrading treatment or punishment. By then the boy was 15. (*The Times*, 26 March 1993)

123 Implementing a recommendation first made in 1933. Probate, Divorce, and Admiralty work were lumped together because they were originally dealt with in courts which applied Roman law. See J. R. Spencer (ed.), *Jackson's Machinery of Justice* (Cambridge University Press, 1989), p. 38.

124 Although in theory the job is open to anyone who has had rights of audience in the High Court for ten years: Courts and Legal Services Act 1990, s. 71(1)(a)(i).

125 Pronounced 'right on' and denoting membership of the Privy Council.

126 Section 2(3).

127 Although they retain their membership of the Privy Council and with it the title 'Rt. Hon.'.

128 Courts and Legal Services Act 1990, s. 71(1)(b).

129 Recent examples include Jowitt, Mantell, Blofeld, Curtis, Brown and Bracewell JJ.

130 With the exception of Junior Counsel to the Crown who by convention do not become QCs; those appointed to these coveted positions know that promotion to the High Court will follow automatically. Lord Justice Butler-Sloss was never a Silk; before becoming a High Court judge she was a Registrar (what would now be called a District judge) in the High Court Family Division.

131 There really is a Mrs Justice Smith. Before her appointment she was known professionally as Miss Janet Smith QC, even though she was married. Her clerk at the High Court is called Ms Smith.

132 Pronounced 'puny' and meaning 'junior'.

133 Because of their robes.

134 At the time of writing, there were two Lords Justices Gibson. There was also a Mr Justice Tucker and a Mr Justice Tuckey.

135 This is despite the fact that a woman becomes a Lord Justice of Appeal on promotion to the Court of Appeal. A lawyer addressing a court of two or three judges which included Dame Elizabeth Butler-Sloss had to address her as 'My Lady' but refer to her when addressing all three judges as 'My Lady, Lord Justice Butler-Sloss'. There are different rules in the Irish Republic. It was reported in April 1991 that the only woman judge in the Irish Republic had ordered lawyers to stop addressing her as 'My Lord' and call her 'Judge' instead. The judge in question was known as Miss Justice Carroll.

136 The author once telephoned the well-known Chancery judge Mr Justice Harman and, after introducing himself, started to ask the judge a question. 'How do you address me?' the judge demanded to know. The author had deliberately side-stepped this pitfall, but he offered to call the judge 'My Lord' if that was what he wished. Mr Justice Harman indicated that this would meet with his approval. 'Well, My Lord . . .' the author continued.

137 Supreme Court Act 1981, s. 9(4).

138 In January and March 1993 non-High Court judges were responsible for more than half the sitting days; in February 1993, for more than two-thirds.

139 Including District judge, stipendiary magistrate and High Court Master: Courts and Legal Services Act 1990, s. 71(2) and Schedule 10.

140 By the Courts Act 1971. The Act abolished Assizes and Quarter Sessions. The judges who sat at Quarter Sessions were generally called Recorders.

141 But 'My Lord' at the Old Bailey. Until a few years ago there was a distinguished barrister on the Midland and Oxford Circuit called Igor Judge QC. If he had become a Circuit judge he would have been called Judge Judge. Fortunately he avoided the fate of Major Major in *Catch 22* (and Constable Constable in a *Carry On* film) and in 1988 he became Mr Justice Judge instead. There is also a judge called Mr Justice Laws and another called Judge Hazel Counsell.

142 Courts and Legal Services Act 1990, s. 74.

143 Just as Circuit judges found themselves doing work which previously had gone to a High Court judge, District judges were given work which would previously have been done by a Circuit judge.

144 From 1 January 1991: Courts and Legal Services Act 1990, *s*. 71(2) and Schedule 10.

145 *Judicial Appointments: The Lord Chancellor's Policies and Procedures*, Lord Chancellor's Department (May 1986), p. 11.

146 See p. 75.

147 *Today's Magistrate*, Lord Chancellor's Department, (1992), p. 2. The title 'Keepers of the Peace' can be traced back even further: in 1195 Richard I appointed certain knights to preserve the peace in unruly areas ('Notes for Speakers I', Magistrates' Association, 19 June 1985).

148 'Notes for Speakers III', Magistrates' Association (22 June 1985).

149 Speech to the Staffordshire and Shropshire branch of the Magistrates' Association, 17 June 1988.

150 Speech to Law Society's conference, Brussels, October 1991, reported in the *Law Society's Gazette*, 23 October 1991, p. 7.

151 Interview with Gerry Northam, *File on Four*, BBC Radio 4, 29 June 1993.

152 As n. 151.

153 *Daily Telegraph*, 17 September 1993.

154 He meant appointing a vicar.

155 Speech by Lord Kilmuir to a branch of the Magistrates' Association, February 1955, quoted by Lord Mackay in a speech to the Hertfordshire branch of the Magistrates' Association, 1 July 1988.

156 See p. 277.

157 Press conference, 28 May 1993.

Chapter 2: What's Wrong with the Judiciary?

1 Interview with David Rose, *The Observer*, 9 May 1993.

2 Speech to the Canadian Institute of Advanced Legal Studies, Cambridge, 13 July 1993.

3 By the author, 26 July 1993.

4 Lord Reid, 'The Judge as Law Maker', *Journal of the Society of Public Teachers of Law*, vol. 12 (1972), p. 22.

5 The common law means simply the principles laid down by the judges in past cases. Those cases which are thought to develop new principles generally find their way into the various law reports, bound volumes of which are to be found lining the shelves of barristers (and the pockets of law publishers). Nowadays reports are available electronically. Courts are generally bound by previous decisions unless they find a way of *distinguishing* them from the case before the court. The House of Lords decided in 1966 that it would no longer have to follow its earlier decisions (Practice Statement [1966] 1 WLR 1234).

6 *The Spectator*, 22 May 1993.

7 *The Times*, 22 October 1993.

8 The term comes from Australia. The author is assured it is genuine.

9 Unfortunately Lord Browne-Wilkinson used the word *cohabitee*. This word is commonly used but is quite wrong: it must mean someone who receives cohabitation. A person who cohabits is a cohabiter, or rather better, a cohabitant.

10 Professor H. L. A. Hart, *The Concept of Law* (Clarendon Press, 1961) p. 12.

11 J. A. G. Griffith, *The Politics of the Judiciary*, (Fontana, 4th edn, 1991), p. 13.

12 As n. 11, p. 18.

13 As n. 11, pp. 19–20.

14 Replying to the author, December 1992.

15 Of the 139 judges appointed between 1832 and 1906, 80 were MPs at the time of their nomination; 11 others had been candidates. Of those 80, 63 were appointed by their own party while in office. See S. H. Bailey and M. J. Gunn, *Smith and Bailey on the Modern English Legal System* (Sweet & Maxwell, 2nd edn, 1991), p. 215.

16 See J. Ll. J. Edwards, *The Law Officers of the Crown* (Sweet & Maxwell, 1964), pp. 309–34.

17 As Lord Templeman did with the Land Registration Act 1988.

18 There is a fuller discussion of judicial review on pp. 194–202.

19 *R. v. Commissioner for the Special Purposes of the Income Tax Acts ex parte*

Stipplechoice Ltd, 21 January 1985 (*The Times*, 23 January 1985).

20 Lord Hailsham, *A Sparrow's Flight* (Collins, 1990), p. 432. Lord Hailsham did not identify the judges concerned.

21 Hansard, House of Lords, 5 February 1985, col. 945.

22 Lord Hailsham, *A Sparrow's Flight*, p. 432.

23 Indeed, Lord Justice Ackner declined to be interviewed by the BBC about the controversy.

24 Lord Hailsham, *A Sparrow's Flight*, p. 431.

25 On 3 November 1987 Lord Mackay said: 'If a person has been appointed a judge and that trust has been placed in him, I think he should be able to decide what to do if he is approached by the media.' (*Daily Telegraph*, 4 November)

26 Lord Mackay took a much more relaxed view than his predecessor about judges speaking out in public. 'I don't go in for criticising individual judges, whatever views they may hold about me,' he said pointedly. (Interview with the author, 18 June 1993).

27 He was also one of the seven judges willing to support Lord Woolf's views on penal policy, discussed later in this section.

28 Interview with the author, March 1993.

29 Hansard, House of Lords, 26 January 1993, col. 1193.

30 The government did not budge.

31 Speech to the Law Society of Scotland, Gleneagles, 21 March 1993.

32 When interviewed by the author, 30 March 1993.

33 In his report on the prison service.

34 *Prison Disturbances April 1990*, Cm 1456 (1991).

35 Lord Woolf, speech entitled 'Crime, Punishment and Rehabilitation', 12 October 1993: see n. 37.

36 27 September 1993.

37 12 October 1993. Lord Woolf was addressing a meeting of the New Assembly of Churches, which is made up of twenty of the largest black-led churches in the country. Its General Secretary, Rev. Carmel Jones, was closely involved with rehabilitating offenders.

38 Michael Howard, speech to Chesham and Amersham Conservative Association, 14 October 1993.

39 17 October 1993.

40 Michael Howard, speech, 14 October 1993.

41 David Maclean, speech to the Cumbria Victim Support annual conference, 16 October 1993.

42 23 October 1993.

43 To the Association of Jewish Ex-Servicemen, 24 October 1993.

44 The Lord Chief Justice, the Master of the Rolls, the Vice-Chancellor of the Chancery Division and the President of the Family Division.

45 An experienced Circuit judge, who spoke on the BBC phone-in programme *Call Nick Ross*, was also warned about his behaviour by the senior presiding judge, Lord Justice McCowan.

46 See p. 62.

47 Hansard, House of Lords, 3 February 1993, cols. 282–3. This time he was unsuccessful. The issue is discussed more fully on pp. 224–32.

48 Until the Lord Chief Justice's appearance on 28 October 1993.

49 And indeed the government won both cases.

50 By the author, press conference, 28 May 1993. Lord Taylor was speaking in a room at the Royal Courts of Justice which was normally used as an additional courtroom. Cameras were allowed in. The Law Society's challenge to the legal aid eligibility cuts was being heard simultaneously in another part of the building.

51 Interview with the author, 30 July 1993.

52 Sir Nicolas Browne-Wilkinson, 'The Independence of the Judiciary in the 1980s', Francis Mann Lecture, November 1987, published in *Public Law* (1988), p. 44.

53 Hansard, House of Lords, 7 April 1989, col. 1331.

54 Press release dated 13 April 1989 issued by the Lord Chancellor's Department on behalf of the Judges' Council.

55 *Public Law* (1988), p. 54.

56 See p. 148. A press release issued by the Lord Chancellor's Department on 8 July 1993 says the Judges' Council 'is a non-statutory body established in 1988 by and on the initiative of the senior judiciary'.

57 By 1993 they had been joined by 'a number of other members of the Court of Appeal and the High Court bench'. In a strikingly uninformative phrase the Lord Chancellor's Department said the council was 'a collegiate body whose purpose is to co-ordinate all aspects of the responsibilities of the judiciary for the administration of justice' (press release, 8 July 1993).

58 23 May 1989.

59 Which were taken into account when the legislation was drafted.

60 The High Court and the Court of Appeal.

61 Unlike the job of Director of Public Prosecutions, for example.

62 Although applicants for the Circuit bench are interviewed by a serving Circuit judge and the head of the Lord Chancellor's Judicial Appointments Group.

63 See p. 80.

64 See n. 44.

65 Although there are plans to consult the Law Society on appointments to the Circuit bench.

66 *Judicial Appointments: The Lord Chancellor's Policies and Procedures*, Lord Chancellor's Department (May 1986).

67 *Judicial Appointments*, (November 1990), p. 2.

68 *The Judiciary in England and Wales* (JUSTICE, 1992), appendix 3.

69 David Pannick, *Judges* (Oxford University Press, 1987), p. 64.

70 As n. 69.

71 *Judicial Appointments* (1990), p. 5.

72 Geoffrey Bindman in *New Law Journal*, 24 July 1992, p. 1036.

73 *Judicial Appointments* (1990), p. 15.

74 As n. 73, p. 16.

75 As n. 73. There seems no logical reason for this distinction.

76 Interview with the author, 18 June 1993.

77 Currently Robin Holmes, a Deputy Secretary.

78 Lord Mackay, speech to the Association of Women Solicitors, 21 April 1993.

79 Senior officials in the Lord Chancellor's Department insist they do not take advantage of visits by candidates to make formal assessments of them. They say that although such a visit may enhance a candidate's chances those who make a bad impression would not 'normally' find it held against them. The officials acknowledge that it is not part of their job to make their own judgment of candidates: they simply assess how a person is regarded by the profession as a whole.

80 *Judicial Appointments* (1990), p. 27.

81 For *Newsnight*, BBC2, 4 December 1990.

82 The chicken wire was subsequently replaced. There is now a row of locked cabinets.

83 At the Law Society's conference, Birmingham, 23 October 1992.

84 Pannick, *Judges*, p. 66.

85 28 September 1987.

86 Lord Taylor, 'The Judiciary in the Nineties' Richard Dimbleby Lecture, BBC1, 30 November 1992.

87 The sub-committee's report was said to have delayed the appointment of its chairman, Sir Peter Webster, to the bench: Robert Stevens, 'Unpacking the Judges', lecture given on 4 March 1993, University College, London. Professor Stevens chaired the JUSTICE committee which reported in 1992.

88 *The Judiciary in England and Wales*, Foreword.

89 As n. 88, p. 29.

90 To the Association of Women Solicitors, 21 April 1993.

91 Lord Mackay, speech at the Lord Mayor's Dinner to HM Judges, 7 July 1993.

92 Robert Stevens, lecture, 4 March 1993.

93 Lord Taylor, 1992 Richard Dimbleby Lecture.

94 The Lay Observer was appointed under the Solicitors Act 1974. His job was to inquire into complaints about the way the Law Society handled complaints against solicitors.

95 The Lay Observer was abolished by the Courts and Legal Services Act 1990 and replaced by the Legal Services Ombudsman.

96 Lord Mackay, speech at the Lord Mayor's Dinner to HM Judges, 7 July 1993.

97 As n. 96.

98 In a consultation paper.

99 Unknown at the time of writing.

100 *The Judiciary in England and Wales*, p. 43.

101 Mr Justice Sachs was the first Circuit judge to be promoted under s. 71(1)(b)(ii) of the Courts and Legal

Services Act 1990 (see p. 45).

102 Courts and Legal Services Act 1990, s. 71(1)(b)(i).

103 *The Judiciary in England and Wales*, p. 17.

104 *Judicial Appointments* (1990), p. 7.

105 Michael Zander, *A Matter of Justice* (Oxford University Press, 1989), p. 116.

106 *The Judiciary in England and Wales*, p. 22.

107 As Sir Henry Fisher did.

108 '. . . subject of course in the case of physical disability to practical considerations.' (Speech to the Association of Women Solicitors, 21 April 1993)

109 Mrs Justice Ebsworth and Mrs Justice Smith were appointed in 1992; Mrs Justice Arden was appointed in 1993.

110 Miss Suzanna Woollam. Judge Advocates, appointed by the Lord Chancellor, officiate at army and RAF courts martial.

111 Carol Taylor, a law centre solicitor, appointed to the London South Region.

112 *Without Prejudice? Sex Equality at the Bar and in the Judiciary*, TMS Management Consultants (November 1992).

113 A postal questionnaire was sent to a random stratified survey of 1,000 members of the Bar and the judiciary. Response rates were 'high for a postal questionnaire, averaging at 56 per cent'. (*Without Prejudice?*, p. ii)

114 Lord Mackay did not know if anyone had encouraged her to apply for silk; he certainly had not.

115 Interview with the author, 18 June 1993.

116 *New Law Journal*, 11 December 1992, p. 1716.

117 Interview with the author, 18 June 1993.

118 Letter from Lord Mackay to Lady Howe JP, 7 November 1990.

119 Interviewed in *The Times*, 27 April 1993.

120 Until 1992 the judge normally rode to court every day dressed in his wig and gown. This practice has now been abandoned.

121 Neither do the judges of the High Court Chancery Division – apparently because their experience of life is perceived to be too limited for them to be let loose on criminal trials.

122 Interview with the author, 18 June 1993.

123 Interview with Marcel Berlins, *Law in Action*, BBC Radio 4, 12 March 1993.

124 *Review Body on Top Salaries: Fifteenth Report*, Cm 2015 (1992), appendix D, table 2.

125 Mr Justice Saville, statement in open court, December 1992.

126 These remarks, and those that follow, are taken from appendices to the *Review of High Court Judges' Work, Deployment and Numbers*, Lord Chancellor's Department (March 1993).

127 Under the Supreme Court Act 1981, s. 9(4), the Lord Chancellor is allowed to appoint Queen's Counsel as Deputy High Court judges 'as a temporary measure to facilitate the disposal of business'.

128 Such fees are not uncommon. In *Havers' Directory of the Bar* (Havers Directories, 3rd edn, 1993) David Pannick QC, who specialises in administrative law, quoted his fees for advocacy as £750–£1,750 a day (and they have probably gone up since then). Very few barristers are prepared to disclose their fees in this way but commercial specialists would generally charge more.

129 Lord Chancellor's Department press release, 5 March 1993.

130 In October 1993 Judge Prosser gave judgment in a test case about Repetitive Strain Injury, a painful affliction of the upper limbs which affects journalists and others. On the evidence before him the judge was not satisfied that the case was proved. He appeared to be saying that this syndrome simply did not exist, which was something of a hostage to fortune. A High Court judge might not have said any more than was needed to dispose of the case (*Mughal v. Reuters Ltd, The Independent*, 2 November 1993).

131 Lord Taylor, press conference, 28 May 1993.

132 The Judicial Remuneration Act 1965 raised the salary of a High Court judge to £10,000.

133 By the Administration of Justice Act 1973.

134 *Review Body on Top Salaries: Fifteenth Report*, Cm 2015 (July 1992), para. 133. A High Court judge would have got

£100,000, a Lord Justice of Appeal £115,000, and a law lord £120,000.

135 Paragraph 45. The *median* pre-appointment income of High Court judges in April 1991 was put at £166,200. The median is the 'middle' figure: the number of barristers earning more than that figure was the same as the number earning less. The *mean* pre-appointment income was much higher: £227,300. The mean is the average: the barristers' total earnings divided by the number of barristers (appendix D, table 3(a)).

136 Hansard, House of Commons, 16 June 1993, col. 556. Some candidates were not expecting to be offered appointments at such an early age.

137 Interview with the author, 18 June 1993. The candidate could have been Anthony Lester QC. It was widely known at the Bar (although Mr Lester would not confirm it) that he had turned down the offer of an appointment to the High Court because at the age of 57, after building up a distinguished practice in the field of public law, he had no wish to spend half his time trying criminal cases on circuit. The Lord Chief Justice was not prepared to reduce this obligation and Mr Lester went to the House of Lords instead as a 'working peer', Lord Lester of Herne Hill.

138 Sir Roger Parker interviewed in the *Sunday Telegraph*, 2 August 1992.

139 *The Times*, September 1992.

140 Speech at the Bar Conference, 26 September 1992.

141 *Review Body on Top Salaries: Fifteenth Report*, para. 45.

142 Press conference, 28 May 1993.

143 Expected to come into force by the end of 1994.

144 Section 3(1). The Act also reduces the amount a judge will receive by effectively basing his pension on the salary received during his last year of office rather than the salary he was receiving at the date of his retirement: see s. 3(3)(a).

145 Debate on the Judicial Pensions Bill, House of Lords, 12 November 1992, Hansard, col. 390.

146 Section 26(1). Section 26(5) says the Lord Chancellor can allow Circuit judges and other minor judicial figures

to stay on until they are 75 if he 'considers it desirable in the public interest'. Judges of the High Court and above who were appointed before the Act came into force can stay on until they are 75. Circuit judges can stay until the age of 72. Before the 1993 Act took effect, retired judges were sometimes invited back if there was a temporary shortage of judge power. Now they are no longer allowed to sit after their final 'retire-by' age of 75: see s. 26(7).

147 Under s. 2 no pension is payable unless the judge is 60 or over and has completed five years' service (unless the retirement is on medical grounds).

148 Interview with the author, *Six O'Clock News*, BBC1, 5 March 1993.

149 *Review of High Court Judges' Work, Deployment and Numbers*, para. 56.

150 The working party consisted of Kennedy, Watkins, McCowan, Scott, Rose LJJ, and Macpherson of Cluny, Johnson, Bracewell JJ, as well as unnamed officials from the Lord Chancellor's Department.

151 Simon Lee, *Judging Judges* (Faber, 1989), p. 207.

152 31 July 1987.

153 Lee, *Judging Judges*, p. 212. It is quoted here with equal self-indulgence.

154 *R. v. Callaghan*, CA(CD), *The Independent*, 29 January 1988. They were cleared by a differently constituted Court of Appeal on 15 March 1991: *R. v. McIlkenny*, CA(CD), *The Times*, 1 April 1991: see p. 311.

155 Conversation with the author, 30 July 1993.

156 The law lords stopped reading out their judgments in 1963, following a practice established by the Judicial Committee of the Privy Council in 1922.

157 Thus depriving legal correspondents of the expenses-paid continental trip which used to be the only way of getting hold of a full judgment until use of the fax machine became widespread.

158 *R. v. McIlkenny*, CA(CD), *The Times*, 1 April 1991.

159 This is in contrast to the press conference given by Judge Pickles at a pub in Wakefield, which incurred the displeasure of the Lord Chancellor (in January 1990, see p. 113). It is, however, the only known case of Professor

Lee's proposal being put into effect.

160 This may be because the respondents have had time to build up a measure of trust.

161 That was done on 6 November 1992 by Sir Stephen Brown, President of the High Court Family Division, in a case where a 14-year-old girl was applying under the Children Act for an order allowing her to live with her boyfriend instead of with her mother.

162 19 March 1987. The man was Winston Silcott who was subsequently charged with the murder of PC Keith Blakelock at the Broadwater Farm estate in London. On 25 November 1991 he was acquitted of the murder after his case had been referred to the Court of Appeal by the Home Secretary.

163 Lord Justice Glidewell in *R. v. British Coal Corporation and Secretary of State for Trade and Industry ex parte Vardy* [1993] IRLR 104.

164 In *Vilvarajah v. Secretary of State for the Home Department* [1990] Imm AR 457 Lord Donaldson MR said that 'with the notable exception of *Law in Action*' press reports of an earlier judgment of his indicated that as far as he could make out 'either no one had read the judgment – this, I am bound to say, included the Secretary of State, who broadcast on the radio at one o'clock – or they did not want to understand the judgment'.

165 On 6 June 1986 Mr Justice Alliott invited reporters into his room to correct a misunderstanding of an order he had made in chambers the previous day. The Forestry Commission were trying to get a hippy convoy to leave the New Forest. The judge explained that he had not said the travellers could remain on the land for a further seven days.

166 *Pepper v. Hart*: see p. 13.

167 Letter to *The Times*, 17 February 1991.

168 There is a simple answer to the judges' plea: if they supported moves to let television news crews film them inside the courts, they would no longer need to film the judges outside.

169 *Newsnight*, BBC2, 4 December 1990.

170 Interview with the author, *The Guardian*, 14 November 1990.

171 25 February 1992.

172 Author's sources. When Lord Lane made some intemperate remarks about government policy at the Lord Mayor's dinner for the judges on 9 July 1991 he saw no reason to alert Lord Mackay by allowing the Lord Chancellor's press office to circulate his remarks in advance. As a result, most of the papers missed his speech.

173 *R. v. Lord Chancellor ex parte Hibbit & Sanders*, Rose LJ and Waller J, *The Times*, 12 March 1993. The court found that the Lord Chancellor had acted unfairly but decided the case involved private law rather than public law and was therefore not within the scope of judicial review.

174 21 March 1993; see p. 281.

175 Discussed on p. 66.

176 Lord Chancellor's Department press release, 8 July 1993.

177 Discussed on p. 71–2.

178 Ask a private secretary where his loyalties lie in a conflict between his minister and the department's Permanent Secretary and he will point out that ministers come and go while Permanent Secretaries are, well, permanent. But a Lord Chief Justice will usually outlast a Permanent Secretary to the Lord Chancellor.

179 *Sunday Telegraph*, 10 February 1991.

180 The first sentencing conference was held in London in 1963.

181 In 1976 Lord Devlin said that the words 'judicial training' occasioned alarm. His remarks are quoted in Zander, *A Matter of Justice*, p. 123.

182 *Judicial Studies and Information: Report of a Working Party* (HMSO, 1978).

183 *Judicial Studies Board: Report for 1979–82* (HMSO, March 1983).

184 See Lord Justice Glidewell, 'The Judicial Studies Board', *Law Society's Gazette*, 7 March 1990.

185 *Judicial Studies Board: First Annual Report of Ethnic Minorities Advisory Committee* (HMSO, September 1992), p. 17.

186 As n. 185, Annex D.

187 See generally *Judicial Studies Board: Report for 1987–91* (HMSO, 1992).

188 Interview with the author, 21 April 1993.

189 As n. 188.

190 As n. 188.

191 *Judicial Studies Board: Report for 1987–91*, para. 3.10. Topics covered

include Injunctions (*Mareva* and *Anton Piller* orders); Order 14 (leave to defend); and the European Court of Justice (references under Article 177).

192 Letter to the author, April 1993.

193 Lord Taylor, speech at the Lord Mayor's Dinner to HM Judges, 7 July 1993.

194 *New Law Journal*, 18 June 1993, p. 895. In fact, an Assistant Recorder would not be given the sort of case in which a ten-year sentence was a serious option. But Assistant Recorders, even very new ones, do send people to prison.

195 Interview with the author, January 1993. At that time David Pannick was himself an Assistant Recorder. He is widely expected to become one of the outstanding judges of the twenty-first century.

196 Interview with the author, 21 April 1993.

197 In *The Guardian*, 11 May 1993.

198 *Royal Commission on Criminal Justice*, Cm 2263 (1993), para. 96, p. 140.

199 Supreme Court Act 1981, s. 11(3), re-enacting provisions derived from the Act of Settlement 1701. J. R. Spencer points out that the statute is obscure and can be read in three different ways: see *Jackson's Machinery of Justice* (Cambridge University Press, 1989 edn), p. 368, n. 3. Moreover, S. H. Bailey and M. J. Gunn suggest there are alternative ways of removing a judge for misbehaviour: see *Smith and Bailey on the Modern English Legal System*, p. 220. There are comparable provisions for removing law lords.

200 Anthony Sampson, *The Essential Anatomy of Britain* (Hodder & Stoughton, 1992), p. 49. Most observers of the legal scene (and some television viewers) will know who Mr Sampson is referring to; it would be prudent to say no more.

201 Supreme Court Act 1981, s. 11. The concurrence of at least one other senior judge is needed.

202 Courts Act 1971, s. 17(4): 'The Lord Chancellor may, if he thinks fit, remove a Circuit judge from office on the ground of incapacity or misbehaviour.' There are slightly different powers to remove District judges: see the end of this section.

203 He was fined £2,000: *The Times*, 6 December 1983.

204 See Lord Hailsham, *A Sparrow's Flight*, p. 429. This anomaly is preserved by the Judicial Pensions and Retirement Act 1993. Section 2(4) says that removal from office shall be treated as retirement. It gives the Lord Chancellor power to decide whether the sacked judge should get his pension before he is 60.

205 'A Place for Punishment', *Daily Telegraph*, 22 March 1985.

206 Quoted in James Pickles, 'Kilmuir Rules – OK', *The Guardian*, 14 February 1986.

207 Judge Pickles's sentiments in 1985 were not very different from those expressed by Lord Taylor in 1993 (see p. 291). But Lord Taylor was Lord Chief Justice and Judge Pickles was only a Circuit judge.

208 James Pickles, *Judge for Yourself* (Smith Gryphon, 1992), p. 173.

209 14 February 1986.

210 Interview with the author, recorded at Judge Pickles's home in Halifax and broadcast 21 February 1986. The judge appeared extremely nervous before the recording but he says he enjoyed it: *Straight from the Bench* (Dent, 1987), p. 61.

211 *Wogan* was a once-popular television chat show, Terry Wogan the eponymous presenter.

212 BBC Television News, 13 March 1989.

213 Pickles, *Judge for Yourself*, p. 157.

214 As n. 213, p. 158.

215 As n. 214.

216 Courts Act 1971, s. 17(4).

217 Delivered in an open letter on 27 November 1990.

218 Pickles, *Judge for Yourself*, p. 172 and appendix 6.

219 Lord Hailsham, *A Sparrow's Flight*, p. 430, quoted in Pickles, *Judge for Yourself*, p. 148.

220 Lord Hailsham, *A Sparrow's Flight*, p. 430.

221 As n. 220, p. 429.

222 He was determined to stay on the bench until he had served the 15 years he needed to qualify for a full pension. It was perhaps fortunate that the qualifying period had not yet been extended to 20 years.

223 To lawyers, a moot is an occasion when students act out a fictitious case

and a judge decides the point of law arising from it. Judge Pickles's application for judicial review might make a good moot.

224 Pickles, *Straight from the Bench*, p. 50.
225 Lord Hailsham, *A Sparrow's Flight*, p. 429.
226 Sir John Donaldson MR, speech to the Law Society Oxford Weekend Conference, 12 April 1987.
227 16 November 1992.
228 Lord Chancellor's Department press release, 16 November 1992.
229 Under s. 11 of the County Courts Act 1984, as amended:
  (4) A person appointed [to the office of district judge] shall hold that office during good behaviour.
  (5) The power to remove such a person from his office on account of misbehaviour shall be exercisable by the Lord Chancellor.
  (6) The Lord Chancellor may also remove such a person from his office on account of his inability to perform the duties of his office.
230 Lord Chancellor's Department press release, 1 June 1993.
231 Reported in *The Guardian* and *The Times*, 28 September 1992.
232 29 September 1992.
233 At the Law Society National Conference, Birmingham, 23 October 1992.
234 Page 97.
235 *The Judiciary in England and Wales* (1992).
236 As n. 235, p. 25.
237 *Royal Commission on Criminal Justice*, Cm 2263 (1993), p. 141, para. 98.
238 England and Wales is divided into six circuits. Each circuit has at least two *presiding* judges, who are responsible for the running of judicial business within the circuit. At each Crown Court centre there is a *resident* judge responsible for the listing of cases and their allocation to individual judges.
239 Speech by Lord Taylor at conference entitled 'Criminal Justice after the Royal Commission', London School of Economics, 27 July 1993.
240 Spencer (ed.), *Jackson's Machinery of Justice*, p. 372.
241 See obituary in *The Times*, 24 November 1993.
242 *Nine O'Clock News*, BBC1, 26 July 1990. He later apologised to their

solicitor and said he had not meant to imply that the Guildford Four were guilty: *The Guardian*, 28 July 1990.
243 *The Independent*, 2 March 1989.

Chapter 3: Lawyers and the Courts
1 *Lord Chancellor's Department Court Service: Annual Report 1991–92* (July 1992).
2 Cases worth less than £25,000 must be tried in the county court and those over £50,000 must be heard in the High Court unless the complexity or importance of the case warrants a transfer up or down. For the background to these changes, see pp. 173–4.
3 *Judicial Statistics 1993*, Lord Chancellor's Department, Cm 2623 (1994).
4 *Small Personal Injury Claims*, a consultation paper on proposals for changes to the treatment of small unliquidated claims in the county court, Lord Chancellor's Department (October 1993). This proposal had originally been put forward by the Civil Justice Review in 1988. It was shelved because, as originally drafted, it would have prevented successful claimants recovering the cost of seeking legal advice. The Lord Chancellor recognised that this would put claimants in small personal injury cases at a particular disadvantage. He agreed that in these cases alone claimants would be able to recover a limited sum to cover specified legal costs.
5 See *The Royal Courts of Justice: an introduction for visitors*, available from the Superintendent's office at the Royal Courts of Justice.
6 And *habeas corpus*, the procedure used to test whether a defendant in custody is lawfully held.
7 As J. R. Spencer suggests.
8 *Judicial Statistics 1992*. The number of new actions was down by 26 per cent while there were 34 per cent fewer judgments (chapter 3, paras. 8, 12).
9 Appendix 9 to the *Review of High Court Judges' Work, Deployment and Numbers*, Lord Chancellor's Department (March 1993).
10 This procedure was used when the *Bowbelle*, a Thames dredger, was sued by relatives of those who died on the pleasure boat *Marchioness* with which it collided in August 1989.

11 'This scarecrow of a suit has, in course of time, become so complicated, that no man alive knows what it means.'

12 Such as the affairs of Robert Maxwell.

13 *The Court of Appeal, Civil Division: Review of the Legal Year 1991–92.*

14 Rules of the Supreme Court (Amendment) Regulations, 1993 SI 2133, made under s. 7 of the Courts and Legal Services Act 1990.

15 Such as the case of Tony Bland (*Airedale NHS Trust v. Bland*); see pp. 29–30.

16 According to the *Royal Commission on Criminal Justice*, Cm 2263 (1993), para. 7, p. 2, although the Justices' Clerks' Society says magistrates deal with almost 97 per cent of criminal cases (briefing paper, September 1993).

17 Such as murder, manslaughter, rape, kidnapping, robbery, wounding with intent, conspiracy and spying.

18 However, a High Court judge can 'prefer a voluntary bill of indictment' and bypass the whole process: see p. 131.

19 About 7 per cent of cases, according to the Royal Commission.

20 *Royal Commission on Criminal Justice*, p. 90, para. 26. The issue is discussed further on p. 340.

21 The figure was 56 per cent: *Judicial Statistics 1992*, chapter 6, para. 13.

22 If he did not appreciate the nature of the charge, or if he was put under pressure to plead guilty, or where on the admitted facts he could not in law have been convicted of the offence with which he was charged.

23 Under s. 36 of the Criminal Justice Act 1988.

24 Discussed on pp. 351–4.

25 Under s. 36 of the Criminal Justice Act 1972.

26 When the procedure was abolished by the Criminal Justice Act 1948.

27 This account is based on William T. West, *The Trial of Lord de Clifford: 1935* (Bridlington, rev. edn, 1990).

28 *Pratt and Another v. Attorney-General for Jamaica and Another*, *The Times*, 4 November 1993 (Lord Griffiths, Lord Lane, Lord Ackner, Lord Goff of Chieveley, Lord Lowry, Lord Slynn of Hadley and Lord Woolf).

29 The title of a book by Peter Reeves (Waterlow, 1986).

30 At the same time; one can easily transfer from one to the other.

31 This account is taken from *Jackson's Machinery of Justice* ed. J. R. Spencer (Cambridge University Press, 1989).

32 Association of Women Solicitors press release, 2 February 1993.

33 Paragraph 2.9: of solicitors with 10 to 19 years experience, 79 per cent of men are partners compared with 55 per cent of women.

34 *Law Society Annual Statistical Report 1993*, published October 1993.

35 This account is taken from *Smith and Bailey on the Modern English Legal System* ed. S. H. Bailey and M. J. Gunn (Sweet & Maxwell, 2nd edn., 1991).

36 In October 1993. Source: Bar Council. The word *counsel* may be singular or plural.

37 They instantly become King's Counsel on the accession of a king.

38 *The Work and Organisation of the Legal Profession*, Cm 570 (1989), para. 9.1.

39 This was one of the first restrictive practices which the Bar ended.

40 Each QC is photographed by a picture agency wearing his or her full-bottomed wig. These pictures appear in the newspapers many years later whenever the QC – by then a judge – says something silly. This reinforces the public misapprehension that barristers and judges wear full-bottomed wigs as a matter of routine.

41 Although it was reported in 1993 that John Warren of 1 High Pavement, Nottingham had the misfortune to receive an offer of silk in error. The Lord Chancellor's letter should have been sent instead to Nicholas Warren of 3 New Square, Lincoln's Inn. He received silk a year later.

42 *The Work and Organisation of the Legal Profession*, para. 9.5.

43 April 1993, p. 4.

44 *New Law Journal*, 9 April 1993, pp. 504–5.

45 *Counsel*, May/June 1993, p. 6.

46 *The Lawyer*, 13 April 1993, p. 1.

47 October 1993, p. 11.

48 In a speech to the Law Society's annual conference, Brighton, 28 October 1993.

49 Son of Lord Hailsham of St Marylebone, Lord Chancellor and heir to the disclaimed Viscountcy of his grand-

father, Viscount Hailsham, also Lord Chancellor.

50 *Legal Services: A Framework for the Future*, Cm 740 (1989).

51 Those who aspired to become Lord Chancellor's Permanent Secretary, if not already barristers, would read for the Bar so they could pick up the honorary silk that comes with the job.

52 Barnstaple, Bodmin, Caernarvon, Doncaster and Lincoln.

53 This is a panel of three law lords who sit to decide whether to grant an applicant leave to appeal. The rule does not apply to the Appellate Committee which hears the appeal itself.

54 It led eventually to the establishment of Licensed Conveyancers under the Administration of Justice Act 1985.

55 Letter to *The Times*, 31 October 1985.

56 Letter to *The Times*, 5 November 1985.

57 Headline in *The Times*, 23 December 1985.

58 *Abse v. Smith* [1986] QB 536.

59 Practice Direction issued 9 May 1986, [1986] 1 WLR 545.

60 Press release issued 9 May 1986.

61 Supplement to the *Law Society's Gazette*, 22 January 1986.

62 Interview with the author for the *Law Society's Gazette*, 16 October 1986, p. 3059.

63 *A Time for Change: The Report of the Committee on the Future of the Legal Profession* (13 July 1988).

64 Though not the High Court.

65 *The Times*, 14 July 1988.

66 13 July 1988.

67 The government's discussion documents and consultation papers were issued in green covers long before the colour acquired ecological or environmental connotations.

68 *The Work and Organisation of the Legal Profession*, Cm 570 (1989).

69 As n. 68, para. 1.12.

70 As n. 68, para. 5.8.

71 Press release, 25 January 1989.

72 Sir Desmond Fennell became a High Court judge in 1990 at the end of his term of office. Sadly he suffered a severe stroke a few months later and had to retire from the bench.

73 But the government dealt with the accusation that it would have too much control over access to the courts by providing that all existing rights of audience would be preserved when the Act took effect.

74 Bar press release, 7 December 1989.

75 Law Society press release, 7 December 1989.

76 See Part II of Schedule 4 to the Act. The four 'designated judges' are the Lord Chief Justice, the Master of the Rolls, the President of the Family Division and the Vice-Chancellor of the Chancery Division.

77 Schedule 4, para 11(7) and s. 17, Courts and Legal Services Act 1990.

78 Bar press release, 31 July 1991.

79 *The Lord Chancellor's Advisory Committee on Legal Education and Conduct: Summary of Advice to the Law Society* (14 April 1992).

80 Author's sources.

81 *The Times*, 26 January 1993.

82 Responsible for lawyers working in prosecuting agencies, government departments and the courts; at that time it had 2,700 legally qualified staff.

83 *The Lord Chancellor's Advisory Committee on Legal Education and Conduct: Advice to the Lord Chancellor on the Law Society's application for authorisation to grant extended rights of audience to solicitors* (2 July 1993).

84 As n. 83, para. 4.57.

85 As n. 83, para. 4.64.

86 Summary of report of *Advisory Committee on Legal Education and Conduct*, para. 14.

87 Bar Council press release, 2 July 1993.

88 *Law Society's Gazette*, 7 July 1993, p. 4.

89 *New Law Journal*, 9 July 1993, p. 983.

90 *New Law Journal*, 21 May 1993, p. 714.

91 Tony Holland, *Law Society's Gazette*, 16 June 1993, p. 30.

92 Lord Griffiths, interviewed by Marcel Berlins, *Law in Action*, Radio 4, 14 May 1993.

93 Lord Chancellor's Department press release, 8 December 1993.

94 Solicitors have long memories. As recently as 1968 (when the author was looking for temporary work) at least one solicitor was advertising for a trainee (then called an articled clerk) at a salary of £0. The advertisement generously added 'no premium required', meaning that the trainee would not have to pay the solicitor for the privilege of working for him. The solicitor himself would certainly have paid a

premium for his own articles of clerk-ship.

95 The Lord Chancellor's Advisory Committee on Legal Education and Conduct, press release, 21 July 1993.

96 *Ershad and others v. Council of Legal Education*, 5 February 1993.

97 *The Committee of Inquiry into Equal Opportunities on the Bar Vocational Course: Final Report*, press release 12 April 1994.

98 Press release, 9 September 1993.

99 Interview recorded in October 1990 and shown on *Newsnight*, BBC2, 4 December 1990; quoted in *The Guardian*, 14 November 1990, p. 23.

100 *Court Dress*, a consultation paper issued on behalf of the Lord Chancellor and the Lord Chief Justice, August 1992.

101 Although many women barristers go for an all-in-one collarette, which is a sort of embroidered soft clerical collar with two bands hanging down. In Scotland advocates wear white bow ties and Queen's Counsel wear what appear to be long cravats.

102 The historical information in this section is based on material written by Professor J. H. Baker of St Catherine's College, Cambridge, for *Court Dress* (see n. 100).

103 The wide ermine cuffs are designed so that the judge can put his hands together and keep them warm while riding in an unheated horse-drawn carriage.

104 When the diminutive and distinguished Lord Justice Watkins VC retired, Lord Taylor remarked from the bench that he was an exception to the rule *de minimis non curat lex*: 'the law does not concern itself with trifles' (Court of Appeal, 30 July 1993).

105 At 1993 prices.

106 Charter 88, Submission to the Lord Chancellor and the Lord Chief Justice, 18 December 1992.

107 Lord Chancellor's Department press release, 30 September 1993.

108 *Royal Commission on Criminal Justice: Crown Court Study*, Research Study no. 19 (HMSO, 1993).

109 Unfortunately, as the survey findings conceded, the survey did not ask whether gowns should be kept and wigs scrapped.

Chapter 4: Access to Justice

1 *The Law Society Manifesto* (Autumn 1993), para. 1.1.

2 *The Heilbron Report: Civil Justice on Trial – The Case for Change*, report of an independent working party set up by the General Council of the Bar and the Law Society, chairman Hilary Heilbron QC, published by the Bar and the Law Society (June 1993).

3 Interview with the author, 30 March 1993.

4 Lord Woolf, George Bean Memorial Lecture, Association of Jewish Ex-Servicemen, 24 October 1993.

5 *Report of the Review Body on Civil Justice*, Cm 394 (1988).

6 *Second Report of the Judicature Commission* (1872).

7 See J. R. Spencer (ed.), *Jackson's Machinery of Justice* (Cambridge University Press, 1989), p. 512.

8 The High Court and County Courts Jurisdiction Order 1991 made under s. 1 of the 1990 Act.

9 Lord Mackay, speech to the Chartered Institute of Arbitrators, Glasgow, 24 September 1993.

10 Hilary Heilbron's mother was the second woman to become a High Court judge. Dame Rose Heilbron practised under her maiden name and shortly before going to university Hilary decided to assume her mother's surname in preference to her father's name of Burstein, which she said people found difficult to spell. In due course, Hilary Heilbron QC will no doubt become the second Mrs Justice Heilbron.

11 *Heilbron Report*, para. 1.7.

12 As n. 11, para. 3.4. The Family Division would remain.

13 Who would remain responsible for the General Business List.

14 Writs used to bear the full name and title of the Lord Chancellor: the issuing offices displayed signs so that solicitors' clerks could fill them in correctly on the printed forms. When the author worked as a solicitor's clerk, the signs said 'Gerald Baron Gardiner' which was easier to copy than, for example, 'Quintin McGarel Baron Hailsham of St Marylebone'.

15 Section 1(10) Courts and Legal Services Act 1990.

16 *Heilbron Report*, para. 10.7.
17 As n. 16, para. 4.8.
18 Before the Heilbron Report was published.
19 Lord Donaldson said that a judge should control the tempo of the hearing from the moment the usher calls for silence. 'Whatever the judge's pace or preoccupations when approaching the court down the judge's corridor, the moment he makes his appearance he must move fast to his seat and at once say "Well Mr So and So" and preferably tell counsel what the point at issue is. Even if his papers are in disarray or indeed he has mislaid them, he must conceal this fact and catch up with counsel later.' (Administrative Law Bar Association lecture, 13 October 1993).
20 *Heilbron Report*, para. 4.10.
21 As n. 20, para. 6.14.
22 Lord Taylor, speech to the Bar Conference, 2 October 1993.
23 As n. 22.
24 *Royal Commission on Criminal Justice*, Cm 2263 (1993), p. 119, para. 2.
25 *Report of the Committee on Death Certification and Coroners*, Cmnd 4810 (1971).
26 Such as allowing the police to take saliva samples by force for DNA testing: see *Royal Commission on Criminal Justice*, p. 3, para. 12.
27 Lord Woolf, 1993 George Bean Memorial Lecture.
28 *Justice and the Individual*, a report by JUSTICE (July 1992).
29 *Small Personal Injury Claims*: a consultation paper on proposals for changes to the treatment of small unliquidated claims in the county court, Lord Chancellor's Department (October 1993).
30 Lord Woolf, 1993 George Bean Memorial Lecture.
31 Lord Mackay, speech to the Chartered Institute of Arbitrators, Glasgow, 24 September 1993.
32 In 1993 the London Court of International Arbitration (originally the London Chamber of Arbitration) marked its centenary with a glittering dinner in the City of London. It aims to provide 'the best possible commercial dispute settlement service for the world's international business community'.
33 Those who remember the days when trade unions went on strike in Britain will recall late-night mediation sessions at ACAS, the government's conciliation service.
34 Another body offering expert mediators is the grandly named British Academy of Experts (established 1987).
35 Sir Alex Jarratt, Centre for Dispute Resolution, press release, 24 September 1992.
36 *The Heilbron Report: Civil Justice on Trial – The Case for Change* para. 9.13.
37 Lord Mackay, speech to the Chartered Institute of Arbitrators, Glasgow, 24 September 1993.
38 Lord Chancellor's Department press release, 10 August 1993.
39 The Law Society hoped to introduce a model agreement so that clients would understand where they stood.
40 Provided the solicitor was an approved member of the Law Society's new Personal Injury Panel: press release, 28 October 1993.
41 Section 41.
42 Court Business Item issued by the Lord Chancellor's Department, February 1989.
43 Except of the lawyers and court staff, who are not mentioned in the 1925 Act.
44 Interview with the author, May 1989.
45 The Courts (Research) Bill, sponsored by Dr Mike Woodcock MP. The bill was debated on 22 February 1991 (Hansard, col. 555).
46 Letter to the author, 5 August 1992.
47 Issued on 7 August 1992.
48 Directions issued 7 August 1992.
49 A civil hearing was also filmed.
50 Where he chaired the Ethnic Minorities Advisory Committee: see p. 105.
51 *Law Commission: Twenty-Seventh Annual Report* (10 March 1993), Law Com. 210, para. 1.12.
52 As n. 51, para. 1.15.
53 As n. 51, para. 1.18.
54 Hence the expression 'public law' which is used interchangeably with administrative law.
55 Clarendon Press, 6th edn, 1988, pp. 4, 5. H. W. R. Wade was Professor of English Law, first at Oxford and then at Cambridge. His book forms the basis of this section and readers are referred to it for more details.
56 In administrative law, over the past

three hundred years.

57 *Ridge v. Baldwin* [1964] AC 40, p. 72.

58 The suspicion was that Lord Mackay deeply disapproved of what his cabinet colleagues had apparently been up to and selected the judge most likely to put them on the spot. But there was no evidence to support this ingenious theory.

59 In the Administration of Justice Bill, 1984. Clause 43 would have prevented an applicant who was refused leave to apply for judicial review the right to make a fresh application to the Court of Appeal. The story is told on pp. 61–2.

60 [1948] 1 KB 223.

61 *Council of Civil Service Unions v. Minister for the Civil Service* [1985] AC 374, p. 410.

62 Wade, *Administrative Law*, p. 409.

63 *Council of Civil Service Unions v. Minister for the Civil Service* [1985] AC 374.

64 Just to make sure, the changes were subsequently given statutory force by the Supreme Court Act 1981.

65 Mandamus, prohibition, certiorari, declaration and injunction.

66 *O'Reilly v. Mackman* [1983] 2 AC 237.

67 The simile comes from Lord Lane, via Lord Woolf: see *Public Law* (1992), p. 221.

68 Law Commission press release, 27 January 1993. The precise figures were 918 in 1981 and 2439 in 1992.

69 Figures quoted by Lord Donaldson, annual lecture, Administrative Law Bar Association, 13 October 1993.

70 *Public Law* (1992), p. 236.

71 A proposition always denied by Sir John May who was appointed to inquire into the first of those miscarriages to come to light: see pp. 306–7.

72 Who would also have to sit as Deputy High Court judges: s. 1(10) Courts and Legal Services Act 1990.

73 Such as Sir Louis Blom-Cooper QC and Anthony Lester QC (later Lord Lester of Herne Hill).

74 Lord Donaldson, annual lecture, Administrative Law Bar Association, 13 October 1993.

75 *Administrative Law: Judicial Review and Statutory Appeals*, Law Commission Consultation Paper no. 126 (January 1993).

76 [1993] 3 WLR 433.

77 *Judicial Review in Perspective* by Maurice Sunkin, Lee Bridges and George Mészáros, The Public Law Project (June 1993).

78 As n. 77, p. 8.

79 Central government accounted for 27 per cent; local government for 35 per cent; courts and tribunals for 32 per cent. *Judicial Review in Perspective*, table 2.3.

80 The European Court of Justice at Luxembourg is frequently confused with the European Court of Human Rights at Strasbourg (which will be discussed in the next section). There is also an International Court of Justice at The Hague – this is the United Nations court, the so-called 'World Court'. Only states may bring proceedings: individuals have no right to be heard. The International Court decides disputes between states in accordance with public international law but cases can only be brought before it if the parties have accepted the court's compulsory jurisdiction because disputes between sovereign states depend ultimately on consent.

81 Since 1 January 1973.

82 European Communities Act 1972, s. 2(1).

83 Not to be confused with the European Commission on Human Rights in Strasbourg.

84 See *Marshall v. S.W. Hampshire A.H.A.* [1986] QB 401; *Foster v. British Gas plc* [1990] 3 All ER 897.

85 The treaty which set up the European Community.

86 Like participants in the 'Miss World' contest, advocates appear wearing their national costume: English barristers addressing French-speaking judges can be seen wearing headphones over their wigs.

87 Just as the Lord Privy Seal is neither a lord nor a privy and certainly not a seal. The expression 'Lord Privy Seal' is used by television producers to denote an over-literal manner of illustrating concepts. It derives from a television sketch in which the three images were used in succession when reference was made to the Lord Privy Seal.

88 It may also help explain the court's judgment, which is generally much

shorter than the Advocate General's opinion.

89 Czechoslovakia was a member until the country was split into two republics at the end of 1992.

90 Figures at 6 September 1993. Source: Council of Europe.

91 It had to look outside Europe because of the rule that no country can have more than one of its citizens on the court: there was already a judge from each of the European countries which were members.

92 Sir Vincent Evans served from 1980 to 1990. Sir John Freeland was appointed in 1991.

93 Unless the European Court of Human Rights is abolished in the meantime. The planned new court, though bearing the same name, would be a different legal entity and its judges would have to be appointed afresh.

94 (1992) 15 EHRR 137.

95 *The Times*, 26 March 1993.

96 Albeit equally badly.

97 *Brogan and others v. United Kingdom* (1989) 11 EHRR 117.

98 23 December 1988. The text can be found in the minutes of the 200th session of the European Commission of Human Rights (16–20 January 1989).

99 *Brannigan and McBride v. United Kingdom, The Times*, 28 May 1993.

100 This was the view taken by Catherine Lalumière, Secretary General of the Council of Europe, in a lecture at St Antony's college, Oxford, on 11 March 1993.

101 Vienna Declaration, Council of Europe, 9 October 1993.

102 Draft Protocol 11, proposed new Article 30 of the Human Rights Convention (4 October 1993), unpublished.

103 Jeremy Greenstock, Assistant Secretary, Foreign Office, press briefing, 21 September 1993. He added that Britain could not imagine that a fully respected complete judicial system would lack an appeal stage.

104 Draft Explanatory Report to Draft Protocol 11, para. 103.

105 Draft Protocol 11, proposed new Article 41 of the Human Rights Convention.

106 Interview with the author, Vienna, 9 October 1993.

107 One only had to ask a question at the closing press conference about the role of the British government for a titter to go round the assembled journalists.

108 Lord Mackay, speech to the Council of Europe summit, Vienna, 8 October 1993.

109 Foreign Office sources said the bad publicity they received in Vienna had strengthened their case.

110 Lord Taylor, 'The Judiciary in the Nineties', Richard Dimbleby Lecture, BBC1, 30 November 1992.

111 Interview with the author, 30 November 1992.

112 Press conference, Vienna, 8 October 1993.

113 Sir Thomas Bingham, Denning Lecture, Bar Association for Commerce, Finance and Industry, 2 March 1993.

114 Sir Leslie Scarman, *English Law – The New Dimension* (Stevens, 1974).

115 For example, in *The Independent*, 30 September 1993.

116 Harry Street Lecture, University of Manchester, 8 November 1991, published in *Public Law* (1992), p. 397.

117 See the case of *Brind v. Home Secretary* 1991 [AC] 696, in which the applicant, a BBC journalist, relied on the principle that where the words of a statute are ambiguous they should be construed so as to observe pre-existing treaty obligations (such as the European Convention on Human Rights). The House of Lords said this presumption did not apply when the words were clear. The law lords therefore refused to overturn the government's ban on the broadcasting of words spoken by terrorists.

118 [1993] AC 534.

119 Speech to Charter 88, 1 March 1993.

120 This was the view of the specialist adviser to the House of Lords Select Committee on a Bill of Rights, HL 176, June 1978; see Michael Zander, *A Bill of Rights* (Sweet & Maxwell 3rd edn, 1985), p. 70.

Chapter 5: Legal Aid

1 Lord Justice Neill in *R. v. the Lord Chancellor ex parte the Law Society*, High Court, *The Times*, 25 June 1993 (see p. 231).

2 This assessment draws on *A Strategy for Justice*, Legal Action Group, (1992). I am indebted to Roger Smith, director of the Legal Action Group and the book's main author.

3 And not just 'those normally classed as poor': *Report of the Committee on Legal Aid and Legal Advice in England and Wales*, Cmd 6641 (1945).

4 A title coined by the author for ease of reference. The full text is printed in the *New Law Journal*, 30 October 1992, p. 1505.

5 Two real-life case histories submitted by solicitors and published by the Law Society in *Justice at a Price*, a report by Beverly Allen, University of Brighton (October 1993).

6 With some exceptions, of which the most notable is defamation. Legal aid would also not be available for the proposed new civil wrong of invasion of privacy.

7 The means test is now carried out by the Benefits Agency; income limits are discussed later in this chapter. As far as capital is concerned, no contribution is payable if the applicant has less than £3,000. Legal aid is not available if the applicant's capital is above £6,750 – or £8,560 in personal injury cases (1993–4 figures). Pensioners can claim certain concessions on capital.

8 Although there was support for a network of offices along the lines of the neighbourhood law centres: see paras 174–8.

9 The North Kensington Neighbourhood Law Centre in West London: see p. 273.

10 Subject to various conditions. The Green Form scheme was later restricted to exclude advice on wills and conveyancing.

11 Unlike Green Form there may be a merits test involved. ABWOR as it is generally called (although not in this book) covers a bail application; a plea in mitigation; representation for someone who may be imprisoned for disobeying a court order; and representation for anyone else the solicitor thinks needs it – though it is not available for committal proceedings or in cases where the client pleads not guilty. It was extended further to cover representation at Mental Health Review Tribunals (but not other tribunals) in 1982; at prison disciplinary hearings in 1984; and for discretionary life prisoners appearing before Parole Board panels in 1992.

12 The duty solicitor schemes are provided free and there is no means test. Anyone in police custody is entitled to ask for a duty solicitor but relatively few do so, much to the relief of the Lord Chancellor's Department which would otherwise have to meet a huge bill.

13 Excluding legal aid in the higher criminal courts. See *A Strategy for Justice*, p. 7.

14 For example, the number of defendants proceeded against in the magistrates' courts rose from 1,780,000 in 1970 to 2,380,000 in 1980.

15 *Report of the Departmental Committee on Legal Aid in Criminal Proceedings*, Cmnd 2934 (1966).

16 As J. R. Spencer remarks in *Jackson's Machinery of Justice* (Cambridge University Press, 1989), p. 482.

17 Michael Murphy, *Legal Aid Eligibility*, Legal Action Group (1989), table 7.

18 *Report of the Legal Aid Scrutiny*, Lord Chancellor's Department (1986).

19 See the government's White Paper, *Legal Aid in England and Wales: A New Framework*, Cm 118 (1987), chapter 4.

20 It re-emerged as part of the proposals for 'franchising', discussed later in this chapter.

21 *37th Annual Report of the Lord Chancellor's Advisory Committee*, HC 233 (20 January 1988).

22 Criminal legal aid is discussed later in this chapter.

23 *Response to the Lord Chancellor's Consultation Paper: Review of Financial Conditions for Legal Aid*, Legal Aid Board (1991), para. 6.

24 Speech by Lord Mackay to the Law Society's annual conference, Birmingham, 23 October 1992, reprinted in the *New Law Journal*, 30 October 1992.

25 Memorandum of 17 February 1993 by the Lord Chancellor to the House of Commons Home Affairs Committee, published in the *Home Affairs Committee Report on Legal Aid*, HC 517 (22 March 1993), appendix 1, para. 21: 'Very few people who now receive criminal legal

aid pay a contribution. Some more will now have to do so after April [1993].'

26 Including income tax, national insurance, council tax, rent or mortgage payments and other housing costs, work-related costs like fares, pension contributions and child-minding and certain discretionary items such as loans and school fees.

27 Commons oral answers, 30 November 1992, Hansard, col. 18.

28 Memorandum of 18 February 1993 by the Law Society and the Bar Council . . . published in the *Home Affairs Committee Report on Legal Aid*, appendix 2, para. 6.

29 Such as the people whose cases are mentioned in this chapter.

30 People getting income support, family credit or disability working allowance qualify automatically on income although they are still not eligible if they have more than £1,000 in capital (or a slightly higher figure if there are dependants). Those with weekly disposable incomes of between £61 and £147 can still get 'assistance by way of representation', provided they can pay a contribution amounting to one-third of the excess over £61.

31 Speech to the Halifax Law Society, 13 November 1992.

32 Speech by Roger Smith, Director, Legal Action Group, 14 November 1992.

33 Memorandum of 18 February 1993 by the Law Society and the Bar Council . . . published in the *Home Affairs Committee Report on Legal Aid*, appendix 2, para. 5. This interpretation was hotly disputed by the government: see p. 267.

34 'The law-courts of England are open to all men, like the doors of the Ritz Hotel' is attributed to Mr Justice Darling. However *The Penguin Dictionary of Modern Quotations* (2nd edn, 1980) thinks this may be a wrongful attribution; the phrase is also attributed to Judge Sturgess in 1928. Of course, he might have been quoting Mr Justice Darling's *bon mot*.

35 Artistic licence: the homeless sleep near the Savoy Hotel in the Strand.

36 From *Justice at a Price*, a report by Beverly Allen.

37 Lord Taylor, 'The Judiciary in the Nineties', Richard Dimbleby Lecture, BBC1, 30 November 1992.

38 *Law Society's Gazette*, 17 March 1993, p. 4.

39 Lord Chancellor's Department press release, 12 November 1992: 'The plans provide for an extra £400 million on legal aid next year . . .'

40 The net cost of legal aid in 1991–2 was £907 million, substantially higher than the estimate (in February 1991) of £698 million.

41 In the *New Law Journal*, 18 December 1992.

42 The planned figure for 1996–7 was £1,633 million, an increase of only 6.1 per cent on the previous year (Lord Chancellor's Department press release, 30 November 1993).

43 In his evidence to the House of Commons Home Affairs Committee the Lord Chancellor gave figures for 'the number of people helped' by the legal aid scheme:

1979–80	903,000
1988–9	2,300,000
1992–3	3,100,000 (estimate)
1995–6	3,700,000 (estimate)

(*Home Affairs Committee Report on Legal Aid*, appendix 1, para. 19)

44 Hansard, House of Lords, 3 February 1993, col. 277.

45 As n. 44, col. 280.

46 As n. 44, cols. 282–3. The full story of what happened to the judges' letter is told on pp. 259–62.

47 From *Justice at a Price*, a report by Beverly Allen.

48 *Law Society's Gazette*, 23 June 1993, p. 4.

49 See p. 219.

50 *Law Society's Gazette*, 24 March 1993, p. 19.

51 *Franchising Specifications*, Legal Aid Board (July 1993), para. 1.2.

52 *The Times*, 22 January 1993.

53 Law Society Courts and Legal Services Committee report for Council meeting on 26 April 1990.

54 Andrew Lockley, Director, Legal Practice Directorate, The Law Society, speech at the Legal Action Group study day, London, 7 May 1993.

55 Interview with the author, June 1992.

56 The Law Society had tried to get ten-year franchises 'to give security and certainty for firms who may have made

57   A total of 2,637 legal aid practitioners told the Legal Aid Board in a survey that they would definitely apply for a franchise in 1993. Of the 97 law centres or advice agencies surveyed, 13 said they would apply and 25 were undecided. Two said they would not apply and the others did not reply (Legal Aid Board press release, 26 July 1993).

a major investment in order to obtain a franchise' (Andrew Lockley, speech, 7 May 1993). As an apparent compromise, it was agreed that everyone granted an initial five-year contract should be offered a new one, probably for three more years, when the original contract expired.

58   A survey of solicitors showed that the most popular categories were matrimonial work and personal injuries. Among advice agencies, welfare benefits and housing were the most popular (see n. 57).

59   An emergency. certificate may be granted when urgent legal action must be taken and there is no time to apply for legal aid in the normal way.

60   This continues after the franchise is granted: firms which are too far out of line can expect to lose their franchises unless they produce 'consistently better outcomes'.

61   In *Franchising: The Next Steps*, published by the Legal Aid Board.

62   *Law Society's Gazette*, 22 October 1992.

63   Printed in the *Law Society's Gazette*, 26 May 1993, p. 34.

64   *The Independent*, 4 June 1993.

65   *Transaction Criteria* by Avrom Sherr, Richard Moorhead and Alan Paterson, Legal Aid Board (HMSO, 1992).

66   *The Lawyer*, 26 January 1993.

67   Richard Moorhead, Avrom Sherr and Alan Peterson, *Law Society's Gazette*, 16 June 1993, p. 20.

68   Andrew Lockley, speech, 7 May 1993.

69   Sherr, Moorhead and Paterson, *Transaction Criteria*.

70   24 October 1992.

71   *The Times*, 22 January 1993.

72   *Law Society's Gazette*, 17 March 1993, p. 5.

73   John Appleby, quoted in Law Society press release, 22 April 1993.

74   Law Society press release, 24 March 1993.

75   Law Society press release, 22 April 1993.

76   *Report of the Departmental Committee on Legal Aid in Criminal Proceedings*, Cmnd 2934 (1966).

77   Legal Aid Act 1988, s. 21(2).

78   Because they were recommended by the Widgery committee: *Report of the Departmental Committee on Legal Aid in Criminal Proceedings*, para. 180. They were applied on a non-statutory basis until the Legal Aid Act 1988 was passed.

79   The full details can be found in the Legal Aid Act 1988, s. 22(2). Other factors may be taken into account.

80   Richard Young, Timothy Moloney and Andrew Sanders, *In the Interests of Justice?*, Institute of Judicial Administration, Faculty of Law, University of Birmingham (September 1992).

81   Before April 1993 the weekly income figure was £65.

82   Writing in *New Law Journal*, 17 July 1992, p. 996.

83   Volume 1, paras. 14.30–31.

84   Speech by Lord Mackay to the Law Society's 1992 annual conference, reported in the *New Law Journal*, 30 October 1992, p. 1505.

85   £4.5 million in 1991–2.

86   *Royal Commission on Criminal Justice*, Cm 2263 (1993), p. 117, paras. 70, 71.

87   HC 330 of 1985–6 quoted in HC 192 of 1991–2, para. 4 (HC is the abbreviation for House of Commons paper.)

88   HC 192 of 1991–2, para. 4.

89   Comptroller and Auditor General's Report (HC 655 of 1990–91).

90   See s. 21(7) Legal Aid Act 1988.

91   Later Sir Thomas Legg KCB QC: he received his KCB a few months before the prime minister announced in March 1993 that in future they would have to be earned.

92   Mr Legg's response should be read aloud in the calm, courteous, charming and well-modulated tones of Sir Humphrey Appleby in *Yes Minister*.

93   *Expenditure on Legal Aid*, Committee on Public Accounts, HC 192 of 1991–2 (May 1992), question 54, p. 9.

94   *Expenditure on Legal Aid*.

95   MCD (92)1, dated 1 April 1992 and signed by E. A. Grant of the Lord Chancellor's Department.

96   Legal Aid Act, s. 21(6) and Legal Aid in

Criminal and Care Proceedings (General) Regulations 1989, SI 1989 no. 344, reg. 23, 24.

97 Interview with the author, June 1992.

98 As n. 97.

99 Lord Chancellor's Department press release, 13 May 1992.

100 'In the light of widespread concern . . . the Lord Chancellor and I have decided that Paragraph 10 should be withdrawn.' Hansard, 8 June 1992.

101 Interview with the author, June 1992, *File on Four*, Radio 4, 30 June 1992.

102 *Means Assessment and Enforcement of Contributions*, Lord Chancellor's Department (December 1992).

103 Legal Aid Act 1974, s. 39(3).

104 Legal Aid Act, 1988, s. 34(9).

105 At 1992 rates.

106 *Legal Aid Board Annual Report 1992–93*, HC 735.

107 As n. 106, table General 6.

108 *Legal Aid: Efficiency Scrutiny*, Lord Chancellor's Department (27 June 1986).

109 Lord Chancellor's Department press release, 15 January 1987.

110 Lord Chancellor's Department information sheet, October 1992.

111 Law Society press release, 12 February 1992.

112 In 1991 standard fees covered only about half the cases heard in the Crown Court (instead of 90 per cent in the magistrates' courts) and the maximum a solicitor stood to lose (on the 'swings') in the Crown Court was £60 compared with about £200 in the magistrates' courts.

113 Law Society press release, 2 December 1991.

114 In his letter to the Lord Chancellor dated 17 December 1991, Mr Ely said he was finding it increasingly difficult to treat standard fees and the 24-hour duty solicitor scheme as separate issues.

115 Lord Chancellor's press release, 21 September 1992.

116 *R. v. Lord Chancellor ex parte Law Society*, *The Times*, 5 May 1993. It was the second time the Law Society had taken a Lord Chancellor to court over legal aid; the previous occasion was in May 1986 when action by the Bar and the Law Society led to an out-of-court settlement with Lord Hailsham. The Law Society's appeal to the Court of Appeal was dismissed: *R. v. Lord Chancellor ex parte Law Society*, *The Times*, 11 August 1993.

117 Lord Chancellor's Department information sheet, October 1992.

118 Interview with the author, *File on Four*, BBC Radio 4, 30 June 1992.

119 Their findings are available in the following publications:
    M. McConville and J. Hodgson, *Custodial Legal Advice and the Right to Silence*, Royal Commission on Criminal Justice, Research Study 16 (1993).
    M. McConville, *The Defence Work of Solicitors in Criminal Cases*, Economic and Social Research Council (1993).
    M. McConville, J. Hodgson, L. Bridges and A. Pavlovic, *Standing Accused* (Oxford University Press, 1993).

120 *R. v. Miller, Paris and Abdullahi* (16 December 1992).

121 Interview with the author, *File on Four*, BBC Radio 4, 30 June 1992.

122 Law Society press release, 27 April 1993.

123 Discussed on p. 224–32.

124 Discussed on p. 247.

125 *The Legal Aid Board's Advice to the Lord Chancellor on the Implications of its Taking Over Responsibility for Criminal Legal Aid in the Magistrates' Courts* (February 1993).

126 But they could still get advice from a solicitor (and perhaps have a letter in mitigation written) under the existing Green Form scheme.

127 5 February 1993, p. 153.

128 *Legal Aid Board Annual Report 1992–93*, para. 6.20.

129 *The Administration of Legal Aid in England and Wales*, Committee on Public Accounts, HC 459 of 1992–3, p. 24, question 239.

130 As n. 129, p. 25, question 244.

131 Hansard, House of Lords, 3 February 1993, col. 283.

132 From *The Independent*.

133 *The Administration of Legal Aid in England and Wales*, p. 51, question 261.

134 As n. 133, p. 53, question 280. The Lord Chancellor's Department is not unique. After he had retired as Lord Chief Justice, Lord Lane wrote a letter to the then Home Secretary, Kenneth Clarke. It took three months and a change of minister before he received

an answer. Lord Lane was told his letter had been 'misrouted', which presumably meant it had been treated as if it was from an ordinary member of the public who might reasonably have been expected to wait three months for a reply.

135 As n. 133, para. 18.

136 The fictional Sir Bernard Woolley GCB recalls in *Yes Minister* that in the 1980s 'all government departments – which in theory collectively represented the government to the outside world – in fact lobbied the government on behalf of their own client pressure group. In other words, each Department of State was actually controlled by the people whom it was supposed to be controlling . . . The Department of Employment lobbied for the TUC, whereas the Department of Industry lobbied for the employers. It was actually rather a nice balance: Energy lobbied for the oil companies, Defence lobbied for the armed forces, the Home Office for the police and so on.' (Jonathan Lynn and Antony Jay, *Yes Minister*, vol. 3, BBC Publications, 1983, p. 97)

137 *Review of Financial Conditions for Legal Aid: Eligibility for Civil Legal Aid.* This was the paper which proposed the 'safety net'.

138 In *R. v. the Lord Chancellor ex parte the Law Society, The Times*, 25 June 1993.

139 Letter dated 8 December 1992.

140 Law Society Courts and Legal Services Committee, report to the Law Society Council meeting, 10 December 1992.

141 Letter from Mark Sheldon to Lord Mackay, 15 December 1992.

142 Andrew Lockley, *Law Society's Gazette*, 16 December 1992, p. 4.

143 Letter from Lord Mackay to Mark Sheldon, 17 December 1992.

144 Law Society press release, 19 January 1993.

145 The job of sitting behind counsel was originally given to trainee solicitors; more recently, it was performed by out-of-work actors.

146 The profession denied that this was a classic example of over-manning: the president of the Law Society, Mark Sheldon, acknowledged that it would mean an inferior service for the client and the chairman of the Bar, John Rowe QC,

said that without someone to assist him, a barrister might need to request an adjournment while he located a witness who was suddenly needed.

147 Henry Hodge, a member of the Law Society's Council, described this suggestion as 'idiotic' (*Law Society's Gazette*, 24 March 1993, p. 19).

148 Information note published by the Law Society, 19 January 1993.

149 As n. 148.

150 Letter from Lord Mackay to Mark Sheldon, 21 January 1993.

151 22 January 1993.

152 By 1993 he and Douglas Hurd were the last remaining cabinet ministers who had been appointed to their posts by Mrs Thatcher.

153 *The Times*, 22 January 1993.

154 Interview with the author, 12 April 1993.

155 In conversation with the author, May 1993.

156 These can only be given if there is enough evidence for a prosecution and the defendant admits the offence: Home Office Circular 14/1985.

157 See 'Buying time for the debate over criminal legal aid' by David Wall and Adrian Wood, University of Leeds, *New Law Journal*, 5, March 1993, p. 324.

158 The Criminal Justice Act 1991, which took effect in October 1992, included a number of measures designed to reduce the prison population.

159 In fact, the Legal Aid Board later confirmed that the volume of magistrates' courts bills had gone down in the third and fourth quarters of 1992–3 compared with the same periods in 1991–2 (*Legal Aid Board Annual Report 1992–93*, para. 3.8). The Board thought this was 'due largely to a reduction in the number of people being prosecuted'.

160 The new estimate is that 283,000 civil legal aid certificates will be granted in 1993–4: see *Home Affairs Committee Report on Legal Aid*, appendix 21.

161 Evidence to the House of Commons Home Affairs Committee, HC 517, question 184.

162 Memorandum of 17 February 1993 by the Lord Chancellor . . . published in the *Home Affairs Committee Report on Legal Aid*, appendix 1, para. 17. Appendix 23 to the same report says

the Lord Chancellor had originally estimated that 58 per cent of households were eligible for legal aid in 1991–2.

163 *Home Affairs Committee Report on Legal Aid*, para. 52.

164 As n. 163, para. 18. There must surely be some overlap between the two figures, as some people who get initial advice under the Green Form scheme will then get full legal aid to pursue a case.

165 As n. 163, para. 53.

166 As n. 163, para. 58.

167 *Lord Chancellor's Advisory Committee on Legal Aid: 40th Annual Report* (7 July 1993).

168 This is a simplified version of the proposal in *Legal Action*, October 1992, p. 8.

169 The new commission could build on the work of the Citizenship Foundation, which runs an imaginative series of 'mock trials' for schoolchildren as part of its 'Law in Schools' project.

170 Some of the Australian legal aid commissions provide classes for women going through divorce or seeking child support: see *A Strategy for Justice*, p. 114.

171 J. Hartnett, quoted in *A Strategy for Justice,* p. 95.

172 On behalf of council tenants, for example.

173 *Legal Action*, October 1992, p. 9.

174 *A Strategy for Justice*, p. 133.

175 *Home Affairs Committee Report on Legal Aid*, para. 54.

176 As n. 175, para. 54.

Chapter 6: Planning Criminal Justice

1 *A New Framework for Local Justice*, Cm 1829 (1992), para. 7.

2 As n. 1, para. 8.

3 An Assistant Secretary is not, as the name suggests, a part-time typist. Still less is the Permanent Secretary a full-time typist. Assistant Secretaries are really quite senior members of the civil service hierarchy.

4 By the Justices of the Peace Act 1949.

5 In 1992 the Home Office handed this uncertain role over to the Lord Chancellor's Department.

6 *Magistrates' Courts: Report of a Scrutiny 1989* (HMSO, 1989).

7 On 18 February 1988 Mrs Thatcher had announced that as far as possible the executive functions of government should be carried out by executive

agencies. Ministers would remain answerable to parliament for an agency's activities but they would delegate day-to-day responsibility to a chief executive who would have substantial freedom to manage staff and resources. Staff would remain civil servants but their work would become more directly focused on the agency's priorities. This was known as the 'Next Steps' approach.

8 Although they had no such doubts about putting the rest of the courts service under the control of an executive agency: see p. 52–3.

9 *A New Framework for Local Justice*, para. 13.

10 *A New Framework for Local Justice*, Cm 1829 (1992).

11 Not to be confused with the Lord Chief Justice's Clerk (currently John Bond).

12 Interview with the author, 21 September 1993.

13 As n. 12.

14 Interview with Clare Dyer, *The Guardian*, 13 July 1993.

15 Speech to Suffolk Magistrates' Association, Ipswich, 9 November 1993.

16 Press release, September 1993.

17 On 21 March 1993.

18 The sections are s. 1(2) and s. 29(1). The quotations are from the marginal notes.

19 Lord Windlesham, *Responses to Crime*, vol. 2 (Clarendon Press, 1993), p. 209.

20 As n. 19, p. 222.

21 Cm 424 (1988).

22 *Punishment, Custody and the Community*, para. 1.5.

23 18 July 1988.

24 It was reported that the American inventor first got the idea from a *Spiderman* comic.

25 *Punishment, Custody and the Community*, para. 3.20.

26 Press briefing, 18 June 1988. Despite a less than successful pilot scheme (reported in 1990 as Home Office Research Study 120), the proposals were solemnly enacted as s. 13 of the Criminal Justice Act 1991. A new pilot scheme is now being planned: see Schedule 8, para. 19, of the Criminal Justice and Public Order Bill.

27 If trends continued: para. 3.2.

28 The Criminal Justice Act 1991 was

brought into effect in October 1992.

29 Lord Windlesham, *Responses to Crime*, p. 224.

30 As n. 29, p. 184.

31 Cm. 965 (1990).

32 *Crime, Justice and Protecting the Public*, para. 1.5.

33 The phrase 'just desserts' appears in paras 1.6, 2.1, 2.3, 2.9 and 2.10.

34 Criminals do get desserts, but just in prison. The Home Secretary, David Waddington, spoke more plausibly of 'just deserts': press release, 6 February 1990.

35 Press release, 6 February 1994.

36 See *The Real Alternative*, NACRO (September 1989), para. 7.16.

37 Andrew Ashworth, *Sentencing and Penal Policy* (Weidenfeld & Nicolson, 1983), pp. 447–51.

38 *Crime, Justice and Protecting the Public*, para. 2.16.

39 The idea of a Sentencing Council was subsequently rejected by the House of Lords (which defeated an amendment to the Criminal Justice Bill in March 1991). It has also been roundly condemned by the Lord Chief Justice, Lord Taylor (in his speech to the Law Society of Scotland, 21 March 1993). He feared it would 'usurp the function of the independent judiciary'. In Lord Taylor's view, there would be a real danger of politicising the sentencing process, creating 'a superfluous extra tier of control between parliament and the judiciary'. However, the Labour Party supports the establishment of a Sentencing Council: *A Safer Britain: Labour's White Paper on Criminal Justice*, The Labour Party (1990), p. 14.

40 *Crime, Justice and Protecting the Public*, para. 2.18.

41 As n. 40, para. 2.19.

42 As n. 40, para. 3.9.

43 Up to the maximum penalty available: para. 3.13.

44 Lord Windlesham, *Responses to Crime*, p. 451.

45 Interview with Patricia Wynn Davies, *The Independent*, 9 February 1990.

46 Lord Windlesham, *Responses to Crime*, p. 250.

47 Press conference, Home Office, 4 May 1993.

48 Letter dated 18 August 1993 to the author's source.

49 Lord Taylor said the judiciary had been consulted about the Criminal Justice Bill but a great deal of what they suggested was not heeded. In House of Lords debates Lord Ackner and Lord Roskill had drawn attention to the clauses which were having to be amended. And there were also behind-the-scenes discussions: Lord Taylor, press conference, 28 May 1993.

50 Interview with John Carvel, *The Guardian*, 19 November 1990.

51 *Crime, Justice and Protecting the Public*, para. 3.9.

52 As n. 51, para. 2.18.

53 Clause 3 of the Criminal Justice Bill, published in 1990.

54 See, for example, John Carvel, *The Guardian*, 10 November 1990.

55 But Mr Patten did not have to eat his words; by the time parts of the Act had been repealed Mr Patten had left the Home Office.

56 Home Office press release, 25 July 1991.

57 Press conference, 28 May 1993.

58 Lord Taylor, speech to the Law Society of Scotland, 21 March 1993.

59 The Home Office answer is that 'this is to cover the borderline case where the offences individually may not be quite serious enough to justify a custodial sentence, but a community penalty is insufficient to reflect their combined seriousness' (*A General Guide to the Criminal Justice Act 1991*, Home Office, para. 2.24). But this does not explain why, say, three not-quite-serious offences committed at the same time should not be aggregated.

60 'Once he has exhausted this mitigation by committing more offences, he too will receive the punishment "commensurate" – as the Act puts it – with the seriousness of the offence, but the punishment will not go on getting more severe if he continues to commit offences after this point has been reached.' Dr David Thomas, *The Guardian*, 30 March 1993.

61 Cm 965 (1990).

62 Section 143 Magistrates' Court Act 1980 as amended by s. 48 Criminal Justice Act 1982.

63 Section 17 Criminal Justice Act 1991.

64 They also risked a fine up to £1,000.

65 *The Times*, 7 April 1993.

66 A Home Office guide to the Act, pro- duced in 1991, says: 'It is well-established practice to mitigate fines for less well-off offenders, but the unit fine system will produce higher fines for well-off offend- ers.' (*A General Guide to the Criminal Justice Act 1991*, para. 2.13).

67 *Sunday Times*, 4 April 1993.

68 Bryan Gibson and Geoffrey Levy, *A Method of Achieving Fair Unit Fines*, Justice of the Peace (1993).

69 Home Office press release, 4 May 1993. Mr Clarke apparently had in mind the case of Vaughan Watkins, mentioned on p. 294.

70 In ss. 1 and 29.

71 By the author, press conference, 4 May 1993. The other quotations in this sec- tion are from the same press conference.

72 *Daily Telegraph*, 7 April 1993.

73 *The Times*, 11 May 1993.

74 See Adam Sage, *The Independent*, 5 May 1993.

75 Speech at NACRO's Youth Crime Section conference, Sheffield, 21 April 1993.

76 Press release, 10 May 1993.

77 *Newsnight*, BBC2, 13 May 1993.

78 BBC *Nine O'Clock News*, 13 May 1993.

79 Press conference, 28 May 1993.

80 See ss. 65, 66 Criminal Justice Act 1993.

81 Lord Taylor, speech to NACRO, 11 November 1993.

82 See p. 65.

83 *The Guardian*, 14 October 1993.

Chapter 7: When Justice Miscarries

1 In January 1980 the Court of Appeal agreed to strike out a civil action brought by the Birmingham Six against police officers who they accused of assaulting them while they were in police custody. The court thought this was 'an attempt to set aside the convictions by a side- wind'. It was. a 'scandal' that the case should be allowed to continue. 'Just con- sider the course of events if this action is allowed to proceed to trial,' said Lord Denning. 'If the six men fail, it will mean that much time and money will have been expended by many people for no good purpose. If the six men win, it will mean that the police were guilty of per- jury, that they were guilty of violence

and threats, that the confessions were involuntary and were improperly admit- ted in evidence and that the convictions were erroneous. That would mean the Home Secretary would either have to recommend they were pardoned or he would have to remit the case to the Court of Appeal. This is such an appall- ing vista that every sensible person in the land would say: "It cannot be right that these actions should go any further." (*McIlkenny v. Chief Constable of the West Midlands* [1980] 2 WLR 689)

2 An earlier draft of this chapter appeared in *Criminal Justice under Stress*, ed. Eric Stockdale and Silvia Casale (Blackstone Press, 1992).

3 Paul Hill had a conviction for murder in Northern Ireland but he was granted bail shortly afterwards pending an appeal.

4 At a press conference in the Home Office.

5 HC 449, 30 June 1994.

6 Many people these days speak of 'foren- sic evidence'. This is a gross error. *Foren- sic* means 'of, or used in, courts of law'. Thus one talks of 'forensic skills', 'foren- sic wigs', 'forensic medicine' and, of course, 'forensic science'. A forensic sci- entist is simply a scientist who examines evidence for the purposes of a court. The evidence he examines is therefore scien- tific evidence. Having said that, the mis- use of *forensic* is now so widespread that it has probably come to mean what people think it means.

7 Judgment delivered by Stuart-Smith, Mann, McCowan LJJ, June 1991. The quotations in this chapter are taken from transcripts of the judgments in the author's possession.

8 15 October 1993.

9 He gave the example of *R. v. Pottle and Randle*, where two peace campaigners were acquitted of helping the spy George Blake escape (June 1991).

10 17 October 1993.

11 *Sunday Telegraph*, 14 November 1993. The apology, with its excessive tautol- ogy ('fully recognise and accept', 'apolo- gise fully and unreservedly') and convoluted syntax ('were for good rea- son quashed . . .'), could only have been written by a libel lawyer. It is under- stood that the newspaper agreed to pay heavy damages to the Birmingham Six.

12 Notably in the *Mail on Sunday*, 4 July

1993; *The Times*, 6 July 1993.

13 Coverage was made no easier by the absence of chapter numbers on each page of the report and the refusal of those responsible for the public address system to provide agreed facilities for broadcasters.

14 Interview with the author, 27 July 1993.

15 Interview with Marcel Berlins, *Law in Action*, BBC Radio 4, 9 July 1993.

Chapter 8: The Royal Commission

1 *Report of the Royal Commission on Criminal Justice*, chairman Viscount Runciman of Doxford CBE FBA, Cm 2263 (1993) (referred to in the remainder of this chapter as '*Royal Commission*').

2 *New Law Journal*, 24 September 1993, p. 1338.

3 Each of these topics will be discussed later in this chapter.

4 *Legal Action*, Legal Action Group, November 1993, p. 7.

5 *New Law Journal*, 24 September 1993, p. 1338.

6 Although Professor Zander said there were about three times as many recommendations designed to assist the defence as there were to help the prosecution.

7 *Preventing Miscarriages of Justice*, Legal Action Group (July 1993). This booklet is the source of other comments in this chapter attributed to the Legal Action Group.

8 Speech at a conference entitled 'Criminal Justice after the Royal Commission', London School of Economics, 27 July 1993.

9 Lord Runciman was Senior Research Fellow of Trinity College, Cambridge.

10 The judge was speaking at a closed academic conference in September 1993. There will be a detailed discussion of these proposals later in this chapter.

11 Speech at 'Criminal Justice after the Royal Commission' conference, 27 July 1993.

12 Discussed on p. 332–5.

13 *New Law Journal*, 1 October 1993, p. 1364.

14 In July 1994.

15 There are important exceptions relating to some road traffic cases and in connection with serious fraud investigations.

16 Although the Royal Commission called it the right *of* silence.

17 *Royal Commission*, p. 50, para. 6.

18 Interview with the author, 14 October 1993.

19 It was specifically mentioned in the commission's terms of reference.

20 *Royal Commission*, p. 52, para. 13.

21 As n. 20, p. 53, para. 19. Emphasis added.

22 As n. 20, p. 54, para. 22.

23 Cmnd 8092 (1981). This was the last Royal Commission to be appointed before Mrs Thatcher came to power in 1979; she clearly did not approve of them and there were none appointed until John Major agreed to set up the Royal Commission on Criminal Justice in 1991.

24 6 October 1993.

25 Sir Nicholas Lyell, speech to the Society of Conservative Lawyers, Blackpool, 6 October 1993.

26 *Royal Commission*, p. 54, para. 23.

27 *The Times*, 27 July 1993.

28 Press release, 18 November 1993.

29 As n. 28. Liberty said it would challenge the government before the European Court of Human Rights but any challenge would inevitably be several years off.

30 Press release, 18 November 1993.

31 Interview with the author, 2 October 1993.

32 *Royal Commission*, p. 57, para. 31.

33 As n. 32, p. 61, para. 54.

34 The Cardiff Three case: *R. v. Miller, Paris and Abdullahi*, *The Times*, 24 December 1992.

35 *Royal Commission*, p. 64, para. 66.

36 As n. 35, p. 65, para. 68. Emphasis added.

37 *The Times*, 27 July 1993.

38 *Corroboration of Evidence in Criminal Trials*, Law Com. 202 (Law Commission, 1991).

39 Part III of the Act.

40 *Report of the Committee on the Distribution of Criminal Business between the Crown Court and the Magistrates' Courts*, Cmnd 6323 (1975).

41 See Julie Vennard, in D. Moxon (ed.), *Managing Criminal Justice* (HMSO, 1985).

42 *Royal Commission*, p. 87, para. 12.

43 As n. 42, p. 87, para. 13.

44 As n. 42, p. 88, para. 18.
45 Speech at 'Criminal Justice after the Royal Commission' conference, 27 July 1993.
46 On 6 July 1993, in answer to the first question at his press conference.
47 *Royal Commission*, p. 88, para. 15.
48 *Law Society's Gazette*, 7 July 1993, p. 3.
49 *Royal Commission*, p. 88, para. 18.
50 Interview with the author, 27 July 1993.
51 As n. 50.
52 *Legal Action*, November 1993, p. 6.
53 As n. 52. Italics in original.
54 Under s. 4 Criminal Justice Act 1987 as amended by s. 144 Criminal Justice Act 1988.
55 Under s. 53 Criminal Justice Act 1981.
56 *Royal Commission*, p. 90, paras. 25–6.
57 *R. v. Johnson, Davis and Rowe*, 18 January 1993.
58 *The Guardian*, 8 October 1993.
59 *Royal Commission*, p. 97, para. 58.
60 As n. 59, p. 99, para. 69.
61 As n. 59, p. 100, para. 70.
62 Michael Zander, *Crown Court Study*, Royal Commission Research Study 19 (HMSO, June 1993), para. 4.12. See also *Royal Commission*, p. 98, para. 64, n. 29.
63 There is also 'charge-bargaining' between counsel, where the defendant says he will plead guilty to a lesser charge if the more serious charge is dropped.
64 [1970] 2 QB 321.
65 J. Baldwin and M. McConville, *Negotiated Justice* (Martin Robertson, 1977).
66 Strictly speaking, all defendants are 'innocent' until they are convicted. Need the barrister have been convinced of the defendant's innocence to have answered in the affirmative, or would a lack of admissible evidence have been sufficient?
67 Affirmative answers would have been obtained from those who were worried that this *might* be such a case as well as those who thought this *was* such a case. Indeed, on one reading, only those lawyers who couldn't care less about their clients would answer 'no'.
68 In Michael Zander, *Crown Court Study*.
69 *Royal Commission*, p. 110, para. 42.
70 Speech at 'Criminal Justice after the Royal Commission' conference, 27 July 1993.
71 *Royal Commission*, p. 113, para. 51.
72 As n. 71.

73 As n. 71, para. 50.
74 In *Alice's Adventures in Wonderland*, chapter 12.
75 *Legal Action*, November 1993, p. 6.
76 Sir Stephen Sedley, *London Review of Books*, 23 September 1993.
77 Clause 48 of the Bill.
78 DNA stands for deoxyribonucleic acid – the genetic material for higher organisms. The technique was developed in Britain by Professor Alex Jeffreys of Leicester University.
79 A block of jelly is prepared with small indentations along one edge. A few drops of a coloured liquid from the biological sample are inserted into each indentation. Under the influence of an electric current, the liquid stain travels slowly along the jelly, leaving behind a distinctive pattern of light and dark areas. The scientist has to decide whether two patterns match.
80 They wanted to discover the chances of two people having similar profiles.
81 Three Home Secretaries supported the change: they included Douglas Hurd, Kenneth Clarke and (presumably) Kenneth Baker: see the somewhat uninformative para. 10 in *Royal Commission*, p. 182.
82 In 1983 it rejected the idea of an independent review body to advise the Home Secretary on the exercise of the prerogative of mercy (*Government Reply to the Sixth Report from the Home Affairs Committee Session 1981–82 HC 421*, Cmnd 8856 (1983)).
83 Under s. 17 of the Criminal Appeal Act 1968.
84 Home Office press release, 20 January 1987. See Joshua Rozenberg, 'Miscarriages of Justice', in *Criminal Justice under Stress*, ed. Eric Stockdale and Silvia Casale (Blackstone Press, 1992).
85 *Royal Commission*, p. 183, para. 16.
86 In his speech to the Conservative Party Conference, 6 October 1993.
87 *The Times*, 27 July 1993.
88 It was the role of the Crown Prosecution Service to bring charges if there was a realistic prospect of a conviction and the prosecution was in the public interest.
89 Although it will no doubt be some years after that before the new authority completes its work on the backlog of cases it will receive from the Home Office.

Index